P9-DMY-754

Brother Against Brother

VIOLENCE AND EXTREMISM IN ISRAELI POLITICS
FROM *ALTALENA* TO THE RABIN ASSASSINATION

EHUD SPRINZAK

THE FREE PRESS

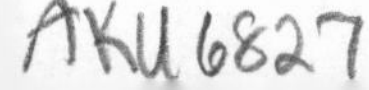

THE FREE PRESS
A Division of Simon & Schuster Inc.
1230 Avenue of the Americas
New York, NY 10020

Designed by Carla Bolte

Manufactured in the United States of America

10 9 8 7 6 5 4 3 2 1

Sprinzak, Ehud.
Brother against brother : violence and extremism in Israeli politics from *Altalena* to the Rabin assassination / Ehud Sprinzak.
p. cm.
Includes bibliographical references and index.
ISBN 0-684-85344-2
1. Political violence—Israel—History. 2. Right-wing extremists—Israel—History. 3. Orthodox Judaism—Political aspects—Israel. 4. Rabin, Yitzhak, 1922–1995—Assassination. 5. Israel—Politics and government. I. Title.
HN660.Z9V57 1999
303.6' 09594' 09045—dc21 98-34983
CIP

This book was published in cooperation with the Jerusalem Institute for the Study of Israel.

FOR SEPHI, DAVID, OPHIR, AND OMER

CONTENTS

PREFACE

This book summarizes nearly thirty years of study and observation of extremism and violence in Israeli public life, a project I wished to complete for a long time. Its actual writing took place during a fateful time for the Jewish state and for me personally, a time in which the reality of Israeli domestic violence overshadowed the darkest chapters of its history. The peak of this incredibly intense period was reached on November 4, 1995, with the tragic assassination of Prime Minister Yitzhak Rabin. My original intent in the summer of 1992, when I began to work on the first version of the book, was to write a policy monograph under the auspices of the Jerusalem Institute for the Study of Israel. The historical part of the study, an in-depth analysis of domestic violence since 1948, was to be followed by alternative potential scenarios of violence and policy recommendations for the minimization of bloodshed. The timing of the project was not accidental. The Labor party under Yitzhak Rabin and Shimon Peres had just won the elections and constituted a peace-oriented government. The directors of the Jerusalem Institute were increasingly concerned about the possibility of intensifying domestic strife and wished to alert Israeli policymakers to the dangers of escalating confrontations. I had more than one reason to share their concerns.

My anxiety over the possibility of Jewish bloodshed was a product of my personal expectations and professional assessment. Personally, I wanted the Rabin-Peres government to aggressively jump-start the long-awaited peace process with the Palestinians. As a concerned Israeli I have long come to believe in the readiness of both sides to live in peace. But professionally I was worried about the consequences of such a move. Just a year earlier, in the last pages of my previous book, *The Ascendance of Israel's Radical Right*, I speculated about the likelihood of civil war in Israel. Though highly unlikely, I concluded, the chances of intense domestic strife were higher under a narrow Labor-Meretz coalition government that would make peace with the Palestinians at the price of a major territorial compromise. Since such a government did, indeed, come to power in 1992, I wished to share with its leaders the little knowledge on the explosive nature of domestic conflicts I had gained from many years of following and studying similar situations worldwide. The decision of the Jerusalem Institute for the Study of Israel to support my project, through the Baruch Yekutieli Fellowship, set me upon one of the most intriguing and painful courses of my life, a close personal and professional interaction with the evolution of Israeli violence between 1993 and 1995.

My concern over the likelihood of domestic violence in Israel grew exponentially in the winter and spring of 1993. While I had no clue regarding the ongoing secret talks with the Palestinians, I had an urge to anticipate what, in my judgment, could be in the making. I consequently decided to do something I had never done before, to publish the policy section of my study before completion of the entire manuscript. The small monograph, *Brotherly War in Israel? Potential Scenarios and Policy Recommendations*, was published by the Jerusalem Institute in April 1993. The possibility of domestic confrontation between the Israeli extreme right and the government, in case of a territorial concession to the Palestinians, was portrayed in great detail, including the likelihood of bloodshed. My major recommendations to the government of Israel were to avoid a conflict of legitimacy with the settlers in Judea and Samaria and to do its utmost to reduce the intensity of such conflict, if it ever **arose**. Along with the critical need to develop a dialogue with pragmatic settlers, I also recommended that the government use an "iron fist" against the small extremist elements within the radical right, whom I expected to flagrantly break the law. A month after its publication, the document was personally presented to Prime Minister Rabin in a lengthy session attended by me and the directors of the Jerusalem Institute . While listening carefully, the prime minister did not seem particularly concerned by the worst-case scenarios portrayed in the document. Like most Israelis, he may not have truly accepted the possibility of domestic bloodshed. Or if he did, Rabin was probably confident of his ability to handle such conflict.

The signing of the Oslo Accords on September 13, 1993, greatly intensified my personal and professional interest in the evolving domestic extremism. The issue was no longer academic, and the project had become more than a scholarly treatment. Entirely preoccupied by the realization of a few of my scenarios, I had gradually become a minor player. In several popular articles in the Israeli press, I warned the government of paying too little attention to the growing rift among the Israeli people. Though fully supportive of the Oslo process, I pleaded with Mr. Rabin to invest more thinking and resources in resolving the evolving domestic conflict before events escalated. Maintaining close contacts with friends and knowledgeable sources within the settler community and the radical right, I also had at that time an open channel to the Prime Minister's Bureau. On the basis of my ongoing talks with the settlers, I wrote several private memoranda to the prime minister with my assessments of the intensifying conflict and recommendations for its alleviation. To my great dismay, I discovered that the dramatic events were far more powerful than my limited ability to make a difference. Particularly damaging in 1994–95 was the Palestinian-Israeli-Palestinian spiral of violence. Terrorism was dramatically on the increase following the massacre by a Jewish doctor of twenty-nine praying Palestinians in Hebron, and the increase in Muslim suicide bombings inside Israel proper. I could not but watch in horror the unfolding tragedy that culminated in Rabin's assassination. I had gradually realized that the only role left for me, an involved yet ivory-tower academic nevertheless, was to document the sad story.

The completion of this project would have been much harder without the support of a number of research institutions, colleagues, and dear friends. I am particularly grateful to the Jerusalem Institute for the Study of Israel and to its directors, Professor Rami Friedman and Ora Achimeir, for their consistent support throughout the preparation of the 1995 Hebrew version of this book. Michal Zmora, the former president of Israel's Tolerance Association, was also involved in that early stage and deserves warm gratitude for her interest and support. The Levi Eshkol Institute, the Shein Center, and the Silvert Institute, all part of the Hebrew University devoted to the study of Israeli society, have for years provided me with grants to study various aspects of Israeli extremist politics. I am afraid it is impossible to mention here the large number of colleagues and students whose wisdom and constructive criticism helped me over the years to refine my arguments and analyses of Israeli extremist politics. I am certain, however, that if they read this book carefully, they will be glad to find their fingerprints throughout. Two of my outstanding supporters cannot remain anonymous, however, even in this short preface: my mentor and colleague, Professor Shlomo Avineri, and my wife, Rikki. Shlomo Avineri, an outstanding scholar, admired teacher, and most loyal friend, has been my intellectual guide for more years than both of us wish to remember. Whenever in doubt, trouble, or uncertainty, Shlomo was there for me. As the first head of the Eshkol Institute, over twenty-five years ago, Shlomo encouraged me to conduct and publish my first study of Israeli extremism. With the same generosity, he kept reading and commenting on my manuscripts, including this one. Rikki, my beloved wife and best friend, may have been spared the trouble of going through my early works, but in the last fifteen years she has repeatedly paid her dues to my obsessive need for constructive criticism. I can only wish myself many more years of such collegiality and friendly support by both Shlomo and Rikki.

The last version of this book benefited from the ideas and suggestions of several colleagues and friends. I am especially grateful to Professors David Ricci, Ira Sharkanski, and Dr. Idit Zevtal for their comments and suggestions. The completion of the manuscript would have been much harder without Steven Mazie, a former student, Wallenberg Scholar, and friend. Steve spent many hours editing, correcting, and improving the text. Thanks also go to my research assistants, Sharona Ehrlich, Tieri Arad, and Darcy Bender for their diligent and devoted work. My two Free Press editors, Mitch Horowitz and Paul Golob, did a great job in putting this book in its final shape. And last but not least is Adam Bellow, former editorial director of The Free Press, who always believed in my work and wanted me to do this book long before I was ready for the task. I wish Adam had stayed with The Free Press through the entire production of this book.

Ehud Sprinzak

U.S. Institute of Peace, Washington, D.C., Summer 1998

Brother Against Brother

INTRODUCTION

It was 5:10 on Friday morning, February 25, 1994. About five hundred Muslims were kneeling in a Ramadan prayer at the great Isaac Hall of the Cave of the Patriarchs in the Israeli-occupied West Bank town of Hebron. An Israeli dressed as a captain in the Israeli Defence Forces, armed with an automatic Glilon rifle, broke into the hall and sprayed the worshipers with live bullets. Fully engaged in their prayers, unarmed and unprepared, the praying Muslims never had a chance. In fewer than three minutes the officer unloaded four magazines containing 111 bullets. Twenty-nine Muslims were instantly killed; over one hundred were wounded. A clog in the assailant's gun ended the surrealistic killing spree before the fifth magazine could be loaded and allowed several unhurt worshipers to throw a fire extinguisher at the killer, bring him down, and beat him to death. In the hysteria, panic, and outrage that spread through the occupied territories as the Hebron tragedy became known, additional violence took place. Palestinians and Israeli soldiers clashed all over the West Bank and Gaza, leaving nine Palestinians dead and nearly two hundred wounded.

The shock of the Hebron massacre multiplied when the killer's identity was discovered. The man turned out to be Dr. Baruch Goldstein, the emergency physician for Jewish settlers in Hebron and the adjacent town of Kiryat Arba, and a devout Orthodox Jew. Goldstein, thirty-seven, father of four, was one of the most respected residents of Kiryat Arba. An able doctor and former town council member, Goldstein was responsible for treating many Jewish victims of Palestinian terrorism. He also at times cared for wounded Arabs; at least one Palestinian resident of Hebron said that Goldstein saved his life. Dr. Goldstein, according to several reports, woke up early the morning of February 25. Dressing in his army uniform and posing as a captain on reserve duty, he attended an early Jewish prayer service at the Abraham Hall of the Cave of the Patriarchs, a shrine sacred to both Muslims and Jews. Sometime after 4:45 A.M., upon the conclusion of his prayers, Goldstein stepped into the Isaac Hall and hid behind a large pillar. According to eyewitnesses, he did not immediately shoot but waited for the traditional Muslim *sojud*, a prayer in which the worshipers kneel in the direction of Mecca.

Goldstein's massacre was immediately described as an unpredictable act of a madman. Israel's prime minister, Yitzhak Rabin, advanced this deranged single-man theory, maintaining that Goldstein was insane. The killer *could not be*, according to the prime minster, just a normal Jew. Speaking before a packed Knesset hall, Rabin said that he was personally ashamed of the massacre and that in his worst nightmares he could not dream of an Israeli perpetrating such a heinous crime. The prime minister's theory of a crazy individual was, not surprisingly, supported by the leading settler organization in the occupied territories, the Yesha Council. The heads of the organization were quick to point out that Baruch Goldstein represented no one but himself, and that the settlers were as shocked by the massacre as anybody else. Accusing Rabin of irresponsibly tolerating Arab terrorism, these right-wing Jews argued that it was the blunders of the government that drove Goldstein to commit the atrocity.

The problem with the crazy-loner theory was that it was not shared by many of Goldstein's close friends in Kiryat Arba. While denying any previous knowledge of the attack plan, they justified the act as a response to Palestinian terrorism. According to this reasoning, the Palestinians had to be taught that Jewish blood is not cheap, and Goldstein's was the only way of getting that message across. But the massacre was not just an act of political-military revenge. It was, according to these colleagues—members or supporters of the radical fundamentalist Kach movement, established by the late Rabbi Meir Kahane—a religious act and a sacred mission. In killing these Muslim enemies of the Jewish people, Goldstein was engaged in *kiddush hashem*, sanctification of the name of God. By avenging the blood of pioneering settlers recently murdered by Palestinian terrorists, Goldstein did what God wanted him to do: he glorified God's name. And the act carried another purpose. In addition to the warning of terror he sent to the Arabs, Goldstein had a message for Rabin and his ministers, to put an end to the peace process with the Palestinians. The fundamentalist and messianic doctor had no doubt that God wanted the government of Israel to abandon the sacrilegious selling of the land of Israel. A number of Baruch Goldstein's friends made it known that in their eyes he was a holy man. According to these associates, Goldstein had conducted a supreme act of *messirut hanefesh* (total devotion), which they themselves should also have done had they had the doctor's courage and sacred sense of mission. One could further detect in these people a sense of guilt about Goldstein's extraordinary personal sacrifice.

At the time of writing this book, four years after the Hebron massacre and especially after the publication of the State Investigation Committee Report regarding the matter, the contours of the atrocious act are relatively clear. There is no question that Dr. Baruch Goldstein conducted the crime on his own and that nobody knew about the plan or assisted in either its preparation or its execution. At the same time it is equally clear that the act was purposeful and premeditated. The Hebron massacre was conducted within an elaborate ideological and political framework that fully justified anti-Arab terrorism. While we will never fully understand the ultimate emotional trigger that ignited this suicidal massacre, it is patently clear that the Kiryat Arba physician planned the attack well in advance, that he wanted to kill as many Muslims as possible, that he was certain that God approved of the killing, and that he hoped and believed that the massacre would stop the peace process. If we add to these facts Goldstein's long and close association with Kach, the Hebron disaster loses its one-time, isolated status. It acquires, instead, a political meaning; it becomes a collective act by proxy, a colossal demonstration of political violence expressing a crisis of an entire fundamentalist milieu. Given the enormous potential damage that the current Israeli-Palestinian peace process holds for Zionist religious fundamentalists, it is not an exaggeration to describe the Hebron massacre as the most extreme reaction of these messianic Jews to the political threat posed to their theological convictions and collective existence.

Despite how stunning the Hebron massacre looked in the spring of 1994, a large number of Israelis still refused to view it as an indication of the deteriorating quality of the nation's civic culture. Dr. Goldstein's operation was, according to this view, an act of war carried out during an external conflict. Although only a few of these observers fully approved of the massacre as a legitimate warlike activity, they saw it as an understandable Jewish reaction to the violent Palestinian culture. The massacre, so the argument went, did not tarnish Israeli democracy. It had nothing to do with the politics of the Jewish state and with the ability of its citizens to handle their own internal differences in a democratic and civil manner. Though living in the undemocratic and bloody Middle East, the Israelis were capable of maintaining their long-cherished culture of civility and nonviolence.

All hopes for Israel's ability to insulate itself from the violence between Jews and Arabs in the occupied territories were brutally shattered on November 4, 1995, in Tel Aviv's Kings of Israel Square. A huge peace rally in support of the government was concluded by the fatal shooting of Yitzhak Rabin, the ninth prime minister of the state of Israel. Rabin, who had just concluded the rally with a big hug from Foreign Minister Shimon Peres and a chat with the rally's organizers, was shot at the door of his armored car. The shooting at the square's "protected" parking lot, from an almost point-blank range, left Rabin with little chance of survival. The prime minister did not suffer much. Almost instantly losing consciousness, he never regained it and died on the operating table in Ichilov Hospital. At 11:10 P.M., the prime minister of Israel was officially pronounced dead.

The assassination of Yitzhak Rabin was neither accidental nor conducted by a madman. The murder was preceded by an unparalleled campaign of political delegitimation against the ruling Labor government and by character assassination of Rabin and Foreign Minister Peres. The ratification of the Oslo Accords with the PLO (signed on September 13, 1993), the failure of the Hebron massacre to stop the implementation of the Palestinian Autonomy Plan, and the repeated acts of Palestinian terrorism drove the Israeli extreme right into deep despair. Mostly expressed in countrywide antigovernment demonstrations, the radicalization of Israel's ultranationalists was particularly expressed in their rhetoric. Not only was the government, duly elected in 1992, an "illegitimate" government, but its leaders had begun to be labeled as "traitors." A wave of Islamic terrorism, begun in November 1993, added a new dimension to the bitterness and fury of the extreme right. Rabin and Peres had increasingly been portrayed as "assassins" and "collaborators with terrorism." The most radical elements of the Israeli extreme right made it clear that they believed that the two architects of Oslo were personally responsible for the violent death of Israeli Jews. By taking the Israeli army out of Eretz Israel territories and by pulling out the Shin Beth, Israel's internal security service, they virtually invited Palestinian terrorists to kill Jews. The question asked increasingly by extremist rabbis was no longer whether the two statesmen were involved in treason. The issue debated by these Halakhic authorities was whether or not the treacherous acts of the two warranted a *din rodef* (ruling about a "pursuer") and a *din moser* (ruling about a "denouncer"). *Rodef* and *moser* are terms that denote individuals directly responsible for the killing of innocent Jews and the surrender of holy Jewish territory. According to Jewish law, *rodfim* and *mosrim* may, in extreme circumstances, be sentenced to death.

Twenty-five-year-old Yigal Amir, who murdered Yitzhak Rabin, was neither a sociopath nor a deranged person. A student of law and computers at Bar Ilan University, Amir was known to his friends as a bright young man. Peers who studied with Amir at the university's Kollel, a special religious academy for the rigorous study of Halakha (Jewish law), testified that the talented student had occasionally outperformed his Talmud teachers. Amir, who in the two preceding years had become increasingly active in the antipeace protests of the Israeli right, shot Rabin in cold blood. His investigators were stunned by the confession that Amir had planned to kill Rabin for a long time and that on at least two earlier occasions he tried to physically approach the prime minister with this purpose in mind. Thrilled by the news of Rabin's death, Amir made it clear that in his opinion Rabin was a *rodef.* The assassin was so sure of his interpretation that he refused to listen to rabbis who tried to dissuade him from jumping to that conclusion. Amir further stunned the Israeli public by stating that he would have loved to gun down both Rabin and Peres. The only reason he did not do so on November 4 was that Peres had left the podium shortly before Rabin, and Amir did not want to miss the opportunity to kill the prime minister.

Though stunning and unprecedented in the Israeli context, the Hebron massacre and the Rabin assassination were not the first atrocities of their kind within the broader picture of the area. The Middle East has recently been associated with a dramatic rise in religious radicalism and extremist fundamentalism. Khomeini's revolution in Iran, the assassination of President Sadat in Egypt, and the ferocious fundamentalist effort to bring down the Mubarak regime by terrorism, the violent eruption of Shi'ite terrorism in Lebanon, the rise to power of Sunni fundamentalists in Sudan, the bloody struggle of Islamic radicals in Algeria, and most recently the dramatic rise of Hamas and Islamic Jihad terrorism among the Palestinians—all contributed to the identification of the region with religious violence and fanatical terrorism. For years, however, there was one exception to this turbulent image—the state of Israel. The Jewish state was perceived as an island of democracy, secularism, pragmatism, and nonviolence. But events of the late 1980s and early 1990s raised the question of whether, within its borders, Israel was in fact isolated from the atmosphere of religious violence that prevailed in most neighboring countries.

Thousands of young yeshiva (Jewish Orthodox seminary) students took to the streets during this period to fight the establishment of a Mormon university in Jerusalem, to stop archaeological digs all over the country, to burn bus stations where "obscene" commercial advertisements had been posted, and to stop the screening of movies on Friday nights in Jerusalem. Such incidents were somewhat reminiscent of fanatical street demonstrations in Tehran or Beirut. The vigilante violence of the young messianic settlers of Gush Emunim (Bloc of the Faithful) in the West Bank, peaking in the 1980 assassination attempts on three West Bank Arab mayors and the 1983 terror attack on the Muslim College of Hebron, approximated the type of religious terrorism that has been highly visible in the Middle-East. The rise to political prominence of Israel's radical right, a marginal group in the first thirty years of the state's existence, is another indication of the changing character and direction of Israel's political culture.

The purpose of this book is to place the Hebron massacre and the assassination of Prime Minister Rabin in a broader historical and cultural perspective. The question the book addresses is not just why and how a Jewish physician could become a political mass murderer and a Jewish student the prime minister's killer but what the political and cultural conditions are within which a large number of Israeli Jews have come to consider violence and assassination legitimate political means. The shocking and senseless atrocities committed by Israelis in 1994 and 1995 did not take place in a vacuum. They were the peak of intense Jewish-Muslim and Jewish-Jewish confrontations in territories captured and occupied by Israel in 1967. The massacre and the assassination were, moreover, a sad indication that the forty-seven-year-old Israeli effort to contain political terrorism and establish a nonviolent democratic society in the Middle East has not been as successful as was once expected.

This book does not examine Israel's external wars and only indirectly addresses the century-old Arab-Israeli conflict. It traces the origins and evolution of domestic extremism and violence in Israeli society, which includes both violence between Jews and between Jews and Arabs. It describes the movements, operations, actors, and ideological reasoning of Israeli extremists since the establishment of the state in 1948. While there are many studies of Arab and Muslim domestic extremism and violence, not a single book comprehensively accounts for Jewish violence in Israel. This study aims to fill that gap. It further tries to show that Jewish politics and violence are not always contradictory terms.

The question of Israeli domestic violence is unfortunately neither just an interesting academic issue nor merely a problem of political and cultural history. The Hebron massacre, the Rabin assassination, and the Muslim violence that preceded and followed both events show how domestic terrorist interaction between Muslim and Jewish religious extremists can damage—and potentially destroy—the peace process. It further indicates the possibility of serious regional and international crises. Though they represent a minority, religious extremists on both sides are heavily armed and enjoy strong support in their communities. Each side is convinced that

God's command is to free the country from the infidels of the other side. In the next decade, whether or not they succeed politically, Muslim and Jewish religious radicals are likely to hold the center stage of their respective societies and attract the attention of the community of nations. In light of the vast importance that Jewish extremism and violence will have in shaping the future of the Middle East, this book introduces and explores the actual forces that are the most likely to play a significant role in Israeli extremism.

This is a study of political history. It seeks to describe and analyze the evolution of the major movements and actors involved in extremism and violence since the formation of the state of Israel. A fundamental presupposition of this study is that political violence does not exist in a vacuum and is not detached from nonviolent politics. Students of politics recognize today that political violence is almost always a behavioral by-product of extremist, extraparliamentary, and extralegal social movements. According to this approach, the study of violence involves not just the systematic observation of the political use of physical force but also the study of the larger milieu of ideological and cultural extremism of the society in question. The scholarly background for this assumption is presented in great detail in the methodological essay at the end of the book. The purpose of the appendix is fourfold: to provide the interested reader with a short historical introduction to the scholarship on political violence, a relatively new subfield in the study of politics; to identify the relationship between violent and nonviolent politics and demonstrate the evolutionary dynamics of violence and terrorism; to elaborate on the concepts and terminology used throughout the book; and to present and justify the analytical skeleton of this book.

Though focused exclusively on the history of Israeli violence, this study is by no means an exercise in revisionist history. My purpose is neither to unmask the "hidden" nature of Israeli politics nor to debunk the effort of the nation's political class to "hide" their brutal use of force. I am convinced that the full story of modern Israel is a tale of construction, not destruction, a story about the building of a free and largely democratic state in a troubled part of the world. What I am trying to show is that the largely successful Jewish endeavor has also had its downside manifested in domestic extremism and violence. The writing of such a book might not have been necessary just a few years ago, but Israel's internal division and bloodshed since the signing of the Oslo Accords have created both the need and the interest. It is, thus, my contention that a present-day portrait of political Israel is incomplete without a systematic examination of the nation's domestic violence.

Although the major goal of this study is to document the political violence perpetrated in Israel since 1948, it also has another purpose—the examination of the alleged demise in the Jewish state of the "ethic of Jewish restraint." A superficial examination of the facts revealed in this study is likely to suggest that Israelis today are a new breed of Jews who, unlike their brothers in the Diaspora, kill without remorse. Readers who form this opinion after reading a few chapters are encouraged to withhold their judgment until the last chapter, where the issue of Jewish exceptionalism is examined from historical and comparative perspectives. After some reflection, I decided to divide the book into two parts, violence in the *first* and *second* "Israeli Republics." This division reflects my agreement with the scholars who argue that the Six-Day War was a watershed in Israeli history and that the dramatic change in the ideological and cultural agenda of the nation justifies the distinction between the Israel that preceded and the Israel that followed June 1967. Largely focused on the major ideological conflicts of the nation and their violent expressions, this book lends, in fact, additional support to the distinction between the two Israeli republics.

The book's structure is as follows.

Chapter one discusses the violent struggle between the Israeli left and right during the birth of the state of Israel in 1948. The confrontation took place during the nation's War of Independence and peaked in the bloody events of *Altalena*, an arms ship brought over by Menachem Begin's Irgun underground and sunk under the orders of Prime Minister David Ben-Gurion. The armed struggle between the army of the newly created state and the Irgun was the closest the nation ever came to civil war. Another significant event of that era, which is discussed at length, is Lehi's (Israel Freedom Fighters) assassination of Count Bernadotte, the U.N. mediator in the 1948 war. This chapter offers both a historical narrative and an assessment of the role of political violence in Israel's formative and most critical year.

Chapter two examines Israeli violence in the first half of the 1950s, in particular that of right-wing and religious origins. It focuses on the rise, activities, and capture of two right-wing antigovernment underground groups and on Begin's 1952 assault on the Knesset following a fierce debate over the issue of Holocaust reparations from Germany. Also discussed is the political assassination of Dr. Israel Kastner, a leader of wartime Hungarian Jewry under German occupation, charged by the extreme right as a former collaborator with the Germans. In addition, the chapter explores violence within the Israeli labor movement exemplified in the conflict between the seamen's union and the Labor party establishment. The intense violence of the early 1950s is portrayed, however, as a remnant of prestate left-right animosities, and is shown retrospectively as a declining trend. This analysis indicates that rather than posing a new and significant threat to the young Israeli government, the violence of the early 1950s was a prestate relic, an expression of old and weakening animosities.

Chapter three introduces the reader to the *haredim*, the ultra-Orthodox Jews living in Israel who take part in national politics yet reject the Zionist state on religious grounds. The chapter focuses on the most extreme religious factions, which to this day refuse to recognize the Israeli state, to speak Hebrew, and to enjoy the state's social benefits. It analyzes the great paradox of these extremists—the gap between their intense denunciation of the Jewish state and their refusal to take up arms against it. This chapter shows, however, that the *haredim* are far from passive. They have waged fierce struggles against transportation on the Sabbath, archaeological digging in ancient graveyards, and the construction of a Mormon university in Jerusalem, as already mentioned. They have also launched campaigns against obscene posters, sex shops, and doctors facilitating human organ transplants. The chapter also surveys internal *haredi* violence: the power struggles among rabbinical courts and the perennial campaign against so-called sexual deviation within the community. Chapter three concludes part one.

Chapter four examines the impact of the Six-Day War on the Israeli collective consciousness, observes the rise of the second Israeli republic, and focuses on the first extremist left-wing responses to the 1967 occupation of the West Bank. It introduces the reader to two new extraparliamentary left-wing movements, Matzpen and Siah, which advocated total Israeli withdrawal from the occupied territories and full recognition of the PLO. The chapter also documents the eruption and dynamics of Sephardi violence in Israel expressed by the Black Panthers, a bitter, alienated, aggressive protest movement in the early 1970s. The violence of the Black Panthers, which brought the discontent of the second generation of Sephardi immigrants into the open, is examined against the background of the 1959 Wadi Salib riots, which were launched by Israel's first generation of Sephardi newcomers. This chapter analyzes the introduction of post-1967 extraparliamentary politics into Israeli public life and identifies the issues that increasingly divided the Israeli public.

Chapter five focuses on Gush Emunim, the powerful settler movement responsible for spearheading Jewish settlement in the occupied territories. The chapter examines the unintended development of religious violence in this pioneering and idealistic movement and the formation of the "Jewish Underground," which conspired to blow up the Muslim Dome of the Rock on Jerusalem's Temple Mount in the late 1970s. The evolution of Gush violence is demonstrated through the increasing friction between Muslims and Jews over Hebron's Cave of the Patriarchs, Nablus, and other West Bank sites. The origins of the terrorist underground are traced to the theological crisis over the 1978 Camp David Accords and the group's messianic convictions. The underground's "side jobs"—the successful attack on Arab mayors in 1980, the 1983 assault on Hebron's Muslim College, and the 1984 attempt to blow up five Arab buses full of passengers—illustrate the unexpected rise of settler terrorism. Also examined in the chapter is the struggle over Yamit, the last settlement to be evacuated in Sinai in the wake of Israel's peace accord with Egypt.

Chapter six examines the ideology, operations, and cultural impact of the late Rabbi Meir Kahane, the most extreme of all modern Jewish preachers. The chapter focuses on Kahane's philosophy of violence, the rabbi's anti-Arab preaching, and the implementation of both by the rabbi's followers in the Kach movement. The chapter also examines the violent interactions between Jews and Arabs in the late 1970s, the spread of militant ultranationalism and "Kahanism" during the Lebanon War, and the election of Kahane to the Knesset. The chapter concludes with the response of Israeli society to the quasi fascism of Kach and the containment of violence following the political murder of Peace Now activist Emil Greentzweig.

Chapter seven considers the violent consequences of the 1993 Oslo Accords between Israel and the PLO in the context of Baruch Goldstein's massacre in Hebron. The chapter describes the shock and confusion created within the settler community by the 1992 Labor electoral victory and the signing of the Oslo Accords. It identifies the tension between moderates and extremists over the proper settler responses to the peace process and Palestinian terrorism. The chapter addresses the classic question of what happens to messianic movements when prophesy fails, and explains the Hebron massacre within the framework of the crisis of messianic fundamentalism. Baruch Goldstein, a dedicated Kahane disciple, is shown to have been a killer by proxy, a representative of an articulated culture of violence that was bound to explode in response to the Oslo Accords and the resumption of Islamic terrorism.

Chapter eight traces the countdown to the Rabin assassination, examining the radicalization of the religious right since the Hebron massacre with special attention to the rhetoric of opinion leaders and rabbis. The movement of the radical right from delegitimation of the government as a political collectivity to the depersonalization, character assassination, and dehumanization of its leaders, Yitzhak Rabin and Shimon Peres, is documented in great detail. While distinguishing between the extremist and pragmatic components of the radical right, the chapter follows the extremist's takeover of the antigovernment struggle and the unwillingness of the pragmatists to curb their militant behavior and rhetoric. Attention is also devoted to the personality of Yigal Amir, Rabin's assassin, and the rulings of *din rodef* and *din moser*, which convinced the young man that in killing Rabin he was following the Halakha. Also discussed is the doctrine of Jewish zealotry, which made it possible for Amir, an obedient Orthodox Jew, to kill without rabbinical authorization.

Chapter nine concludes the book with an examination of the major question implied in its title: is Israeli domestic violence an indication of the end of the famed ethic of Jewish restraint? The chapter explores the issue of Jewish exceptionalism with regard to violence and shows that contrary to common belief, Diaspora Jews, just like their Israeli successors, had occasionally been involved in domestic violence. It is argued, however, that Israeli domestic violence, like Jewish violence in the Diaspora, has not matched the magnitude of Middle East atrocities or even the violence experienced by most Western societies. The chapter concludes with a discussion of the future of Israeli violence and a development of four potential scenarios of domestic violent struggles over the land of Israel.

PART ONE

Extremism and Violence in the First Israeli Republic, 1948–67

1

ON THE BRINK OF CIVIL WAR

Crisis at Year One

On Tuesday, June 22, 1948, at five o'clock in the afternoon, thousands of Israelis witnessed a scene they would never forget. Scattered in the streets surrounding the Tel Aviv beach, onlookers watched a large ship exploding in flames. Some of the ship's Jewish passengers were rescued by small emergency boats; others simply jumped into the water and swam among the bullets flying from the shore. The surrealistic scene, the last moments of the arms ship *Altalena*, would haunt Israeli collective consciousness for many years to come.

The most tragic dimension of the *Altalena* story was not the burning of the ship in front of a large crowd of Israelis and foreigners but the fact that the ship's bitter end was brought about just a few minutes earlier by an Israeli gun shell. The military unit responsible for the disaster, the only heavy gun battery of the young Israeli army, was ordered an hour earlier to sink the ship. The order came directly from general Yigal Yadin, the army's chief of operations. The execution did not take long. After four rounds of shells missed the ship came a fifth, direct hit.[1] In just a few minutes the ship was engulfed in explosions and uncontrollable fire. But the flames were only the beginning of the fighting. Several units of *Altalena* supporters surrounded the larger military contingent and battled them for several hours. Only a strict order from the rebels' commander to stop shooting brought the horrifying scene to a close. Never before or since has the young Israeli state been so close to civil war.

From Port de Bouce to Kfar Vitkin

The ship's tragic voyage began in New York City two years earlier. *Altalena* was a World War II American landing ship purchased by the Hebrew Committee for National Liberation, a Jewish lobbying organization serving as the American branch of Israel's Irgun Zevai Leumi (National Military Organization). The Irgun, the anti-British underground led by Menachem Begin, was very actively engaged in propaganda and fund-raising. With the British Mandate in Palestine drawing to a close, it had become increasingly clear that the next round would see Jews confronting Arabs in a war of life and death. Irgun commanders, like everybody else, knew that without arms the Jews would have no chance. *Altalena* was purchased with the hope of sending a ship full of armed and well-trained fighters to Palestine to help the nation fulfill its dream of independence. The ship's appellation was the pen name of the Irgun's first supreme commander, Vladimir (Ze'ev) Jabotinsky, a legendary Zionist leader and founder of the Revisionist Movement, the Irgun's parent political organization.

Altalena's cargo, a huge load of badly needed arms, was given to the Irgun by the French government. Chaim Ariel, the Irgun representative in France, was very well connected in both the French government and the French underground. He was responsible, to a large extent, for the amicable post–World War II relationship between the former anti-Nazi resistance in France and the anti-British Irgun in Palestine. These friendly relations were to prove priceless in the postwar era, when several of Ariel's friends became highly influential in the French government. Foreign Minister Georges Bidault, a prominent opponent of the Nazis and member of the French resistance, was personally responsible for the arms deal. Furious at the British for driving them out of Syria and Lebanon, the French watched the Jewish struggle in Palestine with great sympathy. In addition, they were increasingly at odds with the rising tide of Pan Arabism in the Middle East and the demand to expel the French presence from North

Africa. A strong and stable Jewish ally in the Middle-East, in French eyes, could be of great help.[2]

While the British tried to block illegal Jewish immigration to Palestine, and even strived to keep Holocaust survivors from getting close to Mediterranean ports of embarkation, the French granted these refugees thousands of entry visas to their country. Keenly aware of British sensitivities and the risk of a confrontation with their World War II ally, the French did everything they could to keep the *Altalena* arms deal secret. Aside from a few defense officials, only the French prime minister and defense minister knew about the plan.[3]

Bidault and his colleagues may have been aware of the controversial status of the Irgun in Zionist Palestine, but they still wanted to help. Having followed the news reports of the aggressive underground, which since 1944 had made the life of the British in Palestine increasingly miserable, they believed it to be a central actor in the Jewish struggle for independence. They were apparently not disturbed that in granting arms to the Irgun, they were taking sides in an intense political struggle. Since its inception in 1937, the Irgun had been a dissident right-wing organization refusing to abide by the instructions of the Jewish Agency, the leading organization of the Jewish community.[4] Since during the Mandate the British were the sole authority in the land and the Jewish community was organized in a voluntary way, the heads of the Jewish Agency had no legal remedy for the Irgun's lack of discipline. Relations went especially sour as the struggle with the British intensified, with the Irgun resorting to violence against them. Although the ultranationalist organization did not fully challenge the national leadership of individuals such as David Ben-Gurion, it was increasingly critical of their postwar liberation strategy. Irgun commanders opposed the 1947 U.N. Partition Resolution, dividing Palestine between the Jews and the Arabs; they believed that Israel should keep more of the biblical Land of Israel. The Irgun warned the government that if it did not fight for full liberation of Israeli land, and if it did not insist that Jerusalem become the capital of Israel, they would fight on their own to expand the borders of the new state.[5]

The *Altalena* arms deal was finalized before the May 14, 1948, termination of the British Mandate and the official declaration of the State of Israel. Its purpose was to bolster the military capabilities of the five thousand Irgun fighters.[6] But the establishment of the state instantly changed the status of the organization. One of the first laws of the newly created state, already subject to massive Arab invasion, mandated the formation of a single army and required all qualified citizens to enlist. The government of Israel made it unequivocally clear that it would not tolerate the continued presence of private militias and that the Irgun would have to be dissolved. Negotiations for the organization's dissolution and its merger with the Israeli army were long and difficult, reflecting years of political disagreement, confrontations, and mistrust. Facing the massive Arab invasion, an Irgun dissolution agreement was nevertheless reached. It obliged all Irgun soldiers to join the army but allowed them to do so with their commanders. It was therefore agreed that the army would approve several intact Irgun battalions. The agreement also stipulated, however, that Irgun arms, ammunition, and military installations be given to the army and that the Irgun must fold as a military organization. Moreover, Irgun independent purchase operations were to cease, and all contacts were to be transferred to the newly created Ministry of Defense. In recognition of the logistical problems involved in the merger and the time required for its completion, it was agreed that a temporary Irgun command would be established to facilitate the agreement's implementation. Since the Israeli government did not claim sovereignty over the city of Jerusalem at that time, the agreement did not include Irgun units fighting in the city.[7]

Altalena's voyage to Israel represented a clear breach of the Irgun dissolution agreement, according to which the ship and its weapons should have been handed over to Israeli officials in France, who should then have brought the operation to completion. But Irgun diehards in France, hostile to Ben-Gurion's government and dissatisfied with the merger, took the arms into their own hands.[8] These Irgun operatives sought to supply Irgun units, who were fighting the Arabs almost empty-handed, with improved stockpiles. They believed the weapons could change the balance of power on the battlefield. A second, perhaps more important reason for not sharing the *Altalena* information with government officials was the secretive nature of the French operation. Any unnecessary noise could have blown up the transaction. They knew, in addition, that the final decision about the arms would be made by Menachem Begin in Israel and that their job was limited to getting the French part of the operation done.

The *Altalena* sailing created another legal problem, however. On June 11, 1948, a truce was declared in Palestine. The truce terms, negotiated by Count Folke Bernadotte, the U.N. peace mediator in Palestine, provided for a ban on the introduction of additional weapons and required that male immigrants of military age would be gathered in camps under United Nations supervision. A U.N. Observing Force was sent to the front to oversee the truce. The *Altalena* landing, planned by the Irgun for late June, would have constituted a clear violation of the truce and put the government of Israel in an embarrassing situation.

Altalena's trip to Israel was full of communications problems. The ship's old transmitter was only partially functional, which often left the Tel Aviv Irgun headquarters, the ship's commander, and the Irgun Paris command post in the dark. The ship left France's Port de Bouce on June 11 without even informing Begin.[9] Secrecy was deemed essential for fear of British or Arab sabotage. But on June 12, the cover was already blown. Both Reuters and the Associated Press reported that about one thousand Jewish volunteers left for Palestine aboard a landing ship full of arms. Begin first learned of the ship's embarkation by tuning in to a BBC radio broadcast early in the morning, a habit he acquired in his long underground career. Fully aware of the cease-fire violation involved in the ship's arrival in Israel, Begin immediately ordered the ship to stop and await instructions. Simultaneously, he informed Ben-Gurion's aides of the ship's presence in the Mediterranean and asked for permission to land.[10]

By June 16, Begin could happily cable *Altalena*, "full speed ahead." This he did after getting a green light from Ben-Gurion's aide, Israel Galilee.[11] The *Altalena* unloading plan involved a night landing in Kfar Vitkin, an unguarded beach twenty miles north of Tel Aviv, and a quick unloading to be completed before sunrise. No one in Israel's top defense leadership seemed to have been particularly concerned about breaking the truce. The Jewish state was receiving nightly loads of military hardware in several other remote locations. *Altalena*'s unloading problem was, in this regard, only a technical matter of preparation and coordination. Difficulties emerged, however over the details of the unloading. While Begin had no intention of using the arms against government forces, he wanted to have a say in their distribution. The Irgun commander, who considered *Altalena*'s five-million-dollar shipment as a great Irgun coup, wanted his men in the army to be proud of their underground's great success as well as to be the first to benefit from the ship's weapons. He also wished to have them symbolically participate in the unloading.[12] There was also the issue of Jerusalem. Since Jerusalem had not yet been annexed by Israel, the Irgun dissolution agreement did not apply there, and several hundred Irgun fighters operated in the city, maintaining independent camps. Begin wanted 20 percent of *Altalena*'s arms to go to these Jerusalem units. Ill-equipped and under enormous Arab pressure, they badly needed any guns they could get their hands on. *Altalena* had everything they needed.[13]

There was no way that Israel's suspicious prime minister could accept the Irgun's demands. For Ben-Gurion, a crusader for the cause of a unitary army and a single line of command, Begin's conditions contradicted everything he believed in.[14] They also sounded suspicious. Mossad (Israel's intelligence service) agents fed the prime minister information about Irgun plans for a potential independent action in the war front. In addition to the early information he had about *Altalena*'s whereabouts in France, Ben-Gurion was told of Irgun fund-raising among wealthy Israelis for a potential future confrontation with the government.[15] He knew that the extremist militia was no match for the Israeli army. But with *Altalena*'s weapons, Begin's five thousand soldiers could be a source of great trouble. And in a struggle with formidable Arab forces, an internal battle with rebel militia was inconceivable. All efforts must be dedicated to winning the war.

For many years, while leading the *yishuv*'s (Jewish community in Palestine) struggle for independence, Ben-Gurion had had to put up with the dissidents. Now, as the prime minister of a sovereign Israel, he had both law and power on his side—there was no need for a compromise. In addition to his political disagreement with the Irgun, the prime minister despised the organization's soldiers. When once visiting the Jaffa front, held by an Irgun battalion, he was saluted by the organization's fighters. Begin was informed that Ben-Gurion got excited and told his aides, "I did not know they have such fellows." But in his personal notebook, Ben-Gurion recorded a very different opinion: "I met an Irgun guard [in Jaffa]," he wrote. "I received their salutes. It may be an accident but they all look like criminals."[16] The prime minister saw only one way of peacefully resolving the *Altalena* crisis. The unloading would be carried out by the army, and all equipment would go to the army's central stores; Irgun soldiers serving in the Israeli army would get their share of the *Altalena* shipment as would all other soldiers in the army. But on June 19, the Irgun-government negotiations over *Altalena* ended in a stalemate. Israel Galilee, Ben-Gurion's envoy, told Begin, "We are taking our hands off the arms' unloading."[17]

In their worst nightmares, neither Begin nor his more suspicious colleagues expected a military attack on the ship. Their immediate concern in the talks with the government was the technical problem of unloading the ship. *Altalena*'s large arms shipment—consisting of five thousand guns, two hundred and fifty Bren machine guns, five machine-gun carriers, a huge amount of ammunition and explosives, and tons of other military equipment—required crates and heavy equipment the Irgun did not possess. The organization's support units, moreover, were no longer functional.[18] This is why the only part of the Kfar Vitkin operation that went smoothly upon the ship's landing was the immigrants' descent to the shore and their quick busing to immigration centers. Matters became more complicated during the unloading of arms. Just as Irgun commanders were starting to unload, they discovered that they were being slowly surrounded by the Israeli army. The arrests of several Irgun volunteers trying to get to the beach, as well as the sound of warning shots against others, created at once a grim situation. Amichai Paglin, Irgun operations chief and the man in charge of the unloading, had always been suspicious of the government's intentions. Sensing a trap, he ordered the ship to be promptly reloaded; gun boxes already on the beach were returned to *Altalena*. Paglin's tentative plan was to take the ship back to sea and find a new landing spot, perhaps in an Arab section of Palestine that could be taken by force. On learning of Paglin's pessimistic reading of the situation, which he did not share, Begin decided to replace his operations chief with Jacob Meridor, a former Irgun deputy commander.[19]

The pace of the *Altalena* confrontation was largely dictated by David Ben-Gurion. The bellicose prime minister was not interested in compromise and insisted on the ship's surrender. To do that he greatly dramatized the situation. Ben-Gurion had known about the Irgun ship for nearly two weeks but did not choose to inform his cabinet ministers until June 20, just before the first unloading effort. The matter was presented to the cabinet as a shocking Irgun conspiracy, which took the government and the army by surprise. It was further described to the ministers as a violation of the truce and an unacceptable challenge to the government's authority. Under those circumstances, which included great time pressure, the cabinet discussed the use of force. Each minister expressed the hope that force would not be necessary but authorized the operation commander to employ whatever means—including force as a last resort—to attain *Altalena*'s full compliance.[20]

On June 21, at 1:15 A.M., Begin received an ultimatum from Israel's chief of staff. Begin was informed of the army's decision to expropriate *Altalena*'s weapons and ordered to surrender the ship within ten minutes. Following a short consultation with Meridor, Begin refused the order and demanded to talk to the military commander in charge. The commander declined Begin's request and both sides alerted their militaries. Surrounded by the much larger force of the Israeli army, Irgun soldiers on the beach moved into combat positions.[21]

The expiration of the ten-minute ultimatum did not, however, lead to an immediate attack; over the next fourteen hours, several Israeli mayors and non-Labor ministers in Ben-Gurion's cabinet tried to negotiate a compromise. The prime minister and his left-wing cabinet ministers held firm and ordered the continuation of army preparations for a showdown with the rebels. Among the preparations was an effort to mobilize the young Israeli air force to bomb *Altalena* and to ready the navy for a concurrent seaside attack on the ship. Many officers, especially within the air force, refused to participate. A large number of them were Jewish volunteers from the United States, Europe, and South Africa who would have no part in what would be the opening salvos of a Jewish civil war.[22]

The magnitude of the crisis became apparent when Irgun soldiers within the Israeli army began to desert their units. Army battalion 57, fully staffed by Irgun commanders and soldiers, left its Sarafend camp and moved toward the Kfar Vitkin beach. The first casualties, two dead and several wounded soldiers, resulted from an armed confrontation twenty miles from Kfar Vitkin between battalion units and army soldiers trying to block their movement. With the failure of mediation efforts and the general mobilization of the army, Irgun commanders saw that they had no chance.[23] Begin, determined to avoid civil war, pushed for a third alternative that would neither involve an armed struggle nor require unconditional surrender. His idea was to move the ship from Kfar Vitkin to Tel Aviv. At Tel Aviv, Israel's largest city and an Irgun stronghold, the rebels could count on large public support. They could also bet that no Israeli leader would dare fire at a Jewish ship in front of thousands of citizens. Landing in Tel Aviv was the Irgun's best option for an honorable middle way.

But just as they were ready to board the small motorboat that would take them to the ship, Irgun commanders on the beach found themselves under artillery and mortar siege. Although most of the firepower did not hit its targets because many soldiers refused to kill fellow Jews, the barrage was heavy and produced a few casualties. On the outskirts of Kfar Vitkin, meanwhile, Moshe Dayan's commando battalion engaged Irgun fighters in battle. Only the restraint displayed by both sides kept the number of casualties to one dead and three wounded.[24] Back on the coast, an attempt to move Begin and a few of his officers aboard *Altalena* was met with fire from the sea, and a few Israeli navy ships joined in the hunt. Only the reluctance of soldiers in the field to fight their brothers prevented June 21 from becoming a bloodbath. Yet the conflict indicated the explosive potential of the *Altalena* dispute. Begin hoped to defuse the situation by sailing to Tel Aviv.

Confrontation on the Tel Aviv Beach

Altalena's last day started with the midnight arrival of the ship at Tel Aviv beach. Irgun supreme commander Menachem Begin and a few of his officers were aboard, as well as the ship's crew, several overseas volunteers, and about forty Irgun fighters. Convinced that Ben-Gurion would not order the army to attack *Altalena* in front of thousands of Tel Avivians, Begin ordered the former World War II ship to get as close to the beach as possible and to land on a rock so that it could not be forced anywhere else. Begin, ready to compromise, believed that time was on his side and expected Ben-Gurion's emissaries to contact him to resolve the situation peacefully. Begin's cautious optimism for a peaceful resolution to the crisis stemmed in large part from his patriotism and conviction that since he never intended to fight Israeli soldiers, the crisis was the result of a misunderstanding. A little more time for clarification would remove all outstanding difficulties. Sooner or later, Begin reassured his men, the ship would be unloaded peacefully.[25]

But the Irgun commander was sadly mistaken. Ben-Gurion, the majority of his ministers, and all the top army commanders greatly mistrusted Begin and considered *Altalena* as a seditious act of the first degree. An early notice of the troubles ahead was posted on *Altalena*'s deck about an hour after its midnight arrival at Tel Aviv. A small boat sent to the beach, apparently spotted by a vigilant observer, was met by heavy fire. The observer saw the boat from his position in Palmach headquarters, the elite brigade of the Israeli army. In addition to its rich military experience, Palmach was also staffed by unswervingly loyal Labor youth whom the government could trust completely. At sunrise it was discovered that *Altalena* had hit a rock in Tel Aviv's busiest beach area. The "landing" site was just in front of the Kete-Dan Hotel, the U.N. peacekeeping force's headquarters. The command and communications centers of several Israeli military units also overlooked the beach area.

Ben-Gurion learned of *Altalena*'s landing by 2:00 A.M. and immediately ordered a special cabinet meeting for noon of that Tuesday. Acting in his capacity as the nation's defense minister, Ben-Gurion went in the morning to the navy's headquarters to find out about contingency plans for *Altalena*. The furious prime minister kept walking nervously from one end of the room to the other, talking angrily to himself: "Where is Yigal [Yadin, operations chief]? If he does not show up soon, I'll have him replaced."[26] Busy at his Ramat Gan headquarters, Yadin did not believe the navy, acting alone, was capable of handling the *Altalena* crisis. Instead, he developed a detailed, comprehensive plan to commandeer the ship. Anticipating a confrontation on the beach between the army and an expected throng of Irgun volunteers, Yadin entrusted the entire operation to the Kiriyati Brigade, the military contingent responsible for the Tel Aviv vicinity. "Operation Unity," as the mission was ironically named, required Kiriyati soldiers to surround and capture Irgun troops positioned near the beach.

Yadin's worst fears about the Irgun were soon actualized. Following the news about the ship's Tel Aviv landing, with Begin aboard, hundreds of Irgun members flocked to the beach. Many of them, already officers and soldiers in the army, deserted their units and came fully armed. Irgun cars with loudspeakers drove through Tel Aviv's streets soliciting a massive presence to support the Irgun on the beach. Yadin soon realized that the Kiriyati soldiers were incapable of carrying out their mission. This was due partly to a manpower shortage but mostly to the refusal of a significant number of soldiers to use their arms against fellow Jews. Given the population density of the area and the large number of streets and alleys, it was virtually impossible to block passage to the beach. The need for a large-scale operation would finally bring Yadin, acting on a strict order from Ben-Gurion, to put in writing detailed instructions for the entire officer corps in the area.

> Purpose:
>
> To bring the enemy present in the vessel docking in front of the Tel Aviv beach (the landing ship) to unconditional surrender by all means and methods at your disposal. Your job is to concentrate the following forces and be ready for the beginning of the operation and opening of fire, according to my order and in line with the instructions of the government of Israel.
>
> The method:
>
> a. The creation of an operational zone as a base for offensive action in front of the landing area of the landing ship.
> b. Organization and securing of areas close to your operational base.
> c. Warning fire.
> d. A demand for unconditional surrender.
> e. If the demand for surrender is refused, a continued operation till it reaches a conclusion. . . .[27]

Yadin's document, defining Irgun men aboard the ship as "enemies," left no doubt that the army had no negotiations in mind and that any *Altalena* movement short of unconditional surrender was to be met by fire. It reflected Ben-Gurion's determination to bring a quick end to the *Altalena* affair, an end that might take many lives. A short communiqué to the press indicated that the cabinet approved of Ben-Gurion's strategy "to demand a complete surrender." Unaware of the government plans, Begin and others aboard *Altalena* kept yelling to the beach, "Soldiers of the Haganah [Labor Movement militia], do not open fire! We have brought arms for both of us! We came to fight together! We are not going to open fire! We shall not lift a finger against brothers! Soldiers of Israel, we have brought plenty of weapons, come get it!" The sounds of Israeli and Jewish songs drifted from the deck.[28]

The lack of any message from the government led *Altalena*'s command to begin unloading the cargo. A boat carrying arms and a dozen armed men was sent to the beach with the additional purpose of starting negotiations with the government. While announcing their intention to unload and asking their supporters in the area for help, *Altalena*'s loudspeakers called upon the soldiers to hold their fire. The announcement was accompanied by a warning that if fired at, *Altalena* men would respond in kind. The first boat made its way to the beach safely, and the men quickly took combat positions vis-à-vis the army. Palmach and Irgun soldiers spoke to one another and even agreed on informal boundaries that would hold as long as there was no firing from the other side. The situation changed dramatically with the arrival of the second boat, however. Under direct instructions from Yadin, Palmach commanders ordered the second boat to return to the ship. When the Irgun sailors refused, gunfire broke out for the first time and both sides suffered casualties. Fire was also directed at the ship. Short cease-fires were negotiated by the local commanders to evacuate the wounded.[29]

Since the Kiriyati brigade was incapable of doing its job, it became clear to Yadin that the fighting on behalf of the government would have to be conducted by the Palmach. But Palmach's command post was manned by auxiliary and support units with only a few fit combatants. One of these was Palmach operations chief, Colonel Yitzhak Rabin. Rabin came to Tel Aviv for a meeting and made an early detour to meet his girlfriend, Lea, who was serving in the Palmach communications center. Instantly the senior officer in the building, Rabin understood the potential danger of Irgun men storming the Palmach headquarters. Rabin reacted quickly, throwing hand grenades at Irgun men who approached the building and ordering several Palmach off-duty combat units to report immediately to the scene. Rabin's superior, Palmach commander Yigal Alon, soon took over. Replacing the incompetent Kiriyati commander, Alon ordered full mobilization. The situation was getting out of hand and casualties were mounting. The men aboard *Altalena*, who showed no intention of surrendering, were not allowed to carry their wounded to the beach for fear they would bring in more guns and ammunition.[30]

The ensuing explosion on *Altalena*, which forced its people to evacuate the ship, was not the only ordeal. Some Palmach and army units continued to shoot at the swimming survivors despite a number of white flags flown on the ship's deck to indicate surrender. Not all the fire was meant to kill, but there were egregious exceptions. Sporadic fighting between Irgun and army units on the beach and in the surrounding streets went on for a few more hours. Several Irgun groups even prevailed over Kiriyati soldiers and took their arms. A major concern of the ship's commanders was the life and safety of Menachem Begin. Irgun chief officers were certain that Begin, their most cherished symbol of defiance, was personally targeted by the government. Faced with intensifying fire and increasing casualties, they desperately tried to persuade their commander to quickly leave the ship. Begin refused, however, making clear he would leave only after all the wounded had been taken ashore. There was no personal hunt, however, for the Irgun commander and, to the relief of his followers, he finally made it safely to the beach aboard a light boat.[31]

Angry, exhausted, and deeply depressed by the aftermath of his stunning defeat, Begin made one of his most emotional speeches ever. Speaking for two hours from a secret Irgun transmitter in Tel Aviv, he told his side of the story. He was occasionally unable to control his emotions and his already broken voice was choked by tears. Categorically denying all government allegations about a possible Irgun conspiracy, Begin described in great detail the lengthy negotiations over *Altalena*. He maintained that there was plenty of time to resolve the problem peacefully had the government only pursued such a path. Insisting that the Irgun had not been given a fair chance to prove its loyalty to the nation and that Ben-Gurion was determined to destroy the ship regardless of Irgun concessions, Begin called the government cynical and charged it with "crime . . . stupidity . . . and blindness." The most significant point in Begin's speech, however, was his appeal to Irgun activists across the country. All Irgun soldiers were instructed by their commander to hold their fire and not to fight back. "As long as the enemy is at our gate, there should be no civil war" was Begin's memorable command. Begin told his men that although in sinking *Altalena*, the government had lost its legitimacy, military resistance—and potential civil war—was not an option.[32]

The public reaction to Begin's dramatic speech was mixed. While many sympathizers were deeply moved by his emotional outpouring and even wept along with him, others felt this was a poor performance. The person they listened to on the radio was not the illustrious rebel who had courageously fought the British and defied their efforts to capture him. The speech revealed a broken man incapable of defending himself and his people. The Irgun commander was especially ridiculed in Labor circles as soft, pathetic, and miserable. Begin was definitely not made of the same material as their resolute leader, David Ben-Gurion, who was determined to assert his authority and prepared even to risk civil war.[33] Weren't they wrong, certain Irgun activists asked themselves, in having taken Begin so seriously for so long?

The sinking of *Altalena* and the military conflict that consumed the life of nineteen Israelis and overseas volunteers led to the collapse of the Irgun dissolution agreement. The army could no longer trust Irgun units that had fought against it on the Kfar Vitkin and Tel Aviv beaches; and Irgun soldiers were unwilling to serve in the army that had sunk their ship and killed their friends. The result of the new situation was "operation purification," a coordinated army effort to arrest Irgun deserters and take control over all the organization's installations. A direct Yadin order, made possible by Israel's emergency regulations authorizing extralegal activities in wartime, led to a massive raid on Irgun bases, camps, clubs, and homes. Weapons, ammunition, and equipment were confiscated. Many Irgun commanders and soldiers were arrested. Refusing to believe that the Irgun would refrain from fighting, army commanders further planned a military assault on Metzudat Zeev, the Tel Aviv nerve center of the Revisionist movement. The attack, launched at dawn, involved the use of firearms and live ammunition. The building was conquered easily; assault units met no resistance.[34]

The campaign against the Irgun reached its peak with the administrative arrest of five members of the organization's supreme command. The arrest, preceded by the apprehension and brutal interrogation of Eliyahu Lenkin and Monroe Fine, *Altalena*'s commander and skipper, included Jacob Meridor, Begin's second in command and Hillel Kook (Peter Bergson), the former head of the Hebrew Committee for National Liberation, which spearheaded the Irgun public relations campaign in the United States. No specific charges were brought against the five detainees. Israel's emergency regulations, a legacy of the British Mandate, authorize government ministers to arrest and imprison, without trial, suspects deemed top security risks. The detention, challenged by the prisoners in the Supreme Court, was upheld by a court majority of two to one. The court, though unhappy with the government's arbitrary act, found no legal way of overruling the emergency regulations. Only massive international pressure, spearheaded by Kook's friends in the American Congress, brought the release of the five after two months in prison.[35]

The tragic end of *Altalena*, the ruthless chase of Irgun soldiers after the ship's sinking, the unnecessary attack on the Irgun civilian center in Tel Aviv, and the arrest of top Irgun leaders were all too much for the non-Labor ministers in the government. Four men, Rabbi Fishman-Maimon, Moshe Shapiro, Yitzhak Gruenebaum, and Peretz Bernstein, were the cabinet representatives of Israel's Zionist-religious community and the political center. During the ship's crisis they tried, but failed, to reduce the tension. Forced by the Labor cabinet majority into a permanent minority, they watched Ben-Gurion's ruthless measures with increasing frustration. The continued repression of the Irgun after the sinking of the ship was for them an undemocratic and illegal operation. No longer willing to bear responsibility for what they considered Ben-Gurion's excessive militancy, they considered leaving the cabinet.[36]

The ensuing resignation of Fishman-Maimon and Shapiro and the intense opposition of Gruenebaum and Bernstein, who chose to stay and fight, was a major blow to Ben-Gurion. The prime minister knew that regardless of the automatic cabinet majority he enjoyed, he badly needed the four ministers to bring a sense of national legitimacy to his government. Eager to avoid the image of a sectarian Labor politician and to present himself as the impartial leader of the entire nation, Ben-Gurion agreed at the end of June to moderate his anti-Irgun crusade. Backing down from his original intention to eradicate the organization and its members, including independent Irgun bases in Jerusalem, Ben-Gurion agreed to the formation of a three-man cabinet committee, led by Gruenebaum, to negotiate with the Irgun for their reintegration into the army. Many Irgun prisoners were released, and tensions were somewhat defused.[37]

But Ben-Gurion never expressed regret about his handling of the *Altalena* affair. Long after he left office, "the old man" thought the sinking of the ship a virtuous act. Many times he referred to the weapon that sunk the ship as the "holy gun" and repeated in numerous variations the summary of the affair he presented to the parliament in 1948,

> Never did a burning of a ship serve the welfare of the *yishuv* so well as the burning of this Irgun ship. . . . The Irgun ship could have blown up our military power and this had to be prevented. . . . What was done to the arms ship was a great salvation made possible by a disaster. While the Irgun is responsible for the disaster, the salvation was brought over by a government not dissuaded by false mercy which could have produced much greater bloodshed. . . . Blessed is the gun which exploded this ship. . . . When we build the Temple, that gun should be placed near the main gate.[38]

Bad Blood: From Arlosoroff's Assassination to the "Season" and Deir Yassin

The armed struggle over the *Altalena* affair need not have happened. If the ship had been brought to Israel just a few weeks earlier, if Menachem Begin and his colleagues had realized Ben-Gurion's determination and yielded to the Israeli army or if Ben-Gurion had been a bit more flexible, the tragedy could have been avoided. But the *Altalena* crisis was not an accident. The confrontation was the culmination of years of animosity, misunderstanding, intolerance, and communication failures between the organized leadership of the *yishuv* and the Irgun.[39]

From their inception, the Revisionist Movement and the Irgun represented a challenge to the Labor Movement, the dominant force in Palestine's Zionist politics beginning in the early 1920s. At stake were deep policy disagreements as to the relations with the British and strategies of Israeli nation building. Since the roots of both ideological camps originated in the nondemocratic eastern Europe of the early twentieth century and their leaders were deeply influenced by the extreme left and right of their countries of origin, the confrontation was hardly held in an atmosphere of civility and mutual respect. Both movements believed they had a monopoly on the truth and all but disregarded the convictions of the other side.[40] The intensification of the conflict in Palestine between the Jews and the Arabs greatly radicalized the internal Zionist debate.

A dramatic turning point in the evolution of the Labor-Revisionist conflict was the 1933 assassination of Chaim Arlosoroff, a young and promising Labor leader. Arlosoroff was murdered at the height of a vicious personal campaign conducted by B'rith Habirionim (Covenant of Thugs), a small and extremist Revisionist group. Active in Palestine since the late 1920s, leaders of B'rith Habirionim were profoundly influenced by Europe's emerging fascism. Also inspired by the ancient Jewish Zealots, who engaged in domestic terrorism during the last days of Jerusalem's Second Temple, they advocated the use of violence for political goals.[41] The campaign of the Zionist extreme right focused on Arlosoroff's attempts to negotiate with the newly formed Nazi government in Germany the possibility of allowing wealthy German Jews to leave with their money provided they used it to purchase German goods and bring them to Palestine. The Revisionist Movement in general and B'rith Habirionim in particular were furious with the agreement. From their perspective it represented a deal with the devil, only helping Nazi Germany to cope with an international trade boycott from world Jewish organizations. While the direct involvement of B'rith Habirionim in the Arlosoroff assassination had never been established and the B'rith's suspects were freed on legal technicalities, the Labor Movement remained convinced that they had assassinated Arlosoroff. The murder led to an unprecedented delegitimation of the Revisionist movement in the powerful Labor press and was responsible for its widespread stigmatization as fascist and terrorist.

"Vladimir Hitler" was the name given by Ben-Gurion to Revisionist leader Jabotinsky during one debate.[42]

The stigma of terrorism and fascism attached to Jabotinsky's followers gained momentum following Irgun's 1937 decision to break *havlagah*, the *yishuv*'s policy of self-restraint against the Arabs. The Irgun was a small militia that in 1929 split away from the Haganah, Labor's main defense organization. In the early 1930s it increasingly came under the spell of Jabotinsky and the Revisionist Movement. Young Jabotinsky followers or Israelis who disliked the restrained struggle of the Labor leadership were natural candidates for the Irgun. The 1936 outbreak of the great Arab revolt, which brought massive terrorism to the small Jewish community in Palestine, forced all Jewish defense organizations to respond. Though public sentiment grew for a retributive response against Arab terrorism, the political leaders of Haganah continued to pursue a policy of self-restraint. This stance of *havlagah* called for aggressive defense against Arab attacks but rejected unequivocally the option of attacks on uninvolved civilian Arabs.[43] Irgun commanders became increasingly critical of *havlagah* and called for a policy of counterterrorism. Led by its commander, David Raziel, the Irgun decided to "break" *havlagah* and engage in massive anti-Arab terrorism.[44] While there was nothing the mainstream leadership could legally do about the Irgun, its terrorism was highly resented. The Labor leadership eschewed terrorism because of both ethical reasons and calculated political considerations of not associating the Jewish community with systematic atrocities. *Yishuv* leaders believed it important to prove to the British and the rest of the world that unlike the Arabs, the Jews were a civilized community and a reliable ally. Irgun terrorism, they believed, would give the enemies of the Jews in Whitehall and other anti-Semitic centers plenty of ammunition for their positions.[45]

Between 1937 and 1939, Irgun fighters resorted to counterterrorism with no remorse. They ambushed and attacked Arab buses and cars, and hid explosives in milk cans and pickup trucks, killing or wounding scores of Arab civilians. Vowing not to let any Arab terror attack go unanswered, the Irgun developed a sophisticated underground infrastructure to sustain their effort.[46] And Irgun's terrorism was not confined to the Arabs. Following its 1936–39 anti-Arab radicalization, the organization had also become increasingly hostile to the British. Their conviction that the British were becoming pro-Arab was strengthened by the brutal interrogations of Irgun prisoners suspected of terrorism. It is highly likely that Irgun terror operations would have eventually been extended to the British without additional reasons, but in the spring of 1939, a special incentive was added. In 1939, the British issued a White Paper imposing severe restrictions on Jewish immigration and calling for the future establishment in Palestine of a single state dominated by Arabs. The White Paper was, for all practical purposes, a death sentence for the *yishuv*. It generated enormous animosity toward the British even among the more moderate parts of the Jewish community. Irgun's answer was anti-British terrorism, carried out through assassination of British officers and placing explosives in British installations.[47]

The tension between the Irgun and the *yishuv* leadership was significantly reduced between 1939 and 1944. Following the outbreak of World War II, the Irgun declared a cease-fire with the British. All operations were suspended and several Irgun members even offered their help in the war effort. Irgun's legendary commander, David Raziel, was killed in 1941 while on a British intelligence mission in Iraq.[48] Meanwhile, Lehi (Israel's Freedom Fighters—an Irgun splinter organization) continued to launch anti-British attacks in Palestine. Lehi, launched in 1940 by Abraham Stern, was a very extremist anti-British terrorist underground, and Lehi guerrillas fought the British during the darkest days of World War II. When everybody else within the Jewish community of Palestine declared a cease-fire with the British and prayed that the Allied forces would survive the 1940–42 Nazi offensive, Lehi fighters placed bombs in British installations and killed British soldiers. Their leaders even sent messages of support to the Nazis and offered their cooperation in the future Nazi world order.[49] Lehi's hopes for replacing the larger and more popular Irgun were not fulfilled, however, and the organization never attracted more than a few hundred followers.

The situation changed dramatically in February 1944, when the Irgun, under its new commander, Menachem Begin, resumed its anti-British struggle. British installations and camps came under attack from both Lehi and Irgun fire. Begin justified this "revolt" by pointing to the British refusal to rescind the infamous White Paper and their closure of Palestine to incoming Jewish refugees. By 1944, when an Allied victory in the war was assumed, Great Britain lost its excuses for mistreating the Jews.[50] Begin's reading of the new political situation, however, was at odds with that of David Ben-Gurion and Chaim Weizmann, the two leading figures of the Zionist movement. Both leaders believed that 1944 could be the year of the political breakthrough long awaited by the Jews. Winston Churchill was a friend and there was a hope that he might become the "Lord Balfour of 1944." In 1917, a year before the end of World War I, the Jews had received from His Majesty's Government the Balfour Declaration, recognizing their right for a homeland in Palestine. Could the Zionists now hope for a Churchill Declaration granting them statehood and independence? The last thing the political leadership of the *yishuv* needed was Jewish terrorism in Palestine, a sure recipe for alienating Churchill's friendly cabinet as well as turning British public opinion against greater independence for the Jews.[51] Menachem Begin, a political neophyte who had been in Palestine only two years, became the epitome of dissident negativism.

The anti-British operations of the dissidents were considered so destructive to the *yishuv* that by the fall of 1944 the Haganah planned to launch a full-scale crackdown on the Irgun and severely damage its operational capabilities. The plan involved informing the British of Irgun activists, detaining many of them in Haganah installations, and damaging their logistical systems. The code name of the operation was Season (a reference to hunting season), and in October 1944 future Haganah participants were offered one-week crash courses.[52] There were still some hesitations, however. Jewish collaboration with the British against other Jews was unprecedented, especially when it involved arrests, long prison sentences, and potential exile. The leaders were also uncertain about the readiness of Haganah members to act against their right-wing counterparts. Then came an event that dramatically aggravated an already grave situation.

On November 6, 1944, in Cairo, Lehi members murdered Walter Edward Guinness, the first Baron Moyne. Lord Moyne was a distinguished member of the British war cabinet and served as state minister for the Middle East. He was also a close friend of Winston Churchill. Lehi commanders killed Moyne because they believed him to be anti-

Semitic and personally responsible for blocking the entrance to Palestine of Holocaust survivors and other Jewish refugees.[53] Moyne's assassination had a disastrous effect on British-Jewish relations. It shocked Churchill and British public opinion; all hopes for another Balfour Declaration were shattered. Britain's prime minister lost all interest in the Zionist cause and began to ignore the question of Palestine. Aware of the enormous damage caused by the Moyne assassination, furious at the brainless dissidents, and fearful of British retaliation against the *yishuv*, the Executive Committee of the Jewish Agency took severe measures. Season contingency plans were taken off the shelf and put into immediate operation. Although Lehi was responsible for the Moyne assassination, it soon became clear that Irgun was the Season's main target. On November 20, 1944, the Histadrut Convention—the parent organization of all Labor political parties—resolved that Irgun members should be surrendered to the British, thrown out of their workplaces and schools, denied hiding places, and detained.[54] The military unit responsible for the operation was made up of the Palmach, the elite force of the Haganah. Palmach volunteers, highly motivated high school graduates, lived in kibbutzim and divided their time between military training and agricultural work. They were the closest thing to a commando unit the Jewish "state in the making" could afford. Highly ideological and committed to socialism, they shared their elders' contempt for the Irgun.[55]

No other period in the history of the Haganah-Irgun conflict had left so much bad blood. Names of Irgun financial supporters, including individuals and institutions, were exposed and given to the British. Hundreds of Irgunists were captured by Haganah activists in the streets or in their homes. A significant number, including senior commanders, were handed over to the British; others were caught by the British themselves after having been tipped off by the Haganah's intelligence services. Many were detained in kibbutzim and brutally interrogated in small, isolated cells. Eli Tavin, a member of the Irgun supreme command abducted in the Season operation, was told, for example, that he had been sentenced to death. Held and tortured for months in a small kibbutz cell, Tavin was told that his death sentence had been commuted three times.[56]

The Season operation was one of Menachem Begin's finest moments. Begin, who was warned in advance by the Haganah of the coming strike, decided not to resist. Irgun members were told that regardless of the "terrible crime" committed against them, they were not to fight back. Begin feared a Jewish civil war, a nightmare he was not ready to be part of as either victim or victimizer. A student of Jewish ancient history, he recalled the trauma of the last days of the Second Temple, when Jews killed Jews. Sharing the traditional Jewish interpretation of the Temple's destruction, Begin believed that the bloody civil war was largely responsible for the collapse of ancient Judea.[57] The Irgun commander, whom the Season organizers failed to capture, was not the only person unwilling to take part in the nascent civil war. Numerous Palmach and Haganah officers also refused to participate in the hunt and were excused. And some leading members of the Jewish Agency's Executive Committee, who did not share Ben-Gurion's passion for ridding the *yishuv* of dissidents, were vehemently critical.[58] But the dissenting opinions represented a minority; the Season continued for nearly five months. While failing to decimate the Irgun or capture its supreme commander, the operation paralyzed the organization and led to a complete suspension of its anti-British activities.

All Season operations came to an end in March 1945. The leaders of the *yishuv* concluded that the Irgun had learned its lesson but were also increasingly frustrated with the British. The Mandate Government did not relax its anti-immigration policy and remained cold to the idea of a Jewish state. In October of that year, the heads of the Jewish Agency, under Ben-Gurion, ordered a massive anti-British sabotage campaign. Haganah commanders were instructed to coordinate activities with the Irgun and Lehi, and both undergrounds found themselves suddenly relegitimized. An unexpected year of cooperation ensued. Acting under the name "United Resistance Movement," the three Jewish militias concentrated on sabotage and conducted several spectacular anti-British operations. But their cooperation did not last long.[59] On July 22, 1946, Irgun members blew up the King David Hotel in Jerusalem, whose southwest wing housed at that time the headquarters of the British administration in Palestine. The destruction of the hotel, one of the most cherished symbols of the British Empire, killed over eighty civilians, including many Jews. It was condemned by the

British and denounced by the leaders of the Jewish Agency. Following the bombing, Ben-Gurion and his colleagues concluded it was no longer useful to work with or trust the political judgment of the erratic and unreliable Begin. Ten months after its formation, the United Resistance Movement was disbanded; each underground returned to its own operational niche.[60]

The year 1947 marked a dramatic deterioration of Haganah-Irgun relations, already badly damaged by the legacy of the Season. The intensified military struggle against the British led the Irgun and Lehi also to extort and blackmail rich Jewish merchants and businessmen in the country's large cities. It also produced bank robberies, intimidation, and coercion against Jews in public places in attempts to spread Irgun propaganda and enlist cooperation in Irgun activities. Jewish motorists were often forced to "lend" their cars for Irgun operations, and school principals were physically "persuaded" to allow the use of their school installations for training and military exercises. The "criminalization" of Irgun and Lehi domestic operations forced the Haganah to provide armed guards at many private firms and organizations. If found guilty, captured Jewish violators were badly beaten by Haganah strongmen. Irgun and Lehi members risked losing their jobs at Labor-related institutions. Intense propaganda was launched against the "dissident terrorists," who seemed to be drifting away from the organized community.[61] As a result of this conflict, the Irgun and Lehi refused to coordinate their anti-Arab military operations with the Haganah. By November 1947, the Jews were engaged in a struggle for life and death against local Palestinians, with the prospect of Arab invasion imminent upon the termination of the British mandate. But the Irgun and Lehi chose to conduct their own operations, dividing and weakening the Jews' already meager resources.

The last outrageous case of dissidents' terrorism that registered in Ben-Gurion's mind before the *Altalena* affair involved Dier Yassin, an Arab village guarding the western entrance to Jerusalem. Largely ignoring its civilian population, the Irgun and Lehi launched an attack on the village on April 9, 1948. In the assault, more than one hundred Palestinian civilians were slain, some of their bodies afterward thrown down a well. Although the deed was immediately repudiated by the Haganah command

and later condemned by the majority of Israeli political leaders, the consequences were far-reaching. News of the massacre circulated rapidly throughout the country and led to a massive Palestinian exodus. Both the Palestinian leaders and ordinary people greatly exaggerated the magnitude of the massacre, convincing many Arabs that the Jews were about to massacre them all.[62] A few days after the Dier Yassin massacre, a convoy of Jewish doctors and nurses traveling via Arab Sheikh Jarach to Hadassah Mount Scopus Hospital was ambushed. Nearly all its ninety passengers, who were trapped in their armored cars, were burnt alive.[63]

The *Altalena* disaster was a direct product of the previous fifteen years of brewing discord among the Irgun, Haganah, and their parent political movements. It especially brought into the open Ben-Gurion's personal hatred of Begin's followers and their "terrorist mindset." When confronted with Arab terrorism, Ben-Gurion would often mention that they reminded him of "our thugs and terrorists, which paved the way to bloody [Arab] attacks in Haifa, King David, the Goldshmidt House, etc."[64] The prime minister mistrusted Irgunists as soldiers and denied them special privileges in the newly formed Israeli army. In April 1948, Ben-Gurion voted against the generous dissolution agreement offered to the Irgun but was a minority voice in his own Zionist Executive.[65] *Altalena* may have caused him consternation, but it also provided a timely opportunity. Israel's warlord would never have missed the chance to establish his authority and teach the renegade Begin a lesson.

The Assassination of Count Folke Bernadotte

While the *Altalena* affair provided Ben-Gurion with a legal excuse to dissolve the Irgun and destroy its military and political infrastructure, it did not terminate the presence of the dissidents in Jerusalem, a city divided in 1948 between warring Jews and Arabs. Irgun soldiers vowed to fight independently for the liberation of the holy city, and there was little the government could do to stop them. Israel had no jurisdiction over Jerusalem according to the U.N. formula and no legal basis for banning Irgun activists. Worse still, Lehi, the smaller but far more radical organization, also maintained several independent bases in Jerusalem.

Lehi's ultranationalists were ready to fight for the integrity of the land of Israel regardless of the political constraints faced by the government. They despised Ben-Gurion's "servile" approach and thrived on the conspiracy theory that the cabinet was ready to facilitate a British return to Palestine. And no piece of land was holier to Lehi than Jerusalem. The group feared that the government would succumb to international pressure and forfeit the holy city.[66] While Ben-Gurion was also interested in keeping Jerusalem, he greatly mistrusted Lehi's lunatic leaders. Afraid that their extremism and political naïveté would spoil his delicate plans for keeping the significant territories that Israel had captured in its War of Independence, Ben-Gurion had many ideas for dissolving Irgun's and Lehi's Jerusalem camps. But the prime minister, who had once ordered the killing of Jews during the *Altalena* crisis, lacked unanimous cabinet support for risking a second crisis and chose not to force the issue.

Ben-Gurion's worst nightmare came true on September 17, 1948. At about 5:30 P.M. he received a short cable from Jerusalem's commander, Colonel Moshe Dayan: " Bernadotte and Serot have been shot at Katamon." Dayan's short message reported a political assassination that threatened to provoke an international crisis. Count Folke Bernadotte, a prominent Swedish diplomat, was the United Nations peace mediator for Palestine. In 1945 he represented the Swedish Red Cross in negotiating with Heinrich Himmler over the fate of Scandinavian captives in the Third Reich. Bernadotte managed to rescue thousands of Christians and Jews from the Nazis. André Serot, a French colonel, was a senior U.N. peacekeeping observer. Just before the fatal trip he had asked to be seated next to Bernadotte to thank him for saving his wife's life during World War II. Serot's wife spent the war in Dachau and owed her survival to the Swedish diplomat. Bernadotte and Serot were the first in a long list of innocents who died while engaged in U.N. peacekeeping, and the assassination shocked the international community.[67]

The Bernadotte convoy of three cars left the U.N. headquarters at the British Old Government House around 4:00 P.M.. Passing through Jerusalem's Greek and German colonies, it climbed up Katamon on its way to Talbiya and turned right at Palmach Street. Just a few seconds after crossing an Israeli military roadblock, the convoy was forced to stop because a jeep with four passengers was blocking the road. Moving quickly to the third car, a new American Chrysler, one attacker thrust the barrel of his Schmeisser submachine gun into the window, pumping bullets into the bodies of the Swede and the Frenchman. The two were rushed to Hadassah Hospital but pronounced dead upon arrival.[68]

In the evening a single-page message was found in the Jerusalem mailboxes of the major news organizations.

> On the 17th of September 1948 we have executed Count Bernadotte. Count Bernadotte served as an open agent of the British enemy. His task was to implement the British plans for the surrender of our country to a foreign rule and the exposure of the *yishuv*. He did not hesitate to suggest the handing over of Jerusalem to Abdullah. Bernadotte acted without interruption toward the weakening of our military efforts and was responsible for the bloodshed.
>
> There will be no foreign rule in the Homeland. There shall no longer be foreign commissioners in Jerusalem.
>
> Hazit Hamoledet [Fatherland Front], September 17, 1948[69]

A short time after his first cable, Dayan informed Ben-Gurion that either Lehi or Irgun men were responsible for the murder.[70] By 8:30 that evening, Secret Service Chief Isser Harel told the prime minister that his sources ruled out Irgun participation. This left the Sternists as the main suspects. Harel was certain that Hazit Hamoledet was a fictitious title selected by Lehi's three-man command to hide the organization's responsibility. It was later discovered that the title was borrowed from a Bulgarian communist underground under the Nazis.[71]

The assassination of the Swedish diplomat, the king of Sweden's nephew and godfather of the heir to the Swedish throne, was the result of a long and careful plan. In the summer of 1948, Lehi commanders became convinced that the U.N. mediator was a British agent. Bernadotte refused to accept the Israeli territorial conquests in the war and was determined to solve the question of Palestine in the spirit of the 1947 Partition Resolution, establishing separate Jewish and Arab states in Palestine. This required the internationalization of Jerusalem and the transfer of the Negev, Israel's large southern region, to Transjordan's King Abdullah.

Bernadotte's plan also included a strong statement about the right of Arab refugees to return to their homes or receive appropriate compensation.[72] Lehi people considered Rhodes, the mediator's headquarters, as the new Munich, the place where Jews would be sold out yet again by the cynical Great Powers. Ironically identifying with Moscow's anti-imperialist propaganda of the time, Lehi's commanders were inspired by Soviet attacks on Bernadotte. A *Pravda* commentary on July 11 read: "Clearly to be seen in the plan proposed by Bernadotte for settling the Palestine problem is the label, 'made in England.' "[73]

Lehi was not the only organization disturbed by Bernadotte's mission. The mediator's plan was resented by the Israeli government, and the Israeli press had become highly suspicious of the man and his team. People in Jerusalem gossiped about Bernadotte's alleged Nazi sympathies. Many others believed that Ralph Bunche, Bernadotte's American deputy, was a State Department agent. Relations between the Israeli authorities and U.N. observers soured as suspicion arose within the army that the observers were spying for the Arabs. "The Israeli press," wrote journalist Jon Kimche, "was full of it, the government officials right up to the top believed it."[74] Israel's leaders had expressed in private serious reservations about the Swede's intentions and were increasingly alarmed by the British and American endorsement of Bernadotte's mediation. But only Lehi, haunted by conspiracy theories, could conceive of an assassination. In Lehi's eyes, Bernadotte was all powerful. His advice, which implied the return of the British through their "puppet king" Abdullah, would be heeded by the great powers. Worst of all, they feared that Bernadotte, an experienced diplomat, would prevail over their spineless leaders.

The decision to assassinate Bernadotte was made by Lehi's three-man joint command, Nathan Friedman-Yelin (later Yelin-Mor), Dr. Israel Scheib (later Eldad), and Yitzhak Yezernitsky (later Shamir), who had led the organization since the 1942 killing of Abraham Stern by the British. In the past they had ordered the killing of several British officials, including the 1944 assassination of Lord Moyne. The killing of Bernadotte was another matter. The assassination of the U.N. mediator would be conducted under the jurisdiction of the state of Israel. Jerusalem may not have been officially annexed yet, but for lack of other authority in the area, the government of Israel had effective control of the Jewish areas. The three were fully aware of the gravity of their act: never before had Lehi denied responsibility for a killing. And never had the three so carefully hid themselves following an operation. While Friedman-Yelin was later captured, Eldad and Shamir remained in hiding for months.[75]

The political thinking that provided the conceptual framework for the Bernadotte assassination was based on Lehi's experience as a revolutionary underground in the 1940s. It was also nourished by the experience of east European revolutionary movements in the first half of the twentieth century. Between 1940 and 1948, Lehi fought the British on the one hand and maintained a legitimation crisis with the Zionist leadership on the other. Despite its small size, which gave the movement no hope of challenging the hegemonic Labor camp, Lehi saw itself as the sole patriotic voice of the nation. Its calling was to revive the ancient kingdom of Israel within the biblical Eretz Israel and to impart this sense of national rejuvenation to the entire nation. Lehi was consequently pleased with the termination of the British Mandate and the establishment of an independent Jewish state. But its commanders were unsatisfied with the state's truncated land and with the political direction of its servile government. Israel's War of Independence, according to Lehi, had only begun.[76]

Vacillating between their old attachment to Europe's radical right and their new fascination with the self-proclaimed anti-imperialist Soviet Union, Lehi chiefs cared least of all about democratic values or procedures. But this antidemocratic foundation required a two-pronged strategy. First the organization had to form a political party and join the newly created democratic politics of Israel. But second, it had to maintain a revolutionary apparatus underground, ready to act in a decisive way—as in the Bernadotte assassination—when ordinary political procedures failed or the government committed treason. Unlike Menachem Begin, who understood the meaning and requirements of Jewish independence and wished to transform the Irgun into a fully legal political party, Lehi heads had many reservations. They appreciated the achievement of national independence but were prisoners of their anti-British, anti-Labor revolutionary ideology. Greatly suspicious of a British-Zionist-Jordanian collaboration that would reduce the size of the Jewish state, Lehi was reluctant to dissolve the underground. The group was convinced of the power of terrorism to change history and wanted to keep the option for violence alive. On occasion they would justify this thinking by using the analogy of Arab irregular forces and their role in Arab politics.[77]

The Bernadotte assassination provided Ben-Gurion with just the excuse he needed to shut down the last Lehi and Irgun camps. The non-Labor cabinet ministers, who were reluctant after *Altalena* to approve of the prime minister's plan to eradicate all Irgun and Lehi traces, were as stunned by the assassination as the rest of the world.[78] They also felt guilty. Could Ben-Gurion have been right? If the Irgun and Lehi had been wiped out earlier, could Bernadotte's life have been saved? Immediately after the murder, Palmach units raided Lehi's three military camps in Jerusalem. Dozens were arrested and many more were simply sent away. Soon it became clear, however, that all the organization's commanders had left the city earlier. Additional arrests were made on the night of the assassination in Tel Aviv and were extended to the rest of the country the following morning. All Lehi's branches, offices, publishing houses, youth clubs, and meeting places were raided and sealed. On September 20, the government issued an "Ordinance to Prevent Terrorism." Lehi and the Fatherland Front were retroactively declared terrorist organizations, which made all their activists and members subject to arrest. A search of the apartment of Friedman-Yelin, who was in hiding, yielded seven Sten submachine guns and rounds of ammunition. Also found were thousands of dollars and a Lehi archive. Friedman-Yelin himself and Mati Shmulevitz, the organization's Haifa commander, were captured on September 29.[79]

The elimination of Lehi's installations, the declaration of the movement as an illegal terrorist group, and the arrest of its activists dealt a serious blow to the organization. But Lehi was not easily decimated. Armed with their long prison experience under the British, Lehi prisoners used their prisoner rights to the fullest possible extent. They ridiculed the inexperienced Israeli military police and took advantage of the reluctance of the prison guards to be tough on Jewish political prisoners. Some of them even managed to escape from the Jaffa prison and resume their underground activities. Lehi also conducted an aggressive propaganda campaign against the government for arresting and jailing Israeli youngsters willing to fight the Arabs. Denying all responsibility for the assassination, they warned against the rise of a Labor police state.[80] The failure of the authorities to arrest Eldad and Shamir, as well as several other top Lehi commanders, also contributed to the incomplete struggle against the group.

The investigation of the Bernadotte assassination was incredibly sloppy, and Israel's Jerusalem police were incompetent. Its officers seem to have been wary of capturing fellow Jews. The assassins were never seriously pursued and were never brought to justice. Three of them drove to Lehi's camp at Lifta, where they were hidden by the organization's religious members. After moving from house to house in Mea Shearim, reuniting with the fourth killer, and lounging about for four days, they were smuggled aboard a furniture truck into Tel Aviv, where they were easily hidden.[81]

In 1949, following significant Swedish pressure on the Israeli government, a blue-ribbon investigation committee was formed to study the Bernadotte assassination and the failure to arrest the assassins. Headed by District Judge Shimon Agranat, the committee included Walter Eitan of the Foreign Ministry and Chief Prosecutor Chaim Cohen. The committee validated the Swedish charge of police negligence and recognized that on the day of the assassination the Jerusalem police failed to adequately pursue the killers. It found further that the police chief investigation officer did not even interview witnesses near the scene or gather relevant evidence. The murder scene was not cordoned off; and no one was stopped from removing the bullets and cartridge cases that the Bernadotte killer dropped in flight. By the time the police had retrieved the items, however, everything had been wiped clean of fingerprints. Bernadotte's car was inspected only after it had been repaired; and no steps were taken by the police to trace the assailants' jeep.[82]

The committee's candid report made it clear that the plan to liquidate Lehi—and not the effort to apprehend the assassins—attracted the most attention during the first few days after the killings. Years later it came out that secret talks were held between Shaul Avigur, Ben-Gurion's aide, and Eldad and Shamir, who were in hiding. An agreement of the latter to stop all subversive operations if Lehi's members would not be discriminated against in the army was achieved. Avigur asked Shamir the names of the assassins, promising that nothing would happen to them, but Shamir refused to give them.[83] Not one member of the hit team would ever spend a night in jail or face a court of justice. For years there was a conspiracy of silence about the Bernadotte assassination, and neither Lehi's leadership nor the assassins said a word. In 1960, the most talkative of all former Lehi commanders, Israel Eldad, approached Gideon Housner, the state attorney general, and offered to tell the truth about the assassination. "God forbid!" was Housner's response. "Do you know the problems you will create for your country?"[84] In 1988, the surviving conspirators gave interviews to the nation's major newspapers, revealing the story. Finally it was found out, for example, that the man who pulled the trigger was Yehoshua Cohen, one of Lehi's toughest fighters and the person who trained Lord Moyne's assassins. Cohen, a member of Kibbutz Sede Boker since the early 1950s, became a close friend of David Ben-Gurion in 1952, when the prime minister retired temporarily and moved to that kibbutz. Cohen was selected as Ben-Gurion's personal guard and walked with him daily for miles. It has never been known whether Cohen shared his secret with Israel's "old man." Yitzhak Shamir, the former Lehi commander and prime minister of Israel from 1983 to 1992, kept silent about the Bernadotte assassination until he published his memoirs in 1994.[85] He never denied involvement though Friedman-Yelin consistently did. The refusal of this former senior Lehi commander to take responsibility for the assassination order infuriated Eldad, who would never again speak to Friedman-Yelin.[86]

The Ordinance to Prevent Terrorism was used against Lehi's senior commanders, but none were implicated in the killing of Bernadotte. The charges involved membership in and leadership of a terrorist organization, for which Friedman-Yelin was sentenced to eight years and Shmulevitz to five. Eldad and Shamir remained in hiding. On February 10, 1949, the State (Temporary) Council granted general amnesty in its last session; all Lehi prisoners and detained suspects were freed.[87] Lehi's political front, the Fighters Party, ran for the Knesset. Only Friedman-Yelin was elected. Bitterly divided over questions of ideology and organization, the "fighters" soon split into Jewish ultranationalists and devotees of the extreme left. The majority, under Friedman-Yelin and Shamir, survived until their 1951 electoral failure and consequent collapse. The minority, under Eldad, focused on ultranationalist education and long-term cultural transformation of the nation. Their most important product was the "kingdom of Israel" philosophy, an ideo-theology obsessed with biblical Eretz Israel and continuing the nation's war of liberation until the state of Israel reached those borders.[88]

The Bernadotte assassination also brought an end to the Irgun as a military organization. Following a long deliberation in the cabinet, all ministers agreed that the organization's Jerusalem branch must be dissolved as Lehi's had been. No one blamed Irgun soldiers for involvement in the assassination or equated them with Lehi murderers. It was decided, however, that the matter should not be left for negotiations; the dissolution came as a government order. Just before the delivery of the dissolution demand, Ben-Gurion's intelligence chief, Isser Harel, convinced the prime minister that if properly addressed, Irgun officers in Jerusalem would not engage in further struggle. Harel's script worked. Twenty-four hours after the ultimatum's delivery, the Irgun ceased to exist.[89] Dejected Irgun soldiers saw that this was the lesser of two evils. With the tragedy of *Altalena* in mind, they realized that Ben-Gurion was not to be tested further; it was incumbent upon the Irgun to fade into history. Watching Haganah soldiers taking over his camp and collecting the weapons, Yehoshua Ophir, an Irgun officer in Jerusalem, commented,

> And at that moment I asked myself: How come the Irgun soldiers, who were not brought down by the mighty British Empire when only armed with pistols and light submachine guns, gave in to the Israeli government when armed with the best weapons? Because the hands of Irgun soldiers were trained to fight foreign occupant and enemy, never to fight their brothers.[90]

The Crisis of Year One in Perspective

The *Altalena* crisis took place under the newly established state of Israel but had its roots in a long-standing *yishuv* conflict between its two major Zionist subcultures: the Labor and the Revisionist movements. The series that began with the Arlosoroff assassination and progressed through the breaking of the Havlagah, the Moyne assassination, the Season, the King

David explosion, and the conflict over Dier Yassin was concluded by the Bernadotte assassination. The crises erupted in a situation Hebrew University Professors Dan Horowitz and Moshe Lissak called "authority without sovereignty," the rise within the *yishuv* of a powerful political center devoid of formal powers. This led the Labor elite to consider itself the only legitimate authority of the Jewish community of Palestine; the Revisionist counterelite, however, interpreted the situation differently. The followers of Jabotinsky, refusing to recognize Labor hegemony, argued that as long as Palestine was under the British Mandate they were entitled to an independent interpretation of Jewish liberation.

But while the *Altalena* incident was admittedly a *yishuv* affair, it was also a defining event of the new state of Israel and the peak of its crisis of transformation from a voluntary community to an orderly state. David Ben-Gurion and Menachem Begin, the dominant figures in the *Altalena* crisis, both contributed to the great tragedy. But in many respects the two men complemented each other in also leaving a legacy of stability and responsibility for the newly created Jewish state. Historians generally concur that Ben-Gurion's actions in the affair were excessively ruthless; it is clear that the Irgun had no putsch plans and that its commander wished to use the weapons only to fight the Arabs. With a touch of flexibility and compassion, Ben-Gurion could have produced a more peaceful settlement to the *Altalena* affair. But by sinking the ship, the first prime minister of Israel sent an unequivocal message to all Israelis and Israeli splinter groups that there would be but one center of civil and military authority in the state and that no dissident action would be tolerated. For a people devoid of two thousand years of sovereignty, a nation of debaters and Talmudic hair splitters, this was a most significant message. The tragedy of the deaths of nineteen Jews and dozens of wounded sent a clear message that would never be forgotten in Israeli politics.

Irgun Commander Menachem Begin, *Altalena*'s major loser, also bore some responsibility for the tragedy. With sharper political instincts he might have allayed the crisis before its tragic end. Had Begin understood Ben-Gurion's obstinacy or learned the lessons of the Season, he might have been more flexible in the early negotiations with Ben-Gurion's aides, or offered a quick surrender after the Kfar Vitkin confrontation. Begin's grave mistake in the *Altalena* affair was his misinterpretation of just how serious Ben-Gurion was.

Begin's reputation did not sink with *Altalena*, though it did take a plunge. Facing the nation beaten and humiliated, the Irgun commander was expected by many of his men to rescue his damaged reputation with renewed struggle. Instead, he ordered his troops to hold their fire and avoid civil war at all costs. There are few examples in modern history of reputable fighting organizations coming under their competitors' attack and not fighting back. But Begin's restraint not only prevented a civil war; it established an important legacy against Jew fighting Jew in the state of Israel. *Altalena*'s victims notwithstanding, a full-blown civil war at Israel's year one would have constituted a tragic break with the long Jewish tradition of forswearing brotherly war. It would have divided the nation and left irreparable scars in the Israeli body politic.

2

VIOLENCE IN THE 1950s

The Eruption of Past Hatreds

The Knesset Under Siege

January 7, 1952, a cold winter day, was one of the stormiest days in the history of the Jewish state. Starting in the morning, Jerusalem was a city under siege. The entire area around the old Knesset building, on the corner of King George and Ben-Yehuda Streets, was sealed off by police roadblocks and barbed wire. All transportation was diverted to peripheral emergency routes. Six hundred policemen armed with clubs, shields, and tear gas were stationed around the building where deliberations were due to start at 4 P.M. Military units were put on full alert, ready for an immediate order to move. Never before, or until after the Rabin assassination, was the site of Israeli sovereignty put under such protection. By evening it was evident that none of the massive emergency measures was sufficient. Thousands of demonstrators clashed with the police, threw rocks at them, and finally tore apart their roadblocks. Charging in the direction of the parliament, they almost broke in. Many of the building's windows were smashed, with stones reaching the main hall and wounding a few Knesset members. The parliament was filled with tear gas that had been used against the attackers, and it was hard to breath. The struggle over the Knesset was long and inconclusive. Finally, the army was called in to help the police push the demonstrators back. Inside the Knesset, the atmosphere was almost as stormy as outside. The session, which was occasionally interrupted but continued nonetheless, was debating one of the most explosive issues to have ever come before the Israeli legislature—the agreement about war reparations from West Germany.

The controversy, which produced the unforgettable demonstration, had started a month earlier. At the beginning of December 1951, the Israeli public was stunned by a government decision to sign a reparations agreement with the Federal Republic of Germany. The agreement, secretly mediated for months between David Ben-Gurion and West German Chancellor Konrad Adenauer, stipulated that Germany would give the state of Israel nearly one billion dollars in compensation for property taken from Jews or destroyed during World War II. The proposed deal was the best thing that could have happened to the newly created state from an economic point of view. Israel was desperately struggling to absorb a huge number of Jewish refugees; the population was about to increase by 100 percent in fewer than three years. The state treasury was empty, and the government needed all the support it could get. However, from a moral point of view, the deal with Germany was shocking. Fewer than seven years had passed since the Holocaust. Signing an agreement with Germany seemed like a calamitous Israeli compromise with the successors of the Nazis, who were still living under Allied occupation. And the opposition perceived and presented the agreement as a most cynical political act. Of course, Prime Minister Ben-Gurion maintained that the Holocaust could never be forgotten or forgiven, and that the agreement was only about stolen property and war damages. He made it clear that in his opinion, building a Jewish state out of the ashes of the nation's greatest historical disaster was part of the will of the deceased. But many Israelis bitterly disagreed with their prime minister. They identified Adenauer's Germany with Hitler's Germany and considered any contact with the Federal Republic as a deal with the devil. In 1949 a *Yediot Aharonot* journalist had written, for example, "we have to inscribe the hatred for Germany in the hearts of our little children and their descendants."[1] Gershom Schoken, the editor of the daily *Ha'aretz*, proposed that a law be enacted prohibiting contacts between Israelis and Germans, including even occasional contacts with German tourists in hotels outside of Germany.[2] A special seal in every Israeli passport stated that it was invalid in Germany. Many Israelis wanted the Jewish people and the Jewish state to maintain a historical ban on Germany, similar to the ban imposed, according to tradition, on Spain after the 1492 expulsion of Spanish Jewry.[3]

The controversy over the reparations agreement stirred the nation's entire political landscape. Antireparations petitions, newspaper ads, protests, and public debates became the order of the day. The left-wing *Mapam* mobilized several surviving legendary Warsaw Ghetto fighters such as Antek Tzukerman, Tzvia Lubetkin, and Haika Grossman for the campaign. It also called upon nationally famous writers such as the poet Abraham Shlonsky and the author Moshe Shamir to join the campaign. There was even a determined opposition to the agreement from within Ben-Gurion's Mapai party. Joseph Sprinzak, the Knesset's speaker, said in a special session of Mapai's Central Committee, "I do not want it to be recorded in Jewish and world history that we took reparations from Germany just as I cannot accept a Torah ruling that a father should be compensated for the rape of his daughter. I think it is a moral absurdity."[4] Azriel Karlibach, *Ma'ariv*'s editor, wrote very emotionally, "What shall I tell my dearest, my burnt ones, my murdered, when they come to me at night?"[5] Several of Ben-Gurion's religious coalition partners were also outraged. The opposition to the agreement portrayed it as blasphemy, an inexcusable move, a desecration of the memory of the six million Jews who died in German concentration camps. The calamity of even considering a deal with Germany unified largely divided Israeli camps. Members of the far right and left vowed never to let it happen. On the morning of January 7, when the Knesset was about to debate the agreement and give the government the green light necessary for starting the actual reparations negotiations, they came to stop it. Armed with the support of both Israel's afternoon dailies, *Ma'ariv* and *Yediot Aharonot*, as well as with a broad sense of national defiance, some of them were even rumored to be planning acts of terrorism against the government.

The January 7 protest against the reparations agreement was conducted in Jerusalem's Zion's Square, just a few hundred meters from the old Knesset building. Many of the demonstrators came directly from Jerusalem's Mount Zion, where Israel's rabbinate conducted special memorial services for the victims of the Holocaust. A large number of them had yellow stars pinned to their sweaters with the letter J (for *Jude* [Jew]) in the middle, to commemorate the special identification badge that European Jews were forced to wear under German occupation. The two main speakers were Professor Joseph Klausner, a famed ultranationalist historian, and Menachem Begin, the former commander of the Irgun and the leader of Herut party. The struggle seemed to have rejuvenated the thirty-eight-year-old Begin. Just a few months earlier he had undergone a personal crisis that almost drove him to early retirement. Herut did poorly in the national elections and its fourteen Knesset seats were reduced to eight. Begin's depression was so deep that for months he did not even appear in the Knesset. His colleagues in the underground were told that their admired commander was no longer interested in politics and that his only wish was to practice law. A signed letter of resignation from the Knesset was in the hands of Begin's friends, and he made arrangements to take the criminal law exam of Israel's bar association.[6]

Ben-Gurion's fateful decision to reach an agreement with the Germans gave Menachem Begin's political life a new meaning. The Holocaust, in which he lost his parents and many other relatives, had played a most significant role in his thinking. One biographer even argued that Begin's hasty escape from Warsaw in 1940, leaving behind family and many of the Betar followers under his command in Poland, had left him with a permanent sense of guilt.[7] For Begin, the reparations agreement was a meta-political issue worth fighting against regardless of all other considerations. His supporters, who were angry at the government, were thrilled to see him back in a bellicose mood. Already in the morning of January 7, on reading *Herut*, the party's daily newspaper, they knew there was going to be a major drama. Almost the entire issue was dedicated to the struggle against the agreement. The paper's front page had a large headline that read, "Remember What Was Done to You by Amalek." During the biblical conquest of Canaan, the Canaanite tribe of Amalek was considered the most treacherous and murderous enemy tribe. The conquering Hebrews were instructed to eliminate its population, including women and children. Maimonides's ruling against taking compensation from murderers, at any price, was also printed on *Herut*'s front page as well as a picture of a tormented Jewish prisoner in a German concentration camp subtitled, "I accuse!" A list of Adenauer's aides with their army records could also be found on the paper's front page. Begin's speech in Zion's square, a long-awaited performance, was one of his most extreme. The thousands of Israelis who listened to him were mesmerized and would soon follow him to the Knesset.

> When you shot us with the gun [during the *Altalena* incident], I gave the order—no! [not to fire back]. Today I shall give the order—yes! This will be a war for life or death. They tell us we only stage anger, but the thousands who are now standing under the heavy rain, are a living testimony that the people's outrage is massively erupting. . . . Today, four years after the beginning of national redemption, the Hebrew prime minister announces that he is going to Germany to take money, that he is ready to sell the dignity of the people of Israel for graft, thereby bringing eternal damnation on the nation. . . . There is no single German who did not murder our fathers. Every German is a Nazi. Every German is a killer. Adenauer is a murderer. All his aides are murderers. But this is their calculation: money, money, money. For a few million dollars blasphemy is about to be committed. . . . Mr. Ben-Gurion has sent policemen who have in their hands, according to our information, German hand grenades and tear gas, the same gases that choked our fathers to death.

Begin was emotionally transformed. He said he was ready to fight and expressed his and his friends' readiness to go "to concentration camps and torture cells." He threatened the government with civil disobedience and tax rebellion. "Liberty or Death," he screamed, "no retreat." He told Ben-Gurion that "your end will be like Ernest Bevin's [Great Britain's hated foreign minister in the late 1940s] end."[8] Leaving Zion's Square, Begin went to the Knesset to participate in the debate. He was followed by thousands of demonstrators who were deterred neither by the rain nor by the police roadblocks. On their way to the Knesset they smashed shop windows and set parked cars on fire. By the end of the day there were nearly three hundred casualties, mostly wounded policemen. About four hundred were arrested. David Ben-Gurion kept his composure until the beginning of Begin's Knesset speech, which stressed the emotional reaction of the crowd outside. "They are a bunch of hooligans," said the prime minister. "You are a hooligan," Begin responded. When the speaker attempted to calm Herut's leader and keep order in the house, Begin responded, "If I do not speak, nobody else will. Only force will get me out of here!"[9] The entire Knesset was in a state of shock and the session was temporarily suspended until Begin agreed to take back his last words. Only then was he allowed to continue.

> This may, perhaps, be my last Knesset speech. . . . There are matters in life which are worse than death itself. This is one of these matters which we are ready to give our soul for, for which we are ready to die. We shall leave our families. We shall tell our children good-bye and there will be no negotiation with Germany. . . . Nations worthy of this title went to the barricades for smaller matters than this one. As for this issue—we, the last generation which suffered repression and the first which enjoyed salvation, we, who saw our parents dragged to the gas chambers, we who heard the voice of the death train wheels, we, in front of whose eyes our elderly father was thrown to the river with 500 additional Jews from glorious Brisk of Lithuania and the river's waters were red with blood, we, in front of whose eyes the murder of our elderly mother in the hospital was committed, we, who witnessed all these unprecedented events in history—are we going to be afraid to risk our life in order to stop negotiations with the murderers of our fathers? We should have been ashamed had we not rebelled against this decision. We are ready for anything, anything, in order to stop this Israeli calamity. I hope we shall stop it. . . .
>
> I know you have force. You have prisons, concentration camps, army police, secret service, guns, machine guns, never mind. Against this matter all force will be broken as glass against a rock. We are going to fight this just matter to the end. Physical force is meaningless in such matters, absolutely meaningless.[10]

The next day, Prime Minister Ben-Gurion broadcast a short radio message to the nation. His aggressive speech, which was full of warnings and threats to the opposition, made it clear that the prime minister was ready for another *Altalena*.

> Yesterday, a vicious hand was raised against the Knesset's sovereignty . . . a preliminary attempt to destroy Israeli democracy. It was announced that Israel's policy would not be decided by the people's elected representatives but by the people of the fist and political assassination. . . . .a wild and incited mob comprised of Irgun members and communists stormed the Knesset and threw rocks at the building. . . . the head and organizer of this "revolt," Mr. Menachem Begin, stood up yesterday in Zion's Square and incited the crowd.

Ben-Gurion went on to describe police restraint, warned the "gangs of thugs" and their leaders that they should not take police restraint for granted, and then concluded forcefully:

> I do not underestimate Mr. Begin's announcement that he is considering a war for life or death. And I, as the nation's Prime and Defense Minister, see fit to tell the nation, do not be intimidated! The state has enough power at its disposal and intends to defend Israel's freedom and sovereignty and stop a takeover by hooligans and political assassins. It is also ready to withstand prolonged terrorism in the country. The army, the police and the independent and peace loving people are the most loyal and effective guarantee that the criminal and insane conspiracy of Herut's hooligans and their communist supporters would never succeed. The State of Israel will neither be Spain nor Syria.[11]

The Knesset debate on the German reparations issue went on for two additional days, but the tension was slowly defused. Military units were still on alert in Jerusalem but very little happened. Organized worker groups from Haifa and Tel Aviv, two strongholds of the Labor movement, came to Jerusalem "to defend" the Knesset. Begin's unruly parliamentary behavior cost him a three-month suspension from parliament. The vote on the agreement was held on January 9, with the government coalition and the opposition conducting a major mobilization of their forces, including a big effort to bring even ill Knesset members to the house. The government won by a majority of sixty-one to fifty. In his diary, Ben-Gurion commented, "Monday, Tuesday and Wednesday were the reparations days—and Begin's failing, tragic and ludicrous putsch. On Tuesday, I broadcasted to the people. On Wednesday, the government position was approved overwhelmingly and with a moral victory."[12]

The last confrontation over the agreement with Germany took place at the end of March, a few days after the beginning of the official negotiations with the Germans. A large protest was organized by Herut party in Tel Aviv, and secret information reaching the prime minister intimated that there might be an assault, at the end of the protest, on several Histadrut buildings. Ben-Gurion, who knew he could muster a large Labor support in the street, decided not to use the police and the army unless the situation became desperate. Instead, he summoned a close aide, Elhanan Yishai, from Kibbutz Alumot. Yishai was informed of the opposition attack plans and told by the "Old Man" that he should put a large number of Ben-Gurion civilian loyalists in the streets. The procedure resorted to was not particularly legal, for Yishai, a citizen with no official position, was briefed on the situation by the Israel Defense Force's chief of staff and by the head of the Shin Beth. He was informed, among other things, about Herut's plan to march through Allenby Street and conclude the demonstration by setting the Histadrut headquarters on fire. But in the early days of the Israeli state, the practice of fighting the opposition using the old methods of *yishuv*'s internal feuds was still common.

Yishai's solution was to mobilize a reserve military brigade comprised of young kibbutz members in plain clothes and to disperse them in the streets of Tel Aviv armed with clubs. Loudspeakers were secretly installed by a special team along Allenby Street, which made it possible to address the crowd if the need arose. The demonstration took place on March 25, 1952. It again featured Begin, whose rhetoric was as extreme as ever: "This is the last time I call upon you, Mr. Ben Gurion: stop, for God's sake, back up! . . . The people do not want reparations from Germany, the people want to pay back, and they will, with the help of God. Are you going to bring goods for Solel Boneh (Histadrut's construction company)? No insurance company will insure these goods. . . . Please order the negotiating team back from Koeln." Just as Begin got excited again, he received an "anonymous" note from Yishai, stating that "about a thousand armed kibbutzniks are spread among the crowd ready to be provoked and strike back." The experienced Begin took the threat seriously. He appealed to the demonstrators to remain calm, and the demonstration was concluded peacefully.[13]

The antireparations activities had some lesser public and more extreme expressions, however. Several former Irgun activists, stationed in Europe, tried to kill the agreement by assassinating Chancellor Adenauer with a letter bomb to his office. On March 28, two twelve-year-old children were approached by two men on a Munich street and given a small package, addressed to Dr. Adenauer at the Chancellor's in Bonn. The children asked a trolley driver about it and were advised to give the package to a policeman stationed nearby. The bomb finally exploded in the Munich police station, killing one policeman and wounding two others. Two letters sent from Zurich and Geneva to several Paris press agencies explained the bombing:

> The Union of Jewish Partisans sent a bomb to Adenauer. This is the first attempt to execute the vengeance of the Jewish people. The book containing the explosives was sent to Dr. Adenauer, the prime minister of the murderous nation. The bomb exploded mistakenly in the hands of one of Dr. Adenauer guards. The German people must know that its crimes are unforgivable. We shall pay them for all their crimes. We have sent the first present, others will follow suit."[14]

Another bombing attempt on German officials associated with the reparations agreement was made on April 1. A heavy package, addressed to the "head of the German reparation negotiating team," which was then meeting in the Hague, was delivered to Amsterdam's main post office. Its size and the lack of a personal address aroused the suspicions of the Hague police, who found, after a careful security check, a large quantity of explosives and the signature "The Union of Jewish Partisans." The last bomb in this series was sent to Chancellor Adenauer on June 24, 1952. A Shin Beth special operations team, active in Europe, exposed the plot and stopped it, thereby preventing a great disaster.[15]

In Israel, a young Herut member and Holocaust survivor, Dov Shilansky, who came to the country aboard *Altalena*, was caught carrying a bomb into the offices of Israel's Ministry of Foreign Affairs. The two-kilo home-made bomb consisted of a battery, an alarm clock, and twenty-three explosive, fingerlike devices. Its detonation in the Foreign Office could have wreaked much damage, but Shilansky did not intend to blow up the building. In his trial he convinced the court that he only wanted to dramatize the situation by sending a desperate message to Ben-Gurion to stop the "great calamity." He was nevertheless sentenced to twenty-one months in prison.[16] In 1988, Shilansky became Israel's Knesset speaker. Former Irgun activists also made plans to put bombs aboard the German ships in the port of Haifa that transported heavy machinery and essential goods as part of the reparations agreement.[17]

The reparations agreement with the Federal Republic was signed on September 10, 1952. The German government agreed to pay Israel $715,000,000 in goods and services, within a period of twelve years. An additional $107,000,000 was to be paid to the General Jewish Committee representing the claims of major Jewish organizations. The reparations from Germany came at a most critical time for the young state and injected much-needed funds into the Israeli economy. They greatly facilitated the absorption of immigration and were directly responsible for the young nation's economic growth.

Lehi's Legacy: The Ultra-Orthodox and Ultranationalist Undergrounds

Most of the struggle against the reparations from Germany was conducted in public. It was an atypical case in which a parliamentary organization, the Herut party, temporarily experienced an uncontrollable urge to express itself in an extraparliamentary fashion. The agreement with Germany was so shocking and the time allotted for public debate was so short that an immediate direct action, which was by no means considered an alternative to parliamentary politics, appeared as the only effective option. There is no evidence that the more conspiratorial and violent operations of former Irgun members, the letter bombs sent in Germany, and the explosives left in German ships were ever authorized by Menachem Begin.

However, Begin's underground Lehi colleagues were another matter. They were always more critical of Israel's established leadership, and they had a revolutionary, antidemocratic streak in their thinking. They were also smaller than the Irgun, less organized, and deeply divided. For these reasons Lehi, unlike the Irgun, failed to transform itself into a stable political party. These reasons were also the cause for the rise of three small underground groups that catered in different ways to the already mythical conspiratorial legacy of Lehi of the 1940s. Two of these underground cells, which named themselves B'rith Hakana'im (Covenant of the Zealots) and Hamachane (the Camp), comprised young ultra-Orthodox Jews. The third did not have an official name, but the press provided two alternative titles: the Tzrifin Underground (the name of the prison in which arrested group members were held), or the Kingdom of Israel Underground (stressing the key ideological symbol of the group).

Members of the underground groups were especially inspired by the writings and personality of Israel Eldad (Scheib), a former Lehi commander and the most influential ideologue of the right wing of the anti-British underground movement. In 1949, following a deep internal division between Lehi's rightist and leftist factions, the organization was dissolved. Former commanders Yitzhak Shamir and Nathan Yelin-Mor moved to the left without much political appeal. Eldad moved to the right and formed *Sulam* (Ladder) magazine, and the Sulam youth clubs. The magazine and the clubs became the hotbed for the pronouncement of the most extreme Zionist interpretation of the time—the call for military expansion of the borders of Israel to the biblical Promised Land. The spiritual origins of the underground movements were laid down in several of Eldad's 1949 electrifying lectures. In these talks, he stressed the need to continue the nation's war of independence until the borders of Israel reached to the Nile River (Egypt) in the west and to the Euphrates (Iraq) in the east. Another theme in Eldad's talks was the need to uphold national honor and fight against disrespect of Israel and Jews by Arabs and other Gentiles. Eldad, a literary and intellectual figure, was probably not personally involved in the illegal operations of these groups, but he was fully supportive of their operations once committed.

B'rith Hakana'im and Hamachane were a strange mixture of Lehi's tradition of revolutionary armed struggle and extreme ultra-Orthodox rejection of the secular state of Israel. Their members were extremely unhappy with the narrow boundaries of the newly created Jewish state but were especially outraged by the attitude of the dominant Labor movement to Orthodox Judaism. Aggressive Sabbath raids into ultra-Orthodox neighborhoods, committed by members of Labor youth movements, created enormous anxiety about the future. An issue that added fuel to the fire was the secular education forced upon children of observant newcomers. The massive absorption of immigrants in the early 1950s gave the government huge power over the lives of hundreds of thousands of penniless new Israelis, especially those coming from the Middle East and North Africa. Government officials believed it was their obligation to free the newcomers' children of the old and "decadent" Diaspora mentality that comprised, among other things, "obsolete religiosity." They accomplished this aim by establishing secular state schools in all immigration absorption centers. There was also a political consideration involved. The socialist parties wished to indoctrinate the immigrant youth into their political culture and saw them as future potential voters. The secular education forced upon children from observant families was increasingly seen by Israel's Jewish Orthodoxy, Zionist and anti-Zionist alike, as a forced conversion. Their rabbis could not forget that all through their history Jews were ready to die rather than convert.

The first underground group was originally started in the summer of 1949 by two yeshiva students who attended an Eldad lecture about the destruction of the Second Temple and its contemporary meaning. The two decided to form an antigovernment underground and name it B'rith Hakana'im. Their first act, which did not draw any attention, was an announcement of the formation of a religious underground in a letter to *Ha'aretz*.[18] They were soon joined by a former Lehi member who helped them in their first sabotage operations against "desecrators" of the Sabbath (Israelis who either drive their vehicles or keep their businesses open on Saturday). These early operations amounted to setting ten coffee shops and two movie theaters on fire. They also left a large amount of broken glasses in a sports arena where soccer was played on the Sabbath. To further publicize the formation of the secret organization, the three decided to paint graffiti on synagogues' walls in Tel Aviv, B'nai-Brak, and Petach Tikva, calling on "religious youth" to join B'rith Hakana'im. A massive burning of several famed restaurants, located in Tel Aviv's crowded Allenby Street, followed. Large graffiti written on the wall in blue chalk read "We are going to fight Sabbath desecrators, B'rith Hakana'im." The successful accomplishment of the Allenby operation, which was heavily reported in the press, led to speculation that the extremist ultra-Orthodox group Neturei Karta (see chapter three) was responsible.[19]

The news about the formation of a religious underground spread quickly in the yeshiva world and led to the recruitment of a larger number of yeshiva students, former religious Lehi members, and several ultra-Orthodox activists. Operations were now expanded to Jerusalem and involved setting on fire Egged buses, traveling on the Sabbath. A spectacular burning of seven cars led to the arrest of two hundred suspects in the nation's capital. All of them were freed, however, for lack of incriminating evidence.[20] The organization, which at its peak had branches in Tel Aviv, B'nai-Brak, Jerusalem, Haifa, and Migdal-Gad, with close to two hundred activists, was built in the best conspiratorial tradition of Lehi. This meant total secrecy, code names for all members, compartmentalization, and the formation of five member cells. Examination and selection of new recruits were conducted by a special admissions committee. Policy and operations were decided on by the underground's command, comprised of the branches' heads. Weapons and explosives were obtained from uncovered Lehi caches but were later lost when most former Lehi members left B'rith Hakana'im to join the newly created Kingdom of Israel underground.

The underground's admission ceremony also followed Lehi rituals. The new candidate was brought to a dark room and seated by a table with a Bible and a gun. Several armed men would then ask challenging questions and explain the tasks involved: "You ought to know that our path is going to be very long, arduous and full of barriers. An unlimited sacrifice for the sacred and elevated goal is expected. Today you enter a zealous framework whose purpose is to establish Torah life in the country by all means necessary." The candidate was later asked to recite a special religious oath, written for the "zealous youth," and was finally told, "as of now you are a soldier in the camp which fights for the elevation of the Torah's honor, respect and rule."[21]

Although the stated goal of B'rith Hakana'im was the initiation of a genuine Torah state, an innovative project by all standards, it emerged as a desperate reaction to a perceived disaster. The young zealots acted out of the conviction that the socialist rulers of Israel were determined to destroy Israel's Orthodox Judaism, a fear shared by a larger Orthodox public. Consequently, the formation of the underground did not excite just young yeshiva students but also touched a very sensitive chord among elderly religious activists, prominent rabbis, and yeshiva heads. The underground won, for example, the support of Jerusalem's highly respected chief rabbi, Tzvi Pesach Frank.[22] A prominent yeshiva head and a member of the Higher Council of Torah Sages of Agudat Israel (Israel's largest ultra-Orthodox organization) once said in front of two hundred students, "The time has come to return to the Maccabee acts and take up guns against the Hellenized." When later severely criticized by other ultra-Orthodox rabbis opposed to the militancy of the underground, he retracted his statement and said he only spoke allegorically and his real meaning was more prayer and Torah studies.[23]

While preparing for further action, the Jerusalem commanders of B'rith Hakana'im learned to their great satisfaction that another Orthodox conspiracy, Hamachane, was being formed in the city with long-range plans for a future Orthodox revolution in Israel. Merger negotiations started soon. B'rith Hakana'im required proof of operational capacity as a condition for future cooperation; Hamachane activists responded by setting twenty-eight taxis and trucks on fire. They also burnt nonkosher butcher shops. Hamachane had, in addition, a special auxiliary women's wing named Judith, whose main tasks were to protest the drafting of girls into the army, to spy and obtain information, and to take medical care of wounded members when terror operations began.[24] But when B'rith Hakana'im's activists correctly suspected that Hamachane was infiltrated by Shin Beth informers, the merger did not occur, saving most B'rith Hakana'im activists from discovery and arrest.

The most dramatic plan of the two ultra-Orthodox undergrounds involved a desperate effort to stop the passage of a bill requiring all Israeli women to serve in the army. The proposed bill led many rabbis to rule that this issue was a clear case of *yehareg velo ya'avor* (be killed rather than sin). B'rith Hakana'im commanders first considered throwing a bomb in the

Knesset, but the idea was later rejected for the fear of many casualties and negative public reaction. Members of Hamachane, who independently debated the same plan, reached the same conclusion. Rather than rejecting the whole idea, they came up, however, with a better tactic, exploding a scare bomb in the Knesset. Their technicians assembled a small bomb capable of producing a large amount of fire, smoke, and noise.[25] Hamachane's only problem was that by the time they concluded their planning, Israel's security services already knew about their planned Knesset provocation. The house's session was stopped abruptly before the vote and a large number of Hamachane activists were rounded up and arrested. This massive arrest, which included many innocent ultra-Orthodox activists, later led to the formation of a state investigation committee to inquire into police brutality and excessive use of force. Only four activists were finally brought to trial. Prime Minister Ben-Gurion, who concluded that the underground was nothing more than an immature act of disoriented Yeshiva students, instructed the state's prosecution to take a lenient attitude. The leaders of the group were sentenced to from three to twelve months in prison.[26] The circumstances that led to the formation of the first underground in Israel's history were described in court by young Mordechai Eliyahu, a key activist and Israel's future chief Sephardi rabbi,

"I felt that Jews suffer from an inferiority complex which leads to their further underestimation by the other side. . . . On Nissan 8, 1950, we met at Yeshivat Porat Yoseph in Jerusalem, and decided to form an organization with the goal of enhancing Jewish pride. Five of us were involved. . . . When I was in Yeshivat Porat Yoseph, I learned for the first time about the educational situation of the immigrant children in the newcomers' camps. . . . I could not tolerate this catastrophe. . . . I believed that we could use the underground to found Torah life in the nation. A few days after the 1951 Independence Day, the Knesset was due to deliberate the Security Service Bill requiring young women to serve in the army. I understood that words were of no help. . . . In the Knesset they must know that large number of people are opposed to the law. . . . We decided to express in the Knesset the outrage of the masses against drafting women to the army."[27]

B'rith Hakana'im, which was not exposed, was shocked by the massive strike against their Hamachane colleagues. After hiding for a few days for fear they would also be arrested, they decided to retaliate. Extremist plans were first considered, including antigovernment terrorism and assassinations. Prudence prevailed, however, and it was decided to wait for a message from Hamachane's remaining activists. A B'nai-Brak secret meeting between representatives of the two organizations led to a temporary halt. Hamachane activists asked that no action be taken until the conclusion of the trial. This led to a quick collapse of B'rith Hakana'im, whose entire raison d'être was antisecular operations.[28] A 1952 effort by "Gideon," the former Jerusalem commander of B'rith Hakana'im, to reorganize the underground led to a short revival. It also led to an effort to put a bomb in Israel's Education Ministry in Jerusalem. The two yeshiva students caught were sentenced to nine years in prison, of which they served only three. This operation was the last associated with B'rith Hakana'im.[29]

The Kingdom of Israel underground was formed in 1951 by former Lehi members who wished to stress the ultranationalist rather than the ultra-Orthodox cause. As mentioned earlier, it was immediately joined by the Lehi faction of B'rith Hakana'im. In 1951, all its activities were devoted to organization, recruitment, and the selection of members, ideological indoctrination, training, and the collection of arms. The movement's founders dreamed about an eventual political takeover but were very unclear about how to make it happen. They therefore started with minor operations intended to draw attention and lead to greater popularity and recruitment. These operations included the burning of nonkosher butcher shops in Tel Aviv. They also included small raids against Jordanian outposts near Jerusalem. The latter were conducted in retaliation for Arab terrorism launched from Jordan. The Israeli-Jordanian armistice line was repeatedly crossed, in those early years, by Palestinian marauders who robbed and occasionally committed murders.[30]

The scope and magnitude of operations were limited, however, by the small number of underground members, which never exceeded two dozen. Most of the activists in the organization were excitable sixteen- to eighteen-year-old boys and girls. They went through intense training in secrecy, conspiracy, and the study of the history of the underground and the Kingdom of Israel ideology. After "passing" the required tests, the new recruits underwent a secret oath-taking ceremony. Most of the initiation rites were held late at night in Tel Aviv's Hadassah Garden Park. The new member was ordered by a masked person to put his or her hand on a gun, read from the Bible the Covenant, and commit his or her life to toppling Israel's government.[31]

By the end of 1952, a new target was added to the underground's hit list, communist diplomatic missions in Tel Aviv. In November, a major show trial was opened in Prague, Czechoslovakia, where several former communist Czech leaders, mostly Jews, were put on trial for allegedly spying for the United States. They were headed by Rudolf Slansky, former Communist party general secretary. The trial, which attracted worldwide attention, stressed the Jewish origins of the accused and the presence of a world Jewish-Zionist-Trotskyist-capitalist conspiracy. It indicated the upsurge in the Soviet block of a blatant anti-Semitic wave. Slansky and eleven others were sentenced to death and executed quickly. Two left-wing Israeli activists, Mordechai Oren and Shimon Orenstein, who were visiting Czechoslovakia at the time, were also among the accused, and they were sentenced to long prison terms. The wave of anti-Semitism that marked the last paranoic days of Joseph Stalin was not confined to Czechoslovakia. On January 13, 1953, the "doctors trial" began in Moscow. Nine Jewish doctors, alleged by the communists to have been members of a "Jewish nationalist organization" directed by the American Jewish relief organization, the Joint, were put on trial for a plot to kill Soviet leaders and destabilize the Soviet Union. Members of the Kingdom of Israel underground felt they had to react. Anti-Semitic persecutors of the Jews were once again raising their heads and the government of Israel, the first instrument of Jewish power in nearly two thousand years, took no action. The first operation took place in the Czech mission in Tel Aviv and involved throwing a hand grenade. This act was, however, just the prelude for blowing up the Soviet permanent mission in Tel Aviv. On the night of February 10, a forty-kilo bomb exploded in the Soviet mission, destroying a large portion of the building. Four embassy workers were wounded, including the minister's wife. The Soviet response, taken within forty-eight hours, was to sever diplomatic relations with Israel.[32]

In April 1953, the world-famous Jewish violinist Jascha Heifetz visited

Israel for a concert series. His rich repertoire included the German composer Richard Strauss. Rightist spokespersons had warned Israeli musicians not to play German music in Israel, particularly music composed by writers sympathetic to the Nazis. This sensitivity to playing German music increased dramatically following the debate about the reparations agreement. Strauss was high on the list of forbidden composers, second only to Richard Wagner, whose anti-Semitism was notorious. Heifetz received several warning letters, but at the advice of Ben-Gurion chose to ignore them. One night, as he was walking to the King David Hotel after the conclusion of his concert, Heifetz was brutally attacked by a young man who hit the violinist's right hand with an iron club. The attacker, a member of the Kingdom of Israel underground, was instructed to permanently damage Heifetz's music-playing hand. On the eve of the attack, Heifetz received a letter that read,

> You ought to know, as we do, that you dared play a Nazi melody in the Holy Land on the eve of Holocaust Memorial Day, a music composed by a partner to the destruction of our people. Why wouldn't you conclude by also playing "Deutschland, Deutschland Uber Alles [the Nazi anthem]? Alas, you, a villain! Beware and never again repeat this crime, for in the name of everything which is dear and sacred to the nation you are damned. Damned. We warn you![33]

In June 1953 following an intense Shin Beth effort, the police started to round up suspects. Significant quantities of weapons, submachine guns, pistols, explosives, and ammunition were discovered in private homes, secret Lehi caches, large milk jars hidden in a cave, in the Valley of the Cross in Jerusalem, and in iron barrels buried near Tel Aviv. The group was declared an illegal terrorist organization (to be tried according to the special antiterror law originally passed after the Bernadotte assassination), and sixteen persons were brought before a special military court. Chaim Cohen, the state attorney general, claimed in court that the suspects were responsible for a long series of sabotage and subversive acts that, in addition to the operations mentioned earlier, included spying on the army and illegally obtaining top-secret state documents. The suspects were also accused of planning future terrorist operations. Many of the allegations were not proven by the prosecution, however, including the blowing up of the Soviet mission in Tel Aviv. Several years later during the Kastner assassination trial (see below), it was discovered that Joseph Menkes, Kastner's assassin and a major underground figure, freed in 1953 for lack of incriminating evidence, had put the bomb in the Soviet building.[34]

In his August 26, 1953, summary, Judge Benjamin Halevy had to stress that "the suspects are not being tried here for their political ideas but for their participation in a terror organization which broke state laws and committed violent acts. The state of Israel cannot allow that five years after its establishment, a terrorist group will break its laws and blow up buildings as was done by several of these men prior to the state's formation." Heavy sentences were given to the convicted. Shimon Bachar was sentenced to twelve years in prison and Yaacov Heruti to ten. The court referred to both men as the founders and commanders of the underground. Several others received from one to seven prison years. The convicted did not serve their entire prison sentences, however. On April 25, 1955, just before Israel's seventh Independence Day, they were all freed by a special decree of the defense minister. At the recommendation of Isser Harel, Shin Beth chief, Prime Minister Ben-Gurion decided to commute the sentences, so that "at the State's Independence Day they could celebrate as independent citizens." The act was celebrated at a special Sulam (Dr. Eldad's organization) party that was concluded by the blessing, "next year in Amman [Jordan]."[35]

B'rith Hakana'im and Hamachane, like the Kingdom of Israel, had dreamed about toppling the secular government of Israel, reestablishing the legendary kingdom of Israel, and redirecting the course of the nation's history. None of these dreams was seriously acted upon, however. In reality, the undergrounds engaged in minor though damaging conspiratorial acts, none of which put the government of Israel at any significant risk. In the final analysis, all three undergrounds were products of protest and the nostalgia of a small number of marginal Israelis who did not feel at home in the newly created state: protest against the secular politics of the socialist government that paid little attention to the needs and anxieties of ultra-Orthodox Jews and totally delegitimized the extreme right; nostalgia for the mythical operations of Lehi, whose members never got over the conviction that they drove the British out of Palestine and laid the foundations for the Jewish state. Years later, Yaacov Heruti, the commander of the Kingdom of Israel underground, reflected on the reasons and circumstances for his underground's formation:

> Upon the establishment of the state we did not reach a sense of mastery. Our feeling was that the *yishuv* was handed a state without appreciating its meaning. Was this the state we dreamt about? We had literally given our blood for it. But somehow it appeared that the government was missing the great opportunity. Under the impact of Sulam's ideas, we therefore felt that something had to be done. Young people with an underground and anti-establishment experience were involved—getting weapons was no problem—with a sense of unguarded state borders. Every day Israelis were being murdered by Arab terrorists. Then came the great anti-Zionist drive conducted in Eastern Europe, the Prague Trials, the Jewish Doctors Trial in the Soviet Union; a drive that involved massive arrests of Jews, the elimination of Jewish writers and artists and their admission of crimes against the Soviet Union, crimes they never committed. And here, everybody bowed in respect to the "Peoples' Sun," Joseph Stalin. We could no longer take it. The time, the people, the means and the ideology—all these added up to an underground where the end justified the means.[36]

The Kastner Assassination

The last stage in the series of tensions that led in the early 1950s to the outbreak of right-wing violence in Israel took place on Saturday night, March 3, 1957. Rudolph (Israel) Kastner, a night editor of *Oikelet*, an Israeli daily published in Hungarian, was fatally shot. Kastner, a Mapai activist and an aspiring politician, died in the hospital fewer than two weeks later. He became the first Jewish victim of political assassination in the state of Israel. Between 1954 and 1955, Kastner stood in the eye of one of the wildest public storms of the young state. The controversy involved a libel trial in which the state attorney general sued a seventy-two-year-old member of the Mizrahi party by the name of Malkiel Greenwald for allegations made against Kastner.[37] During World War II, Rudolph Kastner, a journalist and lawyer, was the head of the Rescue Committee organized by community leaders to save Hungarian Jews. After the 1944 German takeover of Hungary, he conducted a lengthy negotiation with Adolf Eichmann, the top Nazi official responsible for the deportation of the Jews to German concentration camps. The deal sought by Kastner and seriously considered by the Nazis was "blood for goods," saving the life of nearly one million Jews in exchange for ten thousand trucks to be delivered to the German army.

In a brief newsletter he published in Jerusalem in the summer of 1952, Greenwald charged that Kastner collaborated with the Nazis. Greenwald, a Hungarian immigrant specializing in rumors of corruption among Labor leaders and smear campaigns against religious activists he did not like, wrote, among other things, "For three years I have been waiting for the moment to unmask this careerist who grew fat on Hitler's looting and murders. . . . Because of his criminal machinations and collaboration with the Nazis I consider him implicated in the murder of our beloved brothers."[38] According to Greenwald's allegations, Kastner made friends with the Nazis, who then allowed him to save his relatives and a small number of Jewish dignitaries. Kastner let the Nazis use him by not informing Hungarian Jews of the real purpose of the Auschwitz "work camp." Had the Jews been informed of the Nazi extermination plan, many of them could perhaps have escaped to Romania, revolted against the Germans, or sent calls for help to the outside world, all of which could have significantly slowed the Nazi killing. Greenwald also alleged that Kastner, in collusion with some Nazis, stole Jewish money and then helped save the lives of his Nazi partners with favorable testimony at the Nuremberg war crimes trials. The allegations against Kastner were not new, having been voiced at the 1946 Zionist Congress by another Hungarian religious activist. Kastner responded with a libel suit against the accuser, submitted to the Congress's Honor Court. He also wrote a long memorandum accounting for all his wartime activities in Hungary.[39]

Very few people read Greenwald's original newsletter or took his allegations seriously. The advice offered to Kastner by prominent government ministers such as Dov Joseph and Pinchas Rosen was to disregard the matter. State Attorney General Chaim Cohen argued, however, that regardless of Greenwald's shady reputation, Kastner had to clear his name. Such serious allegations could not, according to Cohen, remain unanswered, especially since Kastner hoped to enter the Knesset in the future.[40] Kastner was on Mapai's candidate list for the first and second Knessets. Though he did not get elected, there was a good chance he could be successful in the third elections, to be held in 1955. In the mid-1950s Kastner was a senior official in the Ministry of Commerce and Industry; hence, it was decided that Kastner would be represented by the state's attorney general. Almost everybody on the prosecution side expected an easy win. Little attention was paid by the press to the opening sessions of the trial.

Kastner's and the government's unexpected trouble was created by Shmuel Tamir, a brilliant, thirty-one-year-old attorney hired to defend Greenwald. Tamir, a former Irgun deputy commander in Jerusalem, was exiled by the British to Kenya. He later took part in the establishment of Herut party but because of personal differences was unable to work closely with Menachem Begin. In addition to his great ambition to make a name for himself, Tamir was burning with political and ideological hatred of the Labor establishment. He also shared the Revisionist conviction, born during World War II, that the Labor leadership in Palestine did not really try to save European Jews, and that their only concern was using the destruction of European Jewry for political advantage in Palestine. Just a few months before the publication of Greenwald's newsletter, during the struggle over the reparations from Germany, Tamir published an article in *Herut* (the party's newspaper) under the title "The Minister of Treason and the Minister of Abhorrence." The article, directed at Ben-Gurion, charged the prime minister and his colleagues with a series of crimes including direct collaboration in the extermination of European Jewry.[41] Tamir first became eminent when he served as Yaacov Heruti's (a leading Kingdom of Israel figure) attorney. At that trial he had tried, unsuccessfully, to challenge the state prosecution by playing down the association of that "incompetent group" with terrorism. Judge Benjamin Halevy, who would greatly help him in the Kastner trial, was not impressed.

The Kastner trial provided Tamir with a golden opportunity to put the entire *yishuv* establishment on trial and to crucify its leaders in public. What could not be done in the Knesset or in the streets, owing to Herut's political isolation, might be accomplished in the courthouse. The decision of the government to use the state prosecution in Rudolph Kastner's libel suit played into Tamir's hands, greatly strengthening his argument that everything Kastner did during the war was done under Mapai's direct instructions. If he could only prove that Greenwald's allegations were true, then the entire Mapai leadership would be irreparably damaged. Tamir succeeded. In the trial, which gradually became a major focus of public attention, Tamir showed that Kastner had become excessively friendly with the Nazis, who allowed him free movement and other privileges no other Jew obtained. Tamir also showed that the two trains of rescued Jews were disproportionately filled with Kastner's friends and relatives and that he had failed to tell the rest of Hungarian Jewry about the German extermination plan.[42]

The major breakthrough in the trial occurred when Tamir obtained information from the Nuremberg War Crimes Tribunal proving that Kastner had lied about his testimony there. Greenwald said that Kastner's testimony had helped Kurt Becher, the Nazi German official in Budapest directly responsible for the deportation of Jews. Kastner maintained that at Nuremberg he simply reported his activities during the war, with no special effort to help Becher. The defense found out, however, that Kastner had testified in favor of Becher and that his deposition had saved Becher's life.[43] Tamir's discovery dealt a huge blow to the prosecution's case and ruined Kastner's credibility. He was consequently unable to convince the court that negotiating with the Nazis from a position of powerlessness had put him in an impossible situation. The entire defense line, that Kastner was desperately trying to buy time and postpone the deportation of the Jews until the defeat of Germany, was shattered. Greenwald was found not liable in connection with three of the four charges brought against him. Judge Halevy's 274-page verdict, which was read on June 22, 1955, was devastating. While recognizing the horrible situation of Kastner, who was in no position to save Hungarian Jews, Halevy accepted the defense line that Kastner collaborated with the Nazis. The Germans could never have deceived the Jews about the concentration camps, thereby gaining tranquillity and discipline in the ghettos, without Kastner's silence. By giving the Jewish leader an illusion of power, as well as by "buying him off" with the train that rescued his family and several hundred Jewish dignitaries, the Nazis won his cooperation. In receiving this Nazi present, wrote Justice Halevy, "Kastner sold his soul to the devil!"[44]

A few months after the beginning of the trial, it became clear that the case was much larger than the private war of Dr. Rudolf Kastner. The trial provided the first opportunity for Israelis to confront the Holocaust, which had received little public attention during seven years of inexplicable silence. The trial was especially instrumental in raising the terrible question regarding the failure of the Zionists and other major Jewish organizations either to stop the destruction of Europe's Jews or to reduce its magnitude. The young state had already absorbed many thousands of Holocaust survivors who could not leave their nightmares behind and integrate with the optimistic Zionist culture of the 1950s. The naive expectation that every newcomer would forget the past, make a fresh start, and be content with the new Israeli experience was met by the survivors with a tormented passivity. The Kastner trial provided many of them with the first opportunity to agonize in public and vent their bitterness.

The real significance of the Kastner trial, however, was political. For the Israeli right, still haunted by the shadows of the Season, the sinking of *Altalena*, and the German reparations issue, this trial was a redemptive experience. It was also an opportunity to get even, and nobody was more appropriate for the job than Shmuel Tamir. It would be erroneous to charge Tamir with cynical manipulation of the court, for it appears that until the end of his life he believed that Kastner and his superiors collaborated with the Nazis. But there is no question that Tamir pushed his arguments to the very limit and used the trial to substantiate a conspiracy theory that was largely irrelevant to the case. Tamir was convinced that Kastner represented the Hungarian branch of the Ichud party, which was close to Mapai. He acted in concert with Mapai and collaborated with the Nazis in Hungary, just as Mapai leaders had collaborated with the British in Palestine. The sole purpose of these collaborations was the preservation of political hegemony. Like Kastner, Mapai leaders were interested in silencing the news about the Holocaust. Had they told the public about the Holocaust, people might have rebelled against the British with the demand that they stop the killing. But this scenario would have brought chaos in Palestine and loss of Labor control and power. The Mapai-led Jewish Agency, writes Tom Segev, "was portrayed in this description as the 'Judenrat'[Jews who collaborated with the Nazis] of Eretz Israel; Kastner, who chose the passengers of the 'dignitaries train,' was portrayed as that 'doctor' who, standing on the platform of the concentration camp, made in the waving of his finger a 'selection' between those who go to work and those who die."[45] Several other unresolved cases involving Haganah paratroopers in Europe, who tried but failed to rescue hundreds of thousands of Jews, were very skillfully manipulated by Tamir to substantiate his conspiracy theory. These cases provided additional evidence that Mapai was involved in a major deception and that it never intended to rescue fellow Jews. The political payoff for Tamir's court performance came in the elections of 1955. Following a vitriolic campaign that focused on Mapai's betrayal of the Jews (including the demand to try Rudolph Kastner as a Nazi collaborator), Herut nearly doubled its parliamentary representation and became Israel's second-largest party.[46]

Benjamin Halevy's verdict seems to have sealed Kastner's fate. The Israeli far right had long been convinced that the Mapai establishment harbored traitors, and that Haganah activists involved in the negotiations with the Germans had not tried to save Jewish lives. There are indications that former Lehi members even financed Greenwald's defense.[47] Halevy's ruling that Kastner sold his soul to the devil gave their convictions even greater legitimacy. Not a marginal group but an official Israeli district judge ruled that Kastner was a Nazi "collaborator." Unlike Tamir and Herut members, who shared the same convictions but limited their anti-establishment operations to political propaganda and parliamentary maneuvers, members of the radical right were not yet freed of their anarchist and terrorist traditions. The "Nazi collaborator" had to be executed so that everybody could see how a proud nation treats its traitors. As was later discovered, Kastner was not alone on the hit list of the group that conducted the murder.

The team responsible for the assassination of Kastner was caught and arrested on the night of the murder. It included three individuals known to the Shin Beth: Joseph Menkes, Zeev Eckstein, and Dan Shemer. Another suspect was Yaacov Heruti, the former commander of the Kingdom of Israel. The investigation convinced the police that the suspects belonged to a small conspiracy that kept alive the spirit of the Kingdom of Israel. While Eckstein admitted that he shot Kastner, it was determined that Menkes, a thirty-eight-year-old former Lehi member, was the ringleader of the group. During the 1957 investigation it was also discovered that Menkes was personally responsible for the 1953 bombing of the Soviet mission in Tel Aviv. Eckstein and Shemer were young Israeli reservists captivated by the spell of the extreme right. The investigation of the Kastner assassination also led to the discovery of two arms caches in the Tel Aviv area and to the exposure of a small conspiratorial group in Petach Tikva. The group even had a "death list," assembled over the years. It included Eric Johnston, President Eisenhower's Middle East envoy for water problems; Selwin Lloyd, the British foreign minister; and Kastner. In group discussions, Menkes referred to the government as a "black gang" and to the underground as Lehi. He maintained that the issue of whom to assassinate was less important than the need to instill fear in the heart of Ben-Gurion.[48]

The extreme right reacted to the arrest of Menkes's group with the accusation that Kastner was murdered by the Shin Beth on the orders of the government. The allegation, first made by the sensationalist opposition magazine *Haolam Hazeh*, was based on the fact that Eckstein had previously served as a Shin Beth informer. The logic of the assassination, according to these accusations, was that Kastner "knew too much" about the "collaboration" of Israel's leaders with the Nazis and had to be silenced. After his trial Kastner became, according to this conspiracy theory, a government liability. Fully informed about the undercover activities of Mapai's emissaries during the war, but bitter and badly bruised by Halevy's verdict, he could, perhaps, reveal compromising secrets.[49] Attorney Tamir, who covertly and unethically wrote many of *Haolam Hazeh*'s commentaries on the trial, using the magazine for his political purposes, made a special contribution to the conspiracy theory. He argued that following his trial, the *living* Kastner was an asset for the opposition, because he was a constant reminder of the establishment's "crimes." It was totally illogical, according to this argument, for the right-wing opposition to slaughter its "golden goose"; only the government could have had an interest in eliminating Kastner. Tamir, who twenty years later became Israel's justice minister, never retracted his words. While refusing to discuss the Kastner trial in great detail, he occasionally hinted that at some time in the future he would share his secret information with the public.[50] His premature death in 1986 left the mystery unsolved. Isser Harel, Shin Beth's head at the time, categorically denied the allegation of government involvement. In interviews as well as in several books he wrote after his retirement, Harel admitted that between 1954 and 1956, Eckstein was a Shin Beth informer. At a certain point, however, the young man was so enchanted with his Kingdom of Israel companions that he severed all relations with the secret service, confessed to his new friends about his Shin Beth connection, and volunteered to kill Kastner.

The state attorney general appealed the Kastner decision and won. In January 1958, a few months after the assassination, Israel's Supreme Court, by a majority of four to one, cleared Kastner of most accusations against him by Judge Halevy. Kastner was denounced only for the supportive testimony he gave for Kurt Becher in Nuremberg. The court agreed that Kastner operated under the most impossible conditions, that he acted in good faith, and that he did his best to rescue Hungary's Jews. The justices also ruled that Kastner's selection of those rescued in the Cluj train was reasonable. They mentioned that all Hungarian Jewish leaders, including the Revisionists, approved of Kastner's line. Referring to the failure of most ghetto Jews to rebel against the Nazis, the court rejected Tamir's charge that Kastner was responsible for the passivity of Hungarian Jews. It was extremely critical of Malkiel Greenwald's irresponsible allegations and made uncomplimentary references to Judge Halevy's tolerance of Tamir's unprofessional manipulation of the court.[51]

In 1958 Kastner's three assassins were sentenced to life in prison. Their appeal was rejected by the Supreme Court. Heruti's participation in the conspiracy could not be proved and he received only eighteen months in prison for minor charges. In 1963, however, after serving only five years, all three were pardoned. Prime Minister Ben-Gurion did not agree to support clemency until obtaining the agreement by Kastner's family and a promise from Israel Eldad and Herut Knesset member Yochanan Bader that the three assassins would never engage in illegal underground activity.[52]

Israel's Seamen Rebellion

The phenomenon of bad memories that produced violence in the 1950s was not confined to the conflict between the Zionist right and left. Such memories were also prominent within the Labor movement itself. From 1944, the movement experienced an intense ideological and political division among Mapai, the largest socialist party, and the more radical Achdut Ha'avoda and Hashomer Hatzair movements. The last two united to form the extreme left Mapam party, which was a member of the ruling Labor coalition on the one hand and kept challenging Mapai's hegemony on the other. The major bone of contention was the question of international communism and the role of the Soviet Union. Though committed to Zionism, the Marxist Mapam was increasingly impressed by the performance of the Soviets in World War II and by their global anti-imperialist posture. Mapam held an idealized view of Soviet socialism and a pro-Moscow orientation in the emerging Cold War. Mapam party, and especially the highly suspicious Ben-Gurion, worried about their left-wing ally. From the late 1940s they could not depend on Mapam's full loyalty to the government, and the danger of pro-Soviet subversion kept haunting them. What was of special concern was Mapam's popularity among socialist youth in kibbutzim and pioneering youth movements.[53]

The ideological tension between Mapai and Mapam was especially visible in Hakibbutz Hameuchad, one of Israel's largest kibbutz movements. Many of the kibbutzim involved were established in the 1930s and early 1940s, before the great ideological rift. By the late 1940s they had Mapai and Mapam members who were supposed to share everything but could not agree politically. As long as they faced common enemies, the British and the Arabs, members of these kibbutzim could overlook their differences. But after the British left and the Arabs were defeated, intense communal struggles ensued with bitter feelings and heated debates. In the early 1950s the situation became increasingly intolerable, with intense personal clashes and occasional violent outbursts. The large Hakibbutz Hameuchad crisis was finally resolved by a most painful split. Several communes were broken apart, sometimes violently, into separate Mapai and Mapam kibbutzim. There were numerous tragic cases of family crises in which daughters, sons, and other relatives found themselves living in separate kibbutzim and not talking to one another for years.[54]

An early dramatic, though nonviolent, public confrontation between Mapai and Mapam involved the dissolution of the Palmach brigade of the Israeli army. The Palmach, it should be recalled, was the elite unit of the Haganah. Founded in 1941, the Palmach comprised young volunteers who joined kibbutzim and divided their time between agricultural work and military training. Stationed in the ideological surroundings of Hakibbutz Hameuchad, Palmach units were highly politicized, with strong attachments to Mapam and its internationalist orientation. The brigade, which operated as a semi-independent military unit, subject directly to the chief of staff, excelled during the 1948 war and was by far the most effective and reliable military unit, proving itself during the *Altalena* crisis. Palmach units under Yitzhak Rabin, the deputy commander, surrounded the Tel Aviv beach during the tragic events of June 21, 1948, and were most instrumental in stopping and arresting Irgun volunteers who came to help the besieged ship. Two Palmach companies were responsible for the dismantling of Lehi's Jerusalem bases after the Bernadotte assassination. Following the successful dissolution of the right-wing militias and the IDF's victories on all war fronts, Ben-Gurion decided also to dissolve the Palmach. He wanted to end the special privileges the Palmach had enjoyed as a semi-independent, self-selected military entity and make it a regular brigade subject to the IDF military hierarchy. Ben-Gurion's explanation was that the newly formed Israeli army could not allow a privileged private army to exist, and that regardless of its past accomplishments, the Palmach had to follow the Irgun and Lehi into the fully integrated army.[55]

Mapam's leaders, who were emotionally and politically attached to the legendary unit, were reluctant to accept the prime minister's interpretation. They saw Ben-Gurion's act as a political move aimed at reducing their power and influence in the nation. They also believed that the dissolution was a military mistake. Palmach officers and soldiers deeply resented Ben-Gurion's decision. Over the years they had developed a special esprit de corps. After their enormous sacrifices during the war, which included the death of their best fighters, they felt hurt and humiliated by the decision to disband the unit, and a large number of able Palmach officers resigned from the army in protest. The open wound of the Palmach dissolution would not be healed for years.

Unlike the forced dissolution of the Irgun and Lehi, which took place during the *Altalena* affair and was completed in the aftermath of the Bernadotte assassination, the dissolution of the Palmach did not require force. Palmach commanders obeyed the orders and the act was conducted peacefully. But Palmach veterans remained resentful, and Ben-Gurion's authoritarian governing style in the early 1950s aggravated their feelings. The great ideological debates of the time regarding the nature of the newly created state, the fate of Israeli socialism, and especially the state's position vis-à-vis the Cold War, only made matters worse. The question in the immediate postwar years was not whether some kind of violent conflict would erupt but when and under what circumstances. The explosion finally took place in a series of outstanding labor disputes that came under the name the Seamen Rebellion.

The rebellion started as an ordinary labor dispute between the Israeli sailors' organization and Shoham, a shipping company jointly owned by the Histadrut, Israel's Federation of Labor, and the Jewish Agency. At first, the issue was the sailors' low pay and their small foreign currency allocation. It soon developed, however, into a conflict between the seamen and the powerful Haifa branch of the Histadrut. The key controversy was the question of who was entitled to represent the seamen vis-à-vis the employers—their own union or the Mapai-controlled Histadrut. Although the seamen insisted on having a union of their own that would negotiate their demands directly, the Haifa Histadrut branch considered this claim illegitimate. Only the Histadrut, the representative of all Israeli workers, could rightfully speak for the seamen. Had the issue been just a power struggle between two competitive unions, it would have probably never developed into a large-scale national conflict. But politics was involved, with much at stake for both Mapai and Mapam. The majority of the seamen were former Palmach members who held strong leftist convictions regarding the nature of class struggle and labor disputes. And the Haifa Histadrut branch was not only a union but also a Mapai stronghold. The seamen's demand for their own union appeared to the rather authoritarian

Mapai as a direct challenge to its authority. When the seamen rejected the Histadrut mediation and decided to establish a union of their own and go on strike, conflict was inevitable.[56]

The shutdown of Israel's entire shipping industry was not regarded by the government as a legitimate labor dispute but as a treacherous attempt to paralyze the state fomented by "enemies of the nation and communists." Referring to the conflict in the Knesset, Ben-Gurion asserted, "There was and there is no strike. What is at stake is an effort by the enemies of the state to paralyze the Hebrew navy, an effort strongly supported by several factions for whom the desire to sabotage the state takes first priority. . . . It is for the working public to decide whether it is a strike, not for the Yevsektzia [a Jewish communist organization in the Soviet Union that always represented the party line] and their collaborators in other factions."[57]

The seamen's organization had the support of the entire Israeli radical left of the time, including Mapam activists, former Palmach commander Yigal Alon, and the movement's writers and artists. Mordechai Namir, the Histadrut's secretary general; Joseph Almogi, Histadrut's Haifa chief; and Ben-Gurion were all determined to use any means necessary to impose the Histadrut's authority on the sailors. Substitute seamen were brought to Haifa to replace the striking sailors, creating violent confrontations. Thousands of former Palmach members also came to show their support. One of the government's methods of dealing with the seamen was a mandatory military draft. Many of the striking seamen, who were earlier urged to serve in the nation's commercial navy instead of serving in the army, were ordered to report immediately to their army bases. The pretext was that since they were no longer seamen, they were legally obliged to complete their army mandatory service. The seamen who were considered exemplary Zionist pioneers before the strike were now called "communist agents and black market dealers" by Joseph Almogi. They had to serve in the army like all other Israelis. Violence erupted almost from the beginning. As soon as the first ship, the *Galila*, docked at the Haifa port on October 22, 1951, and declared a strike, substitute seamen tried to board her. A fist fight involving the use of knives ensued and was quickly joined by a large number of policemen.[58] All the company's other ships arrived in Haifa after the *Galila* strike. Massive proseamen demonstrations involving former Palmach members and supporters of Mapam erupted all over the country. The police resort to physical force and the drafting of many strikers into the army led to the spread of the strike to all Israeli ships docking in foreign ports. Israel's entire commercial navy was nearly paralyzed.

The crisis peaked on "black Friday," December 13, 1951. On that day, and probably under a direct order from David Ben-Gurion, hundreds of policemen raided the port. Hours of confrontation between the seamen and the police ensued. Naftali Vidra, the general manager of the Shoham shipping company, later testified about the struggle, "the company was a public venture belonging to the Jewish Agency and Histadrut. The nation was, at that time, still under emergency law and Ben-Gurion, as prime minister and defense minister, had the authority to use this law. Ben-Gurion gave direct orders to the police. . . . the bellicose character of the struggle was determined by the political echelon. . . . At that time I agreed with the operation for there was no way of judging the reality. I believed that I was fighting communist revolutionaries. Today I take exception to the act." Police Inspector General Yehezkel Sahar later admitted, "The matter [forced evacuation] was never discussed in the police general staff meeting. Moreover, I do not recall any operational order issued by the national command. . . . Usually such an operation must be preceded by a serious deliberation and orderly decision regarding the operation and its details. This never took place."[59]

The most ferocious struggle was conducted aboard the ship *Tel-Aviv*. About one hundred policemen, carried by three ships, surrounded the *Tel-Aviv* and tried to climb aboard. They were repeatedly forced back. The *Tel-Aviv*'s deck was heavily fortified with spears and metal poles, making the ship unapproachable. Each of the ship's departments and cells was separately fortified, and a lengthy struggle against the invaders took place aboard. Armed with knives, axes, metal clubs, and barrels of boiling oil, the *Tel-Aviv*'s crew prepared for the worst. The defending seamen were finally convinced by a police trick to lay down their arms. They were told that two policemen were killed and asked to let several others, seriously wounded, come aboard for medical treatment. When the *Tel-Aviv*'s seamen learned that they have been deceived, it was too late. After three hours of intense struggle, all the ship's seamen were subdued and arrested.

Thousands of supporters trying to help the *Tel-Aviv* fought the police in the port.[60] Eyewitnesses testified that "he who was present in the Haifa port on that day could get a glimpse of the hatred of the two political camps, so viciously fighting each other in the kibbutzim; this hatred knows no limits. It is ready to murder, to break skulls with no remorse. It uses axes, knives, throws stones, half blocks and pours boiling oil."[61] Nimrod Eshel, the seamen leader, later said, "We stopped the fighting because it was, after all, a war between Jews, not between Jews and British."[62]

The seamen revolt ended shortly after black Friday. As in similar cases at that time, it was concluded with victory for the government—another example of the rather violent decline of past hatreds, a decline facilitated by the might of Ben-Gurion's government and the prime minister's readiness to use physical force. Noticing the similarity between the repression used against the extreme right and the left, Nimrod Eshel concluded, "in Haifa we experienced McCarthyism. To be a Palmach man was a stain. One had to be apologetic for not being a Mapai member. The same experience was shared by Herut people." "They killed our most beautiful dreams," concluded another seaman.[63]

Political Violence in the 1950s

The repertoire of early Israeli extremist action was rich and diverse. It included subdued extraparliamentary demonstrations, unruly and extralegal protests, rhetorical violence, unintended violence, intended violence, terrorism, and political assassination. Though the situation never deteriorated into civil war or long periods of national instability, there were serious tensions in Israel's early years. However, the questions that come to mind are not simply what happened and why but also why wasn't there more violence, and how did the bitter memories of the past fail to produce larger numbers of Jewish casualties? The questions make sense in the context of the bloodbaths that occurred in other deeply divided and newly independent states. The answer, so it appears to me, is twofold. It has to do with the unique Jewish reluctance to engage in civil war but also with the uncommon resolve of Israel's first prime minister, David Ben-Gurion, to establish and maintain a single center of authority.

A careful examination of the two Lehi-inspired underground groups reveals an inexplicable gap between word and action. It is thus clear that the original desire of the group's members was to overthrow Mapai's "illegitimate" regime. Not only did their leaders express this view but it is also the only logical conclusion from their acts. For if they only wanted to express dissatisfaction with Mapai's regime, there were plenty of public ways of doing so without risking their personal freedom. What could be more natural, according to this revolutionary logic, than to plan and execute a series of political assassinations, especially of David Ben-Gurion, the formidable rival of the Israeli right, the man who ordered the sinking of *Altalena* and never stopped bragging about the "holy gun" that did it? There are no indications that a strategy of assassination was ever seriously considered by the rightist undergrounds. The operations of the right-wing extremists described above did involve planned violence, but its intensity was uncommonly low. The only serious operation undertaken in the early 1950s was the bombing of the Soviet consulate in Tel Aviv, which resulted in few casualties. B'rith Hakana'im, which spoke about a fierce struggle for the establishment of a Torah state in Israel, only burnt cars and butcher shops. The bomb they planned to plant in the Knesset was a scare bomb aimed at hurting nobody. The Kingdom of Israel underground collected a large quantity of arms and explosives but never used them against Jews.

It thus appears that despite their revolutionary rhetoric, none of the rightist "revolutionaries" was able to bring himself to actually killing Jews. The only exception was the murder of Rudolf Kastner, who was executed by a small branch of the Kingdom of Israel. But two points should be noted about this assassination: (1) Despite its political context, the Kastner murder seems to have been less of a struggle for political power and more of a vigilante execution of a Jewish traitor. The assassination of Jewish traitors was, as shown by sociologist Nachman Ben-Yehuda, common among all Jewish militias in the Mandate period, including the Haganah.[64] (2) Kastner's assassination was carried out by a small, marginal offshoot of the Kingdom of Israel. It was executed with almost no relation to the movement's leaders and ideologues. Thus, the evidence indicates that even among former Lehi members this kind of assassination was the exception rather than the rule.

The militancy involved in the riots over the reparations agreement with Germany typified another dimension of right-wing extremist action, an emotional protest that temporarily went out of control. There is no evidence that Herut, a legally elected player in Israel's parliament, planned to abandon the Knesset in favor of systematic extraparliamentary street action. Nor is there any evidence that Menachem Begin, the party's leader, had any kind of putsch in mind. In spite of his militant language and rhetorical violence ("Then [in the *Altalena* affair], I gave the order no! Today, I shall give the order yes! [to fire back at the security forces]"), Begin did not intend to open fire or conduct a violent attack on the Knesset. Begin of the reparations struggle was the same Begin of *Altalena*, a leader full of rage and combative spirit, a bluntly accusatory person of rhetorical violence; but never one who espoused domestic violence or civil war. In addition to the deep resentment against the deal with Germany, a feeling shared by many Israelis, the January–February 1952 protests expressed many years of Irgun bitterness and frustration.

It is important to add, however, that several activists around Begin may have considered a military coup d'état. Shlomo Lev-Ami, a former Irgun commander in 1943, testified that in 1951 a few activists raised the coup idea with him. Lev-Ami refused, however, and argued emphatically that after the long-awaited establishment of a Jewish state, it was inconceivable that opposition parties would use violence to accomplish their political goals.[65] In conclusion, it is evident that the vast majority of former Irgun and Lehi members did not consider terrorism and extreme violence as a real option against Mapai. Most of their violence remained symbolic and rhetorical.

Students of extremist politics have long noticed that one of the primary conditions for the evolution of political violence is the *rational* consideration of its low cost.[66] What is involved is the extremists' perception of the small likelihood of effective government punishment. It is clear, from this perspective, that in addition to their psychosocial reluctance to use violence against fellow Jews, the activists of the right (and the left) had a strong disincentive to resort to violence in the 1950s. David Ben-Gurion, the nation's prime and defense minister, did not leave any doubt in the minds of friends and foes alike that he would act decisively against political extremism. In all the cases reviewed above, he was resolute and unequivocal. Everybody remembered Ben-Gurion's 1948 orders to crush *Altalena*'s "rebellion," and knew that the Old Man was determined to uproot any subversive activity. His tough and unhesitant Knesset response to Menachem Begin during the German reparations riots and especially his orders to the army and the police left no doubt that he *would* use force against extra-legal activity. The ruthless response to the seamen rebellion, a labor dispute conducted within the very bosom of the Labor movement, is another example of Ben-Gurion's unflinching resolve to eliminate what appeared to him as illegal extremism. Whether or not we morally approve of the prime minister's ruthlessness, there can be no question that this style of government made a significant contribution to the decline of political violence in the nation's early days.

3

THOU SHALT PROTEST, NOT KILL

The Case of Haredi *Violence*

Most political violence in Israel has emerged against the background of sociopolitical developments pertaining to Israeli society as a whole and the interactive dynamics of Israel's major public players. This is the reason I have chosen a historical approach in presenting Israeli political violence and in identifying significant eras in the nation's development.One type of political militancy, however, has evolved separately from Israel's major historical events since the early 1950s. This is the branch of violence exercised against the Zionist authorities by the *haredim,* ultra-Orthodox Jews who have never fully accepted Israel's secular government. Most haredi violence is centered in Jerusalem; it ebbs and flows not according to historical trends but to its own internal logic.

The *haredi* community is the oldest religious segment of Israel's Jews, its roots going back to the Old *yishuv* (Jews who settled in Palestine before the dawn of Zionist immigration) and to the traditional eastern European Jewish ghetto. The *haredim* are not a homogeneous social movement or a single theological school but comprise a significant and diverse element of Israeli society with ultra-Orthodox traditions, Hasidic courts, religious seminaries, and prominent rabbis and religious thinkers. While they are united by religious lifestyles and common beliefs, the *haredim* are divided by differences in theological interpretations, countries of origin, and communal traditions. The more extreme among them, members of the *Eda Haredit* (pious community), are middle- and lower-middle-class Jews living in relative poverty under the leadership of very old and conservative rabbis.[1]

What brings the *haredim* together are two fundamental existential elements: (1) an extremist interpretation of Jewish law that insists on strict observance of all the *mitzvot* (commandments) found in the Old Testament; and (2) a theological rejection of Zionism, the guiding ideology of the state of Israel. The importance of these two themes far outshadows internal divisions among the ultra-Orthodox. They set *haredi* society far apart from the rest of the nation—both spiritually and socially. Most *haredim* are different in appearance from other Israelis, behave differently, and even live in separate cities or neighborhoods. They have a world of their own, largely detached from Israel's secular culture.

The *haredim* have various conceptions of the virtuous Jewish life, but almost all of them believe that the people of Israel are still in exile and that Zionism and the state of Israel are meaningless at best and at worst constitute a rebellion against God. The destruction of the Second Temple in 70 C.E. and the ensuing exile (*galut*) of the Jewish nation are not, according to all *haredi* schools, just historical tragedies; they are divine punishment of the people of Israel, a sign from heaven that nonobservant Jews do not deserve a state of their own. Only through full Jewish repentance and strict observance of God's commandments will God forgive and redeem his people. According to ultra-Orthodox belief, heavenly redemption (and real national independence) will take place through the coming of the Messiah, a meta-historical redeemer who will remove at once all the miseries and agonies of the Jews.[2]

The main source of *haredi* political extremism is the community's animosity against Zionism and modern secular culture. According to the ultra-Orthodox, ever since its early pronouncement in the late nineteenth century, Zionism has been a direct revolt against God, a religious sin of the first degree. Secular Jews who desecrated the name of God in their countries of origin dared come to Eretz Israel to establish a secular society and struggle for national independence. This act was both ill conceived and clear apostasy, an outrageous affront, an abrogation of God's direct instructions. God, according to the ultra-Orthodox, made it clear to His people that they were supposed to wait patiently until He decided they were deserving of redemption. He instructed them not to "rebel" against the world's nations and not to initiate massive Jewish settlement in Eretz Israel. Jews were traditionally permitted to come to Eretz Israel to die and to be buried in its holy soil. But they were not allowed to establish a Jewish state. [3]

From Seclusion to Protest: The Legacy of Rabbi Amram Blau

Many *haredi* schools have moderated their attitude toward Zionism and the Zionists over the years and have expressed de facto recognition of the Israeli body politic. Several institutions have in fact become active participants in the Israeli political process through the formation of sophisticated political parties.[4] But for the most extreme sects, the radical members of the *Eda Haredit*, the campaign against Zionism is still understood as a religious struggle and a fight against profanity. These sects include today the divided community of Neturei Karta (Guardians of the City), Toldot Aharon yeshiva, and the followers of the Hasidic Rabbi of Satmar. They live in Jerusalem and B'nai-Brak, with several branches in New York and London, and see themselves as the only legitimate Jews, the gatekeepers of the entire nation. This communal life is clouded, however, by a tragic shadow. Since the Jewish people are seen by all *haredim* as a corporate body whose members are part of an organic whole, the existence of a sinful majority is a great disaster for the pious, for it delays the redemption. The Messiah is fabled to arrive either when all Jews collectively repent or when the entire infidel society is destroyed by God.

The model of *haredi* militancy against Israeli secularism was formed in the first half of the 1950s by Neturei Karta, the most radical component of the *Eda Haredit*. It involved a series of intense demonstrations, especially against using transportation during the Sabbath. In the so-called Sabbath riots of 1950–55, Neturei Karta demanded an end to all Sabbath traffic in and around Mea Shearim (Hundred Gates), the *haredi* enclave in Jerusalem. The riots, held every Saturday for years, shaped *haredi* anti-Zionist hatred. They would start on Friday afternoon with the battle cry, "*Shabbes!*" (Sabbath, in Yiddish) and were directed at secular drivers attempting to cross the area. Neturei Karta activists, led by Rabbi Amram Blau, would start with only a handful of demonstrators. When the police appeared, however, and during the massive beatings and arrests that followed, whole *haredi* communities were mobilized for action. Despite the risks of being beaten or arrested, Neturei Karta always escalated the struggle, developing a reputation as tormented martyrs and building the myth of *haredi* heroism. The Sabbath demonstrations produced significant *haredi* gains. Transportation in the area decreased until it was stopped altogether by an official decree of the City of Jerusalem.[5] The crowded crossroads that was the center of the struggle has since been known as Sabbath Square.

Another historic struggle, launched by Neturei Karta against the threatening secularization of Mea Shearim, was the battle over the David Yelin Community Center. The problem of this youth center, established by the Histadrut's Working Mothers organization, was that it was a coeducational institution aimed at providing extracurricular activities for boys and girls together. Rabbi Blau and his followers saw the establishment of the "quarrel club" as a shrewd attempt by the Laborites to attract and tempt their own children—a socialist conspiracy to destroy the future of their community. A six-month struggle ensued with daily protests and massive police intervention. In their demonstrations, Neturei Karta followers wore a yellow piece of cloth with the Latin letter J (indicating *Jude*—imposed by the Germans during World War II to mark the Jews). The Histadrut finally gave in, allowing admissions to boys only. Their victory became the ultimate proof that a small but determined *haredi* minority can force the mighty Zionist authorities to respect its values and sensitivities.[6] Not all early battles were won, however. In the summer of 1958, Neturei Karta conducted an intense struggle against the building of the first public swimming pool in Jerusalem, which was to be open to both sexes. Several months of rioting, with dozens of *haredim* and policemen wounded, ended in failure. The contested pool was located in a secular neighborhood, and despite Rabbi Blau's determination (which cost him a four-month prison sentence), the battle was lost.

The philosophy behind the violent confrontations, which challenged the dominant secular culture of the 1950s, was promulgated by Rabbi

Blau, the uncontested leader of Neturei Karta, and a few of his associates. They stated that the establishment of the secular state of Israel posed a most difficult challenge to the *haredi* community. Although they live, geographically, within secular Israel, there is no way that they can share the state's cultural and political values. "God is our king and we are His servants. It is our obligation and calling to preserve His teaching, and since we do not recognize the rule of the infidels, because they are rebels against the kingdom of our Creator-King be blessed, it is forbidden to obey and work for a rebellious regime. Our Torah is our constitution and. . . . under no condition can we respect their [the Zionists'] laws."[7]

The establishment of the state, a *haredi* disaster of the first degree, left the pious, according to Blau, with no option but *to seclude themselves and to protest.* The essence of seclusion is a passive separation from the secular. The community must isolate itself in a geographical, social, and spiritual space where a spirit of holiness and the study of Torah can be safely maintained. In addition to geographic and social separation, seclusion calls for avoidance of the everyday Zionist language (Hebrew is a holy language and should be used exclusively in reading the Bible) and refusal to accept Israeli identity cards, serve in the army, and use any Zionist privileges (such as food stamps in time of rationing or government subsidies for education). It even requires an effort to avoid the use of Israeli national currency (whose bills bear portraits of Israel's secular leaders).[8]

Blau did see a major obstacle, however, to *haredi* seclusion: the aggressive presence of the government of Israel. In spite of *haredi* self-isolation, there were ways in which the government could exercise control over the community and hamper its attempts at separation. Certain operations of government agencies are enormously damaging for the community even if they do not enter ultra-Orthodox neighborhoods. When the Zionists build a highway or a soccer park near a *haredi* area (Israeli soccer league games are played on Saturday) or allow advertisements at bus stops showing women in bikinis, *haredim* dread the corruption of their youth. They fear these temptations will spur their children to sin and desecrate the name of God. So *haredim* have to meet these provocations with active *protest and struggle* that bring them out of their enclave and into the political world.[9] When government agencies initiate archaeological excavation in the area of an ancient Jewish graveyard (where the dead are supposed to rest in peace until the coming of the Messiah and resurrection) or approve the building of a Mormon university in Jerusalem (perceived as a center of aggressive Christian proselytization), the strategy of seclusion is no longer meaningful. These calls demand action—to go into the streets, to demonstrate, to yell and scream, to raise hell. What is at stake, according to the radical ultra-Orthodox, is communal Jewish blasphemy, to which the pious, unless they actively protest, are becoming full partners. Nothing the government can do—including arrests and the use of force—can invalidate or end this protest.

It is worth mentioning that since the halcyon days of Neturei Karta, which in the late 1960s were significantly weakened by internal splits, the majority of casualties in *haredi* riots have been *haredim*, not policemen. This is so because *haredi* violence almost always follows a nonviolent demonstration that the police declare illegal. This tactic, which gives the police time to organize and identify the leaders of the protest, has led to many wounded *haredim*. Rabbi Blau, the classical Neturei Karta rebel, turned this *haredi* victimhood in the 1950s into a sacred ceremony that community activists were obliged to take part in. His goal was to unmask the violent Zionist entity and demonstrate to God and to lesser committed *haredim* the total devotion of the believers. Blau, who sought to set an unforgettable personal example, repeatedly subjected himself to the blows of the police and the violence of the Zionists. In his book *The Haredim,* Amnon Levy tells the story of Blau's protest against Sabbath soccer games. "Rabbi Amram approached the ticket counter and blocked it with his head. He was hit repeatedly, screamed at, spat upon, but would not move. He would not let them sell tickets on the Sabbath."[10]

The largest *haredi* protests against Israel's secular institutions were launched in the early and mid-1980s. They involved two lengthy campaigns, a struggle against archaeological excavations in the City of David (ancient Hebrew Jerusalem) and a fierce fight against the construction of a Mormon university—the Israeli branch of Utah's Brigham Young University—on Jerusalem's Mount of Olives. Both struggles, though unsuccessful in the end, involved months of riots, thousands of demonstrators, and a powerful show of *haredi* determination. And yet in *haredi* collective memory, these campaigns pale in comparison to the mythological Neturei Karta heroism of the 1950s. The first decade of nationhood was the worst period for *haredi* Jews living in Israel. The 1950s were a decade of secularization, socialist cultural domination, and intense anticlericalism. They were marked by a crisis of confidence among the ultra-Orthodox and a fear of impending collapse. The original Neturei Karta protesters, who assumed the impossible task of stopping the Zionist deluge, typically numbered only a few dozen, rising to a few hundred in rare cases. The great social and political success of the *haredi* community in the 1970s and 1980s explains, in this perspective, not only the fortunes of *haredi* political parties but also the increasing daring of *haredi* extremism and the larger number of participants in extraparliamentary campaigns. Students of political violence have long identified the connection between the confidence of a community in its power and its readiness to engage in extralegal and antigovernment violent activity.[11]

The recent intensification of *haredi* militancy cannot be appreciated without understanding the territorial dimension of their communal living. Until the late 1960s, the ultra-Orthodox community in Jerusalem succeeded in creating a separate territorial and cultural enclave bordering Arab East Jerusalem. Their seclusion in neighborhoods like Mea Shearim established for the *haredim* an almost completely isolated world from secular Jerusalem. This arrangement was seriously impaired, however, after the Six-Day War of 1967. Following the unexpected unification of East and West Jerusalem, the urban center was moved to the north toward the old armistice line and *haredi* neighborhoods. With the excitement of unification, urban planning surged forward, ignoring ultra-Orthodox needs. Tens of thousands of *haredim* living in the area suddenly faced a situation in which their mores, existential requirements, and growth needs were seriously jeopardized by secular Israelis. The threat was twofold: young and dynamic secular neighborhoods creating unheard of temptations for their youth; and crowded roads introducing heavy traffic on the Sabbath. And the plan to build a large soccer stadium near the area—bound to become a "Sabbath desecration center"—added to *haredi* worries. These events demonstrated for the *haredim* the inability of secular authorities to respect their need for a "culture of holiness" and a world of Torah.[12]

This increasing *haredi* frustration was the background for the great struggle in the 1970s over the main highway to Ramot, a large new neighborhood in northern Jerusalem. The struggle, an expanded version of the Sabbath demonstrations of the 1950s, involved rioting, extensive rock throwing, tire burning, and other violent confrontations with the police. The fight was further intensified by the participation of Ramot's secular residents, who refused to bow to ultra-Orthodox pressure. The struggle over the highway was resolved only when the route was changed to accommodate *haredi* demands. Although it was only a partial victory, this incident reflected newfound *haredi* power. The Likud government of Menachem Begin in the late 1970s showed more sympathy to the ultra-Orthodox than had previous Labor governments, and moderate *haredi* political parties became part of Israel's ruling coalition, giving *haredi* extremists a foot in the door and a better position from which to negotiate with the police.

The growing *haredi* social and political confidence was bound to have an effect on the community's behavior vis-à-vis the authorities and the Israeli public. Since the late 1970s, *haredim* have begun to strike out against secular Israelis living in or near their religious neighborhoods. A recent study sponsored by the Criminology Department of the Hebrew University of Jerusalem, based on dozens of citizen complaints, reveals *haredi* harassment of neighbors—especially harassment of single women—including beating, breaking into homes, and even firebombing isolated apartments.[13] This brand of violence was unheard of in the 1950s, when the *haredi* community felt weak and inferior and only wished to be left alone. In addition to legitimate growth needs, this demonstrated the elevated political status of the *haredim* in the Israel of the 1980s.

Going for the Action: The Dynamics of *Haredi* Militancy

The practice of *haredi* violence depends on the backdrop of the organizational work and rhetorical violence that precede it. Amnon Levy shows that every *haredi* riot starts with an "instigator," a person who identifies a serious and unforgivable religious transgression. The instigator first prints and distributes flyers and posters to be posted on Mea Shearim's public walls. The purpose of this primary publicity campaign is to test the waters and determine the community's response to the blasphemy. If the posters succeed in getting a small demonstration going, then further action is pursued. The most important factor in igniting a larger operation is the recruitment of the community's most respected rabbis. With each rabbi's support comes another wave of activists and yeshiva students who participate in the rioting and facilitate a confrontation with the authorities. Publicity and mobilization techniques are also special. Since the hard core of the *Eda Haredit* do not read the ultra-Orthodox dailies, *Hamodia* and *Yated Neeman* (which are published by moderate *haredi* political parties), the way to reach them over the weekend is through *pashkevilles* (large posters). These notices are glued to the walls just before the Sabbath, assuring the community's full attention. Since tearing posters from the wall is absolutely forbidden on the Sabbath, everybody walking to and from the synagogue will catch a glimpse of them. A final reminder comes a few hours before the demonstration: a car with loudspeakers circles the neighborhood calling on everyone to attend the protest. As with the *pashkevilles*, the appeal is very dramatic. The public is called on to protest, yell, and shake the foundations of the earth against the outrageous blasphemy that has been committed by the evil Zionists. The names of the supporting rabbis, especially if they are members of the *Eda*'s revered rabbinical court, carry plenty of weight and often bring throngs of yeshiva students.[14]

Long before actual violence erupts, then, plenty of excitement, emotional outpouring, and rhetorical violence is aired by *haredi* instigators, denouncing, delegitimizing, and often dehumanizing the secular. The Zionist authorities, especially their police, are presented as villains and persecutors who resemble the worst historical enemies of the Jewish people. And the more extremist the sponsoring group, the more radical the mobilization terminology. The following announcement, posted during the struggle over Ramot's highway, is a typical example of this language.

> Back to Nazi Germany!
>
> Just this last holy Saturday . . . Jerusalem's *haredim* went out to defend the honor of the Sabbath which has been viciously and callously stepped upon by Israel's criminals in Ramot's road, adjacent to the *haredi* neighborhood. Suddenly the Zionist Gestapo storm troopers arrived, the ones who are help-

less against the increasing number of criminal gangs (because we all know that many amongst them take part in these criminal activities). They were very happy, however, to show their force against Jews agonizing over the Sabbath's pain, and mercilessly beat and wounded young and old alike. They were not even ashamed of arresting and dragging sixteen Jews in front of the dirty television, in order to prove their might against "these most dangerous criminals" who still rot in the Zionist-Nazi jail.

And why has this been done? Because out of their pure heart they screamed Sabbath, Sabbath!

But this was not enough for them!

On Saturday night they launched a pogrom in Mea Shearim. They imposed a curfew and all passersby were beaten and arrested.

And as true followers of Hitler, may his memory be cursed, they made tens of Jews stand up against the wall with their face up. He who made a slight move received the full blow of their physical outrage.

Jews! let us help ourselves,

Let all of us, like one person, rebel against this ruthless repression and fight the destroyers of the Sabbath wall. Let us not rest until this shame is removed from our majestic city.

Be ready for the prolongation of the campaign

The suffering and groaning under the Zionist captivity.

One of the most dramatic operations of *haredi* activists in recent time was the campaign conducted in the summer of 1986 against "obscene" advertisement of swimsuits. Had the pictures of beautiful models in minimal bikinis been printed only in Israel's secular press, or confined to secular neighborhoods, we might never have heard *haredi* complaints. But the giant posters were placed in bus stops all over the country with a special concentration in Jerusalem. There was no chance that any passenger, including young yeshiva students, would miss the colorful pictures. This advertisement campaign, conducted by the Israeli agency Poster-Media, led to a *haredi* attack of unprecedented scope, determination, and effectiveness. For several weeks, small teams of *haredi* youngsters launched raids on the affected bus stations, either completely coloring over the pictures or setting afire the bus stop. On the eve of the Jewish holiday of Shavuot in 1986, the students raided 142 bus stops including 102 in Jerusalem. Forty-eight of these were burned to the ground. Despite police preparation for the damage, the campaign met with complete success. The Poster-Media agency lost several hundred thousand dollars in the fiasco, and the company has not since dared to design similar advertisements.[15]

The campaign against bikinis revealed to the Israeli public a previously unrecognized dimension of *haredi* aggression. It also exposed *haredi* activists cut from a different mold from that of Rabbi Amram Blau. In contrast to the ordinary ultra-Orthodox riot dominated by spontaneity and an unintended escalation to violence, the battle against the bus stops required sophisticated planning. An operational headquarters was especially set up for the campaign, with representatives of several action groups. Present were members of the Chastity Guards (described below), representatives of Toldot Aaron yeshiva, the Satmar Hasidics, Rabbi Amram Blau's son, and other *Eda Haredit* activists. A careful surveillance operation was conducted prior to the raids to identify the relevant bus stops and expose police ambushes. *Haredi* sources told journalists that about seven hundred youngsters were recruited for the operation.[16]

The person who coordinated the operation against the bus stops was a young *haredi* activist, Yehuda Meshi-Zahav, who had already been named *Eda Haredit*'s operation chief by the secular press. Meshi-Zahav never hid his great admiration for Rabbi Blau, in the light of whose mythical devotion he grew up. Beginning in the late 1970s, Meshi-Zahav could be seen in almost every demonstration, first as a participant and later as an organizer. The young man never resembled the legendary Blau, however. Neither a rabbi nor an ascetic martyr acting out of awe of God, total devotion, and a sense of a sacred obligation, Meshi-Zahav has been mostly moved by the adventurist and bellicose side of the rabbi's personality. The young activist, who appeared on the scene during a surge of *haredi* confidence, has also been fascinated by modern technology and electronic communication. Unlike the *haredim* of the 1950s and conservative activists of the 1960s who were fearful of modern technology, Meshi-Zahav has become convinced that these instruments could be usefully employed for *haredi* purposes without a religious compromise. This approach, which led him to drive a modern Japanese car and use state-of-the-art communication devices, has been hotly contested by the young man's rivals within the ultra-Orthodox community. But even his harshest critics could not challenge Meshi-Zahav's organizational genius and his operational success.[17]

Yehuda Meshi-Zahav is today's most visible representative of ultra-Orthodox activism. His operational style is marked by a combination of old and new, interweaving the traditional legacy of Neturei Karta with the political and public *haredi* might of the 1990s. Meshi-Zahav's power and legitimacy were originally derived from his grandfather, Rabbi Yoseph Sheinberger. Sheinberger was *Eda Haredit*'s secretary for many years, a very successful fund-raiser, and a powerful figure in the community. A member of the Blau generation, he brought up his children and grandchildren in the heroic tradition of the 1950s. Zvi Meshi-Zahav, Yehuda's elder brother and a "fighter" in his own right, once relayed this nostalgia story to a Jerusalem journalist:

> Every Saturday after Cholent [a traditional Sabbath dish], we would go with the rabbis to protest the desecration of the Sabbath. We were told that driving on the Sabbath is forbidden and everybody who does it must be yelled at, *Shabbes!* The kids would go with Amram Blau, the master, who was everyone's model. We trashed, blocked roads, yelled *Shabbes*. It got into our blood. We observed the adults and tried to imitate them. Later on we would come back to the *heider* [classroom] and share experiences. All the games were focused on this too, games about cops and *haredim*. During Purim [a Halloween-like holiday in the spring], almost every kid would dress up as protesters, holding large posters, wearing sacks and yelling *Shabbes*.[18]

Although he began as a yeshiva student, it was clear to both grandpa Sheinberger and grandson Yehuda that the young Meshi-Zahav was not born for the study of Torah. Both of them benefited from this understanding. Yehuda's activist inclinations earned Sheinberger's support, and the old man took advantage of his grandson's skills to conduct personal struggles within the community. Along with his occasional adventures, which reminded Israelis of a childish imitation of IDF commandos, Meshi-Zahav has been particularly attracted to the media. In his early twenties, he approached the *Eda Haredit* and offered to revive the *EDA*, their failing journal. Meshi-Zahav succeeded in turning this anachronistic vestige into a bold, aggressive magazine. A few years later he established, together with his brother Zvi, a publishing house named after the "sacred Israel Yaacov De-Hahn." De-Hahn, a noted ultra-Orthodox leader, was assassinated in 1924 by the Haganah. Haganah commanders in Jerusalem believed that De-Hahn, a prolific anti-Zionist writer in Palestine and abroad, was so damaging to the Zionist venture in Palestine that he had to be eliminated. The purpose of the newly created publishing house was to commemorate anti-Zionist martyrs from De-Hahn to the fighters against Israeli archaeology. The most attractive best-seller of the series, expected to excite *haredi* youth, is a forthcoming multivolume biography of Rabbi Amram Blau.[19]

The organization of aggressive riots and the manipulation of Israel's secular media have always been Meshi-Zahav's strongest points. More than any previous *haredi* activist, he understands that a successful antisecular protest is one that is extensively covered in the Israeli media. Consequently, he invests a large amount of time and energy in publicizing his activities in advance among newspaper, television, and radio correspondents. Meshi-Zahav is a master of timing, and his demonstrations are staged to fit in Israel's television evening news. He is friendly with the secular press and has plenty of non-*haredi* admirers. Journalists who cannot show up in a Meshi-Zahav riot do not have to worry. They know that one telephone call to Yehuda would give them all the juicy details of the event. An addition to the Meshi-Zahav mystique has been provided by his highly publicized outings such as hiking and rock climbing in the Judean desert—activities rarely pursued by *haredim*.[20] One of Yehuda's recent public relations stunts was an appearance with several yeshiva students in the Jerusalem Arab neighborhood of Silwan during an intense intifada confrontation between the police and local Palestinians. When asked why he came, Meshi-Zahav told the journalists that he wanted to observe new methods of fighting the Zionists.[21]

Meshi-Zahav, despite his many arrests, has also developed close and good relations with the Jerusalem police. This is strange because Israel's police have come to symbolize for ultra-Orthodox extremists the most hated aspect of Zionist authority; *haredi* literature is full of extreme denunciations of the police force. But unlike most of his colleagues who take this propaganda seriously, Meshi-Zahav knows better. He understands that since the *haredim* do not expect to *defeat* the police, and that their real purpose is to strenuously protest Zionist activities, one can do business with the police with both sides winning. An agreement on a noisy (and thus effective) but bloodless demonstration can often be reached. This is why the police allow Meshi-Zahav to legally monitor its communication network (which he can easily scan on his own), and even let him have a recognized station. Meshi-Zahav's code name in the Jerusalem police communication network is "13 black." Meshi-Zahav's strange understanding with the police has had its costs, however. Several *haredi* rivals of the young activist have accused him of being a *moser* (Jew who surrenders Jews to the Gentiles.)[22]

Meshi-Zahav's close contacts with the police was the reason everybody was surprised when he, four other Meshi-Zahav brothers, and a few additional yeshiva students were arrested on February 9, 1989, on suspicion of forming a violent, antisecular underground group called Keshet. Keshet (acronym for Kvutza Shelo Tashlim—a group that would not keep silent) was the code used by an ultra-Orthodox group responsible for fifteen violent assaults launched against anti-*haredi* targets from August 1988 to February 1989. Members of Keshet were involved in blowing up newsstands in B'nai-Brak that sold secular newspapers and magazines. They also threatened and attacked the owners of these shops. Keshet claimed responsibility for the desecration of the graves of Theodore Herzl and David Ben-Gurion. A great commotion was created when several Keshet bombs were found on the Tel Aviv–Jerusalem highway. In several anonymous telephone calls, which whetted the appetite of Israeli journalists, Keshet spokesmen talked about a highly organized *haredi* underground that was planning additional attacks on Zionist police stations and other targets.[23] Several Keshet warning letters, featuring a Star of David with swastika in the middle, further aggravated the situation. The government was charged in these letters with desecrating ancient Jewish cemeteries and staging false political trials for *haredim* protesting these desecrations. The graffiti on Ben-Gurion's defiled grave at Kibbutz Sde Boker in the Negev read, "Wait for us, we have reached this place, look for us, [signed] Keshet."[24]

Although Keshet operations stopped abruptly after the February arrests, the entire group was never discovered. The Meshi-Zahav brothers were freed without being charged. One of the arrested Yeshiva students, Israel Heshin, captured while talking to journalists over the telephone, was later convicted for participating in a few of Keshet's operations. Police investigators concluded that the operations were stopped through massive rabbinical pressure. The group was believed to comprise born-again yeshiva students with possible criminal records and close contacts with secular criminals. These students, it was concluded, did not quite manage to cope with the regimented and highly demanding yeshiva life, and consequently vented their frustration in antisecular violence.

The term Keshet was not born in the late 1980s. Its origins go back to the late 1960s and to the campaign of a small *haredi* organization against pathology doctors conducting "forbidden" autopsies. Though less violent, the original Keshet acted in almost the same fashion as the 1988 group. It made anonymous telephone calls to the doctors involved and sent them scare letters. Keshet reappeared in the early 1970s, this time to squelch the rise of Israeli sex shops. Tel Aviv's first sex shop, the "Eros Boutique," was blown up by a *haredi* bomb.[25] The sociologist Menachem Friedman has argued that this kind of adventurous marginality has always existed among *haredi* yeshivas and that in the early 1950s it was expressed in the operations of B'rith Hakana'im (see chapter two). The two leading ultra-Orthodox rabbis of the 1950s, the "Hazon Eish" of B'nai-Brak and the Rabbi of Brisk, in Jerusalem, had vociferously spoken against this kind of violence. Demanding absolute discipline from their followers, these men helped put an end to *haredi*-organized conspiracy for a long time. Recent eruptions are, according to Friedman, an indication of the great tension between the authority of the elderly rabbis and the hot blood of the unstable students.[26]

Between Zealotry and Limited Violence

Despite the recent rise in the magnitude of ultra-Orthodox riots as well as in the mobilization capabilities of the protesters, the basic parameters of *haredi* violence have not changed since the 1950s. Two elements seem to mark their militancy and set it apart from other forms of Israeli collective violence: first, the doctrine of zealotry, and second, the *haredi* conception of limited violence. Both deserve close attention.

The doctrine of zealotry takes the Jews back to the first biblical Jewish zealot—Pinchas Ben-Eleazar, son of Aharon Hacohen. As told in the Bible, Pinchas, acting in awe of God, killed Zimri, the son of Salu, who had prostituted in public with a Midyanite girl. Pinchas's problem was that the killing was totally unauthorized and that he acted out of an uncontrollable momentary drive. And yet, in spite of the severity of the act, which was denounced, according to the Talmud, by the people's elders, it was forgiven by God. The reason given was that Pinchas "was zealous for my sake among them." Not only did God's anger at the people (many of whom had relations with Midyanite women) disappear but He also ordered an end to the plague, which had already cost the lives of twenty-four thousand Jews.[27] Hot-blooded *haredi* youngsters often see themselves and are perceived by the community as zealots. When they throw rocks at secular drivers, burn sanitation trucks, or brutally attack policemen and archaeologists, they rarely act with rabbinical authorization. Legitimacy comes via the great tradition of Pinchas.

Haredi identification with the doctrine of zealotry is significantly limited, however. The radical ultra-Orthodox do not identify with the most famous Jewish zealots, the extremists who were active at the time of the destruction of the Second Temple in 70 C.E. Those zealots, it should be remembered, were involved in an intense campaign of terror. They not only acted against the Romans, who occupied Judea, but also attacked Jews who wanted to compromise and make peace with the Romans. Those zealots, who caused a terrible civil war and were largely responsible for the destruction of ancient Judea, are seen by the *haredim* as illegitimate messianic zealots. Acting out of an erroneous interpretation of God's will, they tried to force the coming of the Messiah and the redemption of the Jewish people while in fact instigating one of the greatest crises that has befallen the nation.[28]

Although the doctrine of zealotry provides limited legitimacy for *haredi* violence against the secular, it has its complications. The problem with zealotry is that it provides legitimacy to act without rabbinical permission in a voluntary society that totally depends on the authority of these very rabbis. Such a society must face the difficult question of determining where to draw the line and how to define a legitimate zealot. The answers, we are told by Menachem Friedman, have never been formulated. Different rabbis in different eras give different answers. In general, and despite occasional serious tensions, this dialectic of zealotry has never gone out of control or produced serious internal crises. In his book *The Haredi Society*, Friedman argues that the social dynamics of zealotry in the community may be explained by a model of three concentric circles—the small group of active zealots who attend to demonstrations and activate the dynamics of violence; the "passive" zealots who do not take part in the riot but fully identify with its proponents; and the rabbis who occasionally find themselves caught in the dilemma of not having given permission to act and needing to support the action retroactively in the name of the zealotry doctrine. The three circles seem to encompass the entire community, because in one way or another, most *haredim* belong to the passive zealots, even though they personally are neither violent nor particularly interested in political activism. There are a number of reasons why the doctrine of zealotry, despite its many detractors, continues to motivate many *haredim*:

> The overall feeling that their action has a positive dimension; guilt feelings because the zealots risk themselves for *haredi* objectives everybody identifies with; great unease over cooperation with the police and surrendering Jews. The last reason is associated with a traditional Jewish myth that stresses solidarity and mutual support among Jewish believers against the government. Even though the government is now Jewish, it is a secular-Jewish regime, which, from a Halakhic perspective, is worst than a non-Jewish government.[29]

The *conception of limited violence* explains why, in spite of the hundreds of ultra-Orthodox riots held since 1948, *haredi* violence has never directly caused a single death, and the number of serious injuries has been very small. (The sole fatality linked with *haredi* violence was Pinchas Segalov, killed accidentally by the police during a 1956 riot, following an attempt to dissolve a Sabbath demonstration.) The *haredi* conception of limited violence is based on the belief that Jewish life, including the life of the secular, is sacred and that the killing of Jews is absolutely forbidden. This is why extremist ultra-Orthodox symbols such as "Nazis" or "agents of the Inquisition"—dehumanizing terms that in other cultures could trigger extreme violence and terrorism—produce, in this case, only limited violence.

Another reason for the *haredi* restraint is the prohibition to bear arms. According to the ultra-Orthodox understanding of history, the people of Israel have not yet been freed of *galut* (exile), which is a state of godly punishment of the Jews. Being in existential Diaspora requires them to remain loyal to the three oaths—the same oaths sworn by the people of Israel after the destruction of the Second Temple in return for divine protection: not to return collectively to Eretz Israel; to be loyal to the lands and governments of their dispersion; and not to attempt to hasten the Redemption.[30] These oaths, which are binding as long as the Diaspora continues, require the Jews to be passive and patiently wait for the Messiah. *Haredim* are definitely not supposed to take their collective destiny into their own hands and attempt to alter history. The use of firearms presupposes spiritual independence and sovereignty, which the Jews lack. He who uses arms and is in a position to take life may radically shape the life of others. The opposition of *haredi* rabbis to the use of firearms was most clearly expressed in their anxiety over B'rith Hakana'im, the small religious underground that operated between 1949 and 1951 (see chapter two). As was mentioned earlier, there is reliable evidence that the Hazon Eish, the most respected *haredi* authority of the time, referred to these youngsters as *rodfim* (pursuers) who put the entire community at risk of God's vengeance. Under the inspiration of Hazon Eish, Agudat Israel youth issued an antiunderground manifesto that stated, among other things, "Terrorism is an alien branch in the vineyard of loyal Judaism, a rotten fruit of secular political parties which educate for the admiration of the power of the fist and the hands of Esau."[31]

Intra-*Haredi* Violence

The portrait of ultra-Orthodox militancy would not be complete without discussing internal *haredi* violence in conflicts among ultra-Orthodox groups. These conflicts come in two forms: violence among Hasidic groups and supporters of rival rabbis; and enforcement violence aimed at establishing conformity within the ultra-Orthodox community and curbing individual and group deviance.

Although ultra-Orthodox society is voluntary and the number of

Hasidic courts, yeshivas, higher yeshivas, and Diaspora expatriate communities is large, the idea of normative pluralism and the individual right to shape one's own destiny are not recognized. *Haredi* epistemology is monistic; no one denies the existence of one truth. This existential fact and the lack of formal mechanisms of conflict resolution are the reason many controversies, especially conflicts and disagreements among prominent rabbis, occasionally produce communal violence. While the *haredim* do not kill, their repertoire of militancy is large and often very imaginative. It includes such acts as cursing, excommunications, murder threats, publication of hate *pashkevilles*, fake ordering of first aid ambulances, fire brigade, and other bizarre services to the victim's home, publication of fake obituaries, fist fights, physical raids on rival Hasidic courts, and damaging property. Violent raids are especially common among yeshiva students, whose loyalty to their rabbis is absolute and unswerving. These youngsters, who spend as many as sixteen to eighteen hours a day in yeshiva, need outlets to release steam; sometimes these outlets come in the form of aggression and violence.

One of the most intense *haredi* conflicts in recent memory stemmed from the 1980 decision of Belz Hasidim to split from the *Eda Haredit*. Until its withdrawal, the Belz court was the only non-*Eda* member that fully accepted *badatz*, *Eda Haredit* kosher system's court of justice. Belz Hasidim recognized the jurisdiction of *badatz* in all other matters, not only religious dietary issues. This special connection between the extremist *Eda* and the rather pragmatic Belz court, whose members had always participated in Israel's national elections, was made possible by Belz's apolitical nature and nonaffiliation with the political party of Agudat Israel. In 1980, Rabbi Yaacov Weiss, the most revered rabbi of the *Eda Haredit* and the head of *badatz*, issued a decree forbidding *haredim* to send their children to state-financed schools. Weiss's ruling dealt a major blow to the Belz court because their educational system had greatly benefited from the financial support of the Ministry of Religion. Rabbi Issaschar Dov Rokach, the Belz *admore* (Hasidic court head), who was determined to rebuild his court from the devastating ruins of the Holocaust, he decided, in response to Weiss's decree, to sever all Belz relations with the *Eda Haredit* and to found an independent system of religious services.

Rabbi Rokach established a Belz legal association to provide all services previously offered by the *Eda*: a private *badatz*, an independent educational system, a Belz caretaking organization, an independent newspaper (*The Haredi Camp*), homes for the elderly, and so on. These arrangements, especially the newly created kosher system, represented an unprecedented challenge to the real power behind the *Eda Haredit*, the large Satmar court. When Rabbi Rokach visited the United States in 1980, a number of death threats were made by Satmar Hasidim. The threats were taken so seriously that the Federal Bureau of Investigation was requested to provide security for the besieged rabbi. Upon his return to Jerusalem, Rabbi Rokach was welcomed by huge *pashkevilles* announcing, among other things, that "Belz in *gemmatria* [Jewish numerology] means Sodom." A cartoon posted in neighborhood synagogues depicted bear fur around the rabbi's body (Dov, the rabbi's first name, means bear in Hebrew), and horns on his forehead. When Belz established an independent kosher slaughter system, the *haredi* streets were full of *pashkevilles* suggesting that Belz is not kosher, and that he who has eaten meat from the Belz must resanitize all his dishes. Grave family problems ensued. Belz sons studying in *Eda* schools could no longer eat at their parents' dinner tables. Belz students responded by phoning Rabbi Weiss, cursing him, and sending diaper services to his home. The Belz also bugged Rabbi Weiss's telephone lines. The internecine hatred became so intense that *Eda* activists ordered by phone two prostitutes to Rabbi Rokach's home; Rokach's followers responded by sending bread to Weiss's home in the middle of the Passover holidays, during which all leavened food products are strictly forbidden. After this stunt, the Belz court was put under full economic excommunication and fist fights broke out among yeshiva students.[32]

An earlier *haredi* campaign, involving intense coercion and violence, was launched in 1960 against Knesset member Benjamin Mintz, the leader of Poalei Agudat Israel (Aguda Workers), which formed an electoral block with Agudat Israel in the elections of 1959. The Council of Supreme Sages, the highest authority of ultra-Orthodox parties, issued an unequivocal ruling that neither party was allowed to join the government. But David Ben-Gurion, the prime minister at the time, did not give up. After protracted secret negotiations, he convinced Mintz and his party to join the coalition. Mintz was to serve as Israel's post office minister. From that moment on, Mintz's life became miserable. He was cursed, excluded, excommunicated, and became a target of endless harassment and threats. First aid ambulances and fire brigades were repeatedly ordered to his home. Posters and obituaries announcing his death were printed in *haredi* newspapers and spread all over ultra-Orthodox neighborhoods. Dozens of yeshiva students tried repeatedly to attack him; the police provided him with permanent guards. The personal attacks were later extended to Mintz's party. Party officials were harassed during prayer, party offices in Jerusalem were broken into, and incessant threats were presented to party members. Mintz died less than a year after he assumed his government position. While his family believes that he died of a broken heart, the official *haredi* explanation is that he was punished by God for disobeying rabbinical orders.[33]

Another example of intra-*haredi* violence, and the passage from rhetorical to actual violence, was the brutal attack of June 1984 on Knesset member Menachem Porush, an elder ultra-Orthodox statesman who was attacked one Saturday evening while completing Sabbath prayers in a Jerusalem Hotel owned by his family. About fifty youngsters, students of Sefat-Emmet Yeshiva belonging to the Gur Hasidic court, stormed in. Within a few minutes, everyone in the room was badly beaten. Porush himself, then in his sixties, received special treatment. His beard was pulled, his glasses broken, and his ribs badly hurt. He was rushed to Hadassah Hospital's intensive care unit, where he stayed for two weeks. The "Geralach" (nickname for young Gur Hasidics) did not leave the place before tearing it apart, breaking tables, chairs, lamps, and windows. Every Israeli who read *Ha'aretz* (Israel's most respected daily) of the previous day understood the yeshiva students' assault. A few weeks earlier, Porush had been ordered by the Rabbi of Gur to give up his Knesset seat and resign from parliament before his term expired. In the newspaper, Porush was quoted as saying that the eighty-year-old rabbi, by virtue of his advanced age, was no longer competent to tell Porush what or what not to do in the Knesset. What Porush had apparently forgotten was that the Rabbi of Gur was not just another distinguished Torah authority but the leader of Israel's largest Hasidic court and an admired guru with unparalleled spiritual power for his thousands of followers. Several followers of the rabbi found Porush's statement intolerably humiliating and during a Sabbath prayer recalled a similar case that took place in Poland many years earlier and that ended up in a Hasidic assault on the home of the disloyal politician. The hot-blooded yeshiva students who heard the prayer did not wait long. Upon the termination of the Sabbath services they moved in, in full force.[34]

A second type of internal *haredi* use of force involves *enforcement* violence used against individuals perceived by the community as deviants. Like conservative factions of other religions who feel threatened by modernity and secular permissiveness, ultra-Orthodox Jews are often obsessed with sex and take decisive measures against the supposed sexual misconduct of community members. The regulation of personal behavior derives from the *haredi* belief that there exists no private sphere in which the individual may do as he pleases. The community thus fights adultery, forbids the reading of pornographic literature, prohibits visits to prostitutes, and takes steps against meetings between unmarried men and women. The Chastity Guard Committee, the *haredi* organization responsible for fighting sexual deviation, attempts to deter the deviant activity by publicly punishing those who do not respond to warning. The establishment of the committee (which operates primarily in Jerusalem and B'nai-Brak, the two largest *haredi* concentrations in Israel) follows a ruling by Maimonides in the Shulhan Aruch (the authoritative Halakhic code for the proper conduct of the individual Jew). According to Maimonides, special guards should watch gardens, orchards, and caves to make sure that men and women do not eat or drink there together. The Jerusalem committee was established in 1920 by Rabbi Yoseph Chaim Zonenfeld, the first chief rabbi of *Eda Haredit*. In 1937, following the death of Zonenfeld, the committee reorganized itself as the "supreme committee for chastity guarding." The B'nai-Brak branch was only established in the beginning of the 1970s.[35]

Most activists in the Chastity Guard are married and in their thirties or forties. Additional activists are recruited on a temporary basis to partake in special operations. The most important function of the committee is to identify deviant individuals—both men and women—follow them secretly, and act against them if the need arises. Deviance in *haredi* society is a very broad term that covers all extramarital relations (not just adultery). The committee regulates women's fashions and determines the appropriate length of ladies' wigs. Committee activists destroy "obscene posters," confiscate pornographic literature, expel prostitutes from *haredi* neighborhoods, reform deviant girls and boys, and convince (often with physical force) young students who deserted the Torah world or the yeshiva to repent and return. The most common target of the committee are the *shabab* (acronym for "young man, be merry in your adolescence")—young yeshiva dropouts who replace Torah life with immoral activities such as chasing girls, driving fast cars, spending time in secular amusement centers, and getting involved in petty criminal activity. The chastity guards, who have three action teams, receive their instructions from the *badatz* of the *Eda Haredit.* The team involved in surveillance goes to public parks, prostitution centers, and the popular Jerusalem Forest. The activists, disguised as passersby, bring cameras and take photographs of *haredi* youth. Their findings are submitted to the *badatz*, whose rabbis then decide the course of corrective action. The task of the second team is to inform parents and family about the looming trouble and to send a stern warning to those youngsters involved. The third team follows the second and executes *badatz* verdicts. *Badatz* decisions are final and there is no court of appeal.

The Jerusalem and B'nai-Brak Chastity Guards engage in both overt and covert activities. In public, one may encounter committee members, usually Toldot Aharon yeshiva students, in large communal parties and celebrations. The guards mingle among the crowd and approach *haredim* who get too close to girls. These guards are particularly visible during the Purim holiday, when masked and disguised youngsters cavort with young *haredi* females. *Shabab* youngsters who harass women in the streets, visit prostitutes, secretly watch pornographic movies, and drive fast cars are also primary targets. For many yeshiva students, a hint from the chastity guards is all that is necessary to deter further illicit action.

Serious cases of adultery and sexual misconduct require a more secretive approach and more mature activists. In these operations, individuals are covertly identified, named, and—if necessary—physically attacked. Blows are delivered until the culprit cries, "I repent." The Chastity Guards use *gertels*, the prayer belts of the Hasidics, as weapons. They also employ *ma'agalot*, medium-sized sticks for baking *matza*, as clubs. Occasionally blows are administered in a public place such as a *mikve* (purification pool) to publicize the shame and deter others from similar iniquity. After the beatings, the "patients" of the guards are often brought directly to the hospital.

Punishment by physical force, though highly effective, is not the only *haredi* weapon. Other useful instruments are the rumor and the *pashkeville*, which can quickly and effectively create a bad reputation. Such public shame becomes a significant handicap in later trying to secure a spouse. Still harsher punishment entails expulsion from the community, which is implemented following a direct order from the *badatz*. Jerusalem *haredim* are expelled to B'nai-Brak and vice versa. In the most extreme cases, an individual is expelled to the United States, where an American *haredi* foster family adopts him or her and attempts to reform his or her behavior.[36]

The Scope and Limitation of *Haredi* Violence

The material presented in this chapter makes clear that the basic patterns of *haredi* violence were crystallized in the 1950s and have not significantly changed since. Those patterns follow a total repudiation of the Zionist value system, Zionist history, the political institutions of the state, and many of Israel's economic structures, language, and national symbols. The rejection, encompassing a broad political and cultural delegitimation, occasionally produces violent confrontations ignited by extremists but often backed by more moderate *haredim*. These less extreme ultra-Orthodox seem to join the struggle either because of the outstanding issue involved or out of guilt for their own compromises with the Zionists. Since the 1950s, however, *haredi* self-confidence in challenging the secular authorities has grown; *haredi* mobilization capabilities have improved with increasing conviction that it is possible to commit extralegal acts without punishment by the state.

Haredi political violence includes a combination of extraparliamentary tactics, intense rhetorical violence, and occasional escalation to unintended physical violence. The *haredim* do not have a manifest ideology of violence and mostly reject violence as a distinct category of social action. With very few exceptions, antisecular militancy is an extension of a protest against a perceived desecration of the name of God. The ultra-Orthodox are convinced that in most cases, they are only responding to the blasphemy of secular authorities. But the lack of an expressive ideology of violence does not imply that the *haredim* are ignorant of the connection between protest and violence or the conditions under which a tense confrontation with the police becomes physical. This only means that *haredi* authorities—Hasidic leaders, yeshiva heads, and other senior rabbis—do not consider political violence a tenable course of action.

On the activists' plane, however—the young, hot-blooded riot organizers—elements of violence including physical assault are recognized and expected. Individual activists such as Yehuda Meshi-Zahav, the "operations officer" of *Eda Haredit*, specialize in protests and provocative action and plan these confrontations well in advance. Not only do these provocateurs prepare for physical confrontations but they often *manipulate* their elderly rabbis into providing retroactive support for their actions.

What is striking about ultra-Orthodox violence is, in the final analysis, not its intensity but its restraint. If one considers the intense level of *haredi* delegitimation of the state of Israel as well as the threat of Israeli modernity, one must be impressed by the antiviolence taboos of these people. At stake is not just the prohibition against the use of firearms, mentioned above, but also the great hesitation of the rabbis to allow violence or approve of it retroactively. *Haredi* society exemplifies the more general phenomenon of the negative Jewish attitude to brotherly war and intracommunal violence. The *haredi* example is a special case where the violent drives against Israeli society are transformed into *rhetorical violence*. Once rhetoric is involved there are no limits, however. The Zionists are made to look like the most horrible persecutors of Jews in history—the Catholic Inquisition and the Nazis combined.

Their impressive self-restraint does not fully explain, however, the ultra-Orthodox refusal to use violence. It appears that another element must be added—the *haredi* sense of powerlessness and siege mentality. Despite the recent growth of *haredi* learning institutions as well as political power in Israeli society, which seem on occasion to put many Israelis on the defensive, instinctive powerlessness is still a basic component of ultra-Orthodox collective identity. The "erosion trauma," identified by the sociologist Menachem Friedman—the eighteenth- and nineteenth-century sense of the historical collapse of the eastern European ultra-Orthodox

Jewish community, and the perennial uphill struggle against the evil forces of modern secularity have a direct bearing on the power of the *haredim*, on their perception of that power, and on their readiness to get involved in physical confrontation with the Zionists.[37]

Haredi enforcement violence also seems to come out of weakness, not strength. In spite of Israeli secular common sense, which is quick to notice *haredi* aggression and denounce its undemocratic features, the origins of ultra-Orthodox intracommunal violence go back to their sense of powerlessness, mistrust of Zionist justice, inferiority, and siege mentality. Not only are the *haredim* unable to be helped by Israeli legal institutions but they are highly fearful of the corrupting influence of these agencies and the society they represent. Against this background one must understand the desperate effort of such bodies as the Chastity Guards to preserve *haredi* norms and overzealous behavior. The old age of their rabbis, their self-imposed sanctions, and the might of the government just add to their weakness.

Because of their self-imposed restraint as well as their lack of reference to Israel's national issues, the impact of *haredi* militancy on Israeli society has been very small. This is perhaps the reason why the government of Israel has never tried to directly confront the radical *haredim*. Since the days of David Ben-Gurion, this task has been very prudently left to the City of Jerusalem and the Jerusalem police. Ben-Gurion and his successors understood that despite occasional disturbances, *haredi* violence has never had a destructive potential, and that patience, clemency, and understanding were good policy. This is also the reason why the only direct confrontation between the government and the ultra-Orthodox was not about violence but about a sensational early 1960s abduction of a child, Yossele Schuchmacher, whose grandfather insisted on providing him with an ultra-Orthodox education. At that time Ben-Gurion ordered the Shin Beth to confront the *haredim* and use all possible means to find and return the missing child. It appears that the response of the Jerusalem municipality and police to the *haredi* challenge has, with very few exceptions, been adequate and that public order has not been seriously damaged.

PART TWO

The Escalation of Violence in the Second Israeli Republic, 1967–99

4

CHALLENGE FROM THE LEFT

Rebellion in the Periphery

The Six-Day War transformed the map of Israeli political consciousness. The unexpectedly short war, which ended with the complete defeat of three Arab armies and the occupation of territories three times larger than the state of Israel, dramatically changed the nation's political landscape. Only a small fraction of this change involved an extraparliamentary challenge to the government, but it was bound to have significant effects on the entire political system. The most meaningful feature of Israel's new agenda was the division of the nation into two nearly equal political and ideological camps, the maximalists and the minimalists. The maximalist camp organized itself around the ideas of the Greater Land of Israel, the conviction that the Arabs were mentally incapable of making peace with Israel, and the belief that security is solely a function of territory. The minimalist camp supported territorial compromise with the Arabs, strongly believed that the war created realistic opportunities for peace, and was convinced that peaceful agreement, not territories, would guarantee Israel's security.[1]

The intense ideological conflict between Israel's maximalists and minimalists, which has dominated Israeli society ever since, was not immediately expressed by extremism. It mostly involved endless intellectual debates between hawks and doves. Two new ideological organizations—the maximalist Land of Israel Movement and the minimalist Movement for

Peace and Security—represented the two approaches. Activists of both organizations put together sophisticated platforms, organized symposia and public debates, published lengthy pamphlets, and wrote editorials for Israel's newspapers. In doing so they played according to the rules of Israel's traditional politics, which allowed political lobbying of the government but did not tolerate extremist action. While the hawks associated themselves with security-oriented cabinet ministers such as Moshe Dayan and Israel Galilee, the doves maintained almost daily contact with Abba Eban and Pinhas Sapir, cabinet ministers known for their moderate positions. It was against this traditional style that Israel's new extraparliamentary movements would be formed.

Matzpen and Siah: The Rise of the Extraparliamentary Left

Israel's *extraparliamentary* reawakening was triggered by two marginal left-wing movements, Matzpen and Siah. Mostly comprised of students and young activists, both groups represented issues and ideas raised by members of Israel's minimalist camp. They spoke against the unwillingness of the government to make the Palestinians a generous peace offer and protested the aggressive, bellicose anti-Arab posture of Prime Minister Golda Meir and her defense minister, Moshe Dayan. Special attention was given to the "creeping annexation" taking place in the occupied territories, regardless of the government's declared commitment to territorial compromise. Convinced that the Six-Day War had created the best conditions ever for achieving peace between Israel and the Palestinians through Israeli withdrawal from the occupied territories and a fair sharing of old Palestine, the young activists were increasingly unhappy with the conventional lobbying methods of their elders. They were in search of more provocative ways to express their anger, and they planned riots and aggressive demonstrations. Growing up in the 1950s and 1960s, they lived in a cultural and political world that was profoundly influenced by the generation involved in the student rebellions in the West. A number of them were eager to have the kind of student radicalism in Israel that one could observe at the Sorbonne, in Paris, or the Free University of Berlin. Others were secretly envious of the American new left and the antiwar movement. The 1967 war handed these action-hungry youngsters a somewhat similar situation on a silver platter. Israel was perceived to be the United States, and the Palestinians, the North Vietnamese. The rediscovery of the Palestinian issue gave Israel's radicals an opportunity to act like their rebellious peers abroad.

Matzpen was not exactly a new movement. It was originally a Marxist-Trotskyite splinter group that originated in Maki, the Israeli Communist party. In 1962, a few Maki activists decided to break away from the Moscow-controlled party and establish a new movement, Israel's Socialist Organization (ISO). They also resolved to publish an ideological magazine called *Matzpen* (*Compass*), which would challenge conventional party dogmas. Matzpen, a respected Marxist publication, soon became the trademark of the group and its unofficial name. Hardly recognized by the average Israeli in the street, the small circle of true believers was mostly interested in the world communist debate about the nature of socialist revolution and the conflict between the Soviet Union and China. Matzpen shared the Gauchist orientation that adopted a Third World revolutionary platform in the 1960s and idolized militant leaders such as Mao Tse-tung, Fidel Castro, and Che Guevara. The cornerstone of this orientation was an opposition to the Moscow-supported notion of "peaceful coexistence" with the United States and an insistence on the desirability of Trotsky's "permanent revolution." Like other Third World Marxist revolutionary organizations, Matzpen believed that a violent revolution capable of destroying the capitalist world and its imperialist arms was both desirable and feasible.[2]

Matzpen's ideological conflict with Maki, which was the organization's main concern—had direct implications, however, for the group's attitude to the Arab-Israeli conflict. It led Matzpen's ideologues to question Moscow's increasing acceptance of the Jewish state. Israel was, according to Matzpen's revolutionary analysis, part of the "bound for destruction" conservative Middle East. On June 3, 1967, just two days before the outbreak of the Six-Day War, Matzpen collaborated with the Palestinian Democratic Front (a small Palestinian organization not to be confused with Hawatmeh's DPFLP) in publishing a manifesto about the crisis of the Middle East. The document was later published as a commercial advertisement in the *Times of London*, with the sponsorship of the Bertrand Russell Peace Institute. It spoke about the need for totally stripping Israel of its Zionist character and for the establishment in Palestine of a federal socialist state devoid of nationalism. The desired state was presented as an essential stage in the future socialist unification of the Middle East.[3] The heavy ideological language of the document could not conceal that Matzpen, just like many left-wing Palestinian organizations, was calling for the elimination of the state of Israel.

Matzpen's anti-Zionist collaboration with the Palestinians was not an accident but the product of the organization's European branch, which was almost as aggressive as the Israeli home base. Several of the organization's most talented founding members left Israel in the mid-1960s and headed for London, Paris, and Brussels. At the time, Israel seemed not sufficiently exciting for the young revolutionaries, because it was small, conformist, self-centered, security-oriented, and devoid of neo-Marxist revolutionary ambiance. Employment was also a problem for preoccupied Marxists who were more interested in their group activity than in raising families. Leftist European intellectuals and students were very receptive to these Israeli devotees and helped them find part-time jobs and teaching positions that suited their revolutionary preoccupation. Matzpen activists abroad, however, maintained close relationships with their Israeli colleagues and kept the group's name.[4]

The 1967 war and the debate over the Israeli occupation provided Matzpen with political visibility it had never had or expected. The small ideological circle whose previous Marxist hair splitting interested nobody quickly became the most vocal and radical group in the country. Matzpen was among the first groups to protest against the harsh measures and collective punishment used by the Israeli army in pursuing Palestinian terrorists. The first such measures were undertaken as early as August 1967. Several left-wing organizations issued a petition against the administrative arrests of Palestinian activists and the demolition of houses of suspected terrorists.[5] But this moderate beginning did not yet draw attention to Matzpen as an extremist organization.

In November 1967, a member of a militant Palestinian organization, Kaumiun Al Arab, who was suspected of helping a terrorist ring in the occupied territories, was captured in the house of Halil Toama, an Arab Matzpen member. Matzpen activists refused to dissociate themselves from Toama's act and instead launched a public campaign for his release. They published manifestos in Israel's newspapers and organized street demonstrations. One well-reported protest took place at the Hebrew University of Jerusalem, which became the site of many Matzpen operations. None of the protests involved violence, but the uproar they caused was unusual. Particularly controversial was Matzpen's provocative demonstration in March 1968 in front of the court house. Toama, sentenced to nine months in prison, appealed the harsh verdict, and his Matzpen colleagues, wearing shirts with the statement "we are all Palestinian Arabs" came to express sympathy. The simultaneous international campaign for the release of Toama, which was carefully coordinated by Matzpen activists abroad, added fuel to the fire. Letters and petitions were written and demonstrations were held in Italy, the United States, Belgium, Great Britain, Germany, France, Senegal, and Canada. Amnesty International and the International Union of Students were also involved.[6] By the end of 1968 and the beginning of 1969, Matzpen was a name the majority of Israelis loved to hate. From an almost unknown circle of Trotskyite lunatics, the organization became the nation's most provocative and controversial extra-parliamentary group.

Matzpen's years of prominence were 1968–70. Until 1967 the Israeli Socialist Organization was a marginal leftist group in a marginal country. From a Marxist revolutionary perspective, the critical developments in the world had taken place in Latin America, Vietnam, China, and Czechoslovakia. Matzpen activists took a keen interest in these events and discussed them as if their entire life were involved. And yet, to their Trotskyite comrades abroad, just as for themselves, they were a marginal grouplet with little influence on the "real world." The Six-Day War instantly ended this marginality. For the world's leftists, Israel, which had previously been an American puppet, became a senior partner in aggressive imperialism. Its American-supported army destroyed the combined armies of three Third World nations and illegally occupied their lands. The Zionist entity was instantly upgraded to a leading imperialist monster. Another consequence of the Six-Day War was the elevation of the PLO, a Third World liberation organization, to the status of Algeria's FLN and the Viet Cong in the collective thinking of the international left. Everybody in the new revolutionary international expected Matzpen to challenge the Israeli authorities, to identify openly with the PLO, and publicly to defy the government of Israel on all other outstanding issues. Matzpen fulfilled all these expectations, and conservative Israelis occasionally had to read statements like this:

> Israeli Jews ought to eliminate the double contradiction of their relationship with the Arab world. This policy is included in ISO's demand for the de-Zionization of Israel and especially in its demand for the cancellation of all the laws and practices which provide Jews special privileges at the expense of Palestinians. First, it means the elimination of the Law of Return and the readiness to admit all Palestinians wishing to return to Israel or compensate those who do not wish to return for their losses. Secondly, de-Zionization means breaking the bonds of the Israeli nation to imperialism. It also means the end of Israel's military, economic and political dependence on the United States or all imperialist powers, and finally ending Israel's financial dependence on the Jewish communities in these countries.
>
> These steps would lead to a total crisis with the Zionist past. They will demonstrate, for the first time, the readiness of Israel's Jews to live with the Palestinians instead of living against them or at their and other Arabs' expense. It has to, at the same time, be admitted that given Israel's class structure, nothing less than a socialist revolution would be required in order to reach this de-Zionization.[7]

Matzpen activists were careful not to be involved in intentional violence with the Israeli authorities. Their major interest was antigovernment "propaganda by deed," and their unconventional behavior succeeded in drawing attention to their views. While paying their dues to the international antiwar movement by launching occasional anti-U.S. demonstrations and Vietnam solidarity days, their most significant challenge to the government centered on Palestinian human rights. Every publicized act of individual or collective punishment against Palestinian civilians accused of aiding Palestinian terrorists in the occupied territories was protested by Matzpen. So were accidental killings of Palestinians. The Hebrew University campus in Jerusalem and Dizengoff Square in Tel Aviv were often sites of Matzpen demonstrations. Matzpen's really violent confrontations did not involve the authorities but rather their political rivals on both the left and the right. On the left, Matzpen activists repeatedly clashed with members of Maki. May Day and Vietnam Solidarity Day witnessed "intra-Marxist" struggles featuring intense brawls and fist fights over the control of the events. On the right, Matzpen rioters were occasionally attacked by Herut's student organization and other Israeli ultranationalists who considered them traitors.[8]

Matzpen's public discreditation occurred in 1972 with the arrest of a group of six Israeli Jews and Arabs who spied for Syria. The group, the Revolutionary Communist Alliance, was a Maoist splinter organization that left the mainstream movement and decided to close the gap between Matzpen's ideological commitment for the destruction of Israel and its rather nonrevolutionary activities. The public shock over the discovery of the spy ring was intensified because one of its leading members, Ehud Adiv, was born on a kibbutz and served as a paratrooper during the Six-Day War. Native "kibbutzniks," especially those serving in elite units, were never expected to associate with Matzpen. The tale of Adiv's increasing ideological estrangement from his country, his eventual identification with Matzpen and, finally, his radicalization and recruitment as a Syrian spy was heavily reported in the Israeli press and offered further proof of the bizarre nature of this "self-hating" group of Jews.[9]

In retrospect, after almost thirty years of extremist politics and violence, it is hard to understand the uproar and commotion created by Matzpen's few dozen activists. It is true that several of their demonstrations in 1969–70, especially their clashes with rival communist and right-wing groups, led to wild confrontations and considerable violence. But Israel has witnessed much larger violent demonstrations that did not even approximate the commotion surrounding Matzpen. Part of the explanation for Matzpen's impact on the Israeli collective psyche seems to be related to its challenge to the nation's conventional politics and culture. The Israeli public was totally unprepared for the extraparliamentary tactics of the group, which were not in tune with the prevailing style of the national consensus. In the second half of the 1960s, many Israelis may have heard or read of the intensifying student rebellions in the West and their extraparliamentary tactics. But none of these methods seemed attractive or legitimate. Most Israelis unequivocally endorsed the American effort in Vietnam. Faced with Soviet, Chinese, and North Vietnamese pro-Arab positions, they had neither sympathy nor understanding for the antiwar movement and its tactics. Hence, Matzpen's effort to challenge conventional politics was viewed by the vast majority of the nation's citizens as a crazy, illegitimate, and un-Israeli provocation.

But Matzpen's largest challenge to the rules of Israel's politics did not involve its extraparliamentary style. The most stunning effect of the group's activities was their readiness to publicly delegitimize the country and put their politics in the service of Palestinian terrorism. Matzpen's drive to mobilize world opinion against the Jewish state was an ordeal Israelis had never experienced. The state of Israel and its predecessor, the Zionist movement, had always had Jewish opponents. Many were bitterly anti-Zionist and never hid their negative attitude to the idea of a Jewish state. But none of the anti-Zionist movements active *in* Israel had ever dared to oppose the Jewish state among the Gentiles. Moreover, to do so on behalf of Arab terrorists was mind-boggling. Even non-Zionist Israelis understood that the Jewish state was in mortal danger and that its existence could not be taken for granted. By openly campaigning against the state and playing into the hands of its critics, Matzpen broke the rules. Not only had they reached the theoretical conclusion that the Jewish state was doomed and bound for destruction, but they took an active role in making this happen. Although in the post-1967 period Israel's national security was not in any immediate danger, the average Israeli felt threatened by Palestinian terrorism. And young Israeli soldiers were being killed on the Suez Canal front.[10]

While Matzpen's extremist challenge of the Israeli occupation was the most provocative form of political behavior in post-1967 Israel, the group was not alone in the leftist extraparliamentary arena. After 1968, Matzpen had Siah (Israeli New Left) as a more moderate partner to its right. Unlike Matzpen, which existed before 1967, Siah was formed as a direct response to the Six-Day War. In contrast to the anti-Zionist Matzpen, Siah comprised mostly young, sensitive, guilt-ridden Zionists. Members of Siah truly believed that Zionism and Palestinian nationalism could coexist.

They believed that Israeli recognition of the legitimate rights of the Palestinians to their own state and a return to the June 4, 1967, borders in exchange for peace would resolve the protracted conflict.

> The Land of Israel\Filastin is the territorial basis for the self-determination of two peoples; a) the Jewish people some of whom live there and some of whom are scattered in the diaspora, have national aspirations and regard the State of Israel as their homeland and are eager to fulfill their national aspirations by making aliya, and b) equally so—the Arab Palestinian people some of whom inhabit the land and some of whom are scattered in the diaspora, have national aspirations and wish to return. The Jewish right to self-determination has been fulfilled with the establishment of the State of Israel. The right of the Arab Palestinian people has been denied. Today, the Israeli policy of prolongation of the occupation is responsible for the continued denial of this right.[11]

This "national symmetry" theory led Siah to accept what a leading Israeli Labor peace activist, Arye (Lova) Eliav, called "the need for an Israeli Balfour Declaration" addressed to the Palestinians—i.e., a full recognition of Palestinian self-determination in the West Bank and Gaza. It implied a harsh criticism of the government's policies of the time, let alone the position of Israeli maximalists. But unlike Matzpen, Siah never questioned the validity and legitimacy of Zionism. Siah's ideologues attacked the *praxis* of Zionism, i.e., the unnecessary denial of Palestinian self-determination, not Zionist theory.[12]

Siah was a single-issue movement exclusively interested in the Israeli-Palestinian question. A close examination of its ideology and rhetoric suggests that there were few substantial differences among Siah, Labor doves, and the Movement for Peace and Security. The real difference involved the organization's emotional attitude to the government and the degree of its bitterness toward the Labor establishment and Prime Minister Golda Meir.

> The typical features of the occupation are: practical annexation, colonial settlement accompanied by systematic expropriation of Arab population, increasing exploitation of cheap Arab labor in the Israeli economy, enrichment from the war's profits, expansion of the social and ethnic gap, the militariza-

> tion of culture and education in Israel, the growing attack on the democratic freedoms of opposition groups, the rise of secular and religious ultra-nationalism and erosion in the moral values of the Israeli individual.[13]

The disagreements among Siah, the Movement for Peace and Security, and other Israeli moderates who shared the same convictions were emotional and tactical more than ideological. The bone of contention among these movements was not the question of what should be done about the Palestinians but how to get the government to do it. Just like Matzpen, the New Israeli Left did not trust Meir's generation and refused to believe in the effectiveness of the traditional lobbying tactics. The group activists believed that the passage of precious time without change in the occupied territories and the acceptance of the occupation as a given called for an altogether different type of political struggle.

In addition to being a response to the hardships of occupation and "creeping annexation," Siah's formation was nourished by the nation's confrontation with Palestinian terrorism and the 1968–70 War of Attrition with Egypt. These miniwars that dominated the Arab-Israeli agenda of the post-1967 war were costly for the Jewish state. Though immensely powerful and strategically unchallenged, Israel suffered hundreds of casualties in those years. Hardly a week went by without a small number of Israeli soldiers being killed or wounded in Judea, Samaria, Gaza, or the Suez Canal area. Siah activists hoped to channel the growing public concern about these clashes into large and effective protest. They were certain that an increasing number of Israelis believed that the Six-Day War created sufficient conditions for Israeli-Palestinian settlement and that a few peaceful gestures by the strong Jewish state could have saved the lives of many soldiers. For example, a group of Jerusalem high school seniors shocked the nation by sending an open letter to Prime Minister Meir, stating that they were reluctant to join the army for fear they would become additional victims of the unnecessary war.

Siah was formed simultaneously in Tel Aviv and Jerusalem. The Tel Aviv contingent was led by young kibbutzniks studying at Tel Aviv University who decided to break away from Mapam. Long associated with peace overtures toward the Arabs, this left-wing party decided to join the ruling Mapai in a political alliance after 1967. For the young critics, the formation of the alliance signified Mapam's unreserved acceptance of the government's policy of occupation, with which they could not identify. Already unhappy with the Movement for Peace and Security, in which they had been active for a while, the restless activists decided to form their own organization. A group of former Maki members, also unhappy with their party's complacent position on the occupation, would soon join the Tel Aviv group. The Jerusalem contingent of Siah also comprised former activists in the Movement for Peace and Security but at first was unaware of the Tel Aviv organization. Two groups dominated the Jerusalem chapter—Israeli students at Hebrew University, increasingly critical of the government's policies in the occupied territories, and overseas students who volunteered to help the besieged country just prior to the war and found out on their arrival that David had become Goliath overnight. While the Tel Aviv circle was more politically mature, which implied a slow beginning, Jerusalem's inexperienced activists demonstrated many features of impatient, rebellious students including radical rhetoric and a desire for direct action. The two groups soon learned about each other, and the actual merger took place on August 21, 1969, during the commemoration of the first anniversary of the Soviet invasion of Czechoslovakia. Like other international new-left organizations, Siah was as critical of the Soviet Union as it was of the United States and Israel.[14]

Being mostly Zionist and made up of many young military reservists, Siah was less concerned than Matzpen about its confrontations with the police. Consequently, the group's vigils, protests, struggles with settlers, and illicit operations were more militant. Siah members tried to force their way into Hebron to shut down an unlicensed settler restaurant. They staged a symbolic settlement in Golda Meir's courtyard and physically clashed with the police who tried to evacuate them. Several of the organization's most violent confrontations with the authorities took place in the occupied territories. They spread "anti-occupation" leaflets in Judea and Samaria, trying to stop the military government from spraying the West Bank village of Akraba with chemicals, or protesting General Ariel Sharon's expulsion of many Bedouins from Northern Sinai.[15]

Siah's extraparliamentary behavior was not a spontaneous act but a decision taken after numerous meetings and lengthy deliberations. While group members disagreed on many issues, they all agreed on direct action. The consensus was expressed by Reuven Kaminer, a leading Jerusalem activist, who first referred to the organization as an "action group":

> Siah circles are "action groups" with general revolutionary orientation. . . . Experience teaches us that the radicalization of youth and intellectuals in modern societies involves a combination of liberal and democratic slogans with tactics of confrontation, direct action and the evolution of a revolutionary fighting reality.[16]

In another statement, made by members of Siah in Jerusalem, the movement's extraparliamentary method was further explained:

> Siah members are neither in favor of nor interested in violence. They demand, however, the democratic right to demonstrate and would not hesitate to break the law if it is used to limit their democratic right to protest the government's deeds and blunders. . . . This has nothing to do with planned violence.[17]

Like Matzpen, Siah's years as a nationally influential organization were 1969–70. In addition to its extraparliamentary actions with or without Matzpen, which drew significant attention, the organization created a hard core of activists who seriously studied potential solutions to the Israeli-Palestinian conflict and were involved in a thorough process of self-education. Classical Zionist literature as well as Marxist revolutionary texts were studied in small discussion groups to determine their validity for the Israeli case.[18] High school students all over the country showed interest and for a while it seemed that a new and vibrant Israeli peace camp might emerge. This Israeli new left suffered, however, from its beginning with an insurmountable problem, which became increasingly obvious as time went by: *the lack of a Palestinian counterpart.* Siah could not find a Palestinian Siah or similar peace organization to be its partner. Its readiness to share the Land of Israel with the Palestinians remained unreciprocated. And thus, Siah found that it was increasingly difficult to recruit new members and sympathizers. The success of Meir's government in stopping Palestinian terrorism in the West Bank and ending the War of Attrition with Egypt in the summer of

1970 changed the gloomy mood of the country. It had become increasingly difficult for the Israeli peace camp to make a direct connection between the occupation and the daily life of young Israelis. Demonstrating for peace and organizing extraparliamentary activities became difficult. Activists of Siah and Matzpen who tried to revive the good old days found themselves increasingly harassed by the Israeli right as well as by ordinary bystanders. It was only a question of time before Matzpen, like all classical Marxist groups, would split into several factions and fade into oblivion, and before Siah's most talented activists started returning to conventional parliamentary politics.

From Wadi Salib to the Black Panthers: The Eruption of Sephardi Violence

The most significant contribution to Israeli political extremism in the 1967–73 era was made by the Black Panthers, a small and then unknown group of Israeli youngsters who erupted violently in 1971, took the nation by surprise, and left an unforgettable imprint on Israel's collective identity. Despite its meager resources and unsophisticated leaders, the group managed to shake up the Israeli political system and force the government to make major policy changes. Very few extraparliamentary organizations in Israel's history had managed to accomplish so much in such a short time.

The Black Panthers created several precedents in the history of Israel's extremist politics, not the least of which was their aggressive confrontation with the police. The Panthers' uniqueness, however, was their success in translating the anger about Israel's socioethnic gap into effective direct action. Hence, the Black Panthers became a myth in Israeli society that has far outlived the organization itself and is likely to remain alive for years to come. The Panthers flew the flag of Israel's socially deprived Sephardim (Jews born in the Middle East and North Africa—also known in Israel as Oriental Jews), and argued that ethnic discrimination had become an Israeli fact of life. They maintained that, nearly twenty-three years after its establishment, Israel was not the state it pretended to be: a just and egalitarian Jewish society that offered equal opportunities to all, regardless of their country and social origin. The Israeli claim of a successful "ingathering of the exiles" in the newly created Jewish state was openly contested by the

Black Panthers. The Panthers showed, among other things, that while the nation was investing millions of dollars in the absorption of Soviet Jews—which included such luxurious amenities as modern housing and providing jobs and education for the young, as well as numerous material benefits—no one was paying attention to the misery suffered by the immigrants of the 1950s. The immigrants from the Middle East and North Africa, who never received any of these benefits, and who had consequently plunged into a culture of poverty, were proved to have been passed over the second time. The Panthers' spokesmen and the large number of Israelis who identified with them forced Israeli society to recognize that over half of its members were not successfully integrated into the country. The message of the Black Panthers was driven home by a series of uncommonly wild demonstrations that took place between 1971 and 1972. These not only changed the government's social policies but also raised extremist politics and violence to unknown heights.

The 1959 Wadi Salib Riots: The Early Outcry That Went Unheeded

While the Black Panthers were successful in putting the socio-ethnic problem of the oriental Jews on Israel's public agenda, they were not the first to try. Food riots, often led by Jewish immigrants from North Africa chanting the slogan "Lehem, Avoda" (Bread and Work), were an occasional phenomenon in the early 1950s. Most of these riots erupted in tent cities set up temporarily by the Israeli government until better housing for the massive number of newcomers could be found.[19] Although the tent cities were not built exclusively for immigrants from Middle Eastern and North African countries, and European immigrants also suffered from a rough absorption period, food riots and a sense of socioeconomic deprivation were increasingly identified with the former group.

The idea of "second Israel," or a de facto second-class status for non-European Jews, was most clearly fixed in the Israeli mind by the popular play *Cazablan* (The man from Casablanca), which was staged in the late 1950s and written by Yigal Mossinzon. *Cazablan* featured a young Moroccan Jew who served bravely in the army side by side with his Ashkenazi buddies. In the play, Cazablan is very sensitive about his masculinity and is eager to be part of Israeli society, but is constantly rebuffed because of his Moroccan origins, poor neighborhood and childhood friends, who ended up on the wrong side of the law.[20] But neither the food riots nor *Cazablan* nor even the Wadi Salib riots succeeded in making Israeli society understand that the socio-ethnic gap was a serious problem, not a vague malaise.

The Wadi Salib riots were a series of spontaneous demonstrations that took place intermittently for nearly two months in the summer of 1959. The riots broke out in Wadi Salib, a poverty-stricken Haifa neighborhood deserted by the Arabs during the 1948 War of Independence and later inhabited by former tent city residents. At the time of the riots the population of Wadi Salib included nearly fifteen thousand immigrants from North Africa, with a heavy concentration of Moroccan Jews. The Haifa demonstrations soon spread to other centers of North African newcomers. A bitter protest against the socioeconomic discrimination suffered by Sephardim was brought into the open for the first time. Though emotional, violent, and loud, the message sent by the Wadi Salib protesters to the Israeli government was simple and clear: North African immigrants were living in miserable, substandard conditions. The community as a whole, which could not compete with veteran Israelis or with educated Western immigrants, was lagging badly behind. Israel would not fulfill its promises of justice and equality for all. Unless government social policies were changed to accommodate the weaker immigrants from North Africa, there would be more trouble.

The riots started spontaneously after an incident between a local resident and the police. On July 8, 1959, the police shot Yaacov Alkarif, who ravaged a neighborhood coffee shop while drunk. The shootout and the false rumor that Alkarif had died in the hospital led to two days of intense demonstrations. Police cars were stoned and their windows broken. Protesters marched carrying the Israeli flag streaked with black or blood stains. Mapai and Histadrut offices in Haifa were attacked and badly damaged. Unruly marches in Hadar Hacarmel, one of Haifa's most affluent neighborhoods, resulted in many burned cars and destroyed shops. Dozens of civilians and policemen were wounded in the demonstrations, much property was damaged, and thirty-four people were arrested.[21] During the demonstrations flyers were distributed calling on all North African Jews to unite and fight for their rights: "Is our blood cheaper? Let us not forget yesterday's events,"[22] "This is what awaits us of those who become rich at our expense and then move to the posh houses in Hadar Hacarmel. . . . We shall not keep silent. . . . Our blood will not be cheap."[23] Additional leaflets calling on North African Jews to close all shops and refrain from working also appeared. "Let us raid our neighbors in Hadar Hacarmel, our exploiters! All North African Jews, rise up, wake up, open your eyes and see how all other ethnic groups in Israel have succeeded and only we are lagging behind."[24]

The responsibility for the organization of the riots was not immediately clear. A flyer signed by David Ben-Harush, identified as the chairman of the unknown "North Africa's Descendants Union," mentioned that the eruption over Alkarif's case brought into the open "years of accumulated bitterness spread through our community." Mapai's activists in Haifa alleged that the demonstrations had been incited by Herut and the Herut-controlled "National Sephardi Union." Herut's general secretary categorically denied the allegations and produced a statement issued by the Mapai-controlled North-African Immigrant Association, which said, however, that the leaders of the demonstration were Achdut Ha'avoda activists.[25] These allegations resulted from the timing of the riots, a few weeks before Israel's national elections. Worried about electoral repercussions from the riots, especially in their Haifa stronghold, Mapai activists were ready to do anything to defuse the situation. General Moshe Dayan, the illustrious war hero and former chief of staff, who had just joined the Labor party's Knesset list, appeared in Wadi Salib. Soon, Prime Minister Ben-Gurion himself also made a trip to Haifa. To make sure that none of these electioneering events was disrupted by the demonstrators, a score of organized Mapai strongmen, known in Haifa as the "Worker Companies," were sent in to "help" the police handle the demonstration.[26]

After the first day of riots in Wadi Salib, violent demonstrations broke out in Acre and Tel-Hanan. By the end of the first week, North-African immigrants demonstrated in Migdal Haemek. Tension rose dramatically in Beer-Sheba, Beit Shean, and Jerusalem, all locations with large North African concentrations. Order was maintained only by a massive police mobilization. Another round of violent anti-Mapai rallies took place at the end of July in Haifa, Migdal Haemek, Beer Sheba, and other smaller towns. Although there was no sign of national coordination, it was clear that the protest sentiment was shared by large numbers of immigrants. The Wadi Salib commotion did not end until September 29, 1959, when prison sentences for the leading activists were officially announced.[27]

On July 18, 1959, the government decided to form a State Investigation Commission to study the riots and the reasons for their eruption. The commission, headed by Supreme Court Justice Etzioni, comprised a Knesset member, a rabbi, an attorney, and a leading Israeli sociologist. Twenty days of interviewing and deliberations convinced the commission that the Wadi Salib riots had broken out spontaneously, following the neighborhood sense of solidarity with Alkarif's family. The commission concluded, however, that the early spontaneous reaction soon gave way to planned and organized incitement. Ben Harush's "North Africa's Descendants Union" took over and, using leaflets and organized calls to action, was responsible for the prolongation of the protests. The commission maintained, however, that Ben-Harush was not a Herut proxy and that no other political party was involved in the case. The Wadi Salib commission not only investigated the immediate circumstances that led to the riots but also examined the deeper reasons for the unexpected eruption. Acting on the assumption that "a small ember does not become a major fire unless inflammatory material is present," the commission concluded that the poor socioeconomic conditions of North-African immigrants, as well as their bitter sense of discrimination and deprivation, were the deeper causes of the turmoil. It also had harsh words about the physical conditions of Wadi Salib, its unbearable population density, the miserable sanitary conditions, the poor housing, unemployment, and the disproportionally high number of social welfare cases. But the commission ruled that the allegations regarding government discrimination, considered the most crucial issue in 1959, were baseless.[28]

In investigating the organization responsible for the prolongation of the riots, the North-Africa's Descendants Union, the commission discovered that it had been established in late 1958 in preparation for the 1959 national elections. The union's founders were all Mapai aspirants bitter about their inability to get elected to the party's national convention. They complained that North-African immigrants in the party were denied representation because veteran Ashkenazi activists had been elected inappropriately through the party's bureaucratic machine. The young North-African activists who established the union wanted to fight ethnic discrimination and obtain housing and jobs for the unemployed and the poor. The union decided to run in the 1959 elections as an independent list. Its leader was thirty-five-year-old David Ben-Harush, who had come to Israel in 1948 aboard an immigrant ship.

In spite of the publicity the North Africa's Descendants Union received during the riots and its promotion as the only representative of North Africans in Israel, the organization failed miserably. The Israeli press came out unanimously against the Wadi Salib violence, fully supporting the government and police analysis that the case was an isolated incident caused by a few criminals. Most of the other organizations representing Sephardi Jews in Israel were equally hostile to the Wadi Salib rioters. Many Moroccan immigrants who had been successfully integrated into Israeli society voiced their hostility in public.[29] Denying the charges about ethnic discrimination in Israel, they dealt a major blow to North Africa's Descendants Union. No public pressure to bail out the arrested Ben-Harush occurred, and his request to be released to run for the Knesset was denied. Finally, instead of getting elected to parliament, Ben-Harush and a few colleagues were sent to prison for seven to ten months.[30]

The Wadi Salib Commission report, which identified the deteriorating socioeconomic conditions of the Wadi Salib neighborhood but did not perceive Israel's evolving socio-ethnic gap, made very little difference. Ben-Gurion's government, soon to be plagued by the Lavon affair, one of Israel's greatest scandals, had neither the will nor the motivation to act on the document. It was convenient for the government to view the riots as a passing episode, an action by criminal elements interested in diverting the nation's attention from the larger concerns of military security and economic growth. The commission's report was regarded as an additional tool for defusing a highly volatile yet local situation. From this point of view, the report was only a small carrot offered in addition to the large sticks used by the police and the Haifa Worker Companies against the rioters. The suppression of the rioters and the commission's report further convinced the overburdened government that the situation was under control and that other national matters were of greater significance. Israel's social and cultural elites, including the press, did not challenge the government's view and thereby reinforced it. Accordingly, they all bear responsibility for postponing the issue unnecessarily for an additional twelve years.

The Black Panthers' Earthquake

The Black Panthers appeared on the scene on March 3, 1971, when they launched their first public protest. Attended by a few hundred people, the protest brought together a mélange of slum residents, a handful of Matzpen and Siah students, and many bystanders. The demonstration, held in Jerusalem without a permit, stunned the Israeli public. It was the most intense confrontation between demonstrators and policemen in Israel for years and was characterized by unheard of slanderous language and attacks on the government. The Black Panthers, about whom little was known, sounded desperate and wild. Borrowing the name of the notorious American black revolutionary group, the Israeli Panthers were the closest thing to a revolutionary movement Israel's citizens had ever seen in their country. Long aware of the smoldering embers around the unspoken deprivation of the Sephardim, many Israelis and their leaders became seriously fearful of a period of social unrest and uncontrollable violence. Thus, the first reaction to the rise of the Black Panthers was a combination of deep guilt and great fear.

The first Black Panther demonstration, for which they themselves were poorly prepared, shaped their future confrontations with the authorities. It involved a threefold pattern:

1. Demonstrations at any cost, with or without police permission.
2. Extreme denunciation of the government, with special emphasis on Prime Minister Golda Meir.
3. A special type of violent direct action intended to intensify the conflict with the police and drag bystanders into the confrontation.

Even as this book is being written more than twenty-five years after the rise of the Black Panthers, it is still hard to believe that this socio-ethnic earthquake was produced by a dozen uneducated youngsters, aged sixteen to twenty-three, from a poor Jerusalem neighborhood called Morasha. From an early age, the youths, all of Moroccan origin, followed the path of a typical North African raised in Israel's worst slums: growing up in large, poor families that immigrated to Israel in the late 1940s and early1950s; residing in deserted Arab neighborhoods in poor living conditions; seeing the collapse of the father's authority owing to unemployment and inability to speak Hebrew; dropping out of primary school; becoming a juvenile delinquent with a minor criminal record and spending time in juvenile correctional institutions; experimenting with drugs and failing either to serve or to complete full service in the Israeli army.[31]

A group of this sociocultural profile could have hardly challenged the Israeli authorities on its own, let alone created a social earthquake that would unsettle the entire country. And indeed, the success of the Black Panthers cannot be comprehended without understanding two independent encounters the group experienced in its pre-Panther days: a lengthy interaction with the social workers of the City of Jerusalem and a short but effective series of meetings with Matzpen and Siah activists. Contact between several future Panther leaders and the social workers of the City of Jerusalem began in 1963. Helped by young counselors, whose job was to prevent potential street gangs from engaging in criminal activity, the social workers attracted Morasha's youth to a small sport club near their neighborhood. Talking to the social workers in the club, the future Panthers had their first chance to discuss their personal and collective problems, vent their frustrations, and see the larger social picture of their personal miseries.[32] To their great surprise, they soon discovered that they were not the only frustrated members of the club.

In the early 1960s, very few veteran Israelis were aware of the gathering storm within Israeli society, the fast-growing social, economic, and cultural gap between Ashkenazi and Sephardi Jews. This was partly because the early 1960s were years of economic expansion. But at the same time that veteran Ashkenazim were raising their standard of living because of their skills, economic resources, and ability to compete, the Sephardi immigrants, especially the North Africans, were suffering. Lacking the cultural and economic resources necessary to compete, they were left behind. Israel's social workers, in daily contact with the deprived group, had become increasingly aware of the widening socioeconomic gap. Incapable of passing this information on to their uninterested political superiors, they became bitter and frustrated. Identifying with the pain of the Morasha group—which was typical of the second generation of North African immigrants—and yet powerless to help much, they could at least share their critique of the blind and ruthless system with the poor youths.[33] Hence they inadvertently helped channel the outrage of the group into social and political avenues. While not encouraging the future Black Panthers to resort to violence, the social workers gradually made them understand that nobody but themselves was able to help. The future Panthers learned that unless they took dramatic action, their lives would not change. The poorly educated Morasha youths never developed a sophisticated ideology. Even at the height of their success they didn't formulate a coherent program of action. Their long talks with the city's social workers taught them, however, to make demands and not to be intimidated by the politicians or the press.

The immediate trigger for the joint protest of the Morasha group and the social workers was a decision of the Jerusalem City Council to stop financing the street group project, which meant closing the Morasha club. Many council members did not value the educational work done by the street group counselors. Many councilmen were Orthodox or ultra-Orthodox Jews who were highly skeptical of the kind of secular education that could be provided to the young Moroccans. They complained that the counselors often knew about the youngsters' criminal plans but failed to report them. The decision to close the club made the social workers just as angry as the youngsters themselves. The Morasha club's activity now shifted to a larger club on Jerusalem's Hillel Street, and both parties looked for ways to salvage the street group project. The idea of informing the media about the problem and using the ensuing publicity to expose the City Council's decision seemed attractive. Thus, organizing a protest group was an extension of the effort to attract attention and publicity. Neither the Morasha kids nor the social workers thought of the protest as a way of turning Israeli society upside-down or creating a social earthquake. All they wanted was to keep the limited budgets for their project.[34]

The Panthers acquired the "chutzpah" to challenge the Israeli establishment in the streets from Matzpen and Siah, the peace groups involved in extraparliamentary activities in the late 1960s. The encounter between the poor youngsters from Morasha and the young Israeli "revolutionaries" was accidental, for the two groups had little in common. Morasha youths were light years away from the Hebrew University, and the affluent new leftists hardly knew of Jerusalem's North-African slum culture. However, the Hillel Street club, to which all activity was switched after the Morasha club closure, was very close to Ta'amon and the Yellow Tea House, both popular Jerusalem coffee shops where Matzpen and Siah activists gathered.[35] The older members of the Morasha group were influenced by the students who had challenged the Israeli establishment since 1968. The students were also intrigued. Gradually isolated by their increasingly unpopular peace positions, they took a great interest in their new sympathizers. In conversations with the street youths, the leftists immediately identified their great "revolutionary" potential. The affluent challengers of the system, who were in the process of developing a comprehensive new leftist critique of the Israeli system, were pleased to meet its real victims. Like all upper-middle-class socialists, Matzpen and Siah ideologues were more than happy to find a genuine Israeli "proletariat." The meetings, drinking, talks into the night, growing camaraderie, and common consumption of drugs had an effect on the Morasha group. The level of their political consciousness was raised, and they better understood the "oppressive mechanisms" of the Israeli system. But more important, their contacts with Matzpen and Siah provided them with a model of action. Both sides agreed that the Panthers would act independently and that there would be no public association between the organizations. Both understood that the Black Panthers had a powerful issue of social justice capable of creating widespread antigovernment sentiment. They knew that even the remote association of the Panther revolt with the unpopular peace movements could be used by the government to totally destroy the new organization.[36]

The meetings between the peace activists and the future social revolutionaries, which also involved several independent leftist academics, produced the latter group's name. While the Morasha youngsters had never heard of the original Black Panthers, the American revolutionary organization was admired by Matzpen and Siah. The Morasha group had also considered calling themselves the "Tupamoroccanos"—a reference to Uruguay's famed terror organization, the Tupamaros, combined with the Moroccans.[37] But the Black Panther name brought together elements shared by the American and Israeli Black Panthers: dark skin color, a sense of extreme deprivation, intense anti-establishment sentiment, and readiness to resort to violence. Just like the future Panthers, the young leftists realized that the new name was bound to intimidate a large number of Israelis.

In a perspective spanning nearly thirty years, it is clear that the Black Panthers were more about protest than about left-wing politics. Their acute sense of deprivation would have easily taken them to the right had the proper right-wing protest carrier been around. But the Israeli right of 1970 was part of the establishment. Menachem Begin, later considered the greater savior of North-African Israelis, was in the early 1970s a great admirer of Golda Meir. The emerging radical right of the settlers devoted itself to Eretz Israel and hardly noticed the nation's growing socio-ethnic gap. Only years later and after the political failure of the Black Panthers would most of their Sephardi supporters discover the Likud and the great effectiveness of channeling their protest vote to this camp. And it was only after 1977 and the rise of the Likud that the Sephardi protest vote moved decisively to the right.

The Rise and Decline of the Black Panthers

As they learned more about the organization of the new group and its intention to take Israel's socio-ethnic problem to the streets, the authorities became increasingly concerned. Although it had been twelve years since the Wadi Salib riots, the politicians must have had an unhappy recollection of the social earthquake they succeeded in stopping in 1959. A meeting in the prime minister's office, attended by Golda Meir herself, the ministers of police and justice, the nation's top police officers, and Jerusalem's mayor, Teddy Kollek, was hastily arranged. Acting out of the 1950s authoritarian mentality, the group resolved that the planned demonstration must be stopped at once. The police believed they knew how to do it and had in mind a combination of administrative measures and threats.[38] On March 2,

1971, the eve of the planned demonstration, all Panther leaders were summoned to Jerusalem's police headquarters for a "frank and serious talk." At the meeting, they were reminded of their criminal records and told in unequivocal terms that if they made trouble, there was sufficient evidence to arrest and jail them.[39] The patronizing police and their political superiors failed to notice that Israel in 1971 was no longer the same society as in 1959. David Ben-Gurion had been long out of power. The Israeli press had become more open and competitive, with a generation of young, informed journalists closer in age to the Panthers than to the aging cabinet ministers, eager to take on the authorities.[40] The precedents of extraparliamentary politics set by Matzpen and Siah also made it difficult to portray the rioting Panthers as dangerous criminals. The government's last-minute efforts could not stop the gathering storm.

From its beginning, the Black Panther protest was different from any other social action taken in Israel, including the Wadi Salib riots. The Panthers did not apologize or try to be "Ashkenazi-like" nice. They were rude and aggressive, and they used vulgar language. Their entire worldview, modus operandi, and political style were expressed in the first communiqué they distributed on the eve of the first demonstration:

> Enough!
>
> We, a group of screwed-up youngsters, appeal to all those who have had it.
>
> Enough of unemployment!
>
> Enough of 10 people sleeping in one bedroom!
>
> Enough of looking at apartment buildings presently built for new immigrants [from the Soviet Union]!
>
> Enough of being thrown in jail and hit every other day!
>
> Enough of unkept government promises!
>
> Enough of deprivation and discrimination!
>
> How long will they do it to us and we keep silent?
>
> Isolated, we can do nothing. Together we shall prevail!
>
> Demonstrating for our right to be equal to everybody else in this country. Demonstration will be held on Wednesday, March 3, 3:30 P.M. on Jaffa Street in front of City Hall.
>
> The Black Panthers[41]

The first demonstration of the Black Panthers was illegal because the police denied the group a permit, but it was heavily publicized and led to an intense confrontation with the authorities and a high level of violence. The police lost control. Thirteen people were arrested, including members of Matzpen. The second demonstration, also with permit denied, occurred two days later and included several well-known Israeli literary figures who came to support the Panthers' right to be heard. Held in front of Jerusalem's city hall, the demonstration was mostly nonviolent. The only notable moment came when Mayor Kollek, who was hostile and unmoved, implored the demonstrators not to step on the garden in front of his office lest the flowers be destroyed. The Panthers and their supporters could hardly avoid the obvious comparison between the mayor's attitude to people and to flowers in distress. A few days later, following growing public interest in the new phenomenon, the Black Panthers decided to register as a legal association and organize officially. They made it clear that, in addition to their efforts to be heard in the Knesset and in Israeli politics, they intended to keep demonstrating, with or without police permission. During their next demonstration, in which they demanded that their arrested members be released, the Panthers did not hesitate to break into police headquarters to free the men. About twenty demonstrators and five policemen were wounded.[42]

Despite the enormous public reaction to the Black Panthers, which was essentially critical of their violence but sympathetic to their cause, there were no indications that Meir and her colleagues were conscious of the magnitude of the problem. The organization was treated as a group of criminals, which no doubt contributed to its continued aggressiveness and protests. Until its unexpected decline in 1972, the movement organized about ten large demonstrations in Jerusalem. Dozens of smaller protests, put together either by the Black Panthers themselves or by supporting solidarity groups, were held all over the country. The most dramatic confrontation took place on May 15, 1971, in Jerusalem's Davidka Square. "There will be no cease-fire on the poverty front," read a giant poster. For nearly seven hours the city was swept by violence. Cars were set on fire, shop windows smashed, and policemen on horseback chased the rioters. Dozens of wounded protesters and policemen ended their day at Hadassah

Hospital.[43] In another demonstration, a Molotov cocktail was thrown at the police. The Panthers then announced that the perpetrators had gone underground and that the movement's headquarters would soon be moved to a European capital. The Blue-White Black Panther Movement, a Tel Aviv-affiliated organization, announced in August that it would soon declare war on the government of Israel.[44]

Their sense of deprivation and discrimination over a long period undoubtedly had a direct bearing on the Panthers' extremism. But two additional factors contributed to their bitterness: anger at the police—expressed by the slogan *Medinat Mishtar-ra* (a police state [in Hebrew, also an "evil" state]) and a personal vendetta against Prime Minister Meir. It was clear from the outset that although the Panthers expected the police to combine their demand for law and order with an understanding of the social issue, the police only treated them like criminals. Constantly reminding arrested Panthers of their criminal records and ridiculing them for their past personal failures, the police only exacerbated the confrontation.[45]

The Panthers' disdain for the prime minister developed after Meir invited the leaders of the organization to a meeting in her office; they came dressed for business as usual, dirty and unshaven as always. The prime minister, who had neither visited Israel's urban slums in a long time nor recognized the somber reality created there by years of neglect, was dumbfounded. Incapable of listening to their serious arguments about the miserable conditions of North-African immigrants, Meir could offer only personal comments. She continually reminded her interlocutors, most of whom had had no steady job for years, of how unproductive it was not to work or hold a permanent job. She then lectured them about the terrible choice of a name they had made for their organization. Didn't they know that the American Black Panthers supported the PLO and were anti-Semitic?[46] Arguing a few weeks later with people close to her, Meir said that the Panthers "are not nice"—a phrase not forgotten since. The comment served as proof for the Black Panthers and many sympathetic Israelis of the prime minister's lack of interest in social issues and her inability to sympathize with the deprived. The anti-Golda motif became dominant in Black Panther culture and was expressed in such slogans as "Golda, will you please teach us Yiddish" (a German-Jewish dialect spoken by European Jews but unknown to Sephardim), "Golda told us no!" "When will Golda dance at Buzaglo's [a typical Jewish-Moroccan name] wedding?" "Golda, in the Suez Canal [on the battlefront with Egypt] we are all nice," and the famous poster of a naked Meir with angel's wings and the inscription "Golda, will you please fly away?"[47]

A retrospective examination of the political style of the Black Panthers suggests that despite the severe violence of their riots and their aggressive posture, Panther violence, like Wadi Salib violence, expressed powerlessness more than anything else. In spite of their significant impact on Israeli society and their contribution to the reorganization of the government agencies responsible for education and welfare, the Black Panthers were weak ideologically, unsophisticated politically, poorly organized, and, most of all, incredibly inexperienced. They never wanted to take over the government or wished to shape the nation's cultural or territorial boundaries. They were equally uninterested in terrorizing the Ashkenazi population. All the Black Panthers really wished was a place under the sun. Their violence was not strategically planned. It was partly a direct extension of the gang world in which they lived and partly the result of a lack of an alternative. The Panthers were a case of a social pressure cooker exploding after years of neglect, a painful outcry against discrimination and deprivation.

There were several reasons for the Panthers' quick and dramatic decline—which occurred less than a year after the spectacular rise of the organization. By far the most significant reason was internal leadership clashes and the inability to work in concert. Despite the personal and political progress they made, the Panther core group remained what it had been before March 3, 1971: a distraught street gang with many personal and interpersonal problems. Members of the group, who had no experience in organizational or community work, let alone the democratic procedures for holding an orderly meeting, simply did not know what to do. Catapulted within two weeks from social marginality to cultural stardom, they refused to share their glory with anybody who was not originally from the Morasha group. They also would not let professionals help them. Their worst plague, however, was their personal mistrust of one another and their inability to work together. Years of poverty, juvenile delinquency, family conflicts, and clashes with the police had left the Panthers deeply suspicions of one another. Colleagues were constantly being charged with stealing the organization's money, with being ready to be bought by the establishment, with informing the police, and with saying wrong things to the media. Many of these charges were true, for most of the Panthers wished to benefit materially from their new situation. It was, consequently, just a matter of time before the organization would collapse.[48]

The Panthers inability to formulate a strategy of social change and perceive of themselves as a permanent instrument for its implementation was another indication of the organization's death wish. Their weak intellectual skills made it impossible for the original Morasha group to formulate a comprehensive program and stick to it. Once their protests became routine, much of the glory vanished and organizational splits aggravated the situation. By the time the Israeli government finally started to address the nation's socio-ethnic gap seriously, not much of the Black Panther organization was left. Meir was slow to act on the matter, but she did establish the Prime Minister's Commission on the Study of the Problem of Disadvantaged Youth in 1972. The commission, under the leadership of Dr. Israel Katz, the general director of the National Insurance Institute, took its assignment seriously. It divided its work among several subcommittees that employed Israel's best academics on social and ethnic issues. Katz's impressive report, published a year later, left almost no stone untouched. More important, however, was the fact that most government ministries considered the report a blueprint for action.[49] Millions of dollars were now channeled to social purposes, with great emphasis on disadvantaged youth. For the first time, the socio-ethnic gap was identified as a national problem. Israeli governments may not have done enough to close it, but since the Black Panthers, the gap would be impossible to ignore.

The nation's political parties, especially the Herut-Liberal block, also responded to the new challenge, an awakening that led to the political mobility of Israel's Sephardim. Black Panther leaders personally received offers to improve their lot, and a few accepted. The group lowered its violent profile and decided to join Shalom Cohen, a former left-wing radical activist, in the Histadrut and National elections. Fewer than two years after its formation the Israeli Black Panther movement was going through an irreversible decline, dramatically hastened by the tragedy of the Yom Kippur War. All that was left of the Black Panthers was their name and mythical reputation in Israeli society, which has refused to die. Though long detached from Panther activity, former Panther leader Charles Biton, who became a Communist party Knesset member, helped to preserve this tradition.

The Leftist "Rebellion" in Perspective

The quick decline of the Panthers' "violence of powerlessness" and the disappearance of Matzpen and Siah from Israel's extraparliamentary scene demonstrated the resilience of the nation's traditional politics and the survival problems encountered by extremist groups. Although David Ben-Gurion, who had been responsible for the determined enforcement of the parliamentary operative consensus in the 1950s, was no longer in power, his legacy lived on and influenced Israeli politics . While not intellectually equal to Ben-Gurion, Meir was almost as authoritarian as the first prime minister. She refused to listen to anti-establishment critics and bore great hostility toward peripheral challengers of the national consensus. Meir was as hostile to Matzpen and Siah as she was to the Black Panthers. She successfully used all the powers of her office to stigmatize them as antipatriotic and to portray their actions as security risks.

Golda Meir won the battle against the first wave of Israel's extraparliamentary politics. In 1973, on the eve of the Yom Kippur War, Meir's government was as strong as ever. The Israeli public was pleased with its handling of PLO terrorism in the occupied territories and was certain of the army's victory in the War of Attrition with Egypt. The 1967 occupation could no longer be associated with the unnecessary deaths of young soldiers, and the majority of Israelis started to regard the occupation as a fact of life. There was also a sense of relief about the Black Panthers, who were no longer rioting. Many Panther sympathizers were pleased with the official recognition of the existence of the socio-ethnic gap and with the Katz Commission recommendations to overcome it.

The decision of the Black Panthers to run in the Histadrut and Knesset elections, as well as the resolution of many Siah activists to form a political party, Moked (Focus), with a future Knesset orientation, implied a blatant rejection of extraparliamentary politics. Hence I suggest calling the 1967–73 era of Israeli extremist politics "the first rebellion of Israel's extra-parliamentary politics—which failed." In those years Israel witnessed a disturbing peripheral rebellion against the political center. It was beyond the comprehension of Israel's elected politicians that nonelected activists could consider appealing to the public "behind their backs," let alone employ extremist and violent tactics. Hence, Israel's entire political class, not just Prime Minister Meir, rejected the extremists and made their lives so difficult. But the rebellion, which involved direct action and unintentional and some intentional violence, was weak. The participating organizations were powerless, resourceless, and ill-prepared to challenge the authorities seriously. They also faced a self-confident government and a public that had full trust in the leaders who had won the 1967 war. This situation was bound to change, however, much sooner than everybody expected.

5

FROM PIONEERING TO TERRORISM

Gush Emunim and the Underground

The Shock

Most Israelis were stunned when they learned on July 20, 1984, of the election to the Knesset of Rabbi Meir Kahane, a religious fundamentalist and leader of the Kach ("Thus!") party. Nearly twenty-six thousand (1.3 percent) Israelis had voted for the extremist party, known for its call for the immediate expulsion of all Arabs from biblical greater Israel. Two and a half percent of the voters were Israeli soldiers on active duty. Not a few of them remembered that it was Kahane who, since 1974, had publicly advocated TNT, *Terror Neged Terror*, Jewish terrorism against Arab terrorism.

Israelis did not have to wait long before discovering what the new party was all about. A day after the elections, Kahane and his supporters held a victory parade to Old Jerusalem's Western Wall. Marching defiantly through the Arab section of the Old City, Kahane's followers smashed through the market, overturning vegetables stalls, attacking bystanders, punching the air with clenched fists, and telling frightened residents that the end of their stay in the Holy Land was near. This kind of street brutality has been oft-repeated since then, especially following anti-Jewish terror incidents. But instead of being shocked by the violence—until then seen only in old newsreels of pre-1945 central Europe or in modern scenes from Tehran—some Israelis liked what they saw. In fact, support for Kahane increased substantially. Polls conducted between the summer of 1984 and Kach's 1988 disqualification by the Supreme Court revealed support ranging from 2.5 to 7 percent of the populace. Several studies of high school students showed exceptional admiration of Kahane among the young; one found that about 40 percent said they agreed with his ideas and 11 percent said they would vote for him.[1]

The dramatic success of Rabbi Kahane was not the only indication of the unexpected rise of a new Jewish subculture of violence. Just three months earlier, on April 27, 1984, another event shook many complacent Israelis: the uncovering of a plot to blow up five buses full of Arab passengers during a crowded rush hour. Within days, twenty-seven suspected members of an anti-Arab terrorist group were arrested. Soon it was learned that the suspects had been responsible for an unsolved 1980 terror case in which two West Bank Arab mayors were crippled and three others saved only because of a last-minute failure to wire their cars. Several members of the group also admitted responsibility for a score of violent acts against Arabs, including the murderous 1983 attack on the Islamic College in Hebron that took the lives of three students and wounded thirty-three.

The most shocking discovery was that the group had an elaborate plan to blow up the Muslim Dome of the Rock on Jerusalem's Temple Mount, Islam's third most sacred site. The group had made a careful study of the sanctuary's construction, stolen a large quantity of explosives from a military camp in the Golan Heights, and worked out a full attack plan. Twenty-eight precision bombs were manufactured meant to destroy the Dome without causing any damage to its surroundings. The architects of the operation planned to approach the location surreptitiously but were ready to kill the guards if necessary, and therefore had bought special Uzi silencers and gas canisters. More than twenty skilled Israeli reservists were to take part in the operation. Only a last-minute split within the group kept the scheme from being attempted as planned in 1982.

What surprised observers in April 1984 was not so much the existence of Jewish terror as the identity of its members. They belonged to Gush Emunim (Bloc of the Faithful), a fundamentalist religious group committed to establishing Jewish settlements in the West Bank (biblical Judea and Samaria). Though Gush Emunim was an aggressive (and sometimes even illegal) settlement movement, it had never openly embraced an ideology of violence. Its Orthodox leaders asserted a biblically based Jewish claim to Judea and Samaria, but had never advocated deporting the Arab population. Instead they professed the belief that a peaceful and productive coexistence with the Arabs, under benevolent Israeli rule, was both possible and desirable. That any of these highly educated and responsible men, some of them army officers and most of them heads of large families, would resort to terrorism was completely unexpected.

The explosion of religious fundamentalism in 1984, Jewish ultranationalism, aggressive anti-Arab sentiment, and Jewish terrorism revealed the maturation of a significant political and cultural process that had begun in 1967: the rise of the Israeli radical right. The nation's extreme right has since had a dramatic impact on Israel's political culture and institutions. It has led to the second, this time successful, revolt of the Israeli periphery against the political center. It has elevated Israeli political violence to unprecedented heights and meaningfully changed Israel's self-image as well as the image it projected to the world. This chapter examines the evolution of Gush Emunim's extremism and violence; the next focuses on Kach, Rabbi Meir Kahane's party, and the interaction between the Kahanist spirit and Israeli society.

Gush Emunim and the Rise of Settler Extraparliamentarism

Gush Emunim was officially born in 1974 as a reaction to the Yom Kippur War. But the spiritual inspiration for the new movement came directly out of the events of Israel's previous conflict, the Six-Day War of 1967. Israel's swift victory, which brought about the reunification of Jerusalem, the return to Israel of biblical Judea and Samaria (the West Bank), the conquest of Sinai, and the takeover of the Golan Heights, was perceived by many Israelis as an otherworldly event. Zionist religious Jews were especially stunned. The new event did not square with the nonmessianic, pragmatic stand they had maintained for years. It must have been a miracle. The God of Israel had once again showed His might. He came to the rescue of his people in their worst moment of fear and anxiety and, as in the days of old, turned an unbearable situation upside-down. In one strike He placed the whole traditional Eretz Israel—the object of prayers and yearnings for thousands of years—in the hands of his loyal servants.

But while most of the nation, including the religious community, was still shocked and overwhelmed, there was one small religious school that was not. This school centered around Yeshivat Merkaz ha-Rav in Jerusalem and the theology of the Kook family. The head of the Yeshiva, Rabbi Zvi Yehuda Kook, who succeeded the founder of the school (his revered father, Rabbi Avraham Yitzhak ha-Cohen Kook), was preoccupied with the incorporation of the entire Eretz Israel into the state of Israel. His dreams were widely shared with his devoted students and were discussed in many courses and Halakhic deliberations.[2] Following the teaching of his father, and the belief that ours is a messianic age in which the Land of Israel, in its entirety, is to be reunited, Rabbi Zvi Yehuda Kook left no doubt in the hearts of his students that in their lifetimes they were to see the great event. Distinct from the rest of the religious community, the student body of Merkaz ha-Rav was mentally and intellectually ready to absorb the consequences of the Six-Day War—but not before witnessing a unique, seemingly miraculous event.

On the eve of Independence Day in May 1967, graduates of the Yeshiva met at Merkaz ha-Rav for an alumni reunion. As was his custom, Rabbi Kook delivered a festive sermon, in the midst of which his quiet voice suddenly rose, and he bewailed the partition of historic Eretz Israel. His faithful students were led to believe that this situation was intolerable and must not last.[3] When three weeks later, in June 1967, they found themselves citizens of an enlarged state of Israel that included Hebron, Nablus, the Temple Mount, and Old Jerusalem, the graduates of Merkaz ha-Rav were convinced that a genuine spirit of prophecy had come over their rabbi on that Independence Day.

In one stroke a flame had been lit and the conditions ripened for imparting the political ideology of Eretz Israel to a wider religious public, especially young Zionist religious Jews. The disciples of Rabbi Kook became missionaries equipped with unshakable confidence in the divine authority of their cause. They consequently transformed a wide religious community into a radical political constituency. According to the new ideo-theology, the entire historic land of Israel would have to be annexed immediately to the Israeli state, whether by military action or by settlement and the legal extension of Israeli sovereignty. Graduates of Merkaz ha-Rav were the first to settle biblical Judea, moving first to Gush Etzion and then to Hebron a short time later. The settlement in a Hebron hotel, conducted without government authorization, was bound to open a new page in the annals of Israeli settlement.

The new theology of Eretz Israel, and the political spirit associated with it, had one problem, however. The secular government of Israel did not share its convictions and its messianic interpretation of politics. Pragmatic considerations prevailed; Judea and Samaria were not annexed, and Jewish settlement in the new territories was hesitant and slow. The successful establishment of Kiryat Arba, the Jewish city adjacent to Hebron authorized by the government after the evacuation of the first illicit settlement, was not followed by additional settlements. A core group of the future Gush Emunim, Elon Moreh—whose founders first formulated the settlement movement's operational ideology—was diligently preparing itself to settle in the midst of Arab-populated Samaria, but otherwise little happened. However, not until after the 1973 Yom Kippur War, a costly war that greatly damaged Israel's geopolitical stature, did these people feel a need to organize politically. Amid the gloomy public mood occasioned by the first territorial concessions in the Sinai Peninsula (required by the disengagement agreement with Egypt), the founders of Gush Emunim decided to oppose further territorial concessions and struggle for the extension of Israeli sovereignty over the occupied territories.

The founding meeting of Gush Emunim took place in March 1974 at Kfar Etzion, a West Bank kibbutz that had been seized by the Arabs in the War of Independence and recovered by Israel in the Six-Day War.[4] This meeting had been preceded by informal discussions in which leading roles had been played by former students of Rabbi Kook. At first, Gush Emunim was a faction within the National Religious party (NRP), which at that time was a partner in the Labor coalition government. Distrustful of the NRP's position concerning the future of Judea and Samaria, Gush people soon left the party and declared their movement's independence.[5] Since then, they have refused to identify with any political party and have gained a unique political status, a combination of pioneering settlement organization, powerful pressure group, and wild extraparliamentary movement. This combination of inner and outer systemic operation proved highly effective and fruitful.

Under the Labor-led government of Yitzhak Rabin (1974–77), Gush

Emunim pursued three types of confrontation tactics: it protested the interim agreements with Egypt and Syria; it staged demonstrations in Judea and Samaria to underscore the Jewish attachment to those parts of Eretz Israel; and it carried out illicit settlement operations in the occupied territories. Most of these activities involved intense extraparliamentary and extralegal actions, and Gush activists found themselves increasingly confronted by the Israeli army. Owing to the number of activists involved, occasionally reaching several thousand, a serious disruption of the peace had become the order of the day.

The most controversial issue pursued by Gush Emunim was the demand to settle densely populated Arab Samaria. Basing its claim on God's promise to Abraham some four thousand years earlier, Gush Emunim challenged the government's Alon Plan to avoid Jewish settlement in Arab-populated areas at all costs. Gariin (core group) Elon Moreh, already in existence in Kiryat Arba, spearheaded the struggle. Elon Moreh was the biblical name of Jewish Nablus, and the Gariin expressed the movement's resolve to settle and stay in the biblical site forever. Backed by the entire Gush Emunim but without government authorization, the group tried repeatedly to settle the place. Seven such efforts ended in a forced evacuation involving physical encounters with the army. But the Gush did not give up; each settlement effort gained greater publicity and larger pro-Gush mobilization. This battle of resolve and patience, of cunning and pressure was a political struggle between a powerful but divided government and a weak but united Gush. And the struggle ended with Gush Emunim having the upper hand. The ability of Gush activists to get support from within the Labor party and several other powerful organizations finally gave them what they wanted the most: several semi-official settlements in Samaria, the heartland of historic Eretz Israel.[6]

The person who had come to symbolize Gush Emunim's extraparliamentary modus operandi and who had established through these operations a unique pattern of leadership is Rabbi Moshe Levinger, a small, thin, bearded man with a tormented expression and an ascetic aura. A young rabbi at the time, graduate of B'nai Akiva (Zionist religious youth movement) yeshiva and of Merkaz ha-Rav, Levinger was transformed by the Six-Day War and the return of the Jews to the cradle of their civilization. "When I visited Hebron," he would say later, "I underwent an internal turmoil that left me restless for days and weeks."[7] Levinger became the founder of the first illicit Jewish settlement in Hebron (eventually removed), the leader of the newly created Kiryat Arba, and the head of the 1979 reestablished Jewish enclave in Hebron. He also led the Elon Moreh struggle. Levinger had not achieved his Gush prominence and charisma because of his intellectual accomplishments but by never giving up, by enduring physical and mental ordeals, and by personally practicing the greatest "Kookist" virtue of *messirut hanefesh* (complete devotion to the cause). Time and again this man, who could have easily become a high ranking Knesset member or the head of a prominent yeshiva, returned to his private wars on the roads and hills of Judea and Samaria, or to his marches, unarmed, in the streets and alleys of Arab Hebron.[8]

Levinger's practice in settling Hebron, also implemented in the struggle of Gariin Elon Moreh, has remained a classic Gush strategy. Though flexible and open to improvisation, it has four stages: (a) a surprise establishment in the occupied territories of a temporary presence, ostensibly for "worship" purposes; (b) a rigid, highly publicized refusal to evacuate the site on religious grounds, with a generous interest expressed in a "constructive" solution for the alleviation of the "unnecessary tensions" with the army; (c) an agreement to compromise and leave the illicit settlement, provided a small yeshiva is established on the controversial site, or the rest of the intruders are allowed to stay in a nearby military camp; (d) the establishment, a few years later, of a permanent Jewish settlement on the site of the original initiative.[9]

The Likud victory in the elections of May 1977 and the declaration of the prime minister designate, Menachem Begin, that "we shall have many more Elon Morehs" induced Gush Emunim leaders to believe that their extralegal period was over. And indeed, the new regime accorded them full legitimacy. They were allowed to settle Samaria and their settlement organization, Amana, was legitimized as an official Israeli settlement movement. Many of them welcomed this formal admission to the "club" and were happy to shed their extremist image.

But Gush Emunim did not rejoice for long. Despite the movement's expectations, the government did not launch a large-scale settlement program. The constraints of daily policy-making, Begin's failing health, and especially the pressures of the American government, all began to leave their mark on the cabinet. The cabinet was still sympathetic—Minister of Agriculture Ariel Sharon did not conceal his affection for

Gush Emunim—but it gradually became clear that even under a Likud administration the Gush might have to use the extralegal tactics it had devised during the Rabin regime.

Between Messianism and Fundamentalism: The Operative Ideology of Gush Emunim

A close examination of the spiritual world of Gush Emunim, which includes its theology, political ideology, and modes of behavior, suggests that the movement is both messianic and fundamentalist. It is messianic because it maintains that ours is a messianic age in which redemption is a relevant concept and a possible historical event.[10] It is fundamentalist because it endeavors to read the entire historical reality of our time, including the indications for redemption, through the sacred scriptures of the Torah and the Halakha and prescribes on this basis a proper mode of behavior for its members and the nation.[11]

The relation between the messianic components of Gush Emunim and the fundamentalist aspects in the movement's beliefs may well be illuminated by comparing the theologies of the two spiritual fathers of the movement, Rabbi Avraham Yitzhak ha-Cohen Kook—the man who before his death in 1935 established Yeshivat Merkaz ha-Rav—and his son Rabbi Zvi Yehuda Kook, who succeeded him in the Yeshiva and lived long enough to usher in Gush Emunim as a political and social movement. Rabbi Kook senior, by far the more original thinker of the two, believed that the era of redemption of the Jewish people had already begun. It was, he said, marked by the rise of modern Zionism, the Balfour Declaration, and the growing Zionist enterprise in Palestine. Though anchored in Maimonides's understanding of redemption as a sequence of natural events, Kook's interpretation of redemption was original and daring. It signified a marked deviation from the traditional Jewish belief that the messiah could come only through the single meta-historical appearance of an individual redeemer. And there were clearly some elements of heresy in the new interpretation, for it assigned a holy and redemptive status to the secular Zionists—the modern, nonobserving Jews. Kook's argument that the lay Zionists were unknowingly God's true emissaries subjected him to the hostility of the old religious community in Palestine, especially the ultra-Orthodox, who considered Zionism a heresy.[12]

But Kook the father never advocated political fundamentalism or "operative messianism." Writing in the 1920s and 1930s, he wholly supported the vision of the secular Zionist movement, one of slow and prudent progress toward independence. He did not establish a political movement and did not call for a policy-making process based on a daily reading of the Torah. The theology that was studied for years in Yeshivat Merkaz ha-Rav had no immediate consequences and made no exclusivist political demands.[13]

Israel's victory in the Six-Day War transformed the status of Kook's theology. Suddenly it became clear to his students that they were indeed living in the messianic age. Ordinary reality assumed a sacred aspect; every event possessed theological meaning and was part of the meta-historical process of redemption.[14] Though shared by many religious authorities, the view was most effectively expounded by Kook's son, Rabbi Zvi Yehuda, an unknown interpreter of his father's writings before 1967 who became a leader of a fundamentalist movement. He defined the State of Israel as the Halakhic Kingdom of Israel and the Kingdom of Israel as the kingdom of heaven on earth.[15] Every Jew living in Israel was holy; all phenomena, even the secular, were imbued with holiness. Not only Kook's students but also the rest of the nation was expected to recognize the immense transformation and to behave accordingly. The government was counted on to conduct its affairs, or at least part of them, according to Maimonides's "rules of kings" and be judged by these rules and by Torah prescriptions.[16]

The single most important conclusion of the new theology had to do with Eretz Israel, the land of Israel. The land—every grain of its soil—was declared holy in a fundamental sense. The conquered territories of Judea and Samaria had become inalienable and nonnegotiable, not as a result of political or security concern but because God had promised them to Abraham four thousand years earlier, and because the identity of the nation was shaped by this promise. Redemption could take place only in the context of greater Eretz Israel, and territorial withdrawal meant forfeiting redemption. The ideologists of Gush Emunim ruled that the Gush had to become a settlement movement because settling Judea and Samaria was the most meaningful act of human participation in the process of redemption.

The messianic enthusiasm of Gush Emunim and the conviction of the spiritual heads of the movement that redemption was at hand significantly shaped the operative ideology of the movement. In fact, it shaped the lack of such ideology. The heads of the movement, mostly rabbis, were very excited about the government of Israel that had commanded the army to its greatest victory ever. Following Rabbi Kook's theology, they were certain that the government was the legitimate representative of the Kingdom of Israel in the making.[17] Their job, according to this interpretation, was not to contest the government but to settle Judea and Samaria and make sure that on the critical issue of the territories, the nation did not go astray. That is why Gush Emunim was, for many years, equivocal and unclear on three critical political issues: *the Arabs, democracy, and the rule of law*. However, over the years the members of the movement discovered, to their great dismay, that the rest of the world was not as enthusiastic about their prescriptions. There were too many Palestinians in the West Bank who were not thrilled about becoming passive observers of the Jewish regeneration in "Judea and Samaria." There were too many Israelis who were happier with their imperfect democracy than with the mystical and unclear vision of Halakhic redemption. Most important of all, there was an officially elected government whose heads were either not enthusiastic about settling all the West Bank or, even if they were, felt bound by the law of the land and by Israel's international obligations.

The result of the encounter of Gush Emunim with the political reality of the rest of the world had produced a very confused and unsystematic operative ideology. While the leaders of the Gush wished to maintain the constructive and altruistic posture they started with, they realized that redemption could not be reached without pain. Many of them discovered that their fundamentalist nature required them to draw their political inspiration not from the experience of the democratic West but from the tradition of the Torah and the twelfth-century luminary Maimonides. The results have been very significant. The Palestinian Arabs, according to Gush Emunim, do not constitute a nation and are not entitled to collective political rights in Eretz Israel. The land is not theirs. The best they can hope for is to attain the status of what the Torah calls "resident alien," a non-Jewish person who fully recognizes the hegemony of the Jewish nation and enjoys full individual residence rights. But if the Jewish hegemony is not recognized and upheld, then the Palestinians have to be treated *today* as the Canaanites were treated in the old days: they had to be either subdued and subjugated in Eretz Israel or evicted.[18]

Gush Emunim's position on democracy and the rule of law is equally equivocal. In principle, democracy is bound to give way to Halakha theocracy, but this does not have to take place now. If the government of Israel fulfills its prescribed duties—settling all the land and making no territorial concessions to the Arabs—then democracy and the prevailing legal system may be allowed to function. But if conflict between democracy and Zionism (à la Gush Emunim) erupts, then Zionism takes precedence and extralegal action becomes legitimate. The modern state of Israel was not established, according to Emunim's ideologists, to have another legal democracy under the sun. Two thousand years after its destruction it was revived for only one purpose, to redeem the nation and eventually the world. The prescription for this redemption is not written in the charter of the United Nations but writ large in the Torah, the Book of Books.[19]

The Emergence of the Jewish Underground

September 17, 1978, was the lowest point in the short history of Gush Emunim. Prime Minister Begin signed the Camp David Accords with Egypt and the United States, leaving Emunim's people stunned and in disbelief. His agreement to return all of Sinai to the Egyptians, as well as his initiation of the Autonomy Plan (for the Palestinians of the West Bank and Gaza), was inconceivable to them. For many years, these people had led themselves to believe that Begin, the great champion of undivided Eretz Israel, was their best insurance against territorial compromise with the Arabs. Most of them were not Begin's traditional supporters but came to identify with him politically. His commitment to have "many more Elon Morehs" held for them a special appeal.

The Camp David Accords presented Gush Emunim a challenge of unprecedented magnitude. The accords signified that human error (in this case Begin's) was capable of stopping, or at least delaying, the inevitable divine process of redemption. How were they, members of a young and inexperienced political movement, to respond? Even their elderly rabbis were not sure, and most of the reactions indicated despair and confusion.[20] For a while it looked as if Gush Emunim would fold.

The most extreme reaction to the Camp David Accords was not known until the April 1984 arrest of the members of what the press named the "Jewish Underground." When it was first apprehended, and some time after the beginning of its investigation, the group was considered an ad hoc terror team aimed at avenging PLO terrorism. However, it was eventually established that the first contacts of the leaders of the group took place late in 1978 and had nothing to do with revenge against Arab terrorism. The only issue on their agenda was blowing up what they called the *abomination*—the Muslim Dome of the Rock.[21] The idea was brought up by two remarkable individuals, Yeshua Ben Shoshan and Yehuda Etzion. Both men, although closely affiliated with Gush Emunim and its settlement drive, were nevertheless atypical members. More than most of their colleagues, they were preoccupied with the mysteries of the process of regeneration that was about to bring the Jewish people—perhaps in their own lifetime—to their redemption.

The Kabbalistic Ben Shoshan and the zealot Etzion brought the disappointment of Gush Emunim from the Camp David Accords to its peak. The two convinced themselves that the historical setback must have had a deeper cause than Begin's simple weakness. It was a direct signal from Heaven that a major national offense had been committed, a sin responsible for the political disaster and its immense spiritual consequences. Only one prominent act of desecration could match the magnitude of the setback: the presence of the Muslims and their shrine on the Temple Mount, the holiest Jewish site, the sacred place of the First, Second, and Third (future) Temples.[22]

It is not clear when the underground was solidified by the two, and under what conditions. But the most important development in those early years certainly took place in Yehuda Etzion's mind. This energetic young man discovered the writings of an unknown ultranationalist thinker, Shabtai Ben Dov. Ben Dov, who for years was an insignificant official in Israel's Ministry of Industry and Commerce, developed in total isolation a grand theory of active national redemption. Among other notions, the new theory brought life into such ideas as the resumption of the biblical Kingdom of Israel and the building of the Third Temple. The man wrote about territorial expansion, national moral expurgation, and the constitution of Jewish law in Israel. Drawing on the almost forgotten tradition of the ultranationalist poet Uri Zvi Greenberg, but with a post-1967 religious enthusiasm, Ben Dov dared to think the unthinkable—a total and concrete transformation of the nation into a sacred people and a holy state. No one, including Gush Emunim rabbis, had done this before. Etzion, who only slowly absorbed his new discovery of the writings of Ben Dov, decided to devote himself completely to their publication.[23] By 1979, Ben Dov had died after a long illness, but in the mind of Yehuda Etzion, his ideas were very much alive.

Some time early in 1980 a secret meeting was convened by Etzion and his friend Menachem Livni, attended by eight men.[24] This was the first time in which the Temple Mount operation was spelled out in great detail. The main speaker was Etzion, who presented his new redemption theology in its grand contours. He told the group that the removal of the Muslim mosques would spark a new light in the nation and trigger a major spiritual revolution. He appeared convinced that the operation would solve once and for all the problems of the people of Israel. His tone and spirit were prophetic and messianic.[25] The other speakers were more cautious, raising technical as well as substantial political questions. Some did not believe the job could be plausibly carried out, and others worried about the political and international consequences. Livni, a Hebron engineer and captain in the reserves who emerged as the operational head of the group and the most considerate and balanced member, agreed with Etzion in principle. He was, however, apprehensive about the immense consequences. Livni's conclusion, accepted by the rest of the group, was that concrete preparations for blowing up the Dome of the Rock could start immediately, irrespective of a final operative decision. There were so many details to be worked out that the question of a final decision to strike was irrelevant.[26]

Toward Millenarian Terrorism: The Operation That Did Not Take Place

There is no question that the fundamental psychopolitical framework for the emergence of the underground was formed within Gush Emunim long before the pact among Etzion and his friends. This framework was constructed with the ideology of Rabbi Zvi Yehuda Kook, who created within his followers immense expectations. Many observers of Gush Emunim have not failed to identify its behavioral messianic craze, that extranormal quality of intense excitement and hypernomic behavior that produced within many members of the movement constant expectations of progress toward redemption.[27] David Rapoport, who studied the affinity between terrorism and messianism, observed some years ago that "Once a messianic advent is seen as imminent, particular elements of a messianic doctrine become critical in pulling a believer in the direction of terror."[28]

Rapoport argued convincingly that messianism—once it becomes operational—and terrorism imply extra-normal behavior, a pattern of action and orientation predicated on the conviction that the traditional conventions of morality and conduct are not binding. Under certain conditions, which usually imply the failure of an expected redemption to materialize, it is possible, according to Rapoport, for messianic people to resort to extra-normal acts of violence. Either because they want to prove to themselves that redemption remains relevant or because they want to convince God that this is the case, they may opt for exceptional catastrophe.[29] Menachem Livni, the operational "commander" of the underground, described to his investigators how it was all born:

> Shortly after President Sadat's visit to Israel, I was approached by a friend who showed me the picture of the Dome of the Rock on the Temple Mount—to which I shall heretofore refer as the "abomination." My friend argued that the existence of the abomination on the Temple Mount, our holiest place, was the root cause of all the spiritual errors of our generation and the basis of Ishmael's [the Arabs'] hold on Eretz Israel. In this first meeting I did not clearly understand my friend and more meetings were held in which an additional friend joined.[30]

After the crisis of Camp David, most of the members of Gush Emunim, discouraged by the postponement of redemption, turned to old Rabbi Kook's instruction to maintain their allegiance to the Israeli government and passively trust God. But a few Gush activists were not convinced. They gathered around Etzion, Ben Shoshan, and Livni, who all believed they had a better response to the disaster, an act that would alleviate the misery in a single strike.

The spiritual and mysterious nature of the project was described in great detail by many members of the underground. Long before they started to discuss operational matters such as explosives and guns they immersed themselves in Halakhic issues and Kabbalistic spiritual deliberations. Chaim Ben David, who had attended the meetings since 1978, described how he was recruited and how it happened:

> In about 1977 or 1978, I was approached by Gilad Peli from Moshav Keshet in the Golan Heights, a man I have known since 1975 and the advent of his activity within Gush Emunim. He told me to come to Yeshua Ben Shoshan, with whom I had a previous learning experience in Torah subjects. Following the learning part, Yeshua and Gilad discussed with me a plan to remove the Dome of the Rock on the Temple Mount—a plan meant to be part of a spiritual redemption of the people of Israel. The great innovation for me was that this was a "physical operation" capable of generating a spiritual operation. I agreed to join the group and participate in its project. Then came the stages of the meetings and conferences in Yeshua's house as well as in an isolated house . . . owned by Ben Shoshan's relatives. There were many sessions and I am sure I did not attend them all because of my physical distance. The meetings were attended by Menachem Livni, Yehuda Etzion, Yeshua Ben Shoshan, Gilad Peli and myself. There were several sessions in Yeshua's house without his personal presence. . . . In the sessions the spiritual side of the idea was discussed as well as questions relating to the possible acceptance of, and response to, the act by the people of Israel. Then they started to discuss operational matters. The first idea was to bomb [the site] from the air—we had a pilot in our group but it is not clear whether it was serious or just a joke. Finally, it was decided to blow up the mosque with explosives.[31]

In the summer of 1980 the underground was involved in another terrorist effort, an attempt to blow up the cars of several West Bank mayors (discussed below), and it had to suspend temporarily the Temple Mount Operation. But as soon as the commotion over the "mayors' affair" subsided, preparations were resumed for the assault on the Dome of the Rock. Etzion, who masterminded the plan, and Livni, a military demolitions expert, studied the Temple Mount and the Dome of the Rock in minute detail for two years. Following dozens of surveillance hikes to the mount, a careful construction study of the mosque, and the theft of a large quantity of explosives from a military camp in the Golan Heights, a full attack plan was worked out.[32] Since the time of the final Israeli evacuation of the Jewish settlements in Sinai agreed upon in the peace treaty was approaching rapidly, the operation, which could prevent it and reverse the whole peace process, was to take place no later than early 1982.

The underground suffered, however, from one major drawback. None of the individuals involved was an authoritative rabbi. The question of a rabbinical authority had already come up in the first meeting in 1980. Most of the members of the group made it clear that they could not operate without the blessing of a recognized rabbi. But all the rabbis the group approached, including Gush Emunim's mentor, Rabbi Zvi Yehuda Kook, refused to give their blessing. It is not clear how much of the planned strike had been spelled out to these authorities, but Livni, who needed rabbinical approval, was left with no doubt. He *did not* have a green light. When the final date of decision arrived, it was patently clear that only two individuals were ready to proceed—the originators of the idea, Etzion and Ben Shoshan. The grand plan had to be shelved. But in his final word on the issue, Livni, the head of the group, did not appear disappointed or beaten:

> In retrospect it appears to me that the honor of the Temple Mount and the Temple itself, as well as the dignity of the people of Israel, instructs us that this operation should be carried out by a united nation and its government. We, on our behalf, did our best before heaven and earth, as if it was like "open for me a niche a needle wide," and I pray that we shall be blessed to see the building of the Temple in our time. And comments that were made on Rabbi Akiva are true and relevant to all the events and all members involved, "Bless thee, Rabbi Akiva, for being caught following the Torah.[33]

A close reading of Livni's statement suggests a mystical approach. Paradoxically, the statement epitomizes the entire millenarian nature of the underground. Livni does not only speak to his interrogators, he also appeals to God. While somewhat apologetic, he is nevertheless proud and hopeful. He seems to believe that although he and his colleagues did not remove the Dome of the Rock, neither did they shun their apocalyptic mission. In fact, he argues, they did all they could. They identified the national spiritual malaise, they singled out the "abomination" as the root cause of it, they delved into the problem, studied it, and prayed about it, and, finally, they prepared to act. Only inches away from the operation, they did not get God's final signal, his ultimate OK. God, he felt, should know how devoted they were and how serious their mission was. He should be aware of the "needle wide" niche they had opened. Perhaps in the future He would move the government and the nation to concrete action.

Yehuda Etzion and the Theology of Active Redemption

The destruction of Harem Esh Sharif, the Muslim Dome of the Rock, never was on the agenda of Gush Emunim. While many members of this movement had been greatly disturbed by the "desecrating" presence of the Muslims—on the spot to which even most Jews were not allowed to enter, only priests, because of its exceptional holiness—almost none of them thought of blowing up the shrine. The feeling of unease was a product of the paradoxical situation created in 1967. While the reunification of Jerusalem signified the nation's return to its holiest place after two thousand years, it also ruined for religious Jews much of this achievement. The government of Israel, acting out of its sovereign will, decided that Temple Mount must remain, for reasons of political prudence, in Muslim hands.

The fundamentalist members of Gush Emunim managed to live with the paradox because of their "Kookist" theology. They believed that the lay government of Israel was legitimate and holy, that despite its many mistakes it had a bright future. Under the guidance of God, they felt, it was bound to change in time and lead the nation to redemption, just as it had in the Six-Day War. There was a point in struggling against the government on the simple and clear issue of settling Judea and Samaria, but there was no sense in disobeying it on such a sensitive issue as the Temple

Mount. The matter had to be left to God and to His mysterious ways of directing the world.

It was on the issue of the Temple Mount that the underground deviated sharply from Gush Emunim, and the person who solidified the challenge to the official theology was Yehuda Etzion. Twenty-seven years old when he first developed his revolutionary theory, Etzion was a typical product of the movement. While he himself did not study in Merkaz ha-Rav, his rabbi in Yeshivat Alon Shvut was Yoel Ben Nun, one of the most influential graduates of "Merkaz."[34] But something happened to Etzion in the second half of the 1970s. Probably as a result of the "crisis" of Camp David and because of his interest in the mystery of redemption, he discovered a whole new world, the ultranationalist tradition developed by the poet Uri Zvi Greenberg in the 1930s, the tradition of the "Kingdom of Israel."[35]

The unique feature of this vision (which in Etzion's case was redeveloped by the unknown thinker Shabtai Ben Dov) was that it spelled out the notion of *active redemption.* According to Ben Dov, there was no need to wait for another miracle. All the conditions for concrete redemption were already present; one had merely to act. The revolutionary element in Ben Dov's ideology was his concept of redemption. He spoke about building the Third Temple and the institutionalization of Jewish theocracy on Earth. He envisioned a system governed by Torah law and run by a supreme rabbinical court and a Sanhedrin (the Council of the Seventy wise men). None of the leaders and ideologists of Gush Emunim had ever spoken in such concrete terms. None of them had dared to press the issue.[36]

It is not clear whether Etzion would have followed the ideology of Ben Dov had the debacle of Camp David not taken place. But in 1978 he started to develop a thorough intellectual critique of Gush Emunim and the ideology of Rabbi Zvi Yehuda Kook. Etzion's new theology was written down and published only after he was sent to prison in 1984, but there is no doubt that this system inspired his activity within the underground.

The main thrust of the new theory is directed against Kook's subservience to the lay government of Israel. Etzion could not understand why Gush Emunim, which had identified the messianic quality of the present time, should wait until the secular politicians reached the same conclusion. He refused to grant a full legitimacy to "erroneous" rulers who were committing outrageous mistakes. Attacking the spirit of Merkaz ha-Rav, the fountainhead of Emunim's ideology, he wrote,

> The sense of criticism—which is a primary condition for any correction—perished here entirely. The State of Israel was granted in Merkaz ha-Rav an unlimited and independent credit. Its operations—even those that stand in contrast to the model of Israel's Torah—are conceived of as "God's will," or a revelation of His grace. There is no doubt that had the state announced its sovereignty over our holy mountain, driving thereby the Waqf [the Muslim religious authority] out and removing the Dome of the Rock—it would have won a full religious backing. The voice coming from the school would have said "strengthen Israel in greatness and crown Israel with glory." But now that the state does nothing, what do we hear? That these acts are prohibited because it is not allowed. Moreover, letting the Arabs stay is a grace of God since we are, anyway, not allowed into the mount.[37]

Yeshivat Merkaz ha-Rav, and by implication Gush Emunim itself, has become, according to Etzion, a support system of secular Zionism. Narrowing its goal down to settlement only, it does not think in grand terms, does not challenge the inactive government of Israel, and fails to do what God wishes it to do.

What, then, is to be done? What direction should the misled Gush Emunim have taken, had its rabbis read the Torah "correctly"? Following Ben Dov and the ultranationalist School of the "Kingdom of Israel," Etzion maintains emphatically that the Torah portrays the "deserved model" of life as a nation. "This is . . . the proper kingdom of Israel that we have to establish here between the two rivers [the Euphrates and the Nile]. This kingdom will be directed by the Supreme Court, which is bound to sit on the place, chosen by God, to emit His inspiration, a site which will have a temple, an altar, and a king chosen by God. All the people of Israel will inherit the land to labor and to keep."[38]

Etzion's deviation from the standard theology of Gush Emunim is very clear. According to his thinking, it is fully legitimate to portray *now* the contours of the final stage of redemption, including a *theocratic government* centered on the Temple Mount and a country that controls, in addition to present-day Israel, the Sinai, Jordan, Syria, and parts of Lebanon and Iraq. Moreover, it is mandatory to strive now for the fulfillment of this vision, and Gush Emunim or another devoted movement should take the lead in the forthcoming struggle.

Why did Etzion focus on the Temple Mount? How did he justify an operation more incredible and dangerous than any anti-Arab plan ever conceived of in Israel since the beginning of Zionism in the nineteenth century? How does the Temple Mount operation fit into Etzion's general theory of redemption? In a unique monograph, the *Temple Mount*, published while in jail, Etzion explained,

> David's property in the Temple Mount is therefore a real and eternal property in the name of all Israel. It was never invalidated and never will be. No legality or ownership claim which is not made in the name of Israel and for the need of rebuilding the temple, is valid.[39]
>
> The expurgation of the Temple Mount will prepare the hearts for the understanding and further advancing of our full redemption. The purified Mount shall be—if God wishes—the ground and the anvil for the future process of promoting the next holy elevation.[40]

The redemption of the nation was stopped, according to Etzion, on the Temple Mount. Not until its expurgation—a step that had to be taken by the government of Israel but was not—could the grand process be renewed. And since "this horrible state of affairs" was not corrected by the government but rather was backed by it, the task had to be fulfilled by the most devoted and dedicated.

But how did Etzion, a very intelligent and educated man, believe that Israel could go unharmed with the destruction of the Dome of the Rock? How could it conquer Jordan, Syria, parts of Egypt, Iraq, and Lebanon and transform itself, in the eyes of the rest of the world, into a Khomeini-like theocracy? What did Etzion think about the constraints of political reality?

Reading Etzion and talking to him reveals a unique combination of an otherworldly messianic spirit and a very logical mind, a man who talks and thinks in the language of this world but lives completely in another. Etzion's response to these questions is based on the only intellectual explanatory construct possible: a distinction between the *laws of existence and the laws of destiny.*

> Securing and preserving life is an "utmost norm" for all of living nature, for humanity in general—and for us, *Israel,* too. This is indeed a norm that dictates laws, and in the name of which, people go to war. But as for ourselves "our God is not theirs." Not only is our existential experience different from theirs but also from their very definition. For the Gentiles, life is mainly a *life of existence, while ours is a life of destiny,* the life of a kingdom of priests and a holy people. We exist in the world in order to actualize destiny.[41]
>
> The question about the constraints of political reality is relevant only for those who live by the laws of existence. But once adopting the laws of destiny instead of the laws of existence, Israel will be no more an ordinary state, one whose eyes are rolled from hour to hour. . . . She will become the Kingdom of Israel by its very essence. It therefore makes no sense to offer the present state some "good advises," regarding its specific behavior in an isolated "local" situation in the name of the laws of destiny. The stage of this change will take place, inevitably, in the immense comprehensive move of the transformation from the State of Israel to the Kingdom of Israel."[42]

"Operation Temple Mount" was bound, according to Etzion, to trigger the transformation of the state of Israel from one system of laws to another. It was meant to elevate the nation now to the status of the Kingdom of Israel, a kingdom of priests capable of actualizing the laws of destiny and of changing the nature of the world.

From Settler Extralegalism to Vigilante Terrorism

The Jewish Underground became a terror organization on June 2, 1980. On Friday, May 3, a group of yeshiva students returning to Hadassah House in Hebron from a Sabbath prayer had been fired upon by Arabs at close range. Six students died instantly and several others were wounded.

The attack was not an isolated case but came against the background of growing anti-Jewish violence in Hebron and in other parts of Judea and Samaria. The settler community was certain that the attack was masterminded by the Palestinian National Guidance Committee in Judea and Samaria, an unofficial PLO front organization that was allowed by Defense Minister Ezer Weizmann to operate almost freely. It was generally felt that only a massive settler retaliation could put things back in order. Following two unofficial meetings in Kiryat Arba, attended by the communal rabbis, the decision was made to act. Menachem Livni, a local resident, knew whom to contact—his friend and partner in the planned operation at the Temple Mount, Yehuda Etzion. [43] Instead of committing a retaliatory mass murder, in the custom of Arab terrorists, the two decided to strike at the top. The cars of five Arab leaders most active in the National Guidance Committee were to be blown up. The plan was to injure these people severely without killing them. The crippled leaders were to remain a living symbol for a long time to come.

The mayors' affair was crowned with partial success. Two of the leaders involved, Mayor Bassam Shakaa of Nablus and Mayor Karim Khalef of Ramalla, were crippled. Two others were saved because the demolition teams failed to wire their cars. The fifth case ended with an Israeli tragedy. The mayor of El Bireh, whose garage was also set up to explode, was not at home. A police demolition expert rushed to the place had mistakenly activated the explosive device. He was seriously wounded and blinded.

The indefinite postponement in 1982 of the Temple Mount operation signified a major break in the short history of the underground. It meant, for all practical purposes, the removal of the millenarian part of the plan—the aspect so attractive and dear to Etzion and Ben Shoshan—from the agenda. It is therefore not surprising that when the underground struck again in July 1983, the two played minor roles.[44] The operation took place in the Islamic College of Hebron in response to the murder of a Hebron Yeshiva student. It was deadly. Following an open attack on the school, just after its noon break, three students were killed and thirty-three wounded. While logistical support was provided by former group members, the operation itself was carried out by three men who were not involved in the mayors' affair. All three were extremist settlers in Hebron recruited by

Livni (who masterminded the action). The attack was not as sophisticated as the first but otherwise followed the same logic. It was waged in response to a growing wave of anti-Jewish violence, culminating in the murder of a Yeshiva student in broad daylight. It expressed fatalism and a growing frustration with the government's inability to defend the settlers, and it was approved by rabbinical authorities.[45] It was followed by some smaller acts of terrorism.

The emerging Hebronite fatalism was most visible in the last major operation of the group, the one meant to be the most devastating. In a response to a new wave of Arab terrorism—this time not in Hebron but in Jerusalem and near Ashkelon—Shaul Nir, the most aggressive member of the underground, became impatient. This young man considered the earlier attack on the Islamic College a great success. Determined to make it a model operation, he managed to convince the local rabbis that another decisive strike was needed. [46] Armed with their authority, he prevailed over the unsure Livni and made him plan an unprecedented brutal act, the bombing of the men's dormitory on Bir Zeit University in Ramalla. When the operation was suspended owing to a government shutdown of the university, it was replaced by a more ambitious one. Five Arab buses full of passengers were to be blown up in revenge for similar attacks on Israeli buses by Palestinian terrorists. The buses were to explode on Friday at 4:30 P.M., at a time and place Jews were not expected on the road.

The explosive devices were placed under the buses' fuel tanks to cause maximum damage and casualties. [47] Every detail was tended to . . . except one. By 1984 the Israeli Secret Service had finally spotted the Hebron group. Immediately after the completion of the wiring, the whole group was arrested, bringing the secretive part of the story of the first Gush Emunim underground to its end. The open part of the tale continues. Ever since the exposure of the group, a fierce debate about its legitimacy and its significance has been conducted within the movement.[48]

A review of the confessions and testimonies of all the members of the underground, especially Livni and Etzion, suggests that the issue at stake was not primarily religious and that it had only a slight relation to redemption or messianism. The name of the game was revenge. The only association between the Dome of the Rock plan and the acts of terror that actually took place was the identity of the perpetrators. The group that blew up the mayors' cars, and some of those who continued to operate until 1984, were the same who started to prepare themselves, morally and spiritually, to expurgate the Temple Mount. But the motivations and the thinking were totally different. Discussing his participation in the mayors' affair in relation to his main concern, the Temple Mount, Etzion told the court:

> Planning and executing the attack on the murder chieftains took only one month of my life, one month that started with the assassination night of six boys in Hebron, and ended up in conducting this operation. I insist that this operation was right. So right, in fact, that to the best of my understanding . . . even the law that prevails in the State of Israel could recognize its justice or ought to have recognized it as a pure act of self defense. . . . It is unquestionable that in our present reality . . . the reality of the sovereign State of Israel . . . the defense forces of the state had to take care of this matter, quickly, neatly and effectively, so that nobody could have, in his right mind, thought again about such an operation. I do not deny, furthermore, that it was a clear case of undue excess. But the situation at stake was a case in which the "policeman" responsible for the matter not only stepped aside . . . not only ignored the gravity of the case, . . . but developed with them a friendly relationship. . . . This situation, Sirs, was a case of no alternative, a condition that created a need to act in the full sense of the word, for the very sake of preserving life.[49]

No reader familiar with the literature on vigilante movements could fail to detect in Etzion's speech the classic logic of the *vigilante mind*. What Etzion so eloquently told the court was that he took one month of his life, a life otherwise devoted to the approximation of redemption, to become a vigilante terrorist. A vigilante movement, we should recall, never sees itself in a state of principled conflict, either with the government or with the prevailing *concept* of law. It is not revolutionary and does not try to bring down authority. Rather, vigilantism entails profound conviction that the government, or some of its agencies, has failed to enforce its own laws or to establish its own order in an area under its jurisdiction.[50] Backed by the fundamental norm of self-defense and speaking in the name of what they believe to be the valid law of the land, vigilantes, in effect, enforce the law and execute justice. Due process of law is the least of their concerns.[51] When Etzion responded in May 1980 to Livni's request for help in avenging the blood of six Yeshiva students killed in Hebron, he was thinking not of messianism but of vigilantism. He took a short "leave of absence" from his main concern to take care of an altogether different business

But how did Etzion, the messianic dreamer, suddenly become a rough vigilante? What was the psychosocial mechanism that made it possible for him—and also for his millenarian followers in the underground—to switch from their *other-worldly* concern about redemption to the *this-worldly* concern about revenge and law and order? And why was the vigilante terrorism of the members of the underground legitimized by the rabbis of Gush Emunim who refused to support the millenarian terrorism on the Temple Mount?

The answer to these questions, without which a full understanding of the underground is bound to be incomplete, has little to do with either the teaching of Rav Kook or the intellectual climate of Gush Emunim. It concerns, instead, another facet of Gush Emunim, not elaborated upon yet, *the existential extralegalism of the movement* as a "frontier" operation in the West Bank. Gush Emunim, as Giora Goldberg and Ephraim Ben Zadok so aptly remind us, did not produce only strange messianic types—true believers who would walk the hills of Judea and Samaria expecting redemption to be delivered. It equally created a breed of *doers,* rugged frontier men who started their career as illicit settlers and sustained it through a growing friction with their neighboring Arabs.[52] Even before the 1977 Likud rise to power, there was friction with the local Palestinians in places such as Hebron, but after 1978 such friction became almost a daily routine.

While the extraparliamentary nature of Gush Emunim had been a typical feature of the movement since its inception, its vigilante side was not recognized until the early 1980s. Rumors about settler violence against Arabs prevailed, but with no proof. However, in 1982 a committee headed by Yehudit Carp, the state deputy attorney general, studied seventy cases of Jewish anti-Arab violent acts including killing, physical assault, property damage, and the application of armed and unarmed threats. It found that fifty-three out of the seventy cases ended in no action. Forty-three of the files were closed because a suspect could not be found, seven because there were no official complaints, and three because public interest was insufficient to justify prosecution.[53]

The vigilante nature of the settler community was examined in a pioneering study conducted in 1983 by David Weisburd, who found that 28 percent of the male settlers and 5 percent of the females, out of a sample of five hundred, admitted to having participated in some type of vigilante activity. Sixty-eight percent of Weisburd's respondents agreed with the statement that "it is necessary for the settlers to respond quickly and independently to Arab harassments of settlers and settlements."[54] Following another finding, that only 13 percent of those questioned disapproved of vigilantism, Weisburd concluded:

> The vigilantism of Gush Emunim settlers is part of an organized strategy of social control calculated to maintain order in the West Bank. Though a minority of settlers actually participate in vigilante acts, they are not isolated deviant figures in this settlement movement. Rather, those vigilantes are agents of the Gush Emunim community as a whole. They carry out a strategy of control that is broadly discussed and supported."[55]

Weisburd's study of the vigilantism of the settler community, as well as the Carp report and other documented studies, was written and published before the exposure of the Jewish Underground. They nevertheless provide useful factual and analytical perspectives to comprehend the actual terrorism of the group. They tell us that the communal leaders of Kiryat Arba—the Jewish city adjacent to Hebron—who convened after the Beit Hadassah murder of six students were not strangers to communal conflict, anti-Arab violence, or vigilante justice. Extremist rabbis, soldiers and military reserve officers, and rugged settlers—all were used to the idea of communal reprisal. They also knew, as we are told by Weisburd, that the price for previous vigilante acts was very low.[56]

The convergence point between the millenarian orientation of the underground and the vigilante spirit of the settlers that actually produced terrorism was described in some detail by Livni, who told his interrogators that, immediately following the Beit Hadassah murder, it was decided in Kiryat Arba to respond. A special action committee was assigned the job, but its members did not have the "adhesive spirit necessary to act." Livni then approached Rabbi Moshe Levinger, the leading authority in the city, and told him that "for these purposes we have to choose pure people, highly observant and sinless, people with no shred of violence in them and who are disinclined to reckless action."[57] Levinger apparently approved and it was at that point that Livni asked Yehuda Etzion, not a resident of Kiryat Arba, to help him. Only then did the two decide to mobilize the entire group, which until that time was preoccupied with preliminary deliberations about the Temple Mount. The group members were perceived by their leaders to be pure and devoted; they were not terrorists but rather God's emissaries. Their deep commitment and dedication to God and the nation qualified them for the merciless task.

A key to understanding the operations that did and did not take place is the issue of *rabbinical authority*. A careful reading of the confessions and testimonies of the members of the underground does not clarify how much of the *operational* part of the conspiracy was shared by Kiryat Arba's leading rabbis. But it makes clear that none of the operations that took place was opposed by the rabbis and that all the acts were, in fact, blessed by those authorities. The first operation, the mayors' affair, was opposed by Rabbi Levinger, but the reason for his objection was that Levinger preferred an even more extreme action and recommended indiscriminate mass violence. Rabbi Eliezer Waldman, a prominent Gush rabbi and since 1981 a Knesset member, even volunteered, according to Livni, to participate in the first operation. Two other Hebron and Kiryat Arba rabbis were instrumental in inducing Livni to commit the last two operations that involved indiscriminate terrorism.[58] Shaul Nir, the man who conducted the murderous attack on the Islamic College in Hebron, told his interrogators:

> I would like to add that in the time span of three years, I discussed the issue with four rabbis, all of whom expressed their support for warning operations within the Arab public. . . . I also heard the names of an additional three rabbis who stated their support in different stages of the operation.[59]

Rabbinical refusal to support Operation Temple Mount is of crucial importance because it tells us that the radicalization process that finally produced terrorism within Gush Emunim was not marginal but central. It was a by-product of the movement's belief in its own redemptive role and in the necessity of settling Judea and Samaria at all costs. The idealistic and excited people who started in 1968 to settle Judea and Samaria did not go there with violent intentions. None of them expected to become a vigilante, a terrorist, or a supporter of terror within just twelve years. But the combination of messianic belief and a situation of endemic national conflict had within it a built-in propensity for incremental violence—extralegalism, vigilantism, selective terrorism, and, finally, indiscriminate mass terrorism. Had the underground not been stopped in 1984, it might have become the Jewish equivalent of the Irish Republican Army (IRA).

Struggle in the South: The Movement to Halt the Retreat in Sinai

The Jewish Underground provided the most extreme reaction to the Camp David Accords and was a significant step in the formation of the violent culture of Israel's radical right. Nevertheless, these activities had been conducted by only a few individuals in secrecy and—until their 1984 discovery—were not representative of the greater camp. A much larger role in the radicalization of the extreme right had been played by the Movement to Halt the Retreat in Sinai (MHRS), a Gush Emunim front organization formed in 1981 to stop the Israeli evacuation of northern Sinai required by the Israeli-Egyptian peace agreement. As part of its control of the large peninsula conquered from Egypt in the Six-Day War, the government authorized the establishment in northern Sinai of the city of Yamit and several *moshavim* (cooperative settlements). To the dismay of the several thousand settlers who loved the place dearly and had been very successful economically, they learned in 1978 that in four years they would have to leave. As frustrated and angered as they were, the majority did not believe that they were capable of stopping the retreat or had the moral right to impose their will on the entire nation.

Most of the activists of the MHRS neither lived in the Sinai settlements nor cared about the religious sanctity of the area. What brought them to the Yamit area, a territory with no biblical significance, was the fear that the removal of the southern settlements was the beginning of wider territorial compromise. They further convinced themselves that an Israeli government capable of removing Jewish settlements would eventually be ready to make the same deal in Judea and Samaria, the heartland of biblical Eretz Israel. Recognizing in 1981 that the Sinai settlers—mostly secular Labor supporters—did not have the will and determination to fight the government and that the rightist Tehiya party, established in 1979 to stop the government at the polls, did not succeed either, the young leaders of Gush Emunim decided to step in. Hundreds of religious settlers from the West Bank moved to the Yamit region, bringing their families, rabbis, and yeshivas. Some of the newcomers settled in motels in the city and set up camp for a long stay. Others moved illicitly to several *moshavim* that had been evacuated earlier by the army, and occupied their houses. In the last stage of the movement's resistance, it numbered about one thousand activists who managed to penetrate areas closed by the army and settle in its deserted buildings. Several hundred supporters were also stationed outside the border of the closed area, repeatedly trying to outmaneuver the army and get in.[60]

None of the Gush leaders involved in the MHRS believed they had either the power or the will to overcome the Israeli army, and the majority never considered violence. The purpose of the struggle was to create psychological and political conditions under which the political echelon would not instruct the army to evacuate Sinai. Thus, the MHRS leaders came to the conclusion that their objective was to make the price of the retreat higher than the price of Israel's noncompliance with the Egyptian-Israeli peace agreement. This, they believed, could be accomplished through massive civil disobedience in Yamit and intense protests and demonstrations all over the country.[61] This rather rational struggle strategy had, however, a mystical dimension to it, a typical Gush conviction that if sufficient *messirut hanefesh* is demonstrated, God would actively interfere and stop the retreat.[62]

Although they did not plan to conduct a violent struggle against the soldiers, the specter of violence loomed large. An early "preview" of a struggle against evacuation conducted more than a year earlier in the vegetable nursery of Moshav Neot Sinai—the first place to be removed—became very physical despite good intentions. Perhaps a thousand farmers and supporters showed up, including a significant Gush contingent. They refused to evacuate the area, causing a confrontation with the army. When the military used water hoses, the demonstrators stoned the soldiers, threw burning torches, and even threatened to spray them with poisonous chemicals. Only the appearance of two cabinet ministers, including Begin's deputy premier, Yigal Yadin, with a promise to reconsider the evacuation pacified the settlers and ended the violence.[63]

While the early stages of the struggle over Yamit and the neighboring *moshavim* involved only hypernomic religious activity, Torah lessons, Halakhic deliberations, prayers, and ecstatic preparations for the great miracle, the last stage was very physical. The settlers, whose devotion was no operational match to the twenty thousand soldiers confronting them, refused to leave, but they were forcefully dragged out. Many continued to pray and cry until the last moment. Others fortified themselves on the roofs of the buildings and, using nonlethal weapons, would not let the soldiers get near. The military commanders had to devise a special iron cage, moved by gigantic cranes, to outmaneuver the intransigent settlers and remove them.[64] A special struggle tactic was introduced by a small number of Rabbi Kahane's followers who fortified themselves inside one of the city's air defense shelters. As the final days of the evacuation approached, they locked themselves in the shelter with explosives, ammunition, and cyanide capsules and threatened to kill themselves if forced to leave. The entire nation held its breath while Rabbi Kahane himself, at the special request of Prime Minister Begin, finally convinced them to surrender.[65]

When Yamit was demolished by the Israeli army and the area evacuated on April 28, 1984 (the exact date set by the Camp David Accords), it was clear that Begin's grand peace move had won out. It was, however, just as clear that a new Israeli rightist subculture of defiance had come of age. The settlers made a solemn commitment to return to Yamit and clarified, in addition, that territorial compromise involving Judea and Samaria would produce a much larger struggle.[66]

Gush Emunim in an Extraparliamentary Perspective: The Cases of the Yom Kippur Protest Movements and Peace Now

There can be no doubt that Gush Emunim had become since the 1970s the nation's most influential social movement, with an unprecedented impact on government policies and public discourse. Only part of this success can be attributed to the constructive dimension of the movement, being a settler organization involved in concrete "Zionist" nation building and territorial expansion. Another reason for Gush Emunim's success was its ability to surprise and penetrate the Israeli establishment through extraparliamentary tactics. The Gush brought the attack of the Israeli periphery on the political center, an assault started after 1967 by the Israeli extreme left, to the fore. This they did with the help and (later) the opposition of two much smaller and influential extraparliamentary organizations, the Yom Kippur Protest Movements and Peace Now.

There is almost no historical record of the protest movements that emerged in Israel in the wake of the 1973 Yom Kippur War, and most Israelis who lived at the time barely remember their activities.[67] But in the few months of their operations, February-May of 1974, these spontaneous organizations were most instrumental in transforming Israeli politics. Much of the extraparliamentary courage of Gush Emunim, as well as its operational repertoire, was borrowed from these movements—groups that disappeared almost as quickly as they had emerged.

The Yom Kippur Protest Movements, which changed their name to Israel Shelanu (Israel Is Ours) just a short time before they withered away, emerged spontaneously out of a one-man vigil. The man, captain (res.) Moti Ashkenazi, was the commander of an Israeli military outpost on the Suez Canal. Egypt's surprise attack on October 6, 1973, devastated Ashkenazi's stronghold and led to the death of most of his soldiers. Wounded, angry, and frustrated over the army's unpreparedness and complacency prior to the war, Ashkenazi vowed to personally end the career of Defense Minister Moshe Dayan—if he were to survive the Suez Canal inferno. When he did, and started his solitary demonstration in front of the defense ministry, Ashkenazi was soon joined by a large number of Israeli sympathizers who shared his feelings about the war. Without reference to divisive ideological issues (the occupied territories, Palestinians, and peace), the protesters came from the entire landscape of Israeli politics. Defining the tragedy of the Yom Kippur War as *mechdal* (culpable blunder), the activists of the new movement demanded the immediate resignation of Defense Minister Dayan and Prime Minister Golda Meir. Later, these demands became a critique of Israel's entire political system and produced a call for comprehensive political reform.

Three months after their spontaneous rise, the protest movements won their battle. Their nonviolent riots, demonstrations, marches, sit-ins, vigils, and media campaigns proved effective. Following the critical Agranat report, issued by a blue-ribbon state investigation committee looking into the causes of the war, the government ministers resigned. The Meir-Dayan-Eban triumvirate that reigned on the eve of the war left the scene, and a new guard led by junior ministers Yitzhak Rabin and Shimon Peres took over. Having been a spontaneous protest phenomenon and lacking a common ideology, social base, or even interests, the protest movements died quickly. Their most important offspring, the Shinui party (Change), later became instrumental in the downfall of Labor in 1977.

The Yom Kippur Protest Movements contributed much to the rise of Gush Emunim. Inspired by the Kookist theological loyalty to the secular government of Israel, the early Gush Emunim did not challenge the Israeli government in the streets. Its young, impatient activists needed political inspiration and the example of another radical group—lessons they could not get from their rabbis. But the Yom Kippur Protest Movements were something else. The Israelis who joined these movements were not socially and politically marginal. They were neither Matzpen nor Siah types nor even B'nai Akiva graduates. Active in the protest movements were high-ranking reserve army officers, recognized members of kibbutzim and *moshavim*, and prestigious activists of Israel's established Labor movement. Lawyers, doctors, writers, and university professors were also represented in large numbers.[68] Never before had Israeli extraparliamentary action been so legitimate and "in." And as disorganized and short-lived as the Yom Kippur Protest Movements had been, they were very instrumental in tearing apart the mystique of the government and the Knesset. A long tradition of centralized politics, managed by revered national leaders, was irreparably damaged by the tragic war. The road for a more daring (and durable) extraparliamentary challenge to the government was opened by the protest movements; Gush Emunim's able activists simply stepped in.

If the Yom Kippur Protest Movements helped launch Gush Emunim's new politics, the Gush was the parent of Shalom Achshav (Peace Now), Israel's peace movement born in 1978. The young activists of Gush Emunim did not, of course, intend to facilitate the formation of their extraparliamentary mirror image on the left. But once they had established a successful model of extraparliamentary action on the right, it was just a matter of time before the Israeli left would respond. Though it has never matched Gush Emunim's effectiveness, Peace Now has become Israel's most vocal and influential peace organization ever.

Peace Now was formed in March 1978. The immediate reason for the organization's foundation was the slow pace of the Israeli-Egyptian peace negotiations and the fear of many moderates that the great momentum following Anwar Sadat's 1978 visit to Jerusalem was being lost. It was against this background that 348 Israeli reserve officers, most of them young graduates of the Yom Kippur War, wrote a letter to Prime Minister Begin, begging him to waste no time or effort in making peace. Very much like Moti Ashkenazi's personal vigil, which was not intended as a first step to the creation of a new organization, the officers' letter produced a tremor in Israeli society. Before they knew it, the half-dozen organizers found themselves heads of a large, spontaneous, and vocal extraparliamentary movement.[69] Not only had they instantly become Begin's public nemesis during the early stages of the peace negotiations with Egypt, but they also comprised his most vocal supporters when he signed the Camp David Accords. Back from Camp David and already harassed by the first radical right groups, Begin was surprised to find Peace Now activists awaiting him with flowers.

Although they never admitted it, Peace Now's founders responded to the challenge of the Gush. For nearly four years Israel's streets had been dominated by Gush Emunim. Dozens of rallies, marches, and demonstrations—with participation reaching at times into the tens of thousands—made Israelis believe that the extreme right had mastered the extraparliamentary game. The left and its peace camp were seen as weak and ineffectual—at best. While everybody understood that the public was divided between the left and the right, this division was not visible in the streets until 1978. The ability of Peace Now to mobilize tens, even hundreds of thousands of demonstrators is, historically, very meaningful. It showed that the rebellion of the Israeli political periphery against the center was crowned in 1978. Both the Israeli left and right now owned the streets.

Though not sharing the increasing extralegalism of Gush Emunim,

Peace Now learned a great deal from the tactics and experiences of the religious organization. The two movements never set clear membership criteria and let the press estimate the size of their rallies. Since many sympathizers and interested onlookers used to show up at those publicized events, both movements succeeded in creating for themselves a somewhat deceptive image of mass movements. Peace Now was particularly successful in 1982, when nearly four hundred thousand people participated in its commemorative protest of the Sabra and Shatila massacre in Lebanon. Although the number of participants was initially inflated by biased sources, few of the actual participants were movement activists. But the reporting of massive participation help boost the image of Peace Now all over the world.[70]

Peace Now had made a very small contribution to the annals of Israeli political violence. Like many moderate peace movements that had emerged in the West since the 1950s, it has supported moral values and minority rights and rejected aggressive politics. Even when confronting the Likud government, the organization rarely used extralegal methods. Peace Now's most intense engagements involved not the Israeli police but the activists of Gush Emunim. These occurred during the early 1980s, when the organization's activists tried to stop illicit settlements in Samaria or attract public attention for legal settlements that ignored the interests of West Bank Palestinians.

The most significant contribution of Peace Now to Israeli political extremism was made indirectly. While not engaged in violence, the movement reinvigorated the disorderly attack of the periphery on the Israeli center and greatly contributed to emotional politics. It was in this regard an integral part of the fast-growing culture of direct action and, ultimately, violence. Because of its great accessibility to the Israeli and international media, Peace Now became the nemesis of Gush Emunim and Kach, triggering plenty of aggression and hate literature. This rivalry reached crisis proportions in 1983 when a Peace Now activist, Emil Greentzweig, was killed in the course of a peace demonstration.[71] During the 1982–85 Lebanon War, several more radical organizations operated within the milieu of Peace Now. These included "There is a Limit," "Parents against Silence," "Women in Black," and even the Communist "Committee for Bir

Zeit University." More radical than Peace Now in their attitude to the Likud government, these organizations greatly escalated the intensity of Israeli public discourse. Seen by the right as offsprings of Peace Now, which they really were not, these organizations made Peace Now the great demon of the Israeli Right.

A careful examination of the violence of Gush Emunim and the nonviolence of Peace Now suggests smaller differences than are usually assumed. Gush Emunim may have sprung from totally different intellectual sources than Peace Now and may have had a limited normative commitment to Israeli democracy, but it neither was born as a violent organization nor thrived on violence. The number of Gush physical confrontations with the Israeli authorities in its first twenty years was surprisingly small. The major difference in the extraparliamentary activities of both movements involved the target communities they had to deal with, the Israeli public in the case of Peace Now and West Bank Palestinians in that of Gush Emunim. The increasingly militant unwillingness of the Palestinians to play by the Gush rules in Judea and Samaria and the active contribution of PLO terrorism gradually dragged a number of Gush Emunim activists into vigilantism and terrorism. Much of the violence produced by Gush Emunim was therefore not a product of its extraparliamentary politics but of its involvement in a nationalist conflict with the Palestinians.

6

THE KAHANIST CULTURE OF VIOLENCE

Evolution and Containment

A Jewish Fist in the Face of a Gentile Is *Kiddush Hashem*

In 1976, following a brutal terrorist attack on a school in the Israeli border town of Kiryat Shmonah, an attack that took the lives of over twenty children, the late Rabbi Meir Kahane, the leader of the extremist movement Kach wrote a short essay, "*Hillul Hashem*" (desecration of the name of God). In the essay, which was never published and was made available only to Kach members, Kahane presented his answer to the Kookist theology of Gush Emunim regarding the process of heavenly redemption and the origins of the state of Israel. It was also the first time that Kahane fully developed his revenge theory and elaborated on the violence he had propagated since 1969.

> The debate about the religious legitimacy of the State of Israel and its place in our history has already been conducted within religious circles for a long time. It has focused on the penetrating and real question: How can a religious Jew see the hand of God in a state that was established by Jews who not only do not follow the paths of God, but reject Him openly or, at best, are passive to His blessed existence?
>
> The State of Israel was established not because the Jew deserved it, for the Jew is as he has been before rejecting God, deviating from his paths and ignoring His Torah. . . . God created this state not for the Jew and not as a

> reward for his justice and good deeds. It is because He, be blessed, decided that He could no longer take the desecration of His name and the laughter, the disgrace and the persecution of the people that was named after him, so He ordered the State of Israel to be, which is a total contradiction to the Diaspora.
>
> If the Diaspora, with its humiliations, defeats, persecutions, second class status of a minority . . . means Hillul Hashem, then a sovereign Jewish State which provides the Jew a home, majority status, land of his own, a military of his own and a victory over the defeated Gentile in the battlefield—is *exactly the opposite*, Kiddush Hashem [the sanctification of the name of God]. It is the reassertion, the proof, the testimony for the existence of God and His government."[1]

Kahane's essay marked a major disagreement with the prevailing Zionist ideo-theology of the time, the Kookist philosophy of Gush Emunim. According to the elder Rav Kook, founder of Merkaz ha-Rav yeshiva, the state of Israel was created by the Zionists as part of a heavenly plan to redeem the people of Israel. The founding fathers of Zionism who established the secular movement in clear defiance of most Orthodox authorities were, in Kook's view, not sinful heretics who acted against God and abrogated his orders. Although secular and nonobservant, they were unknowingly God's holy emissaries. God Himself acted to revive the nation and in His mysterious way chose to do it through the secular Zionists. The secular state of Israel, according to the Kookist school, is therefore not a sin but a reward, a graceful indication that God has finally decided to forgive all His people, not just the Orthodox faithful. It is holy for its intrinsic value, for what it is and does for the Jews.

In contrast to Gush Emunim, Rabbi Meir Kahane believed that the Gentiles, not the Jews, were responsible for the establishment of the state of Israel. The state was established not because the Zionists deserved it but as a result of the actions of the Gentiles. The perennial humiliation of the Jew by the Gentile world was, according to this theory, also a humiliation of God, since His chosen people were being repeatedly persecuted. Following the Holocaust, God could no longer stand this humiliation and had the state of Israel established as His revenge against the Gentiles. Thus, the Jewish state is virtuous not because of what it does to the Jews but for what it inflicts upon the Gentiles. It is not an expression of reward but of punishment.[2] Gentile persecutors take many forms: Nazis, Blacks, Catholics, Russians, and, of course, Arabs.

Kahane's intense radicalism, passion, and irrevocable commitment to his political struggle seem to have been rooted exclusively in this single element, the insatiable urge to defeat the *goy* (Gentile), to respond in kind for the two millennia of vilification of the Jews. Kahane's hostility to the Gentiles may not be the cardinal presupposition of his political theology, but it is certainly its most dominant emotional and psychological theme. And Kahane *openly* sought revenge. Since the rabbi believed he was expressing the opinion of Halakha and the will of God, the vengeance the Jews are expected to take is, according to him, not simply a personal act but God's revenge for the humiliation He suffered through the desecration of His people.

> Do you want to know how the Name of God is desecrated in the eyes of the mocking and sneering nations? It is when the Jew, His people, His chosen, is desecrated! When the Jew is beaten, God is profaned! When the Jew is humiliated God is shamed! When the Jew is attacked it is an assault upon the Name of God! . . . Every pogrom is a desecration of the Name. Every Auschwitz and expulsion and murder and rape of a Jew is the humiliation of God. Every time a Jew is beaten by a Gentile because he is a Jew, this is the essence of Hillul Hashem! . . . An end to Exile—that is Kiddush Hashem. An end to the shame and beatings and the monuments to our murdered and our martyred. An end to Kaddish and prayers for the dead. . . . An end to the Gentile fist upon a Jewish face . . .
>
> A Jewish fist in the face of an astonished Gentile world that had not seen it for two millennia, this is Kiddush Hashem. Jewish dominion over the Christian holy places while the Church that sucked our blood vomits its rage and frustration. This is Kiddush Hashem. A Jewish Air Force that is better than any other and that forces a Lebanese airliner down so that we can imprison murderers of Jews rather than having to repeat the centuries old pattern of begging the Gentile to do it for us. This is Kiddush Hashem. . . . Reading angry editorials about Jewish "aggression" and "violations" rather than flowery eulogies over dead Jewish victims. That is Kiddush Hashem.[3]

Kahane's use of the formal Halakhic terminology of Hillul Hashem and Kiddush Hashem was hardly the conventional interpretation of these terms. Rather, it reflected Kahane's conviction that Jewish freedom implies the ability to humiliate the Gentile. The stronger the Jew is, the more violent and aggressive, the freer he becomes. Kahane may not have gone as far as George Sorel and Franz Fanon in claiming that violence is a moral force in history or that violence sets colonized and repressed people free, but he shared many similarities with both, especially Fanon.[4] For in a sense he proposed that Jewish independence and a Jewish State are not enough. Jewish sovereignty does not provide a full and satisfactory solution for the Jewish problem, for it only solves the misery of exile.

There is, however, another wound to be healed, the pain of humiliation, the misery of thousands of years of discrimination and victimization, the bleeding memories of generations of vilified Jews, killed for their religion. Kahane did not concentrate solely on the Holocaust, though his profound reaction to the Nazi genocide of the Jews during World War II had been a dominant theme in his actions and writings since the days of the American Jewish Defense League (JDL). The Holocaust was a natural product of anti-Semitism, which could develop in any "normal" nation and is still a historical possibility.[5] According to Kahane, the Holocaust, and the countless pogroms that preceded it, inflicted serious damage on the nation's collective psyche. Jewish independence alone cannot redress the damage. Only revenge, the physical humiliation of the Gentiles, can serve this role. Therefore, Kahane, just as Franz Fanon, was not satisfied with peaceful liberation. A military force that would astonish the world is needed, a Jewish fist in the face of the Gentile.[6]

Catastrophic Messianism

An examination of the style of Kahane's writings and public speeches reveals that his revenge theory and legitimation of Jewish violence are consistently intermingled with a sense of disaster. In his view, Jewish history since the destruction of the Second Temple is nothing but a series of Holocausts, the last of which finally moved God to establish the state of Israel and avenge His desecrated honor. It is therefore not surprising that Kahane's theology of violence was coupled with his emotional sense of catastrophe, a deep conviction that before the Jewish condition will get better, things will become much worse. Long before the evolution of Kahane's pessimistic prophesies regarding the future of Israel, he made himself the prophet of doom and gloom for American Jewry. An essential part of his decision to move to Israel in 1971 was his growing "catastrophic Zionism," a belief that predicted the coming of a new Holocaust and called upon the Jews of the Diaspora to move to Israel before it was too late. Nineteenth-century Zionism, it should be recalled, had a strong catastrophic component. Its most influential theoreticians, Leo Pinsker and Theodor Herzl, concluded that Zionism was the only solution to the physical insecurity of the Jews in eastern Europe at the turn of the century. They convinced many generations of young Zionists that the anti-Semitism of their time would spell the eventual physical destruction or spiritual assimilation of the Jewish People.[7] The doctrine of *Shlilat Hagalut* (Negation of Diaspora) was a direct product of this catastrophic Zionism.

Catastrophic Zionism started to decline—with the exception of Vladimir Jabotinsky's warnings of growing European anti-Semitism in the 1930s—following the evolution of the Zionist enterprise in Palestine and the success of post-1917 political Zionism. The 1948 establishment of the state of Israel, the rising power of American Jewry, and the respectable presence of Jewish communities all over the democratic West have left the thesis of catastrophic Zionism with little power. But Kahane was undeterred. In 1968 he began to talk about the incipient disaster for the Jewish people: it was just a question of time before the enemies of the Jews would overcome their guilt feelings about the destruction of European Jewry and start to plan a new Holocaust. America of the melting pot, the haven of millions of Jewish immigrants, Kahane told his audience, had started to undergo an economic recession in the 1960s, as well as severe moral and social crises. The classical scapegoat, the Jew, would soon be discovered and blamed for the country's ills.[8]

Kahane's catastrophic Zionism was the rationale behind his "program for Jewish survival," the subtitle of his 1972 book, *Never Again*, and his plan to save American Jewry from extinction. While most of the suggestions addressed changes in Jewish life in America, the ultimate step called for immigration to Israel. As much as Jews could help themselves in the Diaspora by returning to full Judaism and by defending their rights and dignity, Jewish life in the Diaspora was doomed. Jewish survival was impossible outside of the state of Israel.[9] And while America of the 1960s was portrayed by Kahane as a troubled land, a modern version of Sodom and Gomorrah, Israel, the modern incarnation of the land of the prophets and great conquerors, was all good. It was the answer to all the Jewish miseries of the time. The young state, which had freed itself by force from British colonialism and built a military machine capable of defeating the Arab nations, was the manifestation of Kahane's early dreams. It provided the only conditions for the breeding of the new Jew, a healthy and complete Hebrew national.[10]

Kahane's 1971 immigration to Israel and his increasing disappointment with its secular culture (and with the refusal of its leaders to listen to him) led to changes in the rabbi's catastrophic theory. In 1973 and 1974 the leader of the JDL wrote two long essays: "Israel's Eternity and Victory" and "Numbers 23:9," in which he first developed his catastrophic Messianism.[11] The theory was based on a single verse from Isaiah—"In its time, I will hurry it [the redemption]" (Isaiah 60:22)—and on its rabbinical interpretation: "If they, the Jews, merit it I will hurry it. If they do not merit it, it will come 'in its time.' " (Talmud tractate, Sanhedrin 93). Redemption, according to this theory, is inevitable. It is part of God's plan and will occur regardless of what the people of Israel do or do not do. But the Jews' actions *will* help determine both how and when the redemption will take place. If the Jews repent, Kahane believed, God will speed up the process, bringing redemption quickly and without pain. But if the Jews are sinful, redemption will come "in its time," that is, following great troubles, wars, and even disasters. The establishment of the state of Israel in 1948 and the 1967 victory in the Six-Day War were unmistakable signs of God's desire to hasten redemption. But following the 1973 ordeal of the Yom Kippur War, which heralded an obstacle on the road to salvation, Kahane warned the people of Israel about the disasters awaiting them should they not respond to God's gesture and return to Orthodox Judaism.

In 1980 Kahane had plenty of time to reconsider his ideo-theology. He was placed on administrative detention for nine months in the Ramla maximum security prison for planning to blow up the Muslim Dome of the Rock on the Temple Mount. In those months Kahane completed two major books, *Thorns in Your Eyes* and *On Redemption and Faith*. He also wrote an essay, "Forty Years," which proposed that Israel was given a forty-year grace period upon its independence in 1948 to repent and prepare for God's redemption. But absent repentance, God would bring redemption through His fury and accompanying disaster. Israel's miraculous victory in 1967 indicated that God had been keeping His promise and that it was now time for the people to fulfill their part. But by 1980, just eight years before the deadline, no repentance had taken place. The nation's time was running out.

> Consider, Jew. If it is indeed true what I say, then the refusal to heed is more than a mere luxury. It is destruction. And then consider a second thing. If it is true that the forty years began with the rise of the State—how many years are left? Too few. So little time to make the great decision that will either bring us the great and glorious redemption, swiftly, majestically, spared the terrible sufferings and needless agonies, or G-d forbid, the madness of choosing the path of unnecessary, needless holocaust, more horrible than anything we have yet endured. As we stand on the crossroads, with one direction, that of glorious life and redemption, and the other, the path of prior tragedy and holocaust, the choice is ours. We are the masters of our destiny if we will only choose the path that the All-Mighty pleads us to walk upon.
>
> My people, my dear and foolish people! We speak of your life and those of your seed, your children and grand children. Choose wisely! The Magnificence is yours for the asking. The horror will be yours for the blindness. Choose life, but quickly; there is little time left. *The forty years tick away.*[12]

In 1980 Kahane thus became Israel's prophet of gloom and doom. Apart from his political programs, which called for the expulsion of the Arabs from Israel and for the Judaization of the country, his books were full of warnings of the coming catastrophe. It is difficult to determine how deeply the leader of Kach believed in his own predictions—whether Kahane's beliefs were more akin to an article of faith of a prophet in the tradition of Jeremiah or to an expression of a troubled person who knew no one took his theories seriously. But Kahane did discuss the issue of catastrophe in private interviews and said that even if he was the prime minister, a catastrophe would still take place if the nation did not repent willingly.[13]

From the Jewish Defense League to Kach: The Radicalization of Rabbi Kahane

Meir Kahane, able and restless young Orthodox rabbi, started his stormy political career in 1968 by establishing the Jewish Defense League. A self-proclaimed vigilante movement aimed at defending lower-middle-class Jewish neighborhoods in New York City, the JDL was primarily concerned with local issues such as crime in the streets and black anti-Semitism.[14] Paradoxically, the inactivity of the Jewish establishment helped Kahane, whose penchant for violence was obvious from the start. The liberal and, by that time, highly successful leadership of the American Jewish community dissociated itself from the vigilante rabbi without offering a solution to the problems he addressed. Consequently, Kahane became attractive to lower-middle-class urban Jews, who suffered from anti-Semitism and violence in the streets. Active in the tumultuous 1960s, Kahane also found a young Jewish middle-class generation looking for an anti-establishment hero.

The ambitious rabbi from Brooklyn was an able speaker, knowing how to pluck the sensitive chords of Jewish anxiety. He spoke bluntly about American anti-Semitism, manifest and latent, and helped assuage his listeners' guilt about the Holocaust. The Jewish establishment was his prime target; he constantly reminded his audience how little the Jewish leadership had done during World War II to stop the killing of Jews in Europe and of how hesitant they now were in fighting black anti-Semitism. "Never Again" became the slogan of the JDL: Never again were Jews to be defenseless.[15]

Kahane's success in mobilizing young Jews for aggressive self-defense against anti-Semitism in America did not escape the attention of several ultranationalist Israelis who believed there was an even more important Jewish cause to fight for, the plight of Soviet Jews. According to Robert Friedman, Kahane's biographer, it was Geula Cohen, former Lehi activist and Herut Knesset member since 1969, who first introduced Kahane to the subject and who was instrumental in forging a secret, semi-official support group for Kahane in Israel, including future prime minister Yitzhak Shamir.[16] Since

1969 the repression of Soviet Jewry and the refusal of the Soviet Union to let its Jews emigrate became the major item on the agenda of the JDL. Soviet diplomats were attacked, first in the United States, then in Europe; Russian artists were harassed; and demonstrations were held in front and inside of Russian agencies. Kahane's extraordinary ability to dramatize this struggle with the use of symbolic and real violence, and to gain media attention, popularized the JDL and facilitated fund-raising and recruitment. In the beginning of the 1970s the league had many thousands of activists in the United States, branches in Europe and South Africa, and admirers in Israel.[17]

For his enthusiastic supporters, Kahane launched a new gospel of Jewish self-transformation and mutual responsibility: "The American Jew, from now on, will become a new person, proud of his origins, capable of defending himself and fully devoted to the cause of his brothers all over the world."[18] Action quickly followed. Though until 1969 most JDL activists used only symbolic violence permitted by law, the league soon became involved in illegal acts and actual violence. After attacking an anti-Semitic radio station, JDL members were sent to jail. In 1970 and 1971 they conducted a score of violent assaults and bombing of Soviet institutions in the United States, including Aeroflot, Intourist, several Soviet cultural centers, Amtorg, Russian diplomatic missions, and the residences of Soviet officials in New York City and Washington, D.C. American firms doing business with the Soviet Union and institutions involved in Soviet-American cultural exchange were also subjected to JDL aggression.[19]

The JDL thus evolved a unique ideology and style, claiming the right to defend fellow Jews wherever they were in trouble. The young rabbi from Brooklyn, already an associate editor of the Brooklyn *Jewish Press*, the largest-selling Anglo-Jewish newspaper in America, would use his weekly column to develop a full-fledged ideology; books based on these essays spread his influence. The key concept of the new philosophy was *ahavat Yisroel* (love of Jewry), a mutuality that implied the obligation to help Jews in trouble, with no reservations or conditions.

> The pain of a Jew, wherever he may be, is our pain. The joy of a Jew, wherever he may be, is our joy. We are committed to going to the aid of a Jew who is in need without distinction, without asking what kind of Jew he is. . . .
>
> We do more, however, than pay lip service to the concept of love of Jewry.

> We act upon it. There is no limit to the lengths to which we will go when necessary to aid a fellow Jew. We must be prepared to give our efforts; we must be prepared to give our money; and, if need be, we must be prepared to give our lives for the Jewish people.[20]

Rabbi Kahane emigrated to Israel in September 1971. He and his supporters have always maintained that this was the logical next step in the realization of his Zionist ideology. But less favorable interpretations point out that by 1971 Kahane had reached a dead end. In the spirit of détente the American administration was by then determined to rein in extreme anti-Soviet activity, and the FBI had made it clear to the rabbi that it had sufficient evidence to send him to prison. He had in fact been given a suspended sentence of four years' probation. The critics maintained that Kahane decided to emigrate to Israel because he was unable to face the decline of his movement—despite claiming ideological advances.[21] Although first declaring his desire to engage only in Jewish education, Rabbi Kahane was not destined to pursue a career in that field. He craved publicity and action in the streets. He was not content with the ideological politics pursued by most of the advocates on the right. Even the most extreme among them could not quite figure out this strange and impatient person who did not join their movements and would not submit to any period of initiation into Israeli public life.

The Israeli public learned in 1972 that the JDL had become fully operative in Jerusalem. Surrounded by a handful of young American supporters who had followed him to Israel, and by a smaller group of young Soviet *émigrés* who admired his anti-Soviet operations, Kahane took to the streets. Besides demonstrations against the Soviet Union, he exploited two new issues: Christian missionary activities in Israel and the sect of American Blacks in Dimona. Though in principle Israelis frown upon Christian missionary activity in their land, there had rarely been serious trouble over this issue. But Kahane was determined to apply the strictest rules of the Halakha prohibiting the presence of Christians in the Holy Land and to evict all missionaries from the country. Similarly, he and his followers aggressively demonstrated against the small black sect that had recently settled in the southern development town of Dimona—claiming to be genuinely Jewish, though they certainly were not. Small and highly isolated, the group went almost unnoticed until Kahane made headlines by drawing attention to it.[22] While doing what he knew best, engaging in extraparliamentary provocations, Kahane was also interested in the Knesset. In 1973 he first ran for the Israeli parliament. With 12,811 votes (0.8 percent), Kahane almost made it.

Rabbi Meir Kahane always had firm opinions on the Palestinians, including Arabs with Israeli citizenship. Never believing in the possibility of compromise, he was consistent in his demand to evict all Arabs from Eretz Israel. But as an American immigrant who had not served in the army or endured Israel's wars, Kahane first demurred on the issue. Less than a year after his arrival, however, in August 1972, JDL leaflets were distributed all over Hebron. The astonished Arab residents learned that the Jewish rabbi was summoning their mayor, Muhammad Ali Ja'abari, to a public show trial for his part in the 1929 massacre of the ancient Jewish community of Hebron.[23] While the show trial was never conducted, a pattern of dramatic anti-Arab Kahanist provocation had been set. In 1972 Kahane initiated an organized operation to encourage the Arabs to emigrate. Promising full compensation for property, he developed his theme that only massive Arab evacuation would solve Israel's problems: just as two people cannot sit on the same chair, so it is impossible for the two nations, Israeli and Palestinian, to coexist in the Land of Israel.[24]

While specializing in symbolic action, Kahane did not shrink from involvement in acts of violence against Arabs. In 1972, following the terrorist massacre on eleven Israeli athletes at the Olympic Games in Munich, he launched an attempt to sabotage the Libyan Embassy in Brussels. He secured the support of Amichai Paglin, Irgun operations chief during the British Mandate. The plot was exposed at Ben-Gurion Airport when a container of arms and explosives was discovered.[25]

Before the Yom Kippur War, Kahane was very much alone among Israel's radical right extremists, and he garnered most of the publicity granted to ultra-right provocations. But after the war the newly formed Gush Emunim began using tactics similar to his. The period after 1973 was thus hard for Kahane—he had a small following and attracted little attention. And Kahane, who had never been able to start constructive ventures (such as settlements) or participate in collective efforts led by others, had a serious problem. His only way to survive politically was to do something no one else had yet done. His solution was to violently polarize relations between Jews and Arabs in the West Bank. Followed by several admirers, Kahane, who had just changed the movement's name from the Jewish Defense League to Kach—an old Irgun theme projecting defiance—moved to Kiryat Arba to exacerbate the volatile relationship between Jews and Arabs; the Kach contingent there had indeed become a time bomb. Although the rabbi himself would eventually move back to Jerusalem, his most devoted students stayed in the town and continued to exert significant influence on its residents. One of them, Baruch Goldstein, became the communal doctor in the 1980s.

Despite his increasing pessimism and extremism, Kahane had until 1977 one soft spot that blocked his total radicalization and alienation from the Israeli normative system: his little-known admiration for Menachem Begin. Kahane grew up within the Revisionist movement of Vladimir Jabotinsky and was an old Betar member. His father, Rabbi Charles Kahane, was very active within the American Revisionist movement. One of Kahane's most vivid memories was Jabotinsky's visit to his home in the late 1930s. As an adolescent in 1947, Kahane picketed Ernest Bevin, Great Britain's minister of foreign affairs, who was responsible for Britain's pro-Arab orientation. The incident resulted in Kahane's first arrest.[26] Menachem Begin, the Irgun's illustrious commander, was one of Kahane's greatest childhood heroes. While Kahane alone did not endorse the Likud in the elections of 1973 and 1977, and ran on his own ticket, he nonetheless supported Begin. In an early 1973 interview he explained that his race for the Knesset had nothing to do with animosity toward Begin; on the contrary, he hoped for a stronger Begin in the Israeli parliament. His argument in those years was that he, as an Orthodox rabbi, was capable of introducing a genuine nationalist religious party, one that would support Begin instead of selling out to Labor.[27] No one was therefore more excited than Kahane when Begin surprised the entire nation by winning the 1977 elections. His elation was captured in his *Jewish Press* weekly column:

> For the first time since its establishment, the State of Israel has as its prime minister potential a man who thinks like a Jew, acts like a Jew, faces television

with a yarmulke on his head, and actually speaks the "one little word" that we have waited to hear from the lips of Ben-Gurion, Sharett, Eshkol, Golda, Rabin and Peres. Menachem Begin, the potential prime minister of Israel, faces the nation and the world and thanks G-d, the one little word that the polysyllabic Eban finds impossible to pronounce. And he reads from the Psalms and thanks the Almighty. Miracle? Miracle of Miracles.[28]

Inevitably, the Camp David Accords were a profound shock to Kahane, and he was at once transformed. The previously admired prime minister of Israel instantly became a traitor in Kahane's eyes. By succumbing to the pressure of the Gentiles, Begin defamed the name of God:

> The heart of the Begin tragedy is that a man who a was symbol, for half a century, of Jewish pride and strength, surrendered Jewish rights, sovereignty and land out of fear of Gentile pressure. It is, in a word, *Hillul Hashem*, the humiliation and the desecration of the name of G-d by substituting fear of the finite Gentile for Jewish faith in the G-d of creation and history.[29]

Kahane was thus relieved of his ideological allegiance to the successor of Jabotinsky. And he was now free from an additional bond, loyalty to Israel's democratic form of government. Kahane was never a great champion of democracy. If a legally elected government under Menachem Begin was capable of solving the pressing problems of Eretz Israel and the Arabs, he might have maintained some allegiance to the system. But now that Begin had proved himself part of a rotten system, the whole secular framework was corrupt. After 1978, Kahane grew even more extreme. His terminology became as radical as the operations of his followers. The prime target of his fulminations became Israel's Declaration of Independence. The 1948 document, which promised equal rights to all the inhabitants of the Jewish state regardless of race, religion, or nationality, was now presented by Kahane as a contradictory document.

Unlike others on the radical right, including Gush Emunim, who felt committed to the declaration, Kahane never agreed that the state of Israel should be committed to general "non-Jewish" humanistic principles such as equal rights. Already in his 1973 book, *The Challenge—The Chosen Land*, he stressed the impossibility of an equal Arab existence in Israel. Profoundly hostile to all enemies of the Jews, Kahane based his prognoses on a simplistic worst-case analysis of the Arab-Israeli conflict: if the Jews did not "take care" of the Arabs first, the Arabs were bound to wipe them out or evict them from Palestine.[30] Before 1978, though, Kahane, as an American immigrant with no part in the heroic Zionist past, did not dare challenge Israel's most cherished document. But the Camp David Accords and the "fall" of Begin removed his last inhibitions. The leader of Kach was ready to confront the Declaration of Independence, calling the document the most damaging statement ever made in the history of Zionism:

> Does "free" mean that they are free to work for an Arab majority in Israel? Does that mean that they are free to give birth to many babies, very many, so that in the future they will be free to establish , by means of their vote, an Arab majority in the Knesset? Does "free" mean an equal right for an Arab majority in the Knesset to decide that the state be named "Palestine"? That the Law of Return which today allows Jews, not Arabs, automatic entrance and citizenship, be canceled? In short, could the Arabs of the Jewish state . . . be free and equal to move to the voting booth in silence, in relaxation, even in complacency, and democratically bring an end to Zionism and to the Jewish state?[31]

According to Kahane, the words *freedom* and *equality* in Israel's Declaration of Independence were meaningless. It was unrealistic to believe that the Arabs can identify with the values of a Jewish state, established on what they consider their own land. It made more sense to expect the Arabs not to forsake the idea of Arab Palestine and to do whatever they could to bring it about, including taking advantage of the Jews' values and generosity.[32]

An Arab Input: Land Day, the "Sons of the Village," and the Progressive Nationalist Movement

Perhaps the most controversial aspect of Rabbi Kahane's approach to the Arab issue was his categorical demand that Israeli Palestinians be evicted. This segment of Israeli citizens, about 16 percent of the Israeli population in the second half of the 1970s, comprised the Arab inhabitants of Palestine who had not escaped from their cities and villages during Israel's 1948 War of Independence. While 670,000 Palestinians left or were evicted, some 150,000 chose to stay. And according to the stipulations of the 1947 United Nations Partition Resolution and the commitment made in Israel's Declaration of Independence, they were offered and received Israeli citizenship. Though emotionally attached to their Arab brothers abroad, Israeli Arabs have been generally loyal to their country. Because of the extensive security measures taken by the new state, the Arabs' social, economic, and political powerlessness, and their rejection by the Arab nations (who considered them traitors for accepting citizenship from the "Zionist entity"), Israeli Arabs have gradually recognized the Jewish state as their permanent home. Many Zionist spokespersons had, in fact, used the Israeli Arabs as a showcase example. They were the ultimate proof that the Jewish state was fully democratic and that with a small amount of goodwill it could be integrated into a peaceful and productive Middle East. Kahane's demand to evict these Palestinians was considered ludicrous in the 1970s. Even those who tacitly supported or "understood" his call for the eviction of the Palestinians of the occupied territories could not quite understand the prudence of his public declarations. The danger that Israeli Palestinians would either sabotage the Jewish state from within or take over through demographic growth seemed remote and unreal.

But new developments in the Arab sector in the second half of the 1970s gave Kahane unexpected support. March 30, 1976, was, in this regard, a special day. A general strike among the Arab population of Israel, intended to protest a large confiscation of Arab lands by the Israeli government, escalated into one of the bloodiest eruptions in the history of the Jewish state. The event, to be later commemorated by the Arabs as "Land Day," began the evening before with a violent confrontation between Palestinian demonstrators and Israeli soldiers. Military trucks carrying soldiers back from training areas near the densely Arab-populated Netofa Valley came upon large Arab roadblocks and burning tires. Then they encountered a barrage of rocks and burning oil cans. Unprepared and panicked, the soldiers opened fire. The Netofa Valley confrontation led to the imposition of a strict curfew on the area that was repeatedly broken by the angry local population. The violence that spread to the lower Galilee and villages such as Sachnin, Tura'an, Ein Mahil, and Kafar Kana was hard to contain. It resulted in the deaths of six Israeli Palestinians and injuries to scores of others, and several dozen policemen were wounded.[33]

The organization responsible for the Land Day initiative, originally planned as a mild protest, was not an extraparliamentary body. It was Rakah, Israel's New Communist List, a nonviolent political party long represented in the Knesset. Rakah's organizers never intended to turn the land struggle into a violent event. Their original idea was to build Arab solidarity over the issue of land confiscation and to express it in legal and legitimate ways. In contrast to the large confiscations of Arab lands conducted by the government in the 1960s, there was no such action in the following years. Israeli Arabs had been led to believe that a dark era in their collective history was gone forever. For this reason they became incensed upon hearing, in the summer of 1975, of the resumption of land confiscations. Rakah, the dominant party among Israeli Arabs, felt an obligation to lead the struggle.

The strategy chosen was twofold: the application of pressure on the government and the mobilization of the Arab public under Rakah's leadership. The group selected for spearheading the struggle was a Rakah front organization, the "Follow-up Committee for the Defense of Arab Lands," composed of Palestinian notables, most of whom were not even party members, and who did not expect a violent eruption. Eli Reches, a leading student of Arab politics, believes that the violent uprising of Land Day came from three sources, none of which had been under Rakah's control: a gap between the sense of power increasingly felt by the Arab population in the 1970s and their sudden discovery of a new deprivation; the internal dynamics of the anticonfiscation struggle in the months preceding Land Day; and the rise of radical organizations that the party could not constrain.[34]

The government's intention to confiscate Arab lands produced a deluge of emotions and memories of the 1950s and 1960s, the years of massive land confiscations. Israeli Arabs, however, had come a long way since those years of powerlessness, misery, and control by the military government. In the mid-1970s, they numbered over 500,000, compared with 150,000 in 1948. The military government, imposed in 1948 and abolished in 1966, was long gone. Their self-image of a small minority subject to arbitrary restrictions and devoid of political options had been replaced by an image of an enlarged, expanding, and unrestricted political bloc. And it was not just a question of numbers. In the 1970s, especially after the decline of the government's authority caused by the Yom Kippur War, Israeli Arabs had undergone intense Palestinization. Expressed by a dramatic rise in self-respect, this trend carried with it a greater sense of legitimacy and power.[35] The renewed land confiscations posed a serious challenge to their newly empowered image, thereby becoming a source of intense anxiety. Israel's Arabs did not perceive the land issue simply as a contest over real estate but as a severe blow to their collective identity. The confiscation was portrayed as an inhumane execution of an illegitimate policy, devoid of justice and decency; the steadfast struggle to keep the land was consequently defined as an act of self-defense. One Knesset member, Tufik Ziad, expressed this feeling when maintaining that "there is no homeland without the land, no home, no school . . . just wandering around looking for a job. In the twentieth century we do not wish to be turned into a wandering people."[36]

The campaign of Israel's Arabs against the land confiscation was also perceived as part of a larger cause, as an element in the newly embarked upon struggle by the Palestinians. Since the late 1960s, Israeli Arabs had been increasingly exposed to the impact of the Palestine Liberation Organization. Although lacking a role in the terrorist campaign of the radical Palestinian movements, Israeli Arabs became increasingly sympathetic to the Palestinian demand for independence, an identification that intensified after the PLO's international success in 1974. Yasser Arafat's organization had long called upon Israeli Arabs to jump off the "Zionist Bandwagon" and start struggling against the government in extralegal ways. These calls played an important role in the radicalization that preceded Land Day.

The immediate dynamics of the struggle against land confiscation on the eve of Land Day had a significant impact on the escalation. Rakah organized the first national meeting against the new policy as early as October 1975. The meeting, which led to the formation of the Follow-up Committee for the Defense of Arab Lands, was attended by representatives of Israel's Arab students, the Negev's Bedouins, and many other public notables. A special effort was made between November 1975 and February 1976 to convince the government to back off from its confiscation plans. Not merely a propaganda campaign, it was a committed effort to communicate to the government the severity of this issue. Establishment of local defense committees followed suit, representing a major public mobilization. The decision to launch Land Day was made only after an official government announcement on February 29, 1976, that two thousand dunams (about five hundred acres) would be confiscated to "develop the Galilee for both its Jewish and Arab inhabitants." During the time leading up to Land Day, as Rakah proceeded with organizing the campaign, the radicalization process gained momentum. Burgeoning expectations for government concessions were created that inevitably deflated, in the face of reality, into great bitterness and anger. The presence of military units in several villages, the preventive arrest employed on radical elements, and the outpouring of emotions augured badly.[37]

It is highly probable, however, that regardless of the intensifying frustration and the explosive potential of the interaction with the government, Rakah would have been able to maintain control in the Arab streets if not for a new presence—the radical Arab groups. These small organizations, which made Rakah appear conservative and establishment, dictated the pace of the escalation, inciting the local population to challenge and attack security officers. The use of extremist tactics such as road blocking, tire burning, and rock throwing, already common in the occupied territories, became prevalent within the Green Line (the pre-1967 Israeli border). The rise of the radical Sons of the Village and the Progressive National Movement reflected the changes undergone by Arab society in Israel since the end of the 1960s: a combination of a strong social protest with intense Palestinization. These significant changes appeared to be filling an Arab nationalist void that had existed since the 1964 outlawing of a nascent Palestinian movement by the name of Al Ard (The Land).[38]

The Sons of the Village movement was formed in 1972 in the village of Um al-Faham. Its founders, university graduates and students, initially focused attention on the communist-controlled local government, which they wished to topple. But in spite of this narrow political perspective, the movement's philosophy highlighted features of Palestinian nationalism and focused on the need of Israeli Arabs to identify with the PLO. More radical than Arafat's organization on several issues related to the struggle with Israel, the group was closer to the Arab "Refusal Front." The Sons of the Village adopted the PLO thesis on the necessity of Israel's destruction, and sought to accomplish this task through "armed struggle," or terrorism. An important stage in the evolution of the organization was its association with Israel's Arab university students. Taking place in the mid-1970s, especially at the Hebrew University of Jerusalem, this development drew the attention of the Israeli public. The Sons of the Village and similar local groups became the effectual detonators for Land Day, triggering the greatest killing of Israeli Arabs since the 1956 Kfar Kassem tragedy.[39]

The eruption of Land Day was quickly contained. Both Jews and Arabs were stunned by the unintentional escalation and vowed to extinguish the fire before it spread out of control. But Land Day underscored a significant change within the Arab population, a passage from passivity to activism. In the Arab milieu, just as in the Jewish arena, extraparliamentary provocations had come of age. Arab protests and riots, considered illegal in the 1950s and 1960s, had now become part of the legitimate repertoire. The extremist groups had become vocal and visible. In 1976 radical students took over Hebrew University's Arab Student Association, resulting in an immediate change of rhetoric, tactics, and political involvement. This student body, hardly noticed until then, began organizing Palestinian folk evenings, field trips to "occupied Sinai," and the publication of newsletters openly supportive of the PLO. The association demanded that Palestinian terrorists be granted the status of prisoners of war, established contacts with Palestinian students in West Bank colleges, and formed the "Progressive Nationalist Movement."

While involving no subversive or violent operations, the new Arab extremism contributed to the rise of intense Arab-Jewish friction on the campuses of Jerusalem and Haifa. Student associations supportive of ultranationalist Jewish parties responded by increasing their presence at the Hebrew University of Jerusalem and at Haifa University. Right-wing radicalization had generally marked Israel's student politics of the late 1970s, and the Sons of the Village as well as the Progressive Nationalist Movement only added a special Arab flavor. Young right-wing activists and future Likud Knesset members Tzahi Hanegbi and Israel Katz, who served sequentially as the heads of the Hebrew University Student Association, used the new Arab extremism as a springboard for their political careers. They craved confrontation and did not hesitate to use brute force to stop what they considered "subversive" activity on campus.[40] The leaders of the Arab groups were only too happy to cooperate, for the increasing focus of the media on the Jerusalem campus made them heroes of the Arab community. Their proudest moment came in 1979 upon launching a highly publicized struggle against "the fascist campaign of the violent Jewish right." The Progressive Nationalist Movement won all eleven seats of the Arab Student Association in Jerusalem. Though never capable of repeating this victory, the movement remained very influential among Arab students well into the 1980s.

Rabbi Meir Kahane did not immediately reap the political dividends of these events. But by the late 1970s he knew he was on the right track. While other right-wing radicals had been vague on the Arab issue, Kahane had already predicted the rise of the new Arab extremism in his 1973 book, *The Challenge*:

> Not only the Arab in the liberated territories sees himself as a "Palestinian," and believes that the Jews stole his land. The Arabs who live in the pre-June 1967 Eretz Israel . . . the Arabs "with equal rights" who enjoy freedom in the Jewish state, think in the same way. He [the Arab] does not see himself as part of the state, for he is an Arab not a Jew, a Palestinian not an Israeli. He feels no loyalty to his government—for he does not see it as his government. He is hostile and is full of hate for the Jewish majority, for in his heart he is a "Palestinian" and an Arab nationalist. . . . But since he suffers from a guilt feeling, for his Israeli citizenship, he is a much more dangerous enemy. . . .
>
> In the coming years we shall witness a growing number of Arab intellectuals whose nationalism will radicalize and become a great deal more extremist. We shall witness a growing number of Arabs who would not find spiritual and intellectual satisfaction in the professions open to them. . . . We shall witness a society whose main blue-collar workers would be Arabs and the others Jews. This situation would produce growing frustration, tensions, demonstrations, strikes, violence, and attempts at subversion and revolution."[41]

Kahane's 1973 predictions proved to be accurate by the end of the decade. Not only was he right about the frustrated young Arab intellectuals who discovered Palestinian nationalism, but he correctly predicted the growing friction between Jews and Arabs in the job market. No competition ever existed between the two sectors in well-paid or even moderate positions, but the early 1980s produced a growing perceived competition for the lower-paying jobs. In 1980–81 Israel's economy started to shrink, and the first to suffer were the country's outlying development towns. High inflation rates destabilized pay scales, and many workers began to demand constant pay increases. Factories and shops that were unprepared for the new situation found Arabs to be an inexpensive alternative to Jewish labor. The Arabs, especially but not exclusively residents of the occupied territories, were willing to work for low pay and without labor unions, and in the nation's developing towns there was a strong perception of a Darwinian economic and cultural competition. The Arabs were seen as willing to work for dismal wages that no Jew would lift a finger for. The result was inevitable, a growing Jewish hostility toward the Arabs—people who "stole" jobs, hostile aliens enchanted with new Palestinian nationalism.[42]

Ultra-Nationalism and Violence in the Early 1980s and the Election of Kahane to the Knesset

Had Meir Kahane been a more balanced and moderate politician, he might well have been elected to the Knesset in 1981, along with the Tehiya leaders. His analysis of the Arab situation was, from the angle of the radical right, realistic. His forecasts were correct. The solution of evicting the Arabs was far more consistent than the suggestions of many of his competitors. But the Kahane of the streets—a bundle of unrestrained emotions, violent eruptions, and insatiable thirst for publicity—was an altogether different person from the analytical Kahane of the books. Apparently those who might have voted for him needed, in addition to good analysis, a credible and legitimate communicator. The leader of Kach did not project this image in 1981, and most of his potential supporters voted for Menachem Begin. By 1984 the situation had changed a great deal.

Begin was gone. Kahane was still an outsider, but the rhetoric of the Likud and the growing radicalism of the Tehiya and Gush Emunim made many of his opinions and beliefs acceptable. Two events in particular, not of his creation, helped the spread of "Kahanism" and played into the hands of its creator: the Likud electoral campaign of 1981 and the intense conflict between the government and Peace Now during the Lebanon War.

The Likud entered the election campaign of 1981 with a serious drawback. The ailing Menachem Begin had for months been hardly functional and his inner cabinet projected intense personal rivalries. Inflation skyrocketed and the polls indicated a large, almost unbridgeable gap between the leading Labor and Likud. Likud leaders who just four years earlier had taken over the government after thirty years of opposition experienced intense anxiety. The specter of a premature return to the Knesset's back benches loomed large in their minds. Nervous and bitter, they were ready to do anything to stay in power. Against this background it was decided to replace Yigal Horowitz, the unpopular finance minister, with Yoram Aridor, soon to become popular by cutting sales taxes on imported goods and appliances. The fear of electoral collapse must have also been the reason for the miraculous recovery of Begin, who not only returned to his 1978 vigorous self but appeared able to relive his bellicose 1950s. Begin, who radicalized his rhetoric against the Syrians and the PLO in Lebanon, would soon order the air attack on the Iraqi nuclear reactor, and was uncharacteristically ready to confront the American administration.

The most significant dimension of Begin's comeback, which filled his old Herut comrades with great jubilation, was his vitriolic attack on the Labor party. Going back almost thirty years, Begin lashed out at Labor and its subsidiary kibbutzim. But unlike his unrestrained campaign against the German reparations and David Ben-Gurion, conducted from total political isolation, Begin was now the prime minister of Israel, a leader of stature and prestige. Stressing Labor corruption and paternalistic attitudes to the Sephardim, mostly exemplified by the kibbutzim's reluctance to share their wealth with the Sephardis of the development towns, Begin helped get the ethnic genie "out of the bottle." Likud's large Sephardi constituency was repeatedly reminded that the people responsible for the rough and paternalistic immigration absorption it experienced in the 1950s—the Ashkenazi Labor party—were trying to return to power to reinstate the same discriminatory policies.[43]

It is not clear whether or not the scrupulous Likud leader really wished the campaign to become violent, but this is exactly what happened. Incited Likud strongmen started to ravage Labor offices and physically attack the party's activists. They were particularly rude to Labor leader Shimon Peres, who in 1981 was the subject of an unprecedented character assassination. There were Likud hecklers everywhere Peres went and he could move about in the countryside only with dozens of bodyguards. The violence reached its peak when Likud operatives ransacked the Petah Tikva offices of the Labor party and pushed burning trash barrels to a Peres election meeting.[44]

The brutality of the 1981 campaign was exacerbated by two exceptional events that gained massive media coverage: the uncalculated attack on Likud activists by former chief of staff Lieutenant General (res.) Mota Gur and the slip of the tongue by comedian Dudu Topaz. Trying to silence Likud hecklers at a Labor election rally, Gur screamed, "We f—ed the Arabs and will f—you the same way." On the contrary, Topaz told a captive audience in a Labor stronghold that he was glad he was surrounded by real Israelis and not by Likud *chach-chahim* (vulgar, lower class oriental Jews). Betraying a supremacist and paternalistic attitude of the Ashkenazi elite toward the oriental "newcomers," long believed by the Sephardim of having remained under the Israeli rhetorical egalitarian veneer, the two incidents turned the elections of 1981 into an ugly Sephardi-Ashkenazi conflict. Labor charges of negative campaigning and election violence, mistakenly believed to be an advantage that would alienate the Israeli middle class, produced additional tension and violence. It may have been appealing to a number of Ashkenazi Jews but simultaneously drove almost the entire Sephardi public into the bosom of the Likud. Begin, the indefatigable street fighter, had never before heard the expression *chach-chahim*, but he knew how to use it. At a huge Likud rally in Tel Aviv on the eve of the elections, he asked the cheering crowd, "Have you heard what he called you?" and then, in his unmatched theatrical manner, which nobody else had ever succeeded in duplicating, Begin reached into his pocket and slowly took out a slip of paper, *"Cha. ..ch . . . cha . . . him."* "Are you *chach-*

chahim?" Begin asked the excited crowed. "No!" was the thunderous reply. Fully aware of the explosive effect of the moment, Begin ordered his enthusiastic supporters to go home instantly to their telephones, call all their relatives and friends, and tell them what the Labor party was thinking of them and what they should consequently do in the voting booths.[45]

Likud's marginal victory over Labor, 48 Knesset seats against 47, which made it possible for Begin to form a narrow coalition government, helped to legitimate the 1981 electoral violence. None of their brutal activists were ever brought to trial and life went on as usual. Shortly after the formation of the government, the Israeli public was mesmerized by a television series that documented the elections. The award-winning series, produced by Chaim Yavin, the nation's Mr. Television, depicted the violence with great accuracy. Most viewers did not seem to care a great deal about the unsavory scenes. They concluded, instead, that in the elections of 1981, violence and rhetorical violence were the winning cards.

Post-1981 era was marked by a growing ideological rift between the Israeli right and left. Begin's new government greatly differed from the previous administration. The relatively pragmatic policy team of Menachem Begin, Yigal Yadin, Moshe Dayan, and Ezer Weizmann, responsible for the spirit of Camp David, was replaced by a hawkish axis: Menachem Begin, Ariel Sharon, and Yitzhak Shamir. Begin was still committed to the full implementation of the peace with Egypt, including the painful evacuation of Yamit and the neighboring *moshavim*, but he was equally determined to tacitly kill the autonomy talks, aimed at producing a compromise in Judea and Samaria. His Camp David strategy had come now to full light, a return of the entire Sinai to the Egyptians in exchange for peace on the southern front and the facilitation of massive Jewish settlement in Judea and Samaria. The November 1981 assassination of Egypt's President Sadat, the Iran-Iraq war, and the Soviet invasion of Afghanistan diverted regional and international attention from the occupied territories and created positive conditions for a massive Jewish drive into the West Bank.[46] No one was better suited for overseeing this venture than Ariel Sharon, Israel's new minister of defense.

The new government's policy resulted in a dramatic escalation of violence in the occupied territories. It also shook up Peace Now, hardly heard from since the signing of the Camp David Accords. Radical Palestinians recruited high school students for demonstrations and rock throwing. Lacking experience in dealing with rioting civilians, let alone students, the army used excessive force, leading to the deaths of sixteen young Palestinians in three months. At the end of November 1981, the IDF responded to rock and Molotov cocktail throwing by blowing up three houses in Beit Sahur, a village adjacent to Bethlehem. Alarmed by the new situation, a group of Peace Now activists went to Beit Sahur to protest the brutal measures. Unknowingly they started a new chapter in the history of the movement. Since there was little doubt about the architect of the new policy, Peace Now began to talk about "Arik's Spring." It did not take long before the situation evolved into a bitter conflict between Peace Now and Ariel (Arik) Sharon.[47]

The confrontation between Israel's aggressive defense minister and the peace movement reached new heights during the Lebanon War. Sharon's desire to find a proper excuse for invading Lebanon, in order to deal the PLO ministate there a crushing blow, was no secret. The only pending questions involved the conditions and justifications for the invasion. A year before the war, a rally of three thousand Peace Now activists protested against staging military activity. The immediate fear in 1981 was that the excuse to go to war would be the Syrian anti-aircraft missile batteries stationed in Lebanon's Beka Valley. The final countdown for the war started in April 1982, and only Begin's strong denials that war was imminent averted Peace Now demonstrations.[48]

The first antiwar protest took place a few weeks after the outbreak of the war, when Peace Now reservists on active duty received a few days' break. The 120,000 demonstrators in Tel Aviv made history: Never before had any Israeli movement dared to protest a war involving most of the Israeli army. The Likud felt betrayed. Labor governments engaged in wars had never faced such opposition and could always count on the automatic support of the opposing camp. But now, upon starting what he considered an unavoidable war against PLO terrorism, Begin, the only peacemaker in the history of the nation, could not count on the loyalty of the opposition. Most activists of the right did not consider Peace Now antiwar activities either acceptable or legitimate. Praises of Peace Now by the besieged

Yasser Arafat in Beirut further exacerbated the situation. In the eyes of the right, the peace activists were simply traitors, Israeli Quislings. Developing the theme of treason, supporters of the government maintained that Peace Now was engaged in "stabbing the nation in the back." While losing his battle with the IDF in Lebanon, Arafat was winning the war in the streets of Tel Aviv, courtesy of Peace Now.[49]

Although the Lebanon situation triggered the rise of extremist and ideological antiwar movements such as Yesh Gvul (There Is a Limit) and Chayalim Neged Shtika (Soldiers Against Silence)—with almost no relation to the large but relatively moderate peace movement—Peace Now was increasingly singled out as the real "enemy from within." Leading activists of the movement started receiving telephone threats and hate letters. Accusations flew regarding the involvement of foreign interests, including secret Saudi financial support. Protesting the war had become a risky endeavor since aggressive supporters of Begin, Sharon, and Kahane began to resort to violence. The large rally sponsored by Peace Now in September 1982, against the massacre of Sabra and Shatila, brought the conflict between the left and the right to unprecedented intensity. Nearly four hundred thousand Israelis protested the killing in Lebanon of several hundred Palestinian refugees and demanded that a state investigation commission study Israeli involvement in the atrocity. The demand to investigate a massacre, clearly executed by the Christian militias, stunned the Israeli right. Most of their activists could not understand why the killing of Muslim Arabs by Christian Arabs was of any concern to Jews. Why had so many Israelis attended the rally? Something was wrong with these "self-hating" Jews.

February 10, 1983, was a tragic day in the history of Israel. Emil Greentzweig, a Hebrew University graduate student, was killed in Jerusalem during a Peace Now demonstration demanding the resignation of Defense Minister Ariel Sharon. Found by the Kahan Commission to have been partially responsible for the Sabra and Shatila massacre, by not taking preemptive measures against the predictable event, Sharon was expected to resign. His reluctance to do so and the hesitation of Prime Minister Begin to fire him led Peace Now, already deeply involved in the antiwar struggle, to launch a large anti-Sharon rally. Just as they reached the prime minister's office in Jerusalem, the rally's leading column was broken up by a single hand grenade. The explosion that occurred four seconds later killed Greentzweig instantly and wounded a score of others. Greentzweig became Israel's first martyr for peace. Twelve years later another peace champion, Prime Minister Yitzhak Rabin, joined this distinguished brotherhood. Author Shulamit Har-even, a member of Peace Now, gave a graphic description of the march and the last moments before Greentzweig's murder.

> Already at the start, marching from Zion Square up Ben Yehuda Street, the demonstrators noticed that this was neither the ordinary clash of opinions nor the usual level of marginal violence. A group of violent people and strongmen had been waiting for the demonstrators even before they gathered; they repeatedly broke into the marchers' lines with a powerful and strong wedge. Screaming, yelling, beating, plenty of beating, crushing in. The police are not prepared for this kind of violence. Here and there you see a policeman struggling against a group of thugs. To my right I see a lovely policeman, looking more like a father of a large family on his way to pick up the kids from the matinee and bring them home. He is trying to stop the deluge in his body, but fails.—The march goes on. Non-stop beating. Spitting. Rocks. A burning cigarette is thrown at Amiram's face. Anat is hard hit. A thug later tries to extinguish a cigarette on Taliah Ziv's face, an artist from the Israel Museum. These are not the ordinary marginal hecklers; somebody must have organized them.—The marching people are holding themselves in check, they do not strike back. There is a strong feeling that the street is on the verge of civil war which must be stopped by all means. I see Yarom, and Zohar, and Alon, Emil, Amos and Shaul, all reserve paratroopers, holding tight each other's hands and staying put, a thin row facing the violent intruders so that the demonstration may go on.[50]

The unruly eruption of Sephardi-Ashkenazi animosities in the 1981 elections and its great intensification during the Lebanon War played into the hands of Rabbi Meir Kahane. The evolution of ultranationalist and ethnic violence was, in fact, more than what "he bargained for." While most of the people involved in the attacks—on Ashkenazi Laborites in 1981 or on Ashkenazi Peace Now activists in 1983—were bitter Begin and Sharon devotees, not Kahane's, they looked more and more like classic Kahanists. Haters of the PLO, pro-PLO Israeli Arabs, and Israeli

"Ashafistim" (PLO-ers) and their "treason" during the Lebanon War, and still suffering from deep-seated ethnic anxieties, they came to consider street violence as legitimate behavior. When two additional conditions were created in the Israeli public arena—the 1983 collapse and resignation of Menachem Begin and the apparent failure of the Lebanon War—a large number of these individuals were ready for the aggressive rabbi. Thus in 1984, frustrated settlers, angry residents of developing towns, young soldiers, and insecure people all over the country—25,906 of them in all—joined forces to lift a ten-year ban from the head of Kach and install Meir Kahane in the Knesset.

Creating a Violent Order

A characteristic element of Kahane's career was that unlike many high priests of violence and catastrophe, his teachings never remained in the books. In fact, many of Kahane's theories had been written after the fact, after the JDL's or Kach's violent operations had already been conducted. Had the extremist rabbi been entrusted with power, he might just as well have created the catastrophe he had been warning against all along. Thus an essential part of the Kahane phenomenon is the conscious attempt on his behalf *to create a violent order*, to shape a Kahane-inspired Weltanschauung in which anti-Gentile violence and terror are part of the rules of the game. Even in the days of the American JDL, Kahane emphasized the importance of physical force. One of the pillars of the JDL's operative ideology was the notion of "Jewish iron." Kahane, it is true, did not invent either the idea or the metaphor: he adopted them from the ideology of Jabotinsky, the ideologue of Revisionist Zionism. The expression *Barzel Yisrael* (Iron Israel), according to Jabotinsky, meant that in the Diaspora or under foreign rule, Jews were no longer to bow to their oppressors but were called upon to respond to them in kind and with physical force, if necessary. It also meant that the sovereign Jewish state should have a strong army, capable of defending it against all threats. Kahane was so impressed with the notion of "iron" and the application of physical force for self-defense that he divided the JDL in America into two groups: the *Chaya* groups and the Scholar groups. (*Chaya* in Hebrew means animal, and

Chaya squads were in charge of the use of violence against the league's rivals.[51]) Teaching his young followers to act and feel like animals, Kahane wanted them to believe that the JDL was the core organization of a new breed, free of the traditional Jewish "ghetto mentality" and that they themselves were like "the Jews of old."

> Once upon a time, the Jew was not a member of the ADL [the American liberal Anti-Defamation League, an organization highly critical of the JDL's violence]—neither in form nor in spirit. It was not in the role of Mahatma Gandhi that the Jews fought at Massada; the men of Bar-Kochba and Judah Maccabee never went to a Quaker meeting. The Jews of old—when Jews were knowledgeable about their religion, when they turned the page of the Jewish Bible instead of turning the Christian cheek—understood the concept of the Book and the Sword. It was only in the horror of the ghetto with its fears, neuroses, and insecurities that the Jew began to react in fright rather than with self-respect. That is what the ghetto does to a Jew.[52]

When he was brought to trial in New York City in 1971, one of the charges against Kahane was illegal possession of guns, ammunition, and explosives. The leader of the JDL, who did not hesitate to ally himself with the Mafia boss Joseph Colombo—who established in New York the fake Italian-American Civil Rights Association[53]—had no problem translating the idea of "Iron Israel" into the actual use of firearms against the enemies of the Jews. Some of his followers, members of the JDL and probably of a *Chaya* squad, planted a bomb in the offices of Sol Hurok, the Jewish producer who brought Russian artists to America. The bomb that set the place ablaze killed a young Jewish secretary who worked for Hurok.[54] It was the beginning of a series of terrorist acts that marked the behavior of the JDL and its splinter groups long after Kahane left the United States. Since the mid-1970s, the JDL has been consistently referred to by the FBI as a terrorist organization.

Kahane never denied his penchant for concrete violence and in his own account of the story of the Jewish Defense League, he devoted a whole chapter to the justification and rationalization of JDL's violence. While making the usual argument that "violence against *evil* is not the same as violence against *good*," and that violence for self-defense is fully legitimate, Kahane reached his famous conclusion that since Jews have been victimized for so long, "Jewish violence in defense of Jewish interest is *never* bad."[55] According to this theory Jewish violence is nothing but an extension of *ahavat Yisroel* (love of Jewry), the natural brotherly sentiment that requires Jews to care for and help one another regardless of the conditions involved.

In Israel, there was no place for further expression of "Jewish iron," since from 1948 the country has been sovereign and Jabotinsky's notion has been realized in the IDF. But unlike Jabotinsky's recognized successors, Kahane apparently had not been satisfied. Though he did not officially form *Chaya* teams in Israel, he maintained that if the state was incapable of action or unready to react in kind against those who spill "so much as one drop of Jewish blood," then it was the duty of individual Israelis to do so . Slowly and without admitting that he was an ideologue of terrorism, Kahane took to legitimizing anti-Arab terror, a message fully absorbed and acted upon by his followers. One of Kahane's historical heroes was David Raziel, the first commander of the Irgun underground in Palestine during the second half of the 1930s. It was Raziel who in 1937 introduced counterterrorism against the Arabs, in opposition to the official Zionist policy of *havlaga* (restraint). Raziel's idea, that uninvolved Arab civilians should pay for what was happening to Jewish civilians, was especially attractive to Kahane.[56] And he did not care to recognize the fact that Raziel's successors, including the admired Menachem Begin, had already renounced indiscriminate terrorism in the 1940s.

In 1974 Kahane first came up with the idea of TNT (the Hebrew acronym for *Terror Neged Terror*—Jewish terrorism against Arab terrorism). In *The Jewish Idea*, he suggested that a "worldwide Jewish anti-terror group" be established and that this group be organized and aided in exactly the same way as the terrorists are aided by the Arab governments. The government of Israel must deny any connection with the group, even while allowing the same training bases on its soil as the Arab states allow their terrorists.[57] Kahane even recommended at the time the application of indiscriminate terrorism against the population of those Arab countries that provide the PLO with financial, political, and military support.[58]

Kahane's idea to apply Jewish counterterrorism did not change much over the years, and in one of his last books he vowed to establish, upon assuming the leadership of Israel, special Jewish antiterror groups that would operate all over the world and help Jews wherever there was trouble, disregarding the local authorities and their laws.[59] Since the government of Israel was not receptive to his proposals, Kahane's followers and other individuals inspired by his ideas soon started to act on their own. Out of fear of the Israeli police and secret services, they did not try to establish a permanent terror organization but, rather, engaged in occasional anti-Arab attacks, using the symbol TNT. Kahane's devotees were actively involved in the intensification of the conflict between Jews and Arabs in the West Bank in the 1970s. Yossi Dayan, for example, a student of Kahane and later the secretary general of Kach, has been caught and arrested several times for provoking the Arabs in the Tomb of the Patriarchs in Hebron. In an interview he once boasted, "I had more trials than the number of stars on the American flag."[60] Before the Intifada (Palestinian uprising, 1987–92), which had changed the rules of public conduct in the West Bank, it was Kahane's followers who usually acted in response to Arab attacks, although by the middle of the 1980s such pretexts as acting only in reaction to Arab violence were decreasingly needed. Craig Leitner, a Kahane student, described a typical mid-1980s operation:

> One day towards the end of July 1984, I agreed with Mike Gozovsky and Yehuda Richter to operate against the Arabs. We left Kiryat Arba in a hired car, headed towards Jerusalem. . . . That night around 23.00, we went to the Neve Yaacov area. Yehuda was driving. Around midnight, we saw an Arab in his twenties walking along the road. I said "let's stop the car." I went out and hit the Arab with my fist on the shoulder. I also kicked him. He escaped into the night. We continued to Hebron and it was decided—I don't remember by whom—to burn Arab cars. We had in our car two plastic bottles containing four-and-a-half liters of gasoline. In Hebron Yehuda stopped the car. Mike took the gasoline and poured it under several cars, maybe three. Following the burning of the cars by Yehuda, we moved, not waiting to see what would happen. Dogs were around and 1 was afraid that they would wake up the neighbors, or perhaps bite us and we would get rabies.[61]

When asked for his reaction to the activities of Leitner and his friends, who later fired on an Arab bus, wounding several innocent passengers, Kahane expressed total approval. He said he was sorry that they would have to spend years in prison and added that, in his eyes, they were Maccabees. Later, Kahane placed Richter, the main suspect in the operation, as number two on his list for the Knesset. Had Kach won two seats in 1984, Richter would have been released, owing to the immunity of Knesset members. When asked once by a journalist whether he would be willing to instruct his followers not to hit innocent Arabs who happened to be nearby the location of a terrorist incident, Kahane responded bluntly by saying, "No, I would not. As long as they are here we are lost. I have no way of knowing if this Arab or another is innocent. The real danger is the demographics [the danger that the Arabs will outnumber the Jews in Israel]."[62]

Kach was intensely violent long before the Palestinian uprising. Its entire posture—the yellow shirts with the black clenched fist, the attacks on Arab families from within the Green Line that move into Jewish neighborhoods, the chasing of innocent Arab workers for the fun of it, the anti-Arab "victory parades," the attempts to break up leftist meetings in a style reminiscent of the 1920s Italian and German fascists—have spelled hooliganism and violence. Especially violent has been Kach's most aggressive local stronghold, the Kiryat Arba branch in the West Bank. Kahane's devoted followers there have initiated countless violent operations against local Arabs since the mid-1970s. Unlike several Gush Emunim activists, who usually resorted to anti-Arab violence in response to previous attacks and who said all along that they were ready to tolerate a peaceful Palestinian presence in the area, Kach members have never concealed their hope for a massive Arab emigration. The only reason for their relative restraint has been their fear of the security forces. In 1986, and following the intensification of Arab-Jewish violence, they established the "Committee for Road Safety," which was to patrol the roads in the area. But the committee that was established as a defensive instrument against Arab rock throwing became during the Intifada a most aggressive vigilante group. Its notorious commander, Shmuel Ben Yishai, publicly said that any incident involving the harassment of Jewish traffic would make him shoot to kill without warning.

> I do not shoot in the air, I shoot to kill. It is stupid to fire the entire magazine in the air! Only the Jews speak about the "purity of the arms." Just a minute! Listen who is talking about morality: Shamir, the biggest terrorist [Yitzhak Shamir, Israel's prime minister, was Lehi's operations chief]? Rabin, who killed Jews on *Altalena*? The Americans who murdered the Indians?[63]

In 1988 Ben-Yishai's statement was no longer an exception among the settlers of Judea and Samaria and the larger non-Kach radical right. Palestinian violence in the occupied territories has "confirmed" what Kahane had been saying about the Arabs (and the Gentiles in general) all along. It was another attempt to "humiliate" the Jews and to "kill" them if possible. For most of these people, it has been an indication that the decisive battle for Eretz Israel has already started. For a few devoted Kahane supporters, it was a sign of a huge gathering storm and a possible beginning of the "pre-redemption" catastrophe that in 1980 was predicted by Kahane to take place within about eight years.

Israeli Society Reacts: The Containment of Violence and Kahanism

The murder of Emil Greentzweig and the discovery of the Jewish Underground had, each in its time, shaken Israeli society. But it was the July 1984 election of Rabbi Kahane to the Knesset that finally convinced the Israeli political elite that the cleavage between left and right and its militant expressions in the street were getting out of control. The danger of internal division that would destroy the nation from within and play into the hands of hostile Arabs was no longer just a theoretical possibility. The realization, furthermore, that the Jewish state, established in the shadow of the Holocaust, now had a quasi-fascist party in its parliament, publicly advocating terrorism as a legitimate means of ridding the country of its Arab inhabitants, was mind-boggling. It is therefore not surprising that the major drive to stop Kahanism since the summer of 1984 was eventually crowned with success. What was surprising at the time was not the expected commitment of the left to this struggle but the determination of the right, including the majority of the radical right, also to join in.

Regardless of the continuation of the settlement process in Judea and Samaria and the intensified disagreement with the Palestinians, the Israeli political right had in the mid-1980s some of its finest civic hours.

A retrospective examination of the events of the 1980s shows that the effort to contain the spread of extremism and violence started right after the Greentzweig murder, with Prime Minister Begin setting the tone. Menachem Begin was the first to denounce the killing of the Peace Now activist, who protested his Lebanon policies, and to do so in unequivocal language. The prime minister was followed by other leaders of the right and, most importantly, by the Israeli police. The police made enormous efforts to capture the assassin and succeeded in doing so after more than a year of a most comprehensive and expensive investigation. Though the murderer, a marginal, partly criminal Jerusalem figure named Yona Abrushmi, was convicted in the case, it took another ten years before he finally confessed and admitted he had been blinded by the rhetoric of Ariel Sharon.

Also of great significance was the confession of a young and promising Likud activist, Tzahi Hanegbi, who, as a leading student activist in the late 1970s, was greatly responsible for the spread of anti-Arab violence on the Hebrew University campus. Admitting publicly that he and his friends went much too far in the practice of their extremism, Hanegbi urged political activists to be careful in what they said and did in the heat of the political debate.[64] The determined right-wing reaction to the Greentzweig murder was an eye-opener. It indicated that regardless of their commitment to Eretz Israel, the majority of Israel's ultranationalists did not really wish to bring their ideological struggle with the left to the brink of civil war. The commitment of the Begin and Shamir governments to the rule of law, despite their agony over the extraparliamentary opposition to the Lebanon War, was reassuring.

Gush Emunim played a larger role than is usually recognized in the containment of violence and Kahanism. As mentioned earlier, the Gush never developed an ideology of violence. The escalation of a number of Gush Emunim members to vigilante violence, particularly members of the Jewish Underground, evolved not from the movement's articles of faith but from the increasing friction with the Arabs. Most Gush settlers, unaware of the existence of the underground and involved only in minor road clashes with the local Arabs, did not see themselves as members of a violent movement. Their self-perception was one of constructive pioneers devoting their lives to the expansion of Zionism against adversary conditions. The discovery of the underground stunned these people, more perhaps than it shocked ordinary Israelis. For years they had honestly rejected Peace Now accusations of Gush anti-Arab brutality, believing them to be malicious lies. But now they were left speechless and defenseless. Most of these activists were consequently bitter and outraged with the anger directed at their own people, the movement's best and brightest. Much of this internal protest was directed, naturally, against the Kiryat Arba rabbis who had authorized the killings.

The discovery of the underground created in fact a rift within Gush Emunim, an open wound hardly healed since. Most of the movement, including its leading rabbis, had rejected the underground both as an idea and in practice. While expressing some understanding for the individual members of the group, who acted in self-defense against a hostile population, the unauthorized killings of civilian Arabs was denounced. Of even greater importance was the question of state authority. The majority of the movement's rabbis reaffirmed their commitment to the state as "the Kingdom of Israel in the making." They strongly maintained that the use of arms against the enemies of the Jews had to be left to the authorities and the army. While insisting on settlers' right to self-defense, when attacked on the roads, they rejected the extension of self-defense to premeditated terrorism. Pragmatic and moderate rabbis such as Tzi Tow, Shlomo Aviner, Yoel Ben Nun, Hanan Porat, Menachem Fruman, Yitzhak Shilat, and many others slowly created an atmosphere in which the term "underground" took on a pejorative connotation.[65] While a small number of Gush diehards such as Rabbis Dov Lior, Moshe Levinger, and Israel Ariel refused to reject settler vigilantism and unauthorized violence, the majority of the movement had gradually distanced themselves from the extremists. Special efforts were made to dissociate the movement from Kach and Rabbi Kahane.

Perhaps the most significant contribution to the struggle against Kahanism and unruly street violence had been made by the leaders of the two major parties, who decided in the summer of 1984 to form a national unity government. There were, to be sure, other and more important considerations leading to the creation of that unprecedented coalition—political reasons devoid of ulterior motives or the desire to fight Kahanism. But the effect of the unity coalition on the struggle against extremism was dramatic. By joining a government committed to ending the Lebanon War, Likud tacitly admitted the failure of the policy that had produced much of the internal violence in the early 1980s. And by its readiness to live with the de facto "creeping annexation" of the West Bank, engineered by Likud governments in the previous years, Labor gave partial legitimation to the large number of settlements established in Judea and Samaria in the previous years. Certainly not involved in an ideological love story, the new political alliance was now ready to take care of the violent extremists.

The most meaningful expression of the new determination to curb extremism was manifested in the anti-Kahanist struggle of Israel's education ministry. Focused on an "education for democracy," the campaign involved hundreds of instructors and tens of thousands of instruction hours. Some of the ideas developed in the state education system were later used by the IDF's chief education officer, who introduced them to the army.[66] The jubilant Kahane, who had expected to thrive under his Knesset immunity, was soon surprised by a special Knesset resolution. Israeli police were authorized by the house to prevent Kahane's provocative visits to Arab villages, considered by movement members their most effective weapon. Acting against the adamant refusal of the rabbi to play by the Israeli rules, the Knesset further amended its Basic Law, stipulating that parties involved in racist incitement and evident antidemocratic practices and ideas could not run for national elections. This dramatic amendment proved in 1988 to be a decisive blow to Kach and Rabbi Kahane. Israel's 1988 elections were conducted under the dark shadow of the Palestinian uprising in Judea and Samaria, a series of events potentially the most "helpful" for the anti-Palestinian Kahane. But the excited rabbi, who had good reason to believe he could triple his Knesset representation, could not run. Kach's appeal to the Supreme Court was rejected by a unanimous court decision.[67] The disqualification of Kach brutally returned the party to its marginal condition of the 1970s, and all Kahane's efforts to challenge the government in the streets ended in failure. At the time of his New

York City assassination, on November 5, 1990, by a Muslim fundamentalist, Kahane was a marginal figure with little national appeal.

While the containment of violence and extremism had become increasingly effective during the second half of the 1980s, it was still incomplete. The 1987 outbreak of the Intifada put many settlers in life-threatening situations and led to a number of local retaliations. Hard-line Gush Emunim activists such as movement Secretary General Daniella Weiss and Guru Moshe Levinger were still involved in occasional confrontations with the Arabs and, inevitably, with the army.[68] Kahane's supporters were busy operating their aggressive Committee for Road Safety. And single events such as the armed attack on civilian Arabs by students of Nablus's Tomb of Yoseph Yeshiva still took place.[69] But given the intensity of the Palestinian uprising and its threat to the very existence of the settlers, these were surprisingly mild developments. Israel's most aggressive extremists were effectively contained. An imaginative Kach challenge idea, the symbolic formation of an alternative Jewish state, the Free State of Judea, to be concretely established on the West Bank after its expected evacuation by the government of Israel, failed miserably.[70] The police raided the offices of the "Free State," confiscated its documents, and put the designated "heads" of its future army through an excruciating investigation. Surprised and unprepared, the architects of the new venture learned to their great dismay that even symbolic delegitimation had become hard to practice.

7

AFTER OSLO

The Crisis of the Israeli Radical Right

The Continued Deradicalization of Gush Emunim Settlers

Israel's 1992 elections dealt a huge blow to the nation's nationalist right. The Eretz Israel camp, which ran for the elections with eight(!) separate party lists—Likud, Tehiya, Moledet, Tzomet, the National Religious Party (NRP), and three single-person lists (Rabbi Moshe Levinger, Yitzhak Modai and Eliezer Mizrahi)—faired poorly. Dominating the Knesset with 44 seats, Rabin's Labor became the nation's largest party. Together with Meretz's 12 seats and 5 Arab representatives, Labor easily established a stable government coalition of 61. While Likud Knesset representation was reduced to 32, Tehiya, Israel's first radical right party, failed to get any of its members elected. Rabbi Levinger, who decided at the last moment to split the radical camp and run with a party of his own, also lost, as did Modai and Mizrahi. The 16 Knesset seats, won by Tzomet, Moledet, and the NRP, were inadequate for the purpose of forming a right-wing coalition and held little political influence.[1]

The right's defeat unexpectedly led to the continued deradicalization of the settlers and Gush Emunim. This development appeared to defy Israel's political logic. Given the peace platform of the newly elected government and its commitment to pursue territorial compromise, one would have expected the radical right to return to its old extraparliamentary tactics and launch an intense anti-Rabin campaign. A government decision to stop the settlement process in Judea and Samaria and freeze all settlement subsidies had always been considered in radical right circles as a casus belli. One would have consequently expected veteran Gush Emunim extremists to remove the more pragmatic operators of Yesha Council and take over the settlement movement. Given the lessons of the 1982 Sinai withdrawal—that the settlers should not postpone the fight until the final moments of evacuation—this development was theoretically likely.

The expected takeover by old warriors such as Rabbi Levinger, Elon Moreh's Benny Katzover, and Kedumim's Daniela Weiss never took place. The extremists were, on the contrary, marginalized and silenced. Held responsible for the great defeat, through splitting the camp and unwittingly helping the left win the elections, they were brutally pushed aside. Rabbi Levinger's hapless campaign to get elected cost him personally very dearly; the leading Gush Emunim settler was informally excommunicated. No one was ready to listen to him or buy his excuses, and Levinger shut himself up in his Hebron house. Daniela Weiss, Levinger's most loyal follower, had no better luck. The Gush Emunim Secretariat, an irrelevant body kept alive only out of respect for Levinger, was finally allowed to die. Benny Katzover, the movement's most charismatic field activist in the 1970s and 1980s, did not even try to get reelected as Samaria's regional head, a position he personally established in the early 1980s. Katzover, not yet fifty, was forced into early retirement.

An additional setback for Gush Emunim extremists was the premature death of Rabbi Yehuda Hazani, head of Mate Ma'amatz (Effort Center). Mate Ma'amatz was for years a one-man ad hoc organization that kept alive the charismatic and extraparliamentary era of the settler movement. Hazani, Ma'amatz's central figure, was a sworn Levinger loyalist who refused to desert the rabbi after the electoral defeat. Hazani's great virtue was his ability to personally bridge the widening gap between the nationalist yeshivas and the settlers and to get the two sides to engage occasionally in extraparliamentary action. Hazani was responsible for the organization and logistics of a large number of protest operations against the Shamir and

Rabin governments. Settler leaders, increasingly unhappy with the tactics of confrontation, had been repeatedly disarmed by the man's genuine enthusiasm and personal association with the legacy of Gush Emunim. Mate Ma'amatz withered in 1993 when Hazani perished after falling off a cliff while hiking in the Judean desert.

Apart from the radical right's shocking electoral defeat, there were three reasons for the deradicalization of Gush Emunim: the "materialization" of the settler community in the 1980s, the rise to power of the "technocrats" of the movement, and the decline of charismatic religious leadership. British writer G.K. Chesterton did not coin his famous phrase, "nothing fails like success," as an account of Israel's settler situation, but it tells well the story of the Gush Emunim community. The settlers had met with great success in establishing a viable community in the West Bank, replete with beautiful settlements and comfortable homes. Many of these settlements were nearly as luxurious as the suburbs of Tel Aviv or Jerusalem, with schools, community centers, and culture and sports facilities far beyond the reach of most Israelis. While these accomplishments gave the settlers a sense of permanence and stability, they had slowly reduced their old combative, anti-establishment spirit. Once lean youth of the 1970s, who fooled and outmaneuvered the Israeli army in the hills of Judea and Samaria, the settlers became in the 1990s the heads of large upper-middle-class families. They had plenty to lose and showed no interest in either fighting the government or following their old warring leaders into the streets. Content with their lot, they believed that they had accomplished Gush Emunim's goal of settling Eretz Israel and that no force on Earth was capable of removing them. While remaining loyal to the original symbols of the movement and occasionally ready to demonstrate for worthy causes, they were hardly available for intense extremist action. In short, the settlers had become soft.

The "bourgeoisification" of Gush Emunim was reinforced by the rise to power of new pragmatic and technocratic movement leaders who were well suited to the new atmosphere of business as usual. This pragmatization, which had begun in the late 1970s, led in the 1990s to the rise of local and regional leaders who cared little about theology or ideology. Frequently seen in the Knesset corridors, these able technocrats were mostly interested in worldly matters and concrete achievements. With upper-middle-class communities to care for, these individuals—increasingly seen and heard in Yesha Council and Amana—were more excited by development budgets and housing projects than by Eretz Israel pep talk. The new pragmatic style was undoubtedly enhanced by the peace of mind provided by continued Likud leadership of the government, especially during Shamir's narrow coalition from 1990 to 1992. But the effects of this technocracy on the settler community were to be felt for many years after Shamir.

A third process encouraging the trends identified above was the decline of Gush Emunim's religious leadership. Since the 1982 death of Rabbi Zvi Yehuda Kook, the legendary head of Merkaz ha-Rav, his yeshiva's political profile steadily shrunk. Merkaz ha-Rav's interaction with Gush settlers, especially through their rabbis, had not been terminated, but the yeshiva's heads, Rabbis Abraham Shapira, Tzvi Taw, and Shaul Yisraeli, showed more interest in Torah education than in politics. Many other nationalist yeshivas followed this model, with an intensifying interest in an ultra-Orthodox rather than an ultranationalist orientation.[2] The combined effect of the three moderating processes was that Gush Emunim became ill equipped to seriously challenge the newly elected Labor government.

The most concrete expression of the decline of Gush Emunim's radicalism involved two new organizations increasingly visible after the elections, Emunim Movement and the Council of Yesha's Rabbis. Emunim Movement—not to be confused with Gush Emunim—was formed after the 1992 debacle and Rabbi Levinger's fall. The purpose of the new organization was to revive the lost spirit of Gush Emunim. The key person in the new organization was Rabbi Benny Elon, a young Beit El settler and head of Yeshivat Orot (Lights), a new yeshiva built in East Jerusalem between Mount Scopus and the Mount of Olives. The purpose of the new movement was to return to Gush Emunim's original 1974 objective of spiritually transforming the nation. Speaking about his new organization, Elon reiterated a movement adage that Gush Emunim "succeeded to settle Judea and Samaria but failed to settle in the hearts of most Israelis." The failure to change public opinion was, according to Elon, the main lesson of the 1992 electoral debacle. It stemmed from Gush Emunim's refusal to cross the Green Line into Israel proper and to invest its energy in massive national education. The hard core of Eretz Israel loyalists became, according to Emunim's leader, so focused on their day-to-day concerns in the settlements that they selfishly deserted their more important calling—the spiritual transformation of the Israeli people.[3]

Elon's idea, advertised aggressively by the new movement, was to cross the Green Line and launch a massive campaign of reawakening. The campaign's targets were what Emunim characterized as the decadent culture and defeatist politics represented by the Labor government. The early months of the new movement were very promising. Elon and his followers raised significant amounts of money and launched their "We Do Not Stop at [the] Green [Line]," campaign. They organized public symposia and Eretz Israel conferences and were especially effective at attracting people to small home meetings. Given the interest of Rabin's government in a negotiated peace with the Syrians, which was bound to involve a retreat from the Golan Heights, Emunim Movement joined the Golan settlers, already in the first stages of their antigovernment struggle.[4] This they did despite significant cultural differences between the secular Golan settlers and their own intense Orthodoxy. The struggle of the Golan settlers was very popular, and active participation in its propagation was politically very useful. Emunim Movement also demonstrated against Arab terrorism and was very involved in the intensifying national debate over the absorption of Soviet immigration, which they greatly supported.

The fly in the ointment of the new movement, which was gaining plenty of media attention, was neither shortage of money nor lack of prestigious supporters. Missing was the genuine excitement of tens of thousands of well to-do settlers, who seemed to be unwilling to return to their boy scouting years. Despite his great enthusiasm, Elon was unable to mobilize mass support or participation. Sensing this settler conservatism and troubled by the excessive publicity of the ambitious rabbi, Yesha heads started quietly to undermine Elon.[5] Suddenly, Elon encountered fund-raising difficulties. The rabbi was quietly informed that his efforts were diverting funds away from the settlements and that he was damaging the larger cause. Respected movement figures, who first agreed to endorse Elon, now quietly rescinded their support. In addition to his troubles with the pragmatic heads of Gush Emunim, Elon was also let down by many of the movement's rabbis. Having little respect for his scholarly accomplishments or rabbinical virtues, these rabbis were increasingly reluctant to crown the young man as their political head. Elon's substantive arguments—about the premature decline of the movement and its docility—fell on deaf ears. A little over a year after its highly advertised and audacious initiation, Emunim Movement ceased to exist.

The Council of Yesha Rabbis was formed in 1990, during the peak of the Intifada, to answer critical questions involving settler responses to Palestinian violence. The leading council rabbis—Shlomo Aviner, head of Ateret Cohanim yeshiva; Eliezer Melamed, from Beit El; and Elyakim Levanon, from Elon Moreh—had never been political types. In fact, they were involved in reducing the movement's political profile. The lack of a rabbinical authority, a supreme guide for all movement settlers, brought these rather shy local rabbis into the fray. They formed the Yesha Rabbinical Council with almost no money or public relations effort. Never defining the new body as a "movement" or an instrument for political mobilization, the founders agreed only to answer pressing questions collectively. The council's contribution to the settler discourse, a monthly four-page newsletter on religious topics, provided specific answers to questions on matters of public concern, with great emphasis on Intifada-related issues.

The 1992 elections, which returned Labor to power, had a very small impact on the Council of Yesha's Rabbis. Its rulings had demonstrated neither rabbinical defiance nor a desire to delegitimize the government theologically. In a response to questions about the danger of the new government's "rolling back the momentum of our Land's settlement," and about the desirability of intense antigovernment operations and extralegal settlement, the rabbis stated:

> God forbid! We are more loyal to the law than anybody else. Everybody with open eyes will see that extralegal actions are only going to damage our entire [settlement] edifice. Instead of fighting against the government, it is wiser to join it, settle there [in specific areas approved by the government for settlement] hundreds of thousands of Jews and establish large cities. The Jordan

> Valley [an area long approved for settlement by Labor ideologues] is a part of Eretz Israel too.[6]

Elyakim Ha'etzni, a leading secular extremist, was shocked by the rabbis' answer. Responding in an article in the settler journal *Nekuda*, Ha'etzni maintained that the rabbinical council " is detached from reality," He continued: "The prognosis is bad because you, Yesha rabbis, disarm Eretz Israel loyalists, fool them, put them to sleep and surrender them, powerless, to their mortal enemies."[7]

Radicalization at the Fringes: Chai Ve-Kayam and the Struggle Center to Stop the Autonomy Plan

While the deradicalization of Gush Emunim was the dominant trend within the Israeli extreme right, it was not the only noticeable trend. Several extremist elements within this camp moved, in fact, in the opposite direction. These included the followers of the slain Rabbi Kahane and two small organizations closer to the Gush Emunim milieu—Chai Ve-Kayam and the Struggle Center to Stop the Autonomy Plan. Both organizations challenged the settlers' complacency and tried to alert the extreme right to the gathering storm. Their leaders also expanded upon the previous understanding of civil disobedience within the extreme right.

Chai Ve-Kayam (Alive and Existing) was established by Yehuda Etzion, the ideologue of the Jewish Underground of the 1980s and the father of the Dome of the Rock demolition plan. Since his arrest in 1984, Etzion had advocated the formation of the "Salvation Movement," a revitalization organization that would replace the decaying Gush Emunim and sever all spiritual relations with the state of Israel. Etzion's ideas implied a rejection of Gush Emunim, just as they expressed a conflict of legitimacy with the Israeli state. The sanctification of secular Zionism and the state of Israel, which marked the early stages of the Gush, was no longer tenable in Etzion's eyes. The failure of the state—already secure and strong—to become Jewish, redeem the land, assert authority against the Arabs, and start building the Third Temple made it illegitimate.[8] According to Etzion, Gush Emunim had failed to understand that the process of redemption had been slowed down by God owing to the secular peace agenda of the Israeli government. So after serving seven years in prison for his role in plotting the Dome of the Rock explosion, Etzion established Chai Ve-Kayam.

The only difference between the Etzion of the Jewish Underground and the Etzion of Chai Ve-Kayam was his conviction that there was no longer room for violence in the 1990s. Etzion, who refused to apologize for the terrorist acts of the underground, never said he was opposed to violence. He admitted, however, that the failed experience of the underground demonstrated the futility of employing violent tactics before the people of Israel were mentally prepared for redemption. The formation of a large revival movement, devoted to preparing Israelis for that day, became Etzion's calling.[9] It was therefore not surprising that Chai Ve-Kayam's first act was to draft an alternative version of Israel's Declaration of Independence. Etzion and his group stripped Israel's revered constitutional charter of the logic of democracy, equality, and human rights and substituted the Bible, Jewish legislation, and the Kingdom of Israel. Unlike many religious Jews, who would have Israel adopt the Halakha—with all its Diaspora connotations—Etzion never speaks of a Halakha state. His is a peculiar form of ultranationalism that associates redemption with the reestablishment of the ancient Kingdom of David.

While neither engaging in violence against the Palestinians nor physically confronting the Israeli security forces, Chai Ve-Kayam activists (whose number never exceeded three dozen) raised the level of antigovernment resistance through incessant efforts to pray as a group on the Temple Mount, an act prohibited by law. Their devotion to the site of ancient Israel's temples has led to many arrests and house detentions of Chai Ve-Kayam members. And it has kept the tensions high at the Temple Mount. By calling upon the settler community—depicted as "betrayed" by the Israeli government—to dissociate themselves from state institutions and to stop paying taxes, Chai Ve-Kayam also contributed to the spread of civil disobedience as a strategy among the settler community. In a short document they call Chai Ve-Kayam's "Identity Card," Etzion wrote,

• We ask every citizen this question: Do you know that your money—taxes and other government tolls—now go toward the establishment of a

PLO state in the middle of your country? Isn't this the time for civil disobedience and refusal to pay taxes to the government which has betrayed the nation's objectives? You must to choose between loyalty to a misguided government and loyalty to your people, God and the Eternity of Israel.

- We ask every civil servant this question: will you cooperate, because of your "legal duties," with a government collaborating with the PLO? Will you join the effort to establish an enemy state? Will you, in order to make a living, join the terrible sinful acts of the leadership? You must choose between loyalty to a misguided government and loyalty to your people, God and the Eternity of Israel.
- Even 120 Knesset members—as well as elections or referenda—cannot change the people's truth. The Eternity of Israel does not lie because He is not a human being. The land is a bequest for the people and its generations. It is a trust in our hands, which one generation does not have the authority to desert and destroy.[10]

The active participation of radical figures such as Rabbi Yitzhak Ginzburg, the head of the extremist Tomb of Yoseph Yeshiva in Nablus, known for sanctioning attacks on civilian Palestinians, foretold Chai Ve-Kayam's potential for extremism and violence.

The Struggle Center to Stop the Autonomy Plan was established in 1991 by Kiryat Arba attorney Elyakim Ha'etzni.[11] It was formed out of Ha'etzni's fear that the government, now headed for the Madrid International Conference, would offer the Palestinians a generous self-rule plan in the West Bank and Gaza. The notion of Palestinian autonomy, first conceptualized by Menachem Begin at Camp David and now renewed by Prime Minister Yitzhak Shamir, was for years Ha'etzni's nightmare. A leading extreme right activist since 1968, Ha'etzni had become convinced that a Palestinian autonomy would inevitably contain the seeds of a Palestinian state and bring an end to the Jewish presence in the occupied territories. Had the occupied territories been annexed to Israel, Ha'etzni would have been less wary of a Palestinian autonomy; without official annexation, in his eyes, disaster was not far off.[12] Ha'etzni's primarily personal struggle played a significant role in the decision of the small right-wing parties, Moledet and Tehiya, to part ways with Yitzhak Shamir, who tried in vain to convince his radical colleagues that he did not intend to implement autonomy and was using the idea only to buy time. Moledet and Tehiya were unimpressed. Refusing to be party to a government that would negotiate a Palestinian entity, the two groups became instrumental in pushing for early elections—a campaign that, a few months later, would prove enormously damaging to their own cause.

After the 1992 Labor victory, Ha'etzni revived the Struggle Center to Stop the Autonomy Plan. He was certain that the newly elected Rabin government would return to the autonomy idea, this time for real. He believed, moreover, that Rabin's autonomy plan would be only a temporary stage on the way to a Labor-negotiated blueprint for a Palestinian state. Fully cognizant of the deradicalization of Gush Emunim and of the government's interest in keeping the settlers at bay, the Kiryat Arba attorney decided to launch an aggressive anti-Labor campaign on his own. While the official target of the Struggle Center was the government, it was the settlers about whom Ha'etzni worried the most. The veteran activist knew that no national opposition to a deal with the Palestinians would be possible without settler mobilization in Judea and Samaria. But to Ha'etzni's chagrin, there were few indications that his message was getting across.

Elyakim Ha'etzni was the first to introduce the language of personal delegitimation into the struggle dictionary of the radical right. As early as 1985, he threatened Prime Minister Shimon Peres with a death sentence for considering the idea of an international peace conference. The threat was made through an analogy to France's Vichy regime and the personality of Marshal Philippe Pétain. Pétain, Ha'etzni reminded Peres, was France's duly elected prime minister in 1940. His decision to surrender and collaborate with the invading Germans was fully legal. Yet after the war, Pétain was sentenced to death for betraying the nation. Only his old age and past heroism led General Charles de Gaulle, France's president, to commute the sentence to life in prison.[13]

Ha'etzni's repeated use of the Pétain analogy was not, however, his primary tactic. Since 1992 he had devoted most of his intellectual energy to the development of a settler version of civil disobedience. Though not particularly original, the attorney's civil disobedience theory responded to the difficulty of devoted secular extremists in identifying with the arguments of the rabbis.

Ha'etzni's justification of civil disobedience starts with the universal proposition that Western civilization has always recognized limits on citizens' obligation to obey human laws. Eminent thinkers from Socrates to Gandhi and Martin Luther King Jr. argued that above the law of every state are higher principles of justice, religion, or natural law that make disobedience legitimate and sometimes obligatory. While Socrates associated disobedience with the right to engage in a free philosophical discourse and to educate the young, Henry David Thoreau placed the limit on slavery and lack of human freedom. Charles de Gaulle, in a case analogous to that of Israel, refused to go along with the surrender of homeland territories to the enemy. Martin Luther King Jr. believed that the inhumanity of racial segregation fully justified civil disobedience. Even members of Israel's Yesh Gvul (There Is a Limit!—a left-wing group active since the 1982 Lebanon War) argued that military service in the occupied territories violated their beliefs and justified disobedience to the law.[14]

Drawing on all these precedents, Ha'etzni asked his readers, friends and foes alike, to respect the right of the settlers to disobey orders involving the surrender of Eretz Israel territories. Israel's settlers, he warned, would refuse to evacuate their settlements despite any agreement the government might conclude with the Palestinians. Had Elyakim Ha'etzni been a preacher or a rigorous moral philosopher, he might have been successful in producing the first Israeli theory of civil disobedience. But the militant maverick from Kiryat Arba had never really been interested in the *moral* nature of the famous tactic—which had led many of its historical adherents to stress *passive* struggle and personal readiness to pay. A close reading of Ha'etzni's essays suggests that his interest was mainly in triggering a massive rebellion against the Labor government, and that the rhetoric of civil disobedience was only a disguise. Ha'etzni's interpretation of civil disobedience had never paid attention to the Palestinian side of the dilemma or considered the plight of people who never chose to live as second-class citizens under Israeli occupation. Ha'etzni failed to notice that civil disobedience theories were developed by the poor and the powerless, usually against oppressive governments—not by mighty colonizers committed to the sacred Land of Israel as if no people had lived there for generations. What Ha'etzni had in mind was not an ethical theory of disobedience but an instrument of popular mobilization that would appeal to educated settlers and legitimize efforts to bring down the government in the streets.

> Of all the struggle steps, imprisonment will be the most critical. The *shnor machine*, representing among Diaspora Jews a deviant and rotten establishment, will stop functioning, for nobody will be ready to contribute and invest in a government persecuting its people.
>
> The devotion radiated by tens of thousands of settlers and supporters—all those accused of having come [to the occupied territories] in order to build "red roofs [a reference to the cozy life of the settlers]" at the expense of the nation's development towns—will bring back to Eretz Israel's camp all those masses of people who left it out of their disenchantment with Likud's corruption.
>
> A process [of disobedience] will feed into an internal process of alienation of the people of Israel from the government, will intensify . . . the message of the demonstrators, rioters, Sabbath strikers, individuals who block the roads, founders of settlements on lands owned by the Palestinian land authority, those who put barbed wires around these lands before their return to the enemy, the jailed, the sentenced, the locked.
>
> This will be the day when this alien government will collapse and a new dawn sheds light on a new Israel, a better Israel, pure and untarnished.[15]

Both Yehuda Etzion and Elyakim Ha'etzni would have liked the status quo of 1992 to remain unchanged. Convinced, however, that the worst was yet to come, they did their best to agitate the settlers and prepare them for acts of government treason. Marginalized by the pragmatists, who did not wish to listen, they knew their time was coming soon.

After Oslo: The Struggle Patterns of Gush Emunim and the Yesha Council

The Oslo Accords, made public in September 1993 and welcomed by the majority of Israelis, stunned Gush Emunim and the heads of the Yesha

Council. As experienced in setbacks as they had become over the years, none of them expected Yitzhak Rabin, Israel's Mr. Security, to recognize the PLO and approve a far-reaching autonomy plan. The settlers' devotion to their cause led them to believe that the Israeli people would never approve of Arafat's "terror organization" and would stop the government in the streets. The positive response of most Israelis to the agreement and their fascination with the Rabin-Arafat handshake on the White House lawn doubled the settlers' shock.

The approval of the Oslo Accords by the nation's majority seems to explain the initial mild response of the Yesha Council to the new reality and its great hesitancy to launch an immediate struggle. A virulent demonstration against the agreement, held on September 7 in Jerusalem, gained the participation of nearly two hundred thousand disgruntled Israelis. This impressive showing had no meaningful follow-up, however. A series of demonstrations in front of the Knesset protesting the official ratification of the accords looked more like a big picnic than a proper answer to a looming disaster.

Unable to put together a popular and effective street struggle, the Yesha Council resorted to a costly public relations campaign based on the slogan *Yesha Ze Kan*—Yesha (Judea and Samaria) Is Here. Launched within the Green Line, the campaign was conducted through thousands of bumper stickers, large street posters, and media advertisement. It tried to convince Israel's citizens that Judea and Samaria, rarely visited by ordinary Israelis since the outbreak of the Palestinian uprising, were close to home and essential for the protection of Israel proper. In addition to this message that Yesha's security was Israel's security—the campaign appealed to the nation's brotherly sentiments. The real message, driven home to hundreds of thousands of Israelis, was, "do not forsake us!"

The sluggish settler struggle caught fire via an unwelcome but highly expected stimulation, Islamic terrorism. Oslo's grace period, which lasted fewer than two months, ended abruptly in late October. A few squads of Muslim terrorists—mostly associated with Hamas and Islamic Jihad—attacked and killed a number of settlers, soldiers, and Israeli civilians, igniting the settler community at once. Triggering an immediate radicalization of the Yesha Council heads, the outbreak of Muslim terrorism led to a "Jewish Intifada," a settler mini-insurrection consisting of a series of attacks on Arab transportation, stoning and destroying hundreds of cars, tire burning, roadblocks, property damage, and even killing.

The event leading to the Jewish Intifada was the ruthless murder of Chaim Mizrahi, a Beit El settler burnt alive by his Palestinian attackers. Settler fury over this atrocity, coupled with accumulated frustration, led to an especially aggressive response. Hundreds of Jews ravaged Arab villages, destroying property and attacking individual Palestinians. Yesha heads, after learning that the Mizrahi murder had been carried out by a Palestinian group belonging to Yasser Arafat's Fatah organization, claimed the government was directly responsible for the murder. Frightened by the prospect of new terrorism, they made a public commitment to fight Palestinian militants with or without governmental approval. A few days after the bloody reaction to the Beit El murder, hundreds of settlers took to the roads during morning rush hour and brought all Arab traffic to a standstill. After a promise from the military commander in the area that the army would act aggressively against terrorists, the settlers agreed to evacuate—but not before declaring their intention to repeat the action in the future. Members of Yesha's moderate rabbinical council subsequently ruled that shooting Palestinian attackers and their collaborators was legitimate. And religious followers of these rabbis were told that no legal barriers should stop them from pursuing their interests.[16]

The settler radicalization, culminating in Yesha Council's decision to use all nonviolent means at its disposal to bring the government down, was further intensified by a new series of killings. A lethal Arab ambush near Hebron led to the murder of Ephraim Ayubi, Rabbi Chaim Drukman's driver. Drukman, a revered rabbinical authority and Gush Emunim founder, somehow survived the attack. The wave of terror peaked in January 1994 with the Kiryat Arba murder of Pinchas Lapid and his yeshiva student son, Shalom. Lapid, a longtime refusnik from the Soviet Union, who finally came to Israel in the early 1970s, was an exemplary figure within the settler movement. A member of the original Elon Moreh group, husband of the popular political militant Miriam Lapid, and father of eleven children, Lapid was a settler legend. The government was virtually powerless to control the emotional eruption of the settler community—especially the irate residents of Hebron and Kiryat Arba.

Hamas's terror campaign, resumed in October and November, created deep fears among the settlers. The prospect of an impending Palestinian autonomy and Palestinian police force convinced the Jewish residents of Judea and Samaria—who had always believed that all Palestinians were terrorists—that terrorism would now be officially recognized by the Rabin government. This led to a hysterical public relations campaign based on the slogan Do Not Give Them Guns. The people of Israel were warned—with ominous posters plastered throughout the country—that thousands of guns, freely handed to the Palestinian police, constituted the liberation and arming of thousands of terrorists. Settler and radical right leaders insisted that if they were to be stopped by armed Palestinian policemen, they would shoot to kill. A plan to create a vigilante settler militia, Hashomer (Watchman), was also unveiled. (Israelis with long memories recalled that the name of the first self-defense organization of the Jewish community in Palestine, a legendary underground organization formed in 1907, was also Hashomer.)

The most significant effects of the terrorist campaign on the settler community was the return of the extremists to politics and the introduction of the language of delegitimation vis-à-vis the Rabin government. Apart from Kahane's followers, who are discussed bellow, two groups were now gaining momentum at the expense of the more restrained Yesha Council: Mate Ma'amatz (Effort Center) and Ha'etzni's Struggle Center to Stop the Autonomy Plan. Mate Ma'amatz, defunct since Rabbi Hazani's death, was now revived under Yitzhak Novik, another Levinger devotee. Inspired by the government's "betrayal" of Eretz Israel and by its inability to defeat Palestinian terrorism, Mate Ma'amatz activists began to recruit yeshiva students for rioting. Ma'amatz's activists were responsible for posters depicting Yitzhak Rabin's face in Yasser Arafat's *kefiya* headdress and labeling the prime minister "traitor!" Soon the titles "assassin" and "murderer" were added and emblazoned on huge banners.

The wave of terror was especially helpful for Elyakim Ha'etzni, the Kiryat Arba attorney. His catastrophic warnings against the coming settler disaster, which had been largely ignored, became more influential in January 1994. More frustrated settlers began to listen to Ha'etzni's appeals and to heed his call to launch a project of political opposition capable of bringing down the government.

> A people whose government committed an act of national treason, collaborated with a terrorist enemy to steal the heart of his homeland, gave this enemy tens of thousands of guns—aimed directly at the heart of its sons and daughters—must be ready to fight. And in this war as in every other war there are risks and casualties. If we do not fight in 1994, no miracle will occur and the year will be as cursed as the previous one.
>
> Rise up and do it! We have done nothing. Protests, demonstrations, "tent cities," even setting roadblocks are insufficient acts against a government conducting national treason. In France, defeated in 1940, when Marshal Pétain gave in to Hitler and made an alliance with him—just as Lieutenant General Rabin did by shaking Yasser Arafat's dirty hand—de Gaulle did not demonstrate in protest. Although the regime was born in a democratic way.... He deserted, rebelled against a Nazi collaborating army.
>
> This is why I am saying it loud and clear: an IDF soldier, though Jewish, who would pull us, our wives, our children and grandchildren from our houses and make us refugees—will, in our view, be conducting a pogrom. We shall look upon him as a violent thug acting like a Cossack. It is no secret that all through Israel's glorious history there were dark and shameful chapters in which Jews beat, tortured, gave in and even put their brothers to death, and leaders led their followers to disaster.[17]

While the more pragmatic Yesha Council did not lose its organizational hold over the settler struggle against the Oslo Accords, it was Mate Ma'amatz and the Struggle Center to Stop the Autonomy Plan that gradually began to dictate the rhetoric of the campaign. Ha'etzni's anti-Rabin posters, increasingly seen in right-wing demonstrations, were even more vitriolic than his *Nekuda* articles. The most nefarious of these posters depicted Rabin as an unsavory Arab, smiling at Arafat and washing his hands in blood. The poster's text associated the prime minister with Palestinian terrorism and assigned him direct responsibility for Jews killed by Hamas violence. And Ha'etzni, although the central figure in the Struggle Center and directly responsible for the organization's style, was not alone. A number of distinguished right-wing individuals declared their support for the organization, not the least among them Colonel (res.) Shlomo Baum, a recognized Israeli war hero of the 1950s. Little effort was made by the Yesha Council to limit the virulence of Ha'etzni's propaganda material. Thousands of copies of the posters were handed to all participants in Yesha antigovernment demonstrations.

After the Rabbi's Assassination: Kahane's Followers Reorganize

The followers of Rabbi Kahane and the hard core of Kach did not share the moderation and pragmatization undergone by the settler community in the 1980s. The Kahanists, who never developed a middle-class mentality, had long wished for total confrontation with the Arabs and believed in the morality of Jewish violence. They needed neither Yehuda Etzion to preach the illegitimacy of the secular state nor Elyakim Ha'etzni to justify the use of civil disobedience. The questions the followers of Rabbi Kahane had to answer, especially after the November 1990 slaying of their rabbi in New York City, were of a more existential nature: would the Kach movement, for a long time a one-man show, survive the death of its leader? Would it maintain its national appeal, partially achieved after years of hard political work by the indefatigable rabbi?

Yes and no. Kahane's assassination on November 5, 1990, by a member of a Muslim fundamentalist ring in New Jersey, dealt the movement a huge blow. Kach lost its national influence and appeal and has been unable to regain it since. The assassination failed, however, to eliminate the militant inner core of the movement. The extremist rabbi, who failed to establish in his lifetime even a single Kach settlement, managed, nevertheless, to form in Kiryat Arba a critical mass of followers capable of carrying on his ideas after his death. The movement's young leaders, most of them in their twenties and thirties, preserved the legacy of the rabbi and rebuilt a movement of dozens of committed activists and a few hundred supporters. They kept alive the key institutions of Kach as well as several of its operational arms. The continued friction with the Palestinians, greatly intensified during the Intifada, proved again to these young people the validity of Kahane's message about the need to confront Gentile violence by Jewish force. Kahanism, they had come to believe, was not simply an abstract philosophy or a lofty ideology but a way of life. Like their slain rabbi, the Kahanists were convinced that nobody but themselves could demonstrate this truth to the "disoriented" Israeli nation.

Since there were few ideological differences among Kahane's disciples, the issue that gripped the small movement in the aftermath of the assassination was the question of succession. The surprising election of Rabbi Abraham Toledano, a computer engineer and instructor in Kahane's Jewish Idea Yeshiva, in March 1991, did not resolve the internal tension. A small group of activists, with a strong concentration of former American members of the Jewish Defense League, left Kach and established Kahane Chai (Kahane Lives). Centered in the Samarian settlement of Tapuach, Kahane Chai was led by the rabbi's youngest son, Benjamin.

The official rationale for the split, which catapulted the young and inexperienced Benjamin Kahane into a leadership position, was Kach's failure to remain loyal to the legacy of the dead rabbi. The betrayal of the rabbi was allegedly epitomized by Kach's decision to seek to qualify for the 1992 Israeli elections. Given the contours of the 1985 law barring racist and nondemocratic parties from participating in national elections, Kach's attempt to get on the ballot required changes in its platform—changes seen as unacceptable compromises by Benjamin Kahane and his friends. Young Kahane's followers maintained that even the slightest change in Kach's platform desecrated the name of the holy rabbi. When Israel's Supreme Court denied Kach's petition to participate in the elections, it became clear that the alterations in the party's platform were purely cosmetic. In reality there was little difference between the two movements. The unstated reason for the split was personal; a few American immigrant activists, headed by Mike Gozofsky, simply refused to accept the leadership of a Moroccan rabbi. Rabbi Toledano, an unknown factor, had never been selected by the slain rabbi as his potential successor.

Kahane Chai met with little success and made little difference. The group failed to match even the size and influence of its parent organization. But it did manage to create an extremely violent Kahanist concentration in Samaria and a handful of activists in Jerusalem. In November 1992, on the second anniversary of Kahane's assassination, two Kahane Chai yeshiva students threw a hand grenade into Old Jerusalem's Butchers Market. Two Palestinians were killed and seven wounded. The eventual capture of the perpetrators, after a year of investigation, sent a stern message to the inexperienced activists. Kahane Chai members learned that they were not immune to the laws of Israel; and they saw that Jewish terrorism carried a high cost.

Rabbi Toledano did not remain Kach's head for long. Less than a year after his election, he resigned amid accusations that several key members had failed him and would not let him reform and reorganize the movement. The 1991 split, along with Toledano's ensuing resignation, uncovered a group of emergent activists who were becoming the movers and shakers of Kach. The extremists involved—Baruch Marzel, Tiran Pollack, and Noam Federman, all Kiryat Arba residents—had no intention of sharing power with former American activists like Mike Gozofsky and David Axelrod. Nor did they like the ideas of Toledano, who sought to raise public respect for Kach and refrained from street hooliganism. The Kiryat Arba trio had propagated dozens of violent incidents and made its mark within the settler community with unceasing provocations.

Although Rabbi Toledano did not approve of the trio's tactics and sought to dispel his movement's reputation for militancy, he did not give up active Kahanism. In November 1993 Toledano was arrested in Ben-Gurion Airport. The police, acting on a tip, searched the rabbi, who was returning from a trip to the United States, and found a mass of military equipment in his baggage, gun silencers, sharpshooting telescopes, bomb-making instructions, parts of machine guns, and devices intended to hide traces of shooting. Despite this damning evidence, the police investigators were unable to prove that Toledano and his colleagues—teachers and students in the Western Wall Yeshiva—were planning an actual conspiracy. None of these investigators believed, however, that the equipment was imported for Halakhic reasons or for the educational program of the Orthodox yeshiva. They concluded that the military materials were intended for emergency use, when the movement would go underground. Toledano and a few friends were sentenced to several years in prison.

Kach's operational arm most involved in the Kahanist challenge to the government and the Oslo Accords was the Committee for Road Safety. This organization, formed in the mid-1980s by Kahane's Kiryat Arba followers, was the "Jewish response" to intensifying Arab violence, rock throwing, and tire burning on the roads of Judea and Samaria. The purpose of this vigilante committee, originally headed by Baruch Marzel and Shmuel Ben Yishai, was to provide protection for Jewish drivers in the Hebron–Kiryat Arba area. Citing the inability of Israel's army to guarantee safe passage for Jewish-owned vehicles, Kahane's people formed a volunteer force to fill the gap. Money for the new organization was raised abroad by Rabbi Kahane. The outbreak of the Intifada increased the demand for the committee's services and led to the expansion of its operations beyond the Hebron area. Committee volunteers were particularly instrumental in protecting Jewish mourners who sought to bury their relatives or visit their graves in East Jerusalem's Mount of Olives. The old Jewish cemetery on the mount had been nearly shut down by the Intifada. Only protected convoys could safely reach the ancient graveyard, a site sacred to Jews for its view of the Temple Mount and its role in the coming of the messiah. Jewish neighborhoods close to Palestinian-populated areas, and yeshivas provocatively erected in Jerusalem's Muslim quarter, also benefited from the committee's work.

Just as in other Kach efforts that started as self-defense vigilante projects but quickly became militant operations, the Committee for Road Safety did not adopt a defensive posture for long. Kach volunteers, who started by protecting Jewish drivers, soon moved on to armed ambushes and revenge raids into Palestinian neighborhoods. Following the arrest of Shmuel Ben Yishai, charged for illegal activities related to the "Free State of Judea," the young Tiran Pollack took over. Pollack had joined the movement a few years earlier, following the murder of two of his sisters in a Jerusalem bus explosion set off by a Palestinian terrorist. When Kach was disqualified for the 1992 elections, Pollack became further radicalized. The committee, Kach's symbol of defiance against the Labor government, was envisioned as the future police force of the Free State of Judea—an entity to be established in the event the leftist government were to evacuate the occupied territories. A drive to recruit additional volunteers followed and the circle of radical settlers widened. Committee members, having been treated with surprising leniency by the security forces, barely attempted to conceal their extralegal activities. Daring even to invite television crews to cover their training exercises, the activists graphically demonstrated their anti-Arab practices to the Israeli public. In a 1993 interview, granted by Kach leader Baruch Marzel, the committee's strategy was plainly spelled out: "We try to heat up the area in order to produce resistance to the Intifada. We move into densely populated Arab areas in order to create provocative contact and immediate Jewish response. We create plenty of friction spots and then solve the problem in our way."[18]

Though the Committee for Road Safety provided Jewish drivers in Judea and Samaria with additional protection, it also contributed to the intensification of Jewish vigilante violence. Committee members, who generally ignored the distinction between guilty and innocent Palestinians, launched ruthless revenge attacks in the Kasbah area and other Hebron neighborhoods. Aware of the risks involved in being caught by the army (when the local commanders did not turn a blind eye), the Kachniks made extraordinary use of electronic radio-wave scanners. The committee's scanners allowed their operators to know exactly where the army patrols were. This essential intelligence made it possible for committee volunteers to conduct instant raids on unprotected Arab neighborhoods and disappear before the army could respond. A typical raid involved two to three cars manned by five to eight committee volunteers. Having verified that the area was clear, the men would conduct lightning strikes against the local residents, turning over vegetable stalls, burning cars, trashing neighborhoods, and bashing bystanders. The committee's cars, usually pickup trucks or vans fortified by bullet-proof windows, came equipped with powerful searchlights and sophisticated communication devices. Armed with clubs, guns, tear gas, smoke grenades, and bullet-proof vests, members of the committee enjoyed free movement in their target neighborhoods. Fearing repercussions from police investigations, members restricted firearms use to intimidation or piercing holes in solar boilers atop Arab roofs. Such raids, which never took more than five to ten minutes, evaded the effective control of the Israeli police. Even if villagers under attack could remember the attackers' faces, it was hard to make reliable testimonies that would sustain the cross-examination of Israeli attorneys. And the fears of settler revenge further reduced the number of witnesses who came forward.

According to the heads of the Committee for Road Safety, nearly one thousand volunteers were recruited for their missions, a success enabled by the transition of the Intifada to terrorism in 1989. About 350 Kiryat Arba activists served as the committee's hard core, but other volunteers, including non-Kach members, made themselves available for occasional operations throughout Judea and Samaria.[19] In an interview granted in 1994, Pollack claimed that between 1992 and 1993 there was a dramatic increase in committee activities. and said further that the organization was involved in about five hundred incidents per year.

The followers of the slain Rabbi Kahane have always been on the fringe of the radical right, while the more pragmatic Yesha Council had distanced itself from extremism. But the dramatic eruption of Muslim terrorism at the end of 1993 and beginning of 1994 gradually pushed the militants to center stage. Nobody was better prepared for a Jewish Intifada than Kach and Kahane Chai. Their rhetoric and practice of violence suddenly appealed to a much larger number of settlers who had never shared their philosophy in the 1980s and early 1990s.

When Prophecy Fails: The Hebron Massacre in Perspective

How did religious messianic Jews respond to the theological crisis brought about by the Labor government and the Oslo peace accords? How did they square the reality of contemporary political events with their messianic belief in the irreversibility of the conquest of Judea and Samaria? Students of religious extremism have long examined the way fundamentalist and messianic movements react to events that contradict their predicted path of salvation. In his classic study, *When Prophecy Fails*, Leon Festinger argued that disconfirmation does not produce movement collapse but instead leads to reinvigorated activity, intensified proselytizing, and reinterpretation of salvation. Festinger showed that while individual believers may become disillusioned and fall into disbelief, messianic collectivities survive. Hyperactive religiosity and group support help members overcome the painful cognitive dissonance of disconfirmation.[20] In his examination of another aspect of the same problem, the relationship between unfulfilled messianism and terrorism, David Rapoport argues that an expectation for imminent salvation and the danger of its disconfirmation may push true believers to catastrophic terrorist acts. In their messianic frenzy they may either try to "blackmail" God, through suicide runs, into keeping His original salvation plan, or prove to Him through extreme acts that His most dedicated servants do not deserve desertion.[21] Following Festinger and Rapoport, it appears that three courses of potential action are available to messianic fundamentalists who face unequivocal disconfirmation: reject the belief and individually drop out of the movement; find a biblical excuse for the setback, accept the inevitable, and slowly turn away from activism to passivism; turn to hyperactive religiosity, including terroristic suicide. All three options could be observed in Israel's messianic camp in the aftermath of the Israeli-PLO agreement. By far, the most extreme reaction was the February 1994 Hebron massacre, committed by Dr. Baruch Goldstein, a longtime Kahane disciple and member of Kach.

There can be no question that the Oslo Accords brought many Gush Emunim and Kach members, individuals obssessed with the redemption of Greater Israel and the coming of the messiah, to a theological crisis. Unlike the *haredim*, Israel's ultra-Orthodox, who never ascribed a whit of religious significance to the secular state, Gush Emunim and Kachniks have come to believe that redemption can take place only when the Jews control all of the biblical Land of Israel, including the entire occupied territories. These messianic activists have been convinced that redemption is both imminent and irreversible.

Troubles with the post-1967 messianic reading of modern Israeli history started as early as the setback of the 1973 Yom Kippur War. The expectation for a linear progression toward redemption has seen many additional challenges, the most dramatic of which came in 1978 when Israel's prime minister, Menachem Begin, agreed to return the Sinai Peninsula to Egypt in exchange for peace. Begin also made a commitment regarding a future Palestinian autonomy in the West Bank and Gaza. Begin maintained, though, that he compromised on Sinai to make peace with Israel's most dangerous enemy, thereby saving Judea and Samaria, the spiritual and historical heartland of Eretz Israel. The disconfirmation of the redemption process, implied in the Camp David Accords, was further moderated by the intense efforts of all Likud governments to settle Jews in the West Bank. Indeed, the relative success of the settlement process was seen by many true believers as a *reconfirmation* of the 1967 messianic promise.

The conditions for the recent and most unequivocal disconfirmation of the hope for redemption came, as already discussed, with the Labor victory in 1992. The Labor party, committed to territorial compromise for peace in the West Bank, ordered a government freeze on settlement in the occupied territories and concluded historic agreements with the PLO. The determination of that Israeli government to recognize the Palestine Liberation Organization, to first implement a Palestinian autonomy in the West Bank and Gaza, and to eventually evacuate most of the territories and facilitate the creation of a Palestinian political entity was the worst nightmare of messianic Zionists in Israel. Labor policies not only turned redemption predictions on their head but also contradicted everything the Gush and Kach had been telling their followers—and the world—for over two decades.

The February massacre in Hebron was an expression of messianism in crisis. It constitutes a prime example of Festinger and Rapoport's third option, the violent and catastrophic reaction to failed prophecy. The massacre also signaled the advent of heightened extremism within Israel's religious radical right—followers of Rabbi Kahane and a few groups in the outer circles of Gush Emunim. It is true that Kach, Baruch Goldstein's organization, had long preached and exercised violence and that it reached a crisis of legitimacy with the government several years prior to the Oslo Accords. It is also true that a number of Kach members had killed innocent Arabs before, without any apparent allusion to a failed prophecy. But the massacre in Hebron was different because of its unprecedented scope and atrociousness. It was committed, furthermore, by an atypical member of the movement, a doctor known for his compassion, a head of a large family and father of four, and a successful, well-respected member of the community. Goldstein, the movement's 1992 candidate for Kiryat Arba's mayor, was referred to by many town residents, regardless of party affiliation, as a *tzadik* (pious man). He was known to have spared no effort or money to help the sick and the needy.

Always ready to help out, whether or not on emergency duty, the young doctor, who never hesitated to drive alone to the area's most dangerous locations, was adored throughout the entire region.[22] Although associated in the Lebanon War with a refusal to treat a PLO soldier, Goldstein saved the life of at least one Hebron Palestinian, hit by Israeli bullets. This community doctor had not been involved in Kach violence before and was never expected by movement members to participate in their routine street hooliganism.

From the information now available about Baruch Goldstein, it is clear that like other dedicated Kahane disciples, already shaken by the 1990 assassination of their beloved mentor, he had undergone since Oslo a personal and theological crisis. Not only was the future of Judea and Samaria put in doubt, but the neighboring Palestinians had become increasingly aggressive and violent. As the community's emergency physician and the doctor responsible for first aid to Jewish victims of terrorism, Goldstein was exposed to the consequences of the disaster more, perhaps, than anybody else. Several victims of the intensifying Muslim terrorism, especially his close friends, Pinchas and Shalom Lapid, died in his arms. There are a number of signs that Goldstein slowly came to the fatalistic conclusion that unless stopped by a most dramatic act, something that would please God and shake the foundations of the earth, the peace process could disconfirm the dream of redemption.[23]

The special State Investigation Committee, formed to study the Hebron massacre, was intrigued by Goldstein's personality. In its official report, the committee tried to explain the contradiction between the doctor's compassionate personality and the incredible and unthinkable massacre he committed. Though far from speculating about the relationship between failed messianism and violence, the committee could not avoid the following observations:

> Goldstein was haunted by a siege mentality, seeing a danger for the existence of the Jewish people and feeling that only an extraordinary act would stop what he considered a most serious deterioration in the nation's condition and the lack of response to the increasing and worsening acts of terror.
>
> He saw himself as a representative of the people of Israel, ordered to act in

> accordance with God's will ("the calling of the individual Jew in this world is to fulfill His creator's wish and to sanctify the name of Heaven").
>
> He must have come to the conclusion that he should carry out an act exceptional in its severity and extremism, which would stop the political process he considered most fatal. According to his understanding, only a serious blow, which would have a worldwide effect, would stop the process. In a leaflet signed by him, Goldstein said, "It is time to wake up from sleep and say enough."[24]

Goldstein, it should be further stressed, was a personal student of Rabbi Meir Kahane and a very methodical individual. Like his rabbi, who in 1983 placed him as the third candidate on Kach's Knesset list, he believed that redemption was inevitable but that it could come in two ways—an easy and smooth one or difficult and catastrophic. In several of his essays, Kahane wrote that the gates of heaven were opened wide in 1967, and that God was ready to instantly redeem the people of Israel. If only they followed the right path, returned to the faith and kicked the Arabs out of Eretz Israel, the Jews could have walked straight to the Kingdom of Israel. If they did not, Kahane warned, redemption would come the hard way, through trials and tribulations, bloodshed, and enormous suffering.[25] There are many signs that following the 1990 assassination of the rabbi, whom he loved dearly, and the disasters since the 1992 elections, especially the Oslo Accords, Goldstein started to step slowly into a desperate messianic defiance. Only a catastrophic act of supreme *kiddush hashem* (sanctification of the name of God) could change, perhaps, the course of history and put it back on the messianic track.[26] And he, a responsible person who never was trigger-happy, had to carry out this exemplary mission. Although it appears that Goldstein did not intend to commit suicide and was ready to spend many years in jail, he was ready to die, if necessary.[27]

The Hebron massacre had a most dramatic and radicalizing effect on Arab and Jewish extremists. As for the Arabs, it appears certain that the massacre triggered a massive Hamas retaliation. There are many indications that Izz-a-Din al-Qassam squads, Hamas's military arm, as well as the Islamic Jihad were determined to engage strategically in anti-Israeli terrorism before the Hebron tragedy. Yahya Ayash, Izz-a-Din al-Qassam's mastermind, the "engineer," was apparently eager to strike. But Goldstein's atrocity instantly upgraded Hamas's retaliation. All inhibitions regarding the killing of innocent Israeli civilians within the Green Line were now removed. Two Hamas car bombs in the cities of Afula and Hadera killed and wounded a large number of Israeli civilians. There was more to come.[28]

The Hebron massacre also had a profound impact on Jewish extremists. Though unprepared and shocked, Israel's pragmatic extreme right blamed the authorities for Goldstein's act. Rabin's government, not the deranged doctor, was responsible for the terrible tragedy. By recognizing the PLO "terror organization" and reducing its own antiterrorist efforts, the government had been instrumental in bringing about a national disaster of high proportions. The Hebron massacre was, according to this fatalistic interpretation, seen by a large number of settlers as just the prelude to a larger storm. Blood and catastrophe were hanging in the air and the time for moderation was gone.

8

TO KILL A PRIME MINISTER

Countdown to the Rabin Assassination

Yitzhak Rabin was pronounced dead at 11:10 P.M., on Saturday, November 4, 1995. Rabin was shot an hour and twenty minutes earlier, just a few minutes after he had delivered a rousing speech at a Tel Aviv peace rally. The huge gathering, planned to demonstrate the popularity of the government's peace policies, was attended by over one hundred thousand cheerful supporters. It was the largest pro-peace demonstration held since the 1992 ascent to power of the Rabin government—an attempt to counterbalance the large number of anti-peace protests held by the Israeli extreme right. An important theme of the rally was nonviolence. The increasing aggression of the extreme right, especially the intensifying use of *verbal* violence, led the rally's organizers to stress peaceful, nonviolent politics. None of the participants in the colorful gathering expected the event to conclude with the first political murder of the Jewish nation's senior leader in nearly two thousand years.

Yigal Amir, the twenty-five-year-old assassin, began his evening with nightly prayers near his Herzeliya home. Following the prayer, Amir washed himself, shaved, and donned a T-shirt that a left-wing activist might wear. After loading his gun with several high-velocity hollow-point bullets, he tested it to make sure there were no blocks. Hiding the gun under his shirt, Amir took a bus to Tel Aviv's Kings of Israel Square. He had plenty of time and circled the square several times. Around 9:10 P.M., the young man was already in the VIP parking lot. Unattended by the policemen in charge, who believed him to be a plainclothes secret agent, Amir waited patiently for the prime minister's descent down the stairway. Then he shot Rabin as the prime minister approached the door of his armored car, at almost point-blank range. The two bullets tore through the prime minister's chest and lungs and left him no chance of survival.[1]

Rabin's assassination did not take place in a vacuum. Although Amir acted alone, his act was the culmination of a process of delegitimization of the Israeli government by Israel's ultranationalists. While the renewed radicalization of the right was triggered by the 1993 Oslo Accords and already involved, as shown above, verbal violence and confrontation tactics, it appears that the final countdown to the assassination had begun in the aftermath of the 1994 Hebron massacre. This chapter attempts to reconstruct the psychopolitical radicalization of the Israeli extreme right that paved the way for a killer like Amir and strengthened his determination to act.

The Crisis of Tel Rumeida and the Rabbinical Ruling on Soldier Disobedience

The Israeli government's immediate reaction to the February 28, 1994, atrocity in Hebron was to outlaw Kach and Kahane Chai. The Kahanist groups, which continued to preach anti-Arab violence and praised Baruch Goldstein as a martyr, were declared illegal terrorist organizations. Their offices were sealed and their propaganda literature confiscated. About ten leaders of these organizations were put under administrative detention, an emergency procedure utilized by the military commander of the area in high-risk circumstances.

While the leaders of the Yesha Council, who never subscribed to the Kahanist ideology, disapproved of the draconian measures taken against Kach and Kahane Chai, they did not make a big issue out of them. Most understood that Goldstein's ideological supporters had to be punished. Government officials were privately told by Yesha activists that the banning of the Kahanist organizations was long overdue.[2] Of much greater concern to the settler establishment was—a by-product of the massacre—

the increasing likelihood that Hebron's Jewish community would be evacuated.

Prior to the February massacre, there were no evacuation plans for the small Jewish community of Hebron. Although he knew that this radical enclave, consisting of 500 Jews living in the midst of 130,000 Palestinians, was the most volatile settlement in the West Bank, Prime Minister Rabin did not have contingency plans for their removal. The Oslo Accords with the PLO stipulated that settlement evacuation would be discussed only in the final stage of the Israeli-Palestinian negotiations and after the implementation of a Palestinian autonomy in Gaza and the West Bank. Neither the PLO nor the Israeli government had legal grounds for demanding an immediate evacuation. But the massacre at the Cave of the Patriarchs, which led to the indefinite suspension of the peace process, created a new reality. It validated the call of many Israeli doves, who considered the settlers anti-Oslo provocateurs, for an immediate evacuation. Evacuation advocates maintained that the removal of Hebron's Jewish community was no longer a Palestinian wish but an Israeli interest. Alluding to the horrible experience of the massacre, left-wing members of Rabin's cabinet warned of still worse future confrontations. They maintained that the continued presence of Jewish provocateurs among Hebron's Palestinians was a recipe for future massacres and a time bomb on the road to peace. Only a decisive government action could, in their view, stop settler provocations and send a reassuring message to peaceful Palestinians and Jews.

In mid-March, the government began to seriously consider evacuating the seven Jewish families living in Tel Rumeida. This small hill in central Hebron had been settled since the mid-1980s by a small number of radical Jewish families. If Jewish Hebron spelled trouble for Arab-Israeli relations, Tel Rumeida was the eye of the storm. Some of the most extreme settlers, such as Kach's head, Baruch Marzel, chose to live there, isolated from the rest of Hebron's Jews and surrounded by thirty thousand Palestinians. Tel Rumeida expressed the ultimate ultranationalist defiance, epitomizing the claim of the Jewish right to settle all of Eretz Israel. Constantly guarded by an entire army company, lest they be butchered by their neighbors, Tel-Rumeida's Jewish residents kept challenging and provoking the neighboring Palestinians.

It was therefore only natural that once considered, the first evacuation of Jews from the area would be conducted in Tel-Rumeida. And indeed, in mid-March 1994, a cabinet majority favored removal of the small enclave. While the issue had not been brought to the attention of the public, it was an open secret. There were indications, furthermore, that Lieutenant General Ehud Barak, Israel's chief of staff, supported evacuation. Government ministers were careful not to associate the coming removal with high politics or the future of the settlements. The argument for the evacuation of Tel Rumeida stressed the need to save Jewish lives and prevent future catastrophes. It was presented as a rescue operation in the interest of the settlers.[3]

The news about a possible removal stunned the settler leaders. An evacuation of Hebron or even of small Tel Rumeida was not interpreted as a benevolent act but was perceived instead as a huge blow to the very heart of the Jewish venture in Judea and Samaria. Hebron, the City of the Patriarchs, second in its holiness only to Jerusalem, was the first settlement site chosen by Jews after the Six-Day War. Hebron's ancient Jewish community had been destroyed in 1929 in a brutal Arab pogrom. When the government of Israel decided in 1968 to evacuate Hebron's illicit settlement, it was able to do so only by establishing Kiryat Arba, a Jewish city adjacent to Hebron. But already by 1979, the settlers, under the leadership of Rabbi Moshe Levinger, were back in the city itself. Taking advantage of the weakness of Menachem Begin, who was outraged by the terrorist murder of a local yeshiva student, they forced resettlement in an old Jewish property in the middle of the city. There was plenty of bloodshed involved in this struggle to settle and stay in Hebron, including intense PLO terrorism and the birth and the first actions of the Jewish Underground.[4] So the possible removal of the Jewish enclave of Tel Rumeida was seen by the settlers as the beginning of the end. If the Rabin-Peres government, already responsible for the Oslo "treason," could evacuate Tel Rumeida, it could evacuate all the settlements in Judea and Samaria.

The looming "disaster" in Tel Rumeida produced one of the most effective mobilization efforts in settler history. Though not officially informed about the planned evacuation, the settlers prepared for the worst. Israel's parliamentary opposition was put on alert. Contingency plans were made for bringing tens of thousands of ultranationalist activists to Hebron to stop the removal by planting their own bodies on the holy ground. Heads of right-wing organizations including many support groups formed earlier within the Green Line were instructed to prepare for an unprecedented ordeal. Numerous lobbyists pleaded with Rabin to spare Tel Rumeida and argued that the danger of another massacre was minimal. Others warned the prime minister of a desperate settler struggle he could not win. Israel's security service, already under investigation for failing to anticipate the Hebron massacre, had become increasingly concerned about Jewish bloodshed.

The most dramatic response to the Tel Rumeida evacuation plan was made by several prominent rabbis, Shlomo Goren, Abraham Shapiro, Shaul Yisraeli and Moshe Tzvi Neria. The four rabbis issued several Halakhic rulings categorically prohibiting evacuation of Jewish settlements in Eretz Israel. Rabbi Goren, Israel's former chief rabbi and a highly regarded Halakhic authority, was the first to rule against settlement removal, in a detailed answer to a question addressed to him in November 1993 by the Council of Judea and Samaria's Rabbis.[5] In an expanded version of that judgment, written in the aftermath of the Hebron massacre, Goren wrote,

> The criminal initiative to evacuate Hebron ought to be met with *messirut hanefesh* [total devotion]. The ruling on such heinous crime, as the ruling on saving life, is "*yehareg velo ya'avor*" [be killed but not sin]. If the government succeeds in its plan, God forbid, the evacuation of Hebron must be responded to by *kria* [cutting one's dress—a sign of death in a family]. . . . According to the Halakha, the meaning of the destruction of Hebron, God forbid . . . is like the killing of people, which requires *kria* like on the dead. . . . This is why we have to give our life in the struggle against this vicious plan of the government of Israel, which relies on the Arabs for its majority, and be ready to die rather then allow the destruction of Hebron.[6]

While Rabbi Goren's ruling, which preceded the Tel Rumeida crisis, produced only a minor controversy, the ruling of Shapiro, Yisraeli, and Neria reverberated throughout the country. The three rabbis were by far the most influential and authoritative in the Zionist religious milieu. While the first two were the heads of Yeshivat Merkaz ha-Rav—Gush Emunim's founding yeshiva—Neria, the oldest of the three, was the historical father of all B'nai-Akiva yeshivas. The shocking novelty of the later ruling was its being addressed to the nation's soldiers. All Israeli soldiers were publicly told that evacuation orders were illegal. They were instructed by the three rabbis to disobey any order to evacuate Jewish settlers from Jewish land.[7]

If the adamant rabbinical opposition to all settlement evacuation had long been known, the rabbis' call for soldier disobedience was unprecedented. No such ruling was made, for example, during the 1982 evacuation of Jewish settlements from northern Sinai. During the 1980s, several left-wing activists preached and practiced refusal to serve in the occupied territories. But the individuals involved, no more than a few dozen soldiers in reserve, were neither leaders nor public authorities and had almost no appeal or influence. They refused to serve and were ready to pay the price by spending time in jail. Rabbis Shapiro, Yisraeli, and Neria had, on the contrary, hundreds of thousands of followers. They were the supreme authorities of thousands of Israeli religious soldiers, mostly graduates of Hesder yeshivas on active duty. These highly motivated soldiers had started in the 1980s to serve in some of the IDF's most prestigious combat units.

The most damaging aspect of the rabbis' ruling was not, however, the potential refusal of a few religious soldiers to participate in Tel Rumeida's evacuation, but its symbolic effect. The presence of highly regarded spiritual authorities who no longer respected the sanctity of the Israeli army was a new development. Long recognized as the nation's only survival guarantee, the IDF has never been seen as just an instrumental institution for compulsory service. Service in the Israeli army had become a moral calling and a virtue. The very rabbis who now called for disobedience were themselves part of the post-1967 religious uplifting of this norm. Very few Israelis missed the profound meaning of the rabbinical ruling, and the issue refused to leave the headlines.

The plan to remove Jews from Hebron, Tel Rumeida, or both did not provide by itself sufficient ground for the dramatic rabbinical ruling. The condition that made the declaration possible was the loss by the Rabin government of the Jewish majority in the Knesset. By the end of 1993, the ruling coalition had lost the support of Shas party, with its 5 Knesset seats. The government was still in control of 61 Knesset members out of 120 and was fully functional, but 5 of the 61 represented Arab parties. The three rabbis argued that although formal citizens, Israeli Palestinians did not have a right to decide the fate of Eretz Israel. Not only was the government, in their view, committing a heinous crime against God and Jewish history but it was ready to do so with the help of Arabs. The fact that public opinion polls also showed dwindling support for the Oslo Accords further convinced the rabbis that they were right. There was, according to them, only one legitimate way of resolving the controversy: dissolving the Knesset and putting the issue to a referendum of the Israeli people. The refusal of the government even to consider the demand for early elections made it, in their eyes, fully illegitimate. There was no reason to expect religious soldiers to obey evacuation orders, no reason to respect the traditional sanctity of the Israeli army.

The rabbinical ruling on soldier disobedience created a public uproar. Prime Minister Rabin was furious. The Israeli left considered the ruling the worst attack ever made on Israel's young democracy. Moderate religious authorities such as Rabbi Amital, the head of the nation's largest Hesder yeshiva, accused Shapiro, Yisraeli, and Neria of having expressed a political rather than a Halakhic opinion. State Attorney General Michael Ben-Yair declared his intention to investigate a charge of illegal incitement. Prominent Likud members, who recognized the potential damage of the rabbinical ruling to the morale of the army, also expressed their great unease. Several members of the National Religious party, who had otherwise admired the rabbis involved, expressed grave concern.[8] Rabbi Ya'acov Ariel, a highly respected Gush Emunim authority, reminded Rabbi Shapiro that during the 1982 struggle over the evacuation of northern Sinai, he himself had ruled that soldiers must obey orders and that only civilians are allowed to practice civil disobedience.

While the rabbinical ruling failed to obtain endorsements from nonreligious Jews, it was approved by the majority of Israel's Orthodox rabbis. Rabbi Eliezer Waldman, the head of Kiryat Arba's Hesder Yeshiva (a yeshiva that combines Torah studies and military training), saluted the ruling and promised "to obey it. This government was born in sin. It depends on the votes of the PLO and has no right to go against any Jewish settlement." Rabbi Dov Lior, Waldman's colleague in the Yeshiva headship and Kiryat

Arba's chief rabbi, was even more adamant. In addition to fully endorsing the decree of the three rabbis, he privately issued a special ruling that Jews should be ready to sacrifice their life over Hebron.[9] One interpretation of Lior's judgment was that suicide was permissible in cases of forced evacuation.

Neither Hebron nor Tel Rumeida was finally evacuated. Drawing on careful evaluations submitted to him, which suggested a high likelihood of violent confrontation with the settlers and possible Jewish fatalities, Rabin decided to let the settlers stay.[10] The message was delivered to Israel's Council of the Chief Rabbinate on April 4, 1994. The messenger was Mota Gur, the Deputy Defense Minister and an official close to the settlers. Toeing the line between their official duty as state rabbis and their respect for Shapiro, Yisraeli and Neria, Israel's chief rabbis, issued this announcement:

> The Council of the Chief Rabbinate has registered with great satisfaction the announcement of Deputy Defense Minister Mota Gur that the government of Israel has no intention of either evacuating Jewish settlers or Jewish settlements. . . . It is therefore clear that the question of military orders to evacuate settlers or settlements—which are against the Halakha—is not on the agenda and the army must be taken out of the political debate.[11]

The relief expressed by the council as well as by several other rabbinical bodies was greatly diluted, however, by a new blow to the settlers. The Gaza-Jericho plan, suspended since the Hebron massacre, was finally implemented in April. Yasser Arafat was allowed to land in Gaza and the Palestinian autonomy became a fact. The extremist rabbinical ruling, which under other circumstances might have been officially reversed, remained in full force. It became, in fact, a symbol of rabbinical defiance. A larger number of Orthodox rabbis, hesitant until then, were now ready to support it openly. On May 3, 1994, a large rabbinical gathering, convened under the title Eretz Israel Rabbinical Union, fully endorsed the judgment over soldier disobedience. Rabbi Nahum Rabinovitz, the head of the Hesder yeshiva of Ma'ale Adumim, called upon his colleagues to take Torah scrolls to the streets of Jerusalem and stay there "until our outcry is heard in Heaven and our message penetrates secular hearts too." Representing more than one thousand rabbis from all over the country, the new body issued an unequivocal warning to the government:

> The so-called peace agreement, made by a government supported by a tiny majority with a critical Arab Knesset vote, is a complete contradiction to peace. The implementation of the agreement may lead, God forbid, to great danger to human life. This is why anyone who can stop this "agreement" and does not do so, breaks the rule "you shall not stand idle when there is danger to your brother!"[12]

Small and large rabbinical gatherings, protesting the peace process and expressing intense delegitimation vis-à-vis the government, continued. About seven such meetings took place in the months preceding the Rabin assassination, each concluding with a harsher antigovernment statement. Thousands of community rabbis, yeshiva heads, and teachers had increasingly committed themselves to the struggle. This amounted to a national mobilization of almost the entire Zionist religious camp, nearly four hundred thousand strong. The campaign was conducted through special prayers, homilies, sermons, and a huge number of pamphlets circulated in hundreds of synagogues. Never before had such an intense delegitimation campaign been conducted in Israel.

The struggle against the legitimacy of his government did not leave Yitzhak Rabin cold. A secular Sabra to the bone, Rabin never liked the settlers and their messianic rhetoric. During his first term as prime minister, he was the target of a large number of Gush Emunim protests. There were also a number of massive confrontations in which the Gush tried to settle in Samaria against the will of the government. The most famous of these confrontations, the one that took place in Kadum in 1975, ended in Rabin's defeat. The prime minister was forced to allow a group of settlers to stay as "temporary workers" in a military camp in Samaria, a concession recognized by everybody as a humiliating defeat for the government. That settler group and many others never left Samaria. Rabin did not forget the Kadum fiasco and always believed he lost the campaign because the settlers worked behind his back and were able to manipulate his defense minister of the time, Shimon Peres, and the chief of staff, Lieutenant General Mota Gur.[13]

Since 1975 Rabin had learned to appreciate the dangerous manipulativeness of the settlers as well as their determination. Convinced that these fanatics were ready to do everything to fulfill their Greater Israel dream, he concluded that he could neither trust them nor take their word at face value. In 1994 and following the intensification of the settler struggle against his peace policies, Rabin lost his patience. Completely unable to understand the settler sense of disaster over the potential collapse of their Judea and Samaria dream, he saw only their antigovernment delegitimation. Unlike President Ezer Weizmann, who had psychologically disarmed many of these angry people by paying occasional visits to their West Bank settlements following terrorist attacks, Rabin remained aloof and cold. He had neither empathy nor sympathy for the people who attacked him and wished to bring his governments down. Repeatedly humiliating them with gestures and name-calling, including the terms "kugelagers" (part of a car's wheel that squeaks), and "propellers" (i.e., people who make a lot of noise and vent hot air), Rabin told the settlers that regardless of their opposition and pain, he was determined to move ahead with the peace process. It was difficult to determine who was the winner of this tragic psychological warfare—Rabin the bitter, personally insecure prime minister who constantly had protesters in front of his house screaming "traitor" and "assassin," or the large number of settlers who felt humiliated and marginalized by their government. What had become increasingly clear was that the settlers' political struggle against Rabin had assumed a highly personal character. They hated him and he despised them.

Din Rodef and *Din Moser*

The rabbis' already intense confrontation with Rabin reached a new height in February 1995. Following an unprecedented series of Hamas and Islamic Jihad suicide bombings inside Israel that took the lives of 87 Israeli civilians, wounded 202, and traumatized the entire nation, the heads of Yesha's Rabbinical Council decided to explore the possibility of putting the government on trial according to *din rodef* and *din moser. Moser* and *rodef,* according to the Halakha, are among the worst kinds of Jews. They betray the community through acts that may result in the loss of innocent Jewish lives. *Moser* is a Jew suspected of providing the Gentiles with information about Jews or with illegally giving them Jewish property. Since the Halakha refers to Eretz Israel as a sacred property of the Jewish people,

Jews are obliged to kill the *moser*. *Rodef* is a person about to commit or facilitate the commitment of murder. The purpose of his immediate execution is to save Jewish life. This rule does not apply to a killer, caught after the murder, who has to go on trial. *Din rodef* is the only case in which the Halakha allows Jews to kill another Jew without a trial.

The fact that the escalation of Muslim terrorism and the indiscriminate targeting of Israeli civilians were largely a response to Baruch Goldstein's massacre was hardly noticed by the ultranationalist rabbis or anybody else within Israel's extreme right. Instead, the right blamed two individuals, Yitzhak Rabin and Shimon Peres, for the loss of the lives of the innocent victims. By ordering Israeli soldiers out of Gaza and Jericho, by allowing the formation of a large, armed Palestinian police, and by relaxing the anti-Palestinian struggle of the nation's security forces, Oslo's two architects made it possible for Hamas and the Islamic Jihad to kill Jews. Their hands were seen as covered with Jewish blood." The rabbis explored the validity of *din moser* and *din rodef* for Rabin and Peres in a long question addressed to forty Halakhic authorities:

> What is the rule about this bad government? Can they be regarded as accomplices to acts of murder committed by terrorists, since in their plans they are responsible for the strengthening and arming of these terrorists? . . . Should they be tried according to the Halakha? And if proven guilty as accomplices to murder, what should their sentence be? If they are, indeed . . . punishable in court, is it the obligation of every individual to bring them to trial in a court of justice, or, for lack of an alternative, in an ordinary secular court? Is it not the obligation of the community's leaders to warn the head of the government and his ministers that if they keep pursuing the agreement, after the terrible experience of stage one (Oslo I), in all of Judea and Samaria, they will be subject . . . to the Halakhic ruling of *din moser*, as ones who surrender the life and property of Jews to the Gentiles?
>
> It is no longer possible to silence the question that bursts out of the broken hearts of many Jews in this country and abroad. . . . We know that the very interest in the issue may stimulate, God forbid, an intense controversy in the nation. Aware of the actual conditions on the ground, we are worried that the situation will get worse, that these questions will be asked by the majority

of the people and that many of the victims [of terrorism] may be filled with sentiments of revenge.[14]

While the letter of the rabbis was formulated as a question addressed to other, more prominent rabbis, it was itself a very incriminating document. The questions about *din rodef* and *din moser* were not presented succinctly and objectively. The long letter was full of harsh statements regarding the government and plenty of presuppositions about its nefarious activities. The causal relation between the government's peace process and Muslim terrorism was stated as a given, and all Palestinians were collectively referred to as terrorists. No distinction was made, for example, between the peaceful PLO and the terrorists of Hamas. There was, moreover, no reference to the possible impact of the Hebron massacre on the eruption of Muslim terrorism. The reader was led to unequivocal conclusions about the criminal responsibility of Rabin and Peres for the suicide bombings. A casual reader might have easily concluded that the three rabbis who drafted the letter—Dov Lior, Eliezer Melamed, and Daniel Shilo—were themselves close to the conclusion that Peres and Rabin qualified for *din moser* and *din rodef*.

The rabbis' letter was not an isolated expression of a few extremist individuals who came to the conclusion that the two Halakhic concepts of *moser* and *rodef* had to be invoked. It was, instead, a reflection of intense scholarly discussion conducted in many extremist yeshivas and religious circles. The writing of the letter was, moreover, not the first time that *din rodef* and *din moser* had been raised in writing. These must have been raised much earlier because already in December 1993, just three months after the signing of the Oslo Accords, Rabbi Ya'acov Ariel, Ramat-Gan's chief rabbi, published in *Hatzofe*, the NRP's official newspaper, an essay on the subject. Ariel's article, written with grave concern over the possible misinterpretation of *din rodef* to the government, did not deny the relevance of the discussion. But its author warned readers against jumping to improper and dangerous conclusions, such as the obligation to kill the head of state.

It is only allowed to hit a "Rodef" when there is no other way of stopping the *Redifa* [pursuance]. He who takes unnecessary drastic measures is considered *shofech damim* [he who sheds blood]. Haven't you considered other

> measures, more realistic, to stop the *redifa*, without assuming that a direct hit is the most appropriate way? Have all other kosher ways to bring the government down or pressure it to change its policies been exhausted? In regard to this question, all kosher ways have not been used. A million telegrams to the prime minister have not been sent yet. Bonfires . . . over the hills and mountains have not been lighted yet. Tens of thousands of people have not yet held a strike. Even a temporary public mourning [*ta'anit*] has not yet been called for. In short, the legal means of shaking up the country from one side to another have not been exhausted. This is why its dangerous steps notwithstanding, it is practically prohibited to refer to this government as *rodef*. Only when the people will do what a normal nation must do in order to repeal the government, and if the government continues to rule by force, it will, perhaps, be possible to define it as *rodef*. But as long as the people have not done it, the government may see itself (erroneously, in your and many other opinions) as the legal representative of the public. This is why practically it does not come under "*din rodef*."[15]

Ya'acov Ariel was not the only rabbi who believed that talk about *din moser* and *din rodef* was dangerous. The highly respected Shlomo Aviner, Beit El's rabbi and head of Yeshivat Ateret Kohanim, also felt that way. He consequently became involved in calming down the excitement of Yesha's Rabbinical Council over this issue. A distinguished member of the group, Aviner urged his colleagues to stop pursuing the *rodef* discussion for fear of fatal consequences.[16] Since the answers to the rabbis' letter were very slow in coming, the task was not so difficult and the council tacitly dropped the issue. The problem with the discussion of *din rodef* and *din moser*, however, was that under the prevailing psychopolitical conditions, it was already too late to extinguish the fire. In extremist yeshivas and messianic circles, Rabin and Peres were increasingly being referred to as *rodfim* and *mosrim*. There was, moreover, little rabbinical effort to actively stop it.[17]

Especially noticeable, in the same context, was the harsh language increasingly used against the Israeli leaders by North American Orthodox rabbis. In a stormy meeting with Schmuel Hollander, Israel's Orthodox cabinet secretary, who visited New York over the High Holy Days, the rabbis compared Yasser Arafat to Adolf Hitler. They told the stunned official that his boss was *moser* and *rodef.*[18] Rabbi Abraham Hecht, the head of New York City's large Sharei Zion synagogue, did not hesitate to say in public what many of his colleagues had been saying privately. In an October 9 interview, he maintained that, "according to Jewish Halakha, Rabin deserves to die. He who intentionally transfers living people, money or property, to strangers, commits, according to the Halakha, a crime punishable by death. Maimonides maintained that he who kills such a person is doing the right thing."[19] In a television interview about this uncommonly harsh statement, Hecht smiled and said it was a *mitzvah* (commandment) to kill Rabin and he was sorry he was personally unable to fulfill it.

Following the assassination of Rabin and the rising interest in the rabbinical authorities who may have legitimized Yigal Amir's act, there were additional indications that many discussions of *din moser* and *din rodef* preceded the murder. Rabbi Yoel Ben Nun, a Gush Emunim founder and longtime critic of the extremist wing of the movement, openly charged several rabbis with authorizing the killing. In a meeting with Israel's chief rabbis, Ben Nun mentioned the names of Kiryat Arba's Dov Lior and Ma'ale Adumim's Nahum Rabinovitz. Ben Nun maintained further that a young rabbi from Gush Etzion, Schmuel Dvir, who in the past several months had made death threats against Rabin, had told other people he knew of the *rodef* ruling of seven prominent rabbis.[20] While none of Ben Nun's charges could be fully substantiated, and he later apologized in public, his allegations exposed the culture of Halakhic defiance that preceded the assassination, including the wide discussion of *moser* and *rodef.* It is unlikely that any of the aforementioned rabbis issued a death sentence on Rabin and Peres, but a number of them allowed their students to believe that Rabin and Peres had more than qualified for the infamous titles. With perhaps the exception of Rabbi Aviner, who forbade his students to use slanderous language against the head of state,[21] rabbis such as Lior and Rabinovitz had increasingly joined the smear campaign. A retrospective examination suggests that it was just a question of time before a hotheaded student was ready to jump to conclusions on his own. The culture of Halakhic character assassination was accurately expressed in the Haredi journal *Hashavua*, an organ that devoted many of its pages to anti-Rabin incitement and occasionally used such terms as "traitor," "madman," and "non-Jew" against him.

> There are today settler groups that favor violence of the first order. They even demand permission to assassinate heads of the government, especially Prime Minister Rabin, against whom there is *din rodef*. The heads of the national *haredim* maintain that an extreme line against the government—which stands under *din rodef*—must be adopted. All speakers with whom we talked tried to maintain that the discussion is totally theoretical and there is no intention to kill Rabin and Peres.
>
> The new situation puts before the *haredi* public alternatives never faced before. One possibility is to forcefully challenge the group that took over the government of the state. There is no reason that we allow the vicious maniacs who run this government to take Jews as sheep to the slaughter. "Rabin is a traitor," says Rabbi Gadi Ben-Zimra, "and I have no problem in saying this. It is clear that the government betrays all values . . . and puts the state in danger."[22]

Baruch Hagever: The Maturation of the Kahanist Counterculture

The 1995 Purim holiday was an occasion for a special radical right ceremony, the anniversary of the Hebron massacre and the death of Dr. Baruch Goldstein. Most Israelis, deeply repelled by the 1994 massacre, knew vaguely about Goldstein's supporters and the special tombstone laid on his grave in central Kiryat Arba. What they did not know, however, was that an entire Baruch Goldstein cult had been formed and that Goldstein's memory had become the rallying point of the disbanded Kahane movement. A surprisingly large number of people had come to consider Goldstein a holy man and an exemplary figure.

In spite of the fears of a major Arab or Jewish provocation, Goldstein memorial services went smoothly. The entire Palestinian area was put under strict curfew, and Kiryat Arba itself was sealed off. Only a small number of local Jews were allowed to participate. Organized by "friends of the family," i.e., Kach and Kahane activists, who could not appear under movement banners, the memorial service was subdued and controlled. The participants prayed for Goldstein and contributed money to religious institutions named after him. They also bought a large quantity of Goldstein memorabilia.[23]

Of much greater significance in the commemoration and preservation of the Goldstein legacy was a 550-page edited volume published in March 1995. Its title was *Baruch Hagever* [*Baruch, the Man*]*: A Memorial Volume for Dr. Baruch Goldstein, the Saint, May God Avenge His Blood.* The volume, edited by Michael Ben Horin, a Golan settler and former president of the "Free State of Judea," had been prepared for months in total secrecy. Although Ben Horin's editorial board failed to convince several prominent Goldstein supporters—such as Kiryat Arba's chief rabbi, Dov Lior, and Rabbi Israel Ariel of Jerusalem's Temple Institute—to contribute to the volume for fear of public condemnation, it was an unusual collection of essays, testimonies, and letters of support. Never before had any Israeli extreme right organization produced such an impressive compendium. The fact that of all right-wing organizations it was the small and defunct Kach and Kahane Chai that were able to put together *Baruch Hagever* was a testimony to the maturation of Israel's small Kahanist counterculture. The majority of the volume's contributors had two things in common: at a certain period of their lives they had supported Meir Kahane and they all admired Baruch Goldstein.

The major theme of the book was conceived by Rabbi Yitzhak Ginzburg, the head of the radical Tomb of Yoseph Yeshiva in Nablus. Ginzburg, a Lubavitcher Hasidic rabbi (follower of the Habad Hasidic Court) who wrote the lead essay of the volume, had never been a formal disciple of Kahane. An extremist thinker in his own right who had specialized in the study of Kabbalah, Ginzburg made the headlines in 1988 by providing Halakhic support for several of his students who had unilaterally shot Arab civilians. Making it clear that there was a huge difference between killing civilian Arabs and Jews, the radical rabbi did not conceal his opinion that under the prevailing security conditions in Judea and Samaria, it was fully legitimate to kill noncombatant Palestinians.[24] As for the Hebron atrocity and Baruch Goldstein, Ginzburg urged his students and readers to be "broad-minded" and consider the positive aspects of the massacre, not just the negative ones stressed by the nation's media and most of its rabbis.

Ginzburg identifies in Goldstein's atrocious act five virtuous aspects: "sanctification of the name of God," "saving life" (of Jews),"revenge" (against Hebron's Palestinians), "cleansing evil," and "struggle for Eretz Israel."[25] Goldstein was not, according to this presentation, a reckless criminal but a pious man of deep religious convictions who wanted to save Jews. Sacrificing his own life for this purpose, he committed the supreme act of *kiddush hashem* (sanctification of the name of God). The Hebron massacre was committed, according to Ginzburg, against the background of increasing information of an upcoming Arab pogrom. It was conducted against a hostile population that had provided enthusiastic support for each act of Palestinian terrorism. The massacre may have seemed wrong, but given the urgent need to save Jewish lives, it was utterly virtuous. There is, Halakhicly, no question that saving Jewish life justifies everything else, including killing Arab civilians:

> About the value of Israel's life, it simply seems that the life of Israel is worth more than the life of the Gentile and even if the Gentile does not intend to hurt Israel it is permissible to hurt him in order to save Israel. In a situation in which there is danger—even though remote—that the Gentile will operate (even if indirectly) to hurt Israel, there is no need to care about him and "thou shall kill the best of the Gentiles. . . ." We are consequently taught that the war referred to is not, necessarily, a real battle, but even a situation of national conflict justifies such killing. Those who may later help another [killer], when forced to by the ruler, deserve to be killed.[26]

Ginzburg's excitement over the Hebron massacre, which he called in another place "a shining moment" that "we" should all be "part of,"[27] assumes in another section of the lecture a seemingly fascist, almost pagan aura. This happens when the Nablus rabbi speaks about the general virtues of "revenge" and about the Jewish virtues of Dr. Goldstein, the ultimate Jewish avenger.

> Now we are getting to the heart of the matter and to the heart of the motivation—revenge. Revenge is not conducted from instrumental considerations,

> from an understanding of its utility. Revenge is a spontaneous reaction operated by the feeling that as long as I do not have the courage to hurt he who hurts me, I can not stand tall. . . . Revenge is stressing my positive essence, the truth in my being. . . . It is like a law of nature. He who takes revenge joins the "ecological currents" of reality. His "true being" meets there the rest of the world. . . . [28] Against this background, revenge is the return of the individual and the nation to believe in themselves, in their power and in the fact that they have a place under the sun and are no longer stepped upon by everybody. It is hard to ignore the excitement and encouragement felt by a large number of people upon learning of the Hebron Massacre, those strata of the population whose flesh is still alive in spite of the intense bleeding caused by all the stabbing wounds against it.[29]
>
> And a word about "the man," about Baruch Goldstein, may God avenge his blood. All those who knew him . . . felt that he acted out of his Jewish being. The act was not an unknown facet of his personality, but an essential part of his "iddishkeit"[sense of Jewishness]. Thus, although we have learned that the revenge is a natural reaction, *this* revenge was felt as pure Jewish revenge and not as an act of rough hooliganism (which is also legitimate). This was not a reaction of a Jewish ignoramus—who should also be blessed—but of a scholar and exemplary man.[30]

While a secular reader of the major essays in *Baruch Hagever* may find it difficult to distinguish between the levels of extremism expressed by the different contributors, there are, nevertheless, significant differences both in style and in substance. Rabbi David Cohen, a yeshiva instructor in the Kahane Chai stronghold, Kfar Tapuah, represents, in this perspective, the most extreme expression of Kahanism in the 1990s, the post-Goldstein Kahanism. It appears that even Kahane did not reach the radical intensity of his students.

> Revenge against the Gentiles is an inseparable part of the process of redemption. This process will peak in the War of Armageddon, in which all the Gentiles will unite to fight the people of Israel. God initiates this scenario in order to take final revenge against the rest of the nations for all the sorrow and pain they inflicted upon the people of Israel all through the generations.[31]

> Revenge is not left to God alone. The revenge executed by the people of Israeli should be understood as God's revenge, since the people of Israel are God's representative in the world. God wants us to take revenge and expects us, just as in the fulfillment of other commandments, to demonstrate our willingness to help Him in the correction of the world.[32]
>
> Revenge is a natural and instinctive human drive. No one is allowed to stop a person from taking just revenge. The individual Jew ought to hope and aspire for revenge and to be happy when he is finally privileged to take it into his own hands or see it in his eyes. Revenge provides the individual Jew with satisfaction and consolation for the troubles the people of Israel suffered for so long from the Gentiles.[33] Revenge is mercy and grace not only for the people of Israel but also for the evildoer himself. Only through the fulfillment of God's cruel commandment would the avenger be rewarded by a full and complete grace and mercy.[34] From an Halakhic perspective, the blood and property of individuals belonging to a hostile population are free game. Jews may exact vengeance upon them without distinguishing the good from the bad. Also, the court does not punish a Jew for shedding the blood of a Gentile, even if the killing was unjust, since the killing of a Gentile is not defined as "murder."

Another notorious contributor to *Baruch Hagever* was the young rabbi Ido Elba, a Kiryat Arba resident. If Elba's essay, "Elaboration of the Rulings about the Killing of a Gentile," had been published just a few months earlier, only a small number of people would have noticed it or cared to comment on its content. Elba had been an anonymous rabbi teaching in an unimportant *kollel* (learning circle) associated with the Cave of the Patriarchs. But by the time his essay was exposed to the public, via *Baruch Hagever*, Elba was already spending time in jail. In September 1994, Shin Beth uncovered a new Kiryat Arba plot. A small group of Jewish extremists centered around two brothers, Eitan and Yehoyada Kehalani, planned and attempted a series of revenge attacks on local Arabs. The conspiracy also involved a young army officer, Oren Edri, later charged with supplying arms and explosives to the group. In attempting to kill a young Arab villager, the Kehalani brothers were caught red-handed, having been spotted by the service, whose agents planted blank bullets in their guns. Both brothers were arrested on the spot. The Shin Beth investigation led, among other things, to the identification and arrest of the Halakhic figure behind the act, Rabbi Ido Elba. [35]

Sharing with the Kahanist counterculture an increasing admiration for Goldstein, Elba took upon himself the task of justifying with scholarship the Hebron massacre. He collected and presented all Halakhic sources that distinguish between killing Jews and killing Gentiles and showed how the two crimes are not equally punishable. Elba also demonstrated that under the conditions prevailing in Hebron, the killing of hostile Palestinians was not only a legitimate option but an obligatory operation. Maintaining that the Palestinians could be considered Amalekites—members of the Canaanite tribe whom biblical Jews were ordered to eliminate—Elba provided the scholarly foundation for the more popular arguments of Ginzburg and Cohen. His conclusion was unequivocal:

> The prohibitions of "thou shall not kill" and "he who sheds human blood" do not apply to a Jew who kills a Gentile and no authoritative prohibition is involved at all. An offensive war, launched in order to kill Gentiles for fear they may attack the Jews, is a legitimate option which must be conducted according to the rules of optional war. An offensive war against Gentiles known to be planning to hurt Jewish life or property, in a way that those Jews will desert their settlement, is an obligatory war, which must be conducted even on the Sabbath. This is the ruling regarding the war against Amalek, the seven nations and the war to conquer Eretz Israel.[36]

A revealing paragraph is found in the introduction of Elba's essay. The passage claimed that Elba did not write the article in order to stimulate concrete attacks on the Arabs. His motive, instead, was to study the Halakha's theoretical stand on the issue of killing Gentiles, and to clarify the issues involved with one of the greatest Halakhic authorities of the time. Rabbi Elba never named that authority in public, but people close to him hinted that the man was Rabbi Mordechai Eliyahu, the former Israeli chief Sephardi rabbi. Eliyahu, who first appears in the tales of this book as the head of the Covenant of the Zealots in the 1950s, had long been known for his extremist opinions. In the mid-1980s, while still chief rabbi, he paid the members of the Jewish Underground a private solidarity visit. He also wrote an official letter supporting the demand to build a synagogue atop the Temple Mount.[37] Rabbi Meir Kahane once confided in private to the author of this book that Eliyahu, one of the only rabbis he really respected, read and approved of all his books.[38]

Ido Elba failed to convince the court that his essay was an Halakhic study devoid of concrete implications. Several letters of support written by prominent rabbis did not help him either. Drawing on undisclosed evidence presented confidentially to the court, the justices sentenced Elba to eighteen months in prison. Convinced of his close association with the Kehalani brothers and their conspiracy to attack civilian Arabs, the justices ruled that Elba's document constituted an illegal incitement.

Most of the essays in *Baruch Hagever* addressed the Jewish-Muslim conflict with a Goldstein-like interpretation of what should be done in time of crisis. There was one noticeable exception, however, an essay written by Benjamin Ze'ev Kahane, the son of the slain rabbi and the young leader of Kahane Chai. The importance of Kahane's contribution lay not in his words about the Arabs but in what he had to say about the Jews. Kahane's argument: had the Jews displayed determination vis-à-vis the Palestinians—expelling them by force and abandoning the fiction of "Jewish democracy"—there would have been no Arab question and no Goldstein tragedy. The problem, according to the younger Kahane, was that a cultural war between the real and Hellenized Jews is forcefully being waged, with the secular Hellenized on the winning side. While young Kahane does not call in the book for a violent Jewish struggle against the "Hellenized," his historical example is very telling. The analogy goes back to the Hasmonean period and the precedents of "pious" Jews slaughtering Hellenized Jews in the name of God. One only has to note that *Baruch Hagever* was avidly read by Yigal Amir, who later spoke about Rabin's cultural war against the real Jews, to understand that young Kahane had identified in his essay the delicate passage between targeting Arabs, which was the "virtue" of Goldstein, and targeting Jews, so tragically expressed by Amir.[39]

> *The problem is not the Arabs—the problem is the Jews.* The truth, the way we look at it, is that there has never been an Arab problem. We could have solved

> that problem in 48 hours, *if only we wanted to.* The real war is not with the Arabs but with the *Hellenized Jews.* All the blood shed by Arab terrorism is "as if" shed by the Arabs; the people really responsible for the bloodshed are Jews scared by the Gentiles and attached to distorted Western ideas.
>
> Today's cultural war is more intense than the Hasmonean one. The Hellenization has penetrated or lives very deeply and its ideas have influenced even the "national" and religious public. The moment of truth has arrived. One possibility is to follow the path of Judaism, the entire Jewish idea, to reject the fear of the Gentile, Western democracy and the idea of co-existence with the Arabs. This way is the condition for the existence of a Jewish state. The other option is the acceptance of the yoke of democracy and the giving up of the dream of a Jewish state. There is no third way.[40]

The publication of *Baruch Hagever* had a larger meaning than the book itself. It was an indication of the maturation of the Kahanist counterculture and its small periphery. This counterculture, probably not larger than a few dozen activists and several hundred supporters, was politically insignificant. It constituted, however, an aggressive, radical spearhead, increasingly allowed to participate and express itself in the large, antigovernment operations of the Israeli opposition. The Kahanist counterculture brought the legitimacy crisis between the settlers and the Labor government to its peak. Comprised of the outlawed Kach and Kahane Chai as well as extremist yeshivas (Ginzburg's Tomb of Yoseph Yeshiva and a small *kollel* in Kiryat Arba, Menucha, and Rachel), the Kahanist counterculture publicly expressed its desire to engage in anti-Arab terrorism and to try Mssrs. Rabin and Peres for treason.

Outlawing Kach and Kahane Chai and the inability of their members to openly fly their original banners led to the rise to fame of Eyal (Israeli Fighting Organization), a new Kahanist organization. Eyal was formed two years earlier by a Tel Aviv University student, Avishai Raviv. First making a name for himself by demanding the resignation of the Arab head of Tel Aviv University's Student Association on the grounds that an Arab cannot be trusted, Raviv was eventually expelled from the university. He moved to Kiryat Arba, where he and a small number of activists started to attract media attention through provocative anti-Arab rhetoric and aggressive ceremonies against Jewish traitors. Eyal claimed to be more militant and radical than the original Kahane movement. In addition to admiring the slain Meir Kahane, Eyal activists expressed loyalty to Abraham Stern and the legacy of the anti-British undergrounds in Palestine. New recruits for the organization were expected to swear allegiance on Stern's grave. The oath included a solemn commitment to fight the nation's enemies, including the enemies within. Raviv proposed contingency plans for expelling Hebron's Arabs in the event the government of Israel pulled out, and even staged special horror shows for Israel's television networks. Masking their faces, armed Eyal activists moved in the Arab Casbah of Hebron and exercised in front of the camera terrorist acts against the local population.[41] Raviv and his vocal friends joined the other Goldstein admirers in becoming the major promoters of the character assassination of the nation's top leaders. Responsible for the mass production of vicious anti-Rabin posters, they were also involved in the printing of Rabin's picture in Nazi uniform.[42]

Before the Assassination: The Rabbinical Struggle Against Oslo II, the Rise of Zo Artzenu, and the "Pulsa Di Nura"

The process of delegitimization undergone by the radical right vis-à-vis the Rabin government reached a new peak in the summer of 1995. At issue was the implementation of Oslo II, the second stage of the agreement between Israel and the PLO. Stipulating that the Palestinian autonomy should now be expanded to seven major West Bank cities and several hundred villages, Oslo II significantly reduced Jewish control over Judea and Samaria. And it provided for the introduction of thousands of armed Palestinian policemen to the area. The Israeli right was increasingly frustrated; the Gaza-Jericho autonomy, contrary to the expectations of the right, seemed to be working well, and Arafat's police had not become a terrorist gang. Against this background, most settler demonstrations, planned to attract the attention of the public and intimidate the government, were less and less effective. Efforts by right-wing leaders such as Knesset member Hanan Porat to call for early elections fell on deaf ears.

A dramatic response to the new challenge was launched again by the spiritual authorities of the settlers. After a lengthy consultation, which included hearings of senior military officers, a distinguished rabbinical body ruled that it was illegal to evacuate military bases in Judea and Samaria and that soldiers should disobey such orders. The ruling was an aggressive extension of the previous decree, made over a year earlier, instructing soldiers to disobey settlement removal orders. The significant difference was that the rabbis had now expanded their judgments to purely military matters. Everybody recognized that there is a huge difference between civilian settlements and a military compound. No civilian rabbi in Israel had ever ruled, or claimed to be competent to rule, on technical matters involving the location of military bases. The rabbinical statement, which had behind it fifteen prominent rabbis including Rabbis Shapiro, Neria, and Ya'acov Ariel, read:

> We hereby determine that there is a Torah prohibition to evacuate IDF bases and transfer the place to the Gentiles. . . . A permanent military camp is a Jewish settlement in the full sense of the term. Its uprooting and desertion into the hands of the Gentiles goes under the same rule as the removal of an Eretz Israel settlement which is prohibited by law. It is therefore clear that no Jew is allowed to take part in any act aiding in the evacuation of a settlement, camp or a military compound.
>
> Never before has the army put its soldiers in a situation in which they had to act against their conscience. We call upon the government and the army to avoid putting soldiers through a decision involving a choice between the army's orders and loyalty to their ethical convictions.[43]

The new rabbinical ruling created a stronger commotion than the one made fifteen months earlier. Israel's president, Ezer Weizmann, who had been particularly attentive to the settlers' agony, was furious. Weizmann, a respected former general, refused to admit to his mansion a representative group of rabbis who came to explain. He demanded categorically that the new ruling be called off. The state attorney general declared his intention to try the rabbis for incitement. Hebrew University professor Aviezer Ravitzky, a leading Orthodox academic, stated that the ruling implied the symbolic collapse of "the Israeli social contract." Writing in *Yediot Aharonot*, Israel's largest daily, Ravitzky charged the rabbis with expressing "an extremist political position characteristic of a minority group, not the opinion of Israel's religion." Ravitzky doubted that a majority of Hesder Yeshiva soldiers would follow the reckless judgment; nevertheless, he warned against the danger of insubordination.[44]

While loud voices of anger were expressed by a group of army generals, a number of Yeshiva students said they would not follow the rabbis. Prime Minister Rabin made it clear that soldiers who followed the rabbis' order would be instantly court-martialed. Infuriated, Rabin told the journalists:

> It is unheard of that the democratically elected government will be forced by rabbis, using the Halakha to instruct soldiers to disobey orders. There has never been anything like this in Israel's past history. It is one of the worst things possible that a small number of rabbis, who do not represent the majority of Israeli rabbis, can make such a decision. It is unthinkable that we shall turn Israel into a banana republic. The entire Knesset, not just the government, ought to reject this matter.[45]

The public uproar over the new rabbinical ruling did not move any of the major signatories to apologize or retract their statement. Nor did it reduce the commitment of Israel's ultranationalists to bringing down the illegal government in the street. It led, on the contrary, to further radicalization. The division of Israeli Jews in the summer of 1995 was as wide as ever.

The intensifying frustration over the inability of the rabbis or the Yesha Council, the leading settler organization, to derail the peace process led to the meteoric rise of a new radical right movement, Zo Artzenu (This Is Our Land). Zo Artzenu was formed by two relatively unknown settlers, Moshe Feigelin and Schmuel Saket, residents of Ginot Shomron, an affluent bedroom community close to the Green Line. They were soon joined by Rabbi Benny Elon, the former head of the defunct Emunim Movement. Zo Artzenu's contribution to the antipeace struggle involved new measures of aggressive civil disobedience and new campaign rhetoric. Between July and October 1995, the activists of the new movement engaged in illicit settlement, roadblocking of the nation's major highways, and aggressive protests in front of government offices. Zo Artzenu drew attention to several other protest groups such as Women in Green, already active in places like the affluent town of Efrat.[46] In the summer of 1995, the activists of the new organization set the agenda of the radical right and dictated its style of struggle.

Though it gained notoriety in the summer of 1995, Zo Artzenu was originally formed in December 1993. Responding to the post-Oslo helplessness of Yesha Council, Feigelin and Saket suggested challenging the Israeli-Palestinian agreements by launching a massive wave of illicit settlements. Having secured partial financial support from the council, they recruited a number of activists and launched Operation Duplicate. The crux of the operation was the instant establishment of a twin settlement next to each existing West Bank settlement. The organization's master plan involved the formation of about 130 new illegal strongholds, staffed either by volunteers from within the Green Line or, temporarily, by the residents of the neighboring settlements. Each of the strongholds was expected to become a settlement eventually, thereby significantly increasing the number of Israeli residents of the occupied territories. The architects of the plan maintained that the Israeli army would not have enough soldiers to effectively stop every new stronghold and that the "phony peace process" would simply crumble.[47]

Launched between December 1993 and March 1994, Operation Duplicate ended in failure. Members of Zo Artzenu managed to establish a few new strongholds, confront some units of the army, and attract a few headlines, but the grand strategy faltered. Feigelin and Sacket failed to turn their organization into a mass movement, and only a small number of settlers were ready to actually "duplicate" their settlements in nearby areas. Most disappointing, however, was the attitude of Yesha Council. While lending an initial endorsement to Zo Artzenu, the council became increasingly skeptical. The two individuals involved were "outsiders," not fully trusted members of the settler movement. The fantastic operation they conceived—the establishment of 130 new settlements—appeared overly ambitious and unrealistic. The plan risked intense confrontations with the army, an eventuality the settler leadership did not seek. Also at risk was the *de facto* expansion of existing settlements—a trend that proceeded with the government's tacit approval. Following a handful of settler-soldier confrontations, which produced a few hundred arrests, Yesha Council decided to withdraw its support. In spite of the large amount of funds raised for the project and the founders' commitment to see it to its fruition, Operation Duplicate simply withered away.[48]

By the summer of 1995, the level of settler frustration had reached new heights. Outraged, bitter, and eager to improve their lot, the established settler leaders did not have new ideas for waging their struggle. The peace process seemed unstoppable, and many activists became increasingly fatalistic. This was the time for Feigelin and Saket and an opportunity to test Zo Artzenu's ideas with Operation Duplicate II. Begun on August 8, the sequel operation involved the establishment of thirty new strongholds as twin settlements in the West Bank. Thousands of eager activists were now ready to start extralegal operations and disobey the army's evacuation orders. Hundreds were arrested and sent to prison. Settler-soldier confrontations were now heavily reported in the press, and a formidable protest movement was quickly developing.[49]

Boosted by their growing impact on the Israeli media, the heads of Zo Artzenu decided to bring their campaign across the Green Line. The idea was to start disrupting life and public order in Israel proper, telling the government that unless it suspended the peace process, its own operation would be literally stopped in the streets. Operation Roadblock, conducted by several thousand Zo Artzenu volunteers, was a military-style mission that acted in an almost military fashion. Spreading out to nearly eighty road junctions across the country and coordinated by Rabbi Benny Elon flying above in a chartered helicopter, these activists succeeded in disrupting transportation for several hours. Nearly three thousand policemen were needed to clear the roads and highways. The clearing was not completed before 130 activists had been arrested, including Moshe Feigelin, the movement's head.

While fulfilling their expectation of gaining publicity, Zo Artzenu heads failed in their main objective of making their struggle popular inside Israel proper. Stuck for hours on the roads, most Israeli drivers did not appreciate the disorder. Instead of becoming sympathetic to the antipeace struggle, they became increasingly hostile. Operation Roadblock proved to be counterproductive, making Zo Artzenu unpopular countrywide. Later efforts to repeat the disruption on September 13 and 29, the second anniversary of Oslo I and the signing day of Oslo II, showed decreasing effectiveness. Fewer volunteers were ready to participate in the unpopular activities within the Green Line, and none of the operations' objectives was reached. Another provocative venture, an ambitious plan to have hundreds of thousands of Israelis turn off their lights all over the country, failed miserably. No serious disruption was reported by Israel's Electric Company and the event had little impact. Asked about the failure, Feigelin responded, "We cannot fail, since we have nothing to lose."[50]

The intense attention given to Zo Artzenu, as well as its increasing role in shaping the agenda of the radical right, was not achieved solely because of the organization's disruptive tactics. Of special attraction for the media were the new faces and unrecognized voices. The most active members of Zo Artzenu were Americans who had immigrated to Israel. In their interviews with the media, they stressed commitment to the American tradition of civil disobedience. Many young Israelis learned for the first time about the civil rights movement, Martin Luther King Jr., and the struggle against the Vietnam War. Dominated by liberal and left-wing journalists, Israel's media loved the new images, which were a far cry from the conservative and messianic rhetoric of Gush Emunim. Zo Artzenu activist David Romanoff told this to a reporter:

> We are free of past memories and do not suffer from deep-seated Israeli inhibitions and commitments. This is what we had absorbed in American universities in the demonstrations against the Vietnam War. I was deeply impressed by Martin Luther King's argument that above the state's law, there is a superior moral law. I remember going to Columbia University in support of Jewish students acting to free Zion's prisoners [in the Soviet Union]. At that time I witnessed students striking against the Vietnam War. Our methods of "civil disobedience," or "refusal to obey the law," were very effectively used there."[51]

Heavily reported in the foreign press, Zo Artzenu's rhetoric was particularly effective with an American audience. The young movement succeeded in establishing nearly forty American support groups, with special concentrations in Seattle, Miami, and New York. Much of the funding for the big operations came from the United States. Also attractive for Americans was the effort to justify the struggle against the Israeli government in the language of American democracy. Moshe Feigelin, born to Australian parents but married to an American, commented on the new phenomenon:

> There is an American approach to freedom which does not exist in this country and I live among Americans who know the real meaning of individual freedom. Freedom does not mean that the government, which won the elections, is free to do whatever it pleases. This is how things are conducted in Israel, which is not a democracy but a "dictatorcy." When a person who barely wins the majority moves to take the most precious objects of the Jewish majority in the country, and speaks in the name of democracy, he cannot expect his actions to go without resistance. The reason the opposition comes mostly from American immigrants is because they understand the meaning of democracy.[52]

While insisting on the right of the Jews to disagree with their government and engage in civil disobedience in matters most dear to them, there was little Zo Artzenu activists were ready to say about the rights of the Palestinians. When asked of his opinion about the connection of Martin Luther King Jr. as a role model for the movement's demand to deny a Palestinian the right of self-determination, Rabbi Benny Elon was candid:

> My understanding is derived from the conception of "Jewish and Democratic State." Yes, I am an American in my aspiration for a democratic state, but no, I am not an American in the sense that I think ethnically and I wish for a Jewish state. Everybody is, thus, allowed to vote, but it must be inscribed in the fundamental laws that this is the state of the Jewish people. No legal government should therefore be established here without a Jewish majority.[53]

Echoing the civil disobedience ideas of attorney Elyakim Ha'etzni, who was glad to join forces with the new movement, Feigelin, Zo Atzenu's chairman, was very critical of the protest tactics practiced by most settler organizations. Only a *real struggle*, i.e., uncompromising civil disobedience and the readiness of a large number of people to be arrested, could mobilize the masses against the government and effectively stop the peace process:

> What is a *real struggle*? A struggle is an operation planned to put the government in an impossible situation. A real struggle is a struggle in which the government's challenger has plenty of ammunition and a chance to keep fighting until the expected victory.
>
> What is a *protest*? Everything else. Demonstrations against passing events (such as Arafat's visit), rallies, bumper stickers, articles, hunger strikes and all other important activities . . . conducted according to rules acceptable to the government.
>
> Under the present system of government which is a democratic tyranny (because it puts its opponents at the mercy of an army of terrorists armed by it), the effectiveness of protest is extremely limited and there is no other way but struggle.
>
> The major problem is that those who have assumed leadership positions in the struggle refused until recently to recognize the seriousness of the new situation. This is why they have been unable to stop or even slow down the process of disintegration. There were, indeed, meaningful accomplishments such as stopping the Hebron evacuation and keeping Arafat in Gaza, but these were only tactical achievements. Strategically speaking, i.e., halting the process which takes us to the void, we have not been successful. Worse yet, the process has been intensified. . . .
>
> How should the struggle be conducted? Once a real struggle is launched, a large number of settlers and supporters will be ready for *messirut hanefesh*. . . . These people are ready to go through lengthy arrests and loss of income. But they will not leave their homes for partial truths or "like struggles." Those who can take hits without responding, take humiliations without answering—perhaps even smile (such Christian qualities!), must be selected. With the help of these people, it may, perhaps, be possible to stop the destructive process we are presently undergoing. . . .
>
> In order to conduct this kind of struggle, there is neither a need of hundreds of thousands nor tens of thousands. Just a few hundred people, clear

> about the struggle's objectives, ready for *messirut hanefesh* and supported by a solid ideological and political leadership, will suffice.
>
> The role of the masses is to provide broad legitimacy to this fighting group—which will make the life of the government miserable—through ordinary protest methods. These masses will provide moral and financial support for the fighters who are likely to find themselves in prison. The writer of this article can testify from personal experience, how demonstrations outside the prison cell, and mobilization of a large public support had unequivocally reduced the regime's ability to repress Zo Artzenu's prisoners.[54]

Zo Artzenu failed to bring down the Israeli government in the street. It was very successful, however, in greatly intensifying the atmosphere of delegitimation surrounding the government. The movement's operations served as rallying events for the entire hard core of the radical right, whose number reached into the hundreds. In addition to thousands of yeshiva students, bused over from their seminaries, it was possible to meet in these events former members of the now-illegal Kach and Kahane Chai, as well as a few Eyal activists. Present also were students of the extremist Tomb of Yoseph Yeshiva in Nablus and Hebron, and Kiryat Arba radicals, a large number of veteran Gush Emunim types, and radical students and activists from within the Green Line, such as Yigal Amir. All of them mingled, argued a lot, vented frustrations, and shared struggle experiences. Old and new posters and slogans—"Rabin and Peres are Traitors," "Assassins," "Collaborators of Terrorism"—were the order of the day. Not a few of the activists started to speak and chant freely about the need to execute the "traitors."

On October 6, 1995, just two days after the holiday of Yom Kippur, an odd group of extremists gathered in front of the prime minister's Jerusalem residence. The purpose of the meeting, convened by Avigdor Eskin, a former Kach activist, was to conduct the traditional ceremony of Pulsa di Nura against Yitzhak Rabin. Pulsa di Nura (in Aramaic, blaze of fire) is the most severe death curse that can be made against a Jewish sinner. The imposition of this mystical punishment is very rare and is performed, if at all, by Kabbalistic rabbis. The curse ceremony is so mysterious that it is not even mentioned in official writing, with instructions about its conduct said to be passed orally from father to son. The execution of the curse is not a simple matter. Ten rabbis and community heads have to convene in a synagogue, fast for three days, then make the curse at midnight. The cursing operation is considered dangerous because if made against an innocent person, it strikes back at the cursers. The curse text, which is read after a long ceremony focused on a mystical dialogue with the angels of destruction, reads:

> Angels of destruction will hit him. He is damned wherever he goes. His soul will instantly leave his body . . . and he will not survive the month. Dark will be his path and God's angel will chase him. A disaster he has never experienced will beget him and all curses known in the Torah will apply to him.[55]

It is not known whether all the formal requirements of the Pulsa di Nura were fulfilled by the group convened before Rabin's mansion. The fact that Israeli citizens, although very few and very extreme, considered its invocation and preparation during Yom Kippur was, however, very telling. It indicated that the verbal violence directed at Rabin in the fall of 1995 had become serious enough to include death wishes. It showed, furthermore, that given the risks involved in a false Pulsa di Nura, the rabbis involved felt very confident. This is what Avigdor Eskin, the organizer of the ceremony and its propagator to the media, had to say after the assassination:

> Just before Yom Kippur we found out that in addition to its readiness to surrender Hebron to our enemies, the Rabin government was willing to give them partial control over the city's Jewish cemetery. Upon hearing this, I concluded that all red lines had been crossed. Following a consultation with a few rabbis, we decided to conduct the ceremony known as Pulsa di Nura.
>
> This prayer is not a death sentence against anybody, but an appeal for Heavenly arbitration. The purpose is, indeed, that one side—either the curser or the cursed—will be hit, but the decision is in the hands of Heaven. He who wishes to curse an innocent person will get hurt for doing so. We simply brought our trial of Rabin before Heavenly systems.[56]

Another indication that the conflict between Rabin and his political opponents was quickly getting out of control was made a week later, at Netanya's Wingate Sport Institute. Upon a visit he paid to a gathering of

Israeli citizens of Anglo-Saxon origin, Rabin met an aggressive group of hecklers. In contrast to past experiences with this crowd, which had never gone beyond verbal violence, the Wingate confrontation looked very much like a physical assault on the prime minister. Rabin was not shielded by his guards before being physically approached by one of the hecklers.[57] It became apparent at that time how easy it could be to walk up to the prime minister with or without his security detail present.

Yigal Amir—A Profile of a Jewish Zealot

The assassination of Prime Minister Rabin stunned the nation. Naturally the peace camp, whose activists had come to despise the rhetorical violence of the Israeli right, was shocked. Stunned also was the extreme right, including most of the individuals who had either used that rhetoric or allowed it to be expressed in their rallies and demonstrations. There are many indications that the vast majority of the organizations and individuals who spoke the language of delegitimation and engaged in character assassination did not really wish to see Rabin dead. The possibility of a Jew killing the nation's top leader, who was also the hero of the 1967 war, in which Israel greatly expanded its borders, was inconceivable to them. It further appears that even the Kahane supporters and the few messianic types close to their extremism, who may have wanted to see Rabin dead, were not mentally ready to murder him.[58]

Yigal Amir was an exception to the rule, a true believer convinced that the killing of the prime minister was a godly order. Amir was a loner who felt uncomfortable as a registered member of any ideological movement or close yeshiva cell. But Rabin's assassin participated in many of the activities of the anti-Oslo extraparliamentary opposition and ran with the hard core of the extremist messianic right. Amir's personal convictions, reinforced by his radical friends, told him that only an extraordinary operation could save the people of Israel from the gathering storm. This is how he explained the assassination to his investigators:

> Without believing in God, I would never have had the power to do this—i.e., the belief in the after world. In the last three years I have understood that

> Rabin is not the leader who could lead the people. . . . He did not care about Jews, he lied, he had a lust for power. He brainwashed the people and the media. He came up with ideas such as a Palestinian State. Together with Yasser Arafat, the murderer, he was awarded the Nobel Peace Prize, but he failed to address his people's problems. He divided the people. He marginalized the settlers and did not care about them. I had to save the people because the people failed to understand the real conditions, and this is why I acted. He used repeatedly the term "victims of peace." Soldiers had been killed in Lebanon and the government did not respond because there was a political process. . . .
>
> If not for a Halakhic ruling of *din rodef,* made against Rabin by a few rabbis I knew about, it would have been very difficult for me to murder. Such a murder must be backed up. If I did not get the backing and I had not been representing many more people, I would not have acted.[59]

In his confession to the interviewers of the state investigation committee, Amir said that the media ignored the protests and demonstrations of the right. He told the investigators that had the protest operations been properly covered by the media, he might not have assassinated the prime minister.[60]

Amir, a slight, dark-skinned, dark-haired son of Yemenites, was born in Herzeliya in 1970 to a lower-middle-class family. Amir's mother, Geula, the dominant figure in an eight-child family, was a longtime kindergarten instructor in Herzeliya's Neve Amal neighborhood. She was known for extremist views, expressed, among other things, in a pilgrimage she made to Baruch Goldstein's grave in Kiryat Arba. The father, Shlomo, a deeply committed Orthodox Jew, specialized in calligraphic writing of Jewish holy books. Most of the family's modest income came from Geula's private kindergarten, located in the family's back yard.[61] Yigal's primary education was obtained in a *haredi* elementary school belonging to Agudat Israel. His secondary education was in Yeshivat Hayeshuv Hehadash, a *haredi* yeshiva in Tel Aviv. According to a number of reports, Amir was an exception in the yeshiva, for unlike most of his peers he was interested in military service. After graduation, he parted company with his classmates and moved to the Hesder Yeshiva of Kerem de-Yavneh, near Ashdod. Nothing in this early training indicated future exceptional radicalism. Kerem de-Yavneh, a large, highly respected high yeshiva, was always known for the relative moderation of its instructors and graduates.

Amir's military experience was obtained in Golani Brigade, a leading combat unit in the Israeli Defense Forces. Golani friends of the assassin testified that while serving in the occupied territories during the Intifada, the young man tortured local Palestinians and took pride in his deeds.[62] Unlike the majority of the extreme right activists, who move to settlements in Judea, Samaria, and Gaza, or continue studying in a high yeshiva after completing military service, Amir went back to Herzeliya. He registered for Bar Ilan University's law school and was chosen for a special education program in the former Soviet Union. As part of a group of former Hesder students, he was selected to teach Hebrew to young Jews in Riga, Latvia.[63]

Amir's political views became greatly radicalized during his tenure at Bar Ilan, Israel's only religious university. He started to take classes after the September 1993 Oslo Accords and seemed to have ignited at once. Though enrolled in two prestigious university programs, law and computers, the young man devoted even more time to the university's *kollel*, a respected institution for the rigorous study of Halakha. But Amir's free time was increasingly spent in right-wing political action. He became the driving force behind the student protest activities at Bar Ilan University, many of which took place on the nearby highway bridge. Amir was also responsible for organizing university discussion groups about the future of Eretz Israel.[64]

In 1993 Amir first obtained his Bereta (double-action) gun, later to be used in the killing of Rabin. To qualify for a gun license, Amir had to prove to the Interior Ministry that he was residing in a settlement outside of the Green Line. And indeed, he obtained a temporary Shavei Shomron address. It was around that time that he started organizing student support groups for several Yesha settlements. Starting in Netzarim, an isolated Gaza Strip village, Amir soon shifted his efforts to Hebron. The government's threat to evacuate Tel Rumeida had a profound impact on the young man. Determined to fight both the Israeli government and the Palestinian population, Amir started to organize solidarity weekends in Hebron. Dozens of Bar Ilan students, sometimes hundreds, would come for the weekend to express their commitment to the holy city. They held Sabbath services together, prayed, sang, and mingled with the local radicals.[65] Amir told investigators that his hidden agenda in these activities was to identify and recruit individuals willing to defend the settlements by force if the government decided to evacuate them.

Amir's obsession with the campaign of the radical right brought him in touch with several organizations and a large number of leading activists. He showed up at most Zo Artzenu operations, participated in the large rallies, and was visible in several settler confrontations with the army. At the university, Amir seemed to have been particularly friendly with Avishai Raviv, Eyal's leader and a well-known provocateur.[66] After the Rabin assassination, when he was identified as a Shin Beth informer, Amir said friends warned him of Raviv and he was cautious about him. Once approaching Benny Katzover, the Gush Emunim veteran radical leader, Amir was bitter and critical of the settlers' lack of determination. He told Katzover that the mischievous government could be toppled only by force.

In spite of his increasing radical involvement, Amir still did not become a registered member in any recognized protest group. He either did things on his own or acted in concert with a small group of friends, mostly Bar Ilan students, who heard him speak repeatedly of *din rodef* and of the obligation to kill Rabin and Peres. No one, including Avishai Raviv, the Shin Beth informer, took him seriously. Raviv's failure to report Amir's statements about Rabin were later the reason for the rise of the baseless conspiracy theory that people within the service were responsible for the assassination because "they knew but did nothing." Yigal Amir's closest friend, who shared all his political convictions, was his younger brother, Haggai. Haggai Amir, later put on trial as an accomplice in the murder, was an amateur technician crazy about special weapons. Raiding Amir's house after the assassination, the police discovered a small but very sophisticated arms cache comprising hand grenades, bullets, and explosives. Haggai had manufactured the hollow-point bullets used for the assassination.[67] A third person close to the Amir brothers and their conspiracy was Dror Adani, a Beit Haggai settler with family in Herzelia. Adani met Yigal Amir in the Hesder Yeshiva, and the two served together in the army.[68] There were indications that in addition to their discussion of the need to assassinate Rabin, about which only Yigal was totally serious, the group had other violent plans. These included punishment raids on West Bank Arabs and an attack on Palestinian terrorists freed by Israel in the context of the peace process. The Amir brothers entertained, in addition, several spectacular ideas of killing Rabin. They discussed preparing a car bomb or injecting nitroglycerin into the house's water system.[69]

Two other Bar Ilan students, Hila Frank and Margalit Har Shefi, also belonged to Amir's close circle. They participated in many of Bar Ilan's demonstrations and attended several of the Hebron solidarity weekends. It appears that Yigal Amir conducted serious talks with Har Shefi, in which he tried to include her in an antigovernment underground. Learning of his desire to kill the prime minister, an idea she rejected, Har Shefi told the young man she would join only if no violence were involved.[70] But under Amir's influence, Har Shefi asked her Beth El Rabbi, Shlomo Aviner, whether Rabin qualified as a *rodef*.

Yigal Amir admired Baruch Goldstein, who also acted on his own. He is said to have decided at Goldstein's funeral that he also had to conduct an exemplary act. *Baruch Hagever*, the volume commemorating Goldstein's act, was one of the few books found in Amir's library.[71] In his investigation Amir said: "*Din moser* and *din rodef* is the Halakhic ruling. Once it is a ruling, there is no longer a problem of morality. If I were involved now in the biblical conquest of the land, and as said in Joshua, I would have had to kill babies and children, I would have done so regardless of the problem of morality. Once it is a ruling, I do not have a problem with it."[72]

It is almost certain that Yigal Amir had no unequivocal rabbinical sanction to kill Rabin. Rabin's assassin told his investigators that he had discussed the issue of *din rodef* and *din moser* with several rabbis but none of them was ready to give him a green light. When asked about his opinion of these rabbis or other rabbis he admired, Amir said he was disappointed with the rabbis because they were all "soft and political." Rather than ruling on this matter according to the Halakha, Amir said, the rabbis introduced irrelevant political considerations into the discussion. Amir also told his investigators that he admired no prominent rabbi in this generation. The decision to kill Rabin thus was taken by the young man alone. Amir believed he was fully cognizant of the relevant Halakhic law and had a sufficient understanding of the misery of the Israeli people to act on his own.[73]

The Halakhic instrument that ultimately convinced Amir he should kill Rabin was the ancient Jewish doctrine of zealotry. This doctrine maintains that under the most extreme circumstances, a God-loving Jew can kill another person without asking permission. As shown in chapter 3, the tradition goes back to Pinchas, the son of Elazar, who killed, during Exodus, another Jew. That person, Zimri, the son of Salue, was among many Israelites who made love in public with young Midianite women against God's orders. In killing Zimri, young Pinchas committed an unauthorized murder of a fellow Jew and had to be severely punished. Yet not only was his act forgiven by God, "for he was zealous for my sake among them," but God instantly terminated a plague that had already killed twenty thousand Jews.[74] Pinchas's entire line of ancestors were made priests of Israel. The prophet Elijah is also described in the Bible as a zealot who killed in his wrath four hundred priests of Baal, a Canaanite god.

The Jewish doctrine of zealotry had never been fully institutionalized nor could it ever be. This is why the concepts of "zealot" and "zealotry" always remained unique, exceptional, and extraordinary. According to Rabbi Shaul Yisraeli, an act of zealotry qualifies as such if it is conducted in an utmost emergency, if it is clear that the act is guided by total awe of God, if the actor is ready to risk his life in the name of God, and if no possibility of personal gain is involved.[75]

Yigal Amir convinced himself that in killing Rabin he was acting in the best tradition of Jewish zealotry. He was sure that in order to save the land and the nation, Rabin had to die. He was certain that this was God's will, which other believers recognized but were hesitant to carry out.[76] While it is evident that he did not wish to die, Amir was ready to give his life if self-sacrifice were the only way to serve God's will. He certainly understood that he would spend his life in prison. After admitting to his investigators that no particular rabbi had authorized his act, Amir told them about the biblical precedents of Pinchas and Yael (who murdered the warlord Sisera). He also told the investigators that before he committed the murder he read the Balak portion, the passage in the Hebrew Bible that tells Pinchas's story and the killing of Zimri.[77]

According to the assassin's psychological evaluators, Amir's is a complex personality of a highly intelligent young man who sought love and admiration at any price. He had a desire to prove to himself, his mother, his friends, and others that he could go further than anybody else. He admitted that he was afraid someone else would kill Rabin, and thereby steal his chance for fame; "I wanted a thinking person to do this. I was afraid an Arab might kill him. I wanted Heaven to see that a Jew had done this."[78] The district psychologists found out that from a young age, Amir was a loner who refused to take orders. He acted against the consensus, thought very highly of himself, and believed he had original solutions that no one else recognized.[79] From his court testimony it was revealed that Amir spent little time at home as a boy. He studied in schools far from home and did not play soccer on the playground with the other kids. A Jewish Agency report on Amir, made after he failed to qualify as a summer camp instructor in the United States, identified him as "an uptight personality, unfit for team work, inflexible and low on a sociometric scale."[80]

In his testimony, Amir discussed his training, self-discipline, and faith in reason:

> My general world view is based on the path of the Torah, on the 613 *mitzvot* [commandments]. This leads to complete control of the body, the passions, the physical and emotional drives. The Torah is reason. He who acts emotionally acts like an animal. This is my morality. This is Judaism's general view and I implement it."[81]

Amir described his struggle for excellence through his computer science study. He told the court that law and criminology, which he had originally chosen as majors, quickly bored him and led him to skip classes. So he turned to the study of the really challenging computer science. "One can learn of my approach to life from the example of computers. Every subject in life is determined by the war between the passion and the intellect, and there are things I 'push aside.' I often sin and I know I am wrong. But finally I overcome. Slowly I advance without looking to either left or right and with no ability to stop."[82]

Amir zeroed in on Yitzhak Rabin after the first Oslo Accord and would not let his "evil" image go. Loyal to his method, he identified the goal and moved to accomplish it in stages. The ability to kill Rabin was built by "a self-courage test." Amir told the interviewers of the State Investigation Committee: "I never chased Rabin. I did not believe I would ever do this. I always thought I was just talking, that I would never have the strength to do this, even though I knew it had to be done. I said, 'Rabin should be killed' and I would smile. Nobody believed that a legitimate fellow, very nice, very logical, funny guy, would kill Rabin. Even I, myself, did not know I would kill Rabin." Rabin's assassination may have been, from this perspective, the act of a megalomaniac seeking to demonstrate his strength of will in public.[83]

Uriel Weil, a clinical psychologist who also examined Amir, identified an additional dimension to Rabin's killing—Amir's depressive personality, which had been sensitized by his dogmatic ideology. Amir "had within him depressive elements which preceded his act. Emotional drives, including rage and frustration, may have burst out despite his effort to fully control his emotions and act only according to pure reason."[84] Amir's only girlfriend, Nava Holtzaman, a pretty and religious woman, left him in January 1995 after five happy months to marry a good friend of his. Amir, who attended the wedding, is said to have gone into deep depression over this.[85] Yigal's father, Shlomo Amir, said after the murder that had his son married Nava, he would never have committed the crime. Geula Amir also spoke about her son's deep depression after the split. Amir's brother, Haggai, also did not believe that Yigal, under normal circumstances, was capable of murder. He confirmed the reports that following the break with his girlfriend, Yigal went into deep depression. It was after the break with Nava that he started to talk about sacrificing himself.

Amir testified in court that before he committed the murder, he prayed that he would succeed in killing Rabin without hurting himself because he did not want to be a dead hero. He was quick to give the police his identity card, lest there be a mistake about his identity. Amir seems to have wished that all who did not believe he was capable of murdering the prime minister—friends, family, girls who did not return his affection—would know that he did indeed do it, that he was the best.[86]

Amir's depression deepened with the advance of the peace process and the ineffectiveness of the right-wing protests. He began to feel a growing obligation and a heavenly calling to commit the extreme act. The unique mixture of mysticism and religious rationalism was reaching an explosion. A reading of Amir's friends' testimonies suggests that many warning signs indicated that Amir was serious about his conviction that Rabin should die. Yigal took Haggai on numerous visits to Rabin's house, and the two discussed many ways of killing the prime minister. Amir told his investigators that on at least two previous occasions, he was armed and ready to kill Rabin. But on both occasions he had a "sign from Heaven" not to act. On one such occasion Rabin did not show up; on another, he was heavily protected by security. On the night of November 4, Amir received the "go" sign. He easily negotiated the Kings of Israel VIP parking lot and waited patiently for forty minutes. According to Amir's testimony, God made it clear that He wanted Rabin dead.[87]

Rabin's killing was made possible by a serious security blunder. Just a few months before the assassination, Israel's Shin Beth chief, Karmi Gilon, met with several settler leaders in a session devoted to a portrayal of the prime minister's potential assassin and to the service's plea that the leaders restrain their rhetoric and action in opposition to the government. The participants in the meeting were told that Israel's security service was gravely concerned about an ideologically motivated single assailant from central Israel. In the months before the secret meeting, and especially in the summer and fall of 1995, the service became increasingly concerned with the radicalization of the extreme right. Special attention had been given to the discussions about *din rodef* and the talks, known to have been conducted in small radical circles, about the need to kill Rabin and Peres. The risk of political assassination by a Jewish extremist was understood months before Rabin was killed.[88]

One report about a possible assassination of Yitzhak Rabin was made by two acquaintances of Yigal Amir—Hila Frank and Shlomi Halevy. Frank, a Bar Ilan law student, was a member of Amir's small activist group. She took part in several Hebron weekends and knew Yigal well. Like other close associates, Frank had heard Amir speak often of the obligation to kill the prime minister. And like all of them, she did not take him seriously. Except once. During one conversation, Amir told Frank of his readiness to kill the prime minister and of a confession he had already made in the synagogue. Fully aware that confession is a serious matter because it indicates one's preparedness to die soon, Frank felt she now had to warn the authorities. Following an examination of the issue with Shlomi Halevy, who happened to serve in Israel's military intelligence, the two decided to break their silence. Since they were friends of Amir and unsure of the seriousness of his statements, Frank and Halevy agreed to report the matter without identifying Amir by name. Halevy told his military commander that when in the public bathroom of Tel Aviv's Central Bus Station, he heard two people speaking about a plot to kill the prime minister. According to Halevy's report, the two spoke about a small, dark, Orthodox, curly-haired Yemenite Bar Ilan student from Herzeliya, who expressed an interest in killing the prime minister. Following the report of Halevy's commander to the police, Halevy himself was summoned. He told the investigators the same story and denied, again, any knowledge of the individual involved.[89] The information was passed on to the Shin Beth, which filed it without additional investigation. The service's explanation for not pursuing Halevy's report further was that they had received hundreds of similar warning signals and were incapable of pursuing them all. Halevy's failure to mention Amir by name gave his report low priority in the Shin Beth.

Although the service's chiefs were not aware of any concrete plan to execute the prime minister, it is difficult to argue that the writing was not on the wall. Reports like Halevy's made it clear that the radical right was growing more bitter and frustrated by the day, and that the language of political assassination had become common. But despite all this advance knowledge, Rabin was poorly protected. The VIP parking lot was not sealed off to the crowd. Amir slipped in unhindered, as did a few other interested onlookers. Neither Shimon Peres, who could have been shot as easily as Rabin, nor Rabin himself was completely surrounded by bodyguards. A large number of personal guards were present but they were not alert. Flanking both Rabin and Peres on their sides—but allowing access from the back—the security team offered no protection from close-range, point-blank gunfire. It was a miracle that Shimon Peres did not join Rabin in their march to their cars. Israel could have lost not one but both great architects of the Oslo peace accords.

9

JEWS WHO KILL?

Some Afterthoughts on Israeli Political Violence

The Hebron massacre and the Rabin assassination undoubtedly had a traumatic effect on a large number of Israelis. The reaction of most Jews and non-Jews who have long cultivated the image of the civic-minded, nonconfrontational, hesitant Jew was that these atrocities were fundamentally un-Jewish. A more refined version of the same reaction was expressed in the argument that the state of Israel, an unprecedented experience in two thousand years of Jewish history, gave birth to a new breed of Jews—"Gentilized," unrestrained, and even ruthless. The belief that Diaspora Jews are incapable of committing such acts was implied in many of the shocked responses to the news from Israel. But is it really the case? Has the Israeli political culture created a new breed of merciless Jews not subject to the famed Jewish ethic of restraint, Jews who, unlike their Diaspora brethren, kill without remorse?

Although the question of Jewish violence has rarely been subjected to a systematic treatment, the issue of "tough Jews" and the use of force and power by Diaspora Jews have been the subject of two major books published in the United States in the last decade: David Biale's *Power and Powerlessness in Jewish History* and Paul Breines's *Tough Jews.*[1] Both studies are highly relevant to the issue under consideration because they challenge the common belief that between the Bar Kokhba Revolt (A.D. 135) and the beginning of the Zionist venture in Palestine (1882), Jews did not resort to physical force, practice military activity, or engage in systematic criminal and political violence.

One of Biale's major arguments is that the portrayal of Diaspora Jews as victims who only sought salvation in prayer or flight and who accepted death in lieu of fighting for their lives is erroneous. Biale's many examples go back to late antiquity and the early Middle Ages, in which Babylonian and Iraqi Jews were involved in armed uprisings, and to western and central European Jews who retained the right to bear arms and did contest their opponents. Biale also documents cases in which Jews in medieval Europe were expected by the local rulers to participate actively in their community's defense.[2] He reminds us of the case of Shmuel ha-Nagid, a poet and military leader who commanded the Muslim armies of Grenada in the eleventh century. Biale refutes, in contrast to the common historical memory, the impression of Polish Jews helplessly slaughtered during the seventeenth century by the Ukrainian Cossacks of Bogdan Chmielnitski, showing that there was in fact armed resistance. Chmielnitski's major target was not Polish Jews but the Polish landowners served by Jews; apparently there was plenty of opposition to the attacks, involving a large number of Jews fighting alongside Poles. Lower-class Jews were especially involved in this physical resistance.[3]

Two tales of Jewish atrocities in antiquity, not referred to by Biale but mentioned in Christian chronicles of the time, tell the stories of the massacres of Christians in Jerusalem and Antiochia (Syria). The first case involved the Jewish community of Jerusalem during the Persian conquest of the city (614). A large number of Byzantine Christians were handed over by the Persians to the city's Jews, who brutally slaughtered them in revenge for centuries of repression.[4] Bar Ilan University's Elimelech Horowitz believes that the number of dead reached four thousand.[5] Jewish insurgents who rebelled against the Byzantines in Antiochia six years later mimicked these atrocities. In addition to killing and setting ablaze many Christians, they also tortured the city's Patriarch and mutilated his body.[6]

Putting in historical perspective the Hebron massacre committed by Baruch Goldstein during the holiday of Purim, Horowitz suggests further that Jews often used this holiday to take revenge against hated Gentiles.

The story of Purim, as told in the book of Esther, recalls the great Jewish revenge against Haman and his allies, the Persian officials who planned to kill all the Jews of the country but ended up hanging on a rope. There are numerous commentaries on Diaspora Jews who hanged or otherwise killed individual Christians during Purim celebrations.[7]

Paul Breines, whose major interest is the normative restoration of the image of the "gentle Jew," is particularly specific about the presence of "tough Jews" in modern Europe and the United States. Breines reminds us of the Jews who became soldiers in New Amsterdam in the seventeenth century, of the six hundred Jews (including twenty-four officers) who served in the American War of Independence, of the two thousand who participated on the British side in the Boer War, and of the hundreds who, like Captain Alfred Dreyfus, served as officers and soldiers in the French army.[8] He also refers to the large Jewish participation in the socialist revolutionary movement since the late nineteenth century, including their disproportional presence in terrorist organizations such as the Narodniya Volya (People's Will) in Russia and the Fighting Organization of the Social Revolutionaries, a historical fact ignored in most discussions of Jewish meekness.[9] Leon Trotsky, the first commissar of the Red Army, had no "Jewish" hesitations whatsoever in heading the massive terror campaign that followed the Russian Revolution and in justifying it in a theoretical essay on terrorism.[10]

Breines's discussion of the rugged "Jewish cowboy" and the tough "Jewish gangster" in America is particularly illuminating. He recalls the German Jews who emigrated to the United States after the revolution of 1848 and became not only successful businessmen but also genuine cowboys in the American West. Citing Fred Rochlin's study of Jewish cowboys' achievements, Breines writes about the many illustrations of gun-toting Jews riding tall in the saddle, the numerous Jewish sheriffs and mayors in the second half of the nineteenth century, and even mentions Josephine ("Josie") Sarah Marcus, who became the wife of the notorious gunman Wyatt Earp.[11] While showing that the Wild West did not generate a Jewish criminal subculture among its tough Jews, Breines reminds us that the American cities of New York, Chicago, Boston, Philadelphia, and Newark certainly did.

Although most educated people remember the infamous names of

Dutch Schultz, Bugsy Segal, Meyer Lansky, and Moe Dalitz, notorious Jewish gangsters active on the East Coast between the 1930s and the 1950s, Breines shows that the high time of "kosher" gangsterism was at the turn of the century, when eastern European Jews, along with Irish and Italian immigrants, were filling the tenements of New York City. At that time Jewish crime and gangsterism was not limited to a few notorious names. To the great dismay of veteran Jewish immigrants already integrated into the American middle class, it was a meaningful social phenomenon encompassing a large number of individuals and families. Relying on Jenna Weissman Joselit's study of Jewish crime in America, Breines mentions the Theodore Bingham report of 1908, issued by the New York City Police Department, which disclosed the extensive presence of Jews in the city's criminal underworld. The report was originally denied by a number of prominent Jews and communal leaders, who sought to discredit the commissioner and his evidence. But all denials were put to rest in 1912, "when Herman 'Beansy' Rosenthal, a notorious gambler, was murdered by several Lower East Side Jewish youths. The follow-up investigation revealed the involvement of more than a dozen Jews in a series of underworld murders, an episode that rocked New York Jewry to its very core."[12]

Biale and Breines do not discuss at length the question of Jewish intracommunal violence, but historians who do, expand upon the numerous cases of intra-Jewish conflict. Hebrew University's Israel Bartal, Bar Ilan's Elimelech Horowitz, and Ben-Gurion University's Ze'ev Greese assert that Diaspora Jewish history was full of communal violence, but Jewish historians had intentionally done their utmost to conceal it. These historians list a large number of *haredi*-like acts of nonlethal violence involving Hasidic courts in eastern Europe but also describe many cases of actual killings. Greese mentions the story of Rabbi Avraham Cohen, an innovative Polish rabbi in Lvov who was poisoned by young zealots after his several attempts to modernize the community. The legitimizing instrument for this killing was none other than *din rodef.* This was apparently not a one-time event.[13] Over ninety years ago, the historian Shaul Ginsburg wrote that if the Dnieper River could have spoken, it would have told the story of hundreds of Jewish *mosrim* drowned in its water. A large number of the victims were professional informers executed for passing information on Jews to Gentile rulers. But the mock trials and lynchings indicated that many of the cases were related to political conflicts between Hasidic, enlightened, and Orthodox Jews.[14] Another indication of the frequency of these executions is implied in a special 1838 memorandum sent by General Dimitry Gabrielovitz Bibikov, the governor of South West Russia, and addressed to all district governors under his jurisdiction. Referring to information from synagogues and yeshivas, the general wrote,

> In these places there are incidents which end with dead Jews. This crime is especially serious since it is committed in places designated for prayer and religious worship. The acts assume the form of vigilante justice made by courts of Jewish rabbis and are based on their false doctrine of eliminating "mosrim" who reveal the crimes of their co-believers. They are so successful in hiding the investigations they conduct, that the identity of the victims, let alone the guilty judges, remains unknown.[15]

Breines's erudite documentation of the presence of "tough Jews" in modern history leads him to two important conclusions: (a) the sociopolitical conditions of Diaspora Jews, not simply their existential "ghetto mentality," greatly determined whether or not they resorted to physical force; (b) the image of the gentle, nonviolent, meek Jew who despises the use of force and takes pride in his physical frailty never fully reflected a historical reality. This Jewish self-image was, in fact, an artificial creation of a long succession of Halakhic sages and communal leaders who had transformed an historical necessity into a virtue. By far the most compelling depiction of this virtue in modern times can be found in Jean-Paul Sartre's tribute to Jewish culture in his *Anti-Semite and Jew:*

> The Jews are the mildest of men . . . passionately hostile to violence. That obstinate sweetness which they conserve in the midst of the most atrocious persecution, that sense of justice and of reason which they put up as their sole defense against a hostile "brutal, and unjust society" is perhaps the best part of the message they bring to us and the true mark of their greatness.[16]

My reading of Biale and Breines, as well as the numerous examples of Jewish violence identified by other historians, does not suggest a total rejection of the historical phenomenon of Jewish exceptionalism. The relevant writers do not refute that Diaspora communal life was largely devoid of aggression and brutality and that the ethic of Jewish restraint was a dominant feature of the Diaspora *Weltanschauung*. Biale's and Breines's contribution lies in showing that the Diaspora experience was not completely devoid of violence and brutality, and that under certain social and political circumstances a number of Jews had engaged in fighting and killing and even committed atrocities. While many of these operations were not committed against fellow Jews or within Jewish communities, there are, as shown above, plenty of examples of brutal acts committed by Jews against Jews.

It is my contention that the Israeli experience with political violence as documented in this study follows more or less the patterns of collective behavior identified by Biale and Brienes. One would have to admit that since the turn of the century Israeli Jews have committed acts of domestic violence, climaxing with the Hebron massacre and the Rabin assassination. But on balance, their violence has been largely restrained. Considering the violent region within which Israeli Jews have resided since the beginning of the Zionist venture—the Middle East and the hostile Arab world—as well as the deep ideological divisions among them over critical issues such as religion, the borders of the state, and the state's political structure, the volume of violence documented in this study is neither shocking nor great. It may perhaps be unfair to compare Israeli violence to the domestic atrocities committed in the neighboring Arab countries of Egypt, Syria, Iraq, and Jordan (not to mention Lebanon), in which a democratic culture never took root. But even a comparison with French society during the war in Algeria, the United States of the 1960s, and Italy and the German Federal Republic of the 1970s sets Israelis apart in their nonpractice of violence.

Having long observed violent movements in several Western societies, I am convinced that had the Frenchmen, Italians, Germans, Americans, and most likely any other Westerners been subject to existential threats as well as divisive issues similar to the ones experienced by the Israelis, blood would have flooded their streets. Though the violence and extremism documented in this study show that Israeli Jews have been subject to the same rules of radicalization and violence that govern other nations, the brutalities committed by their extremists pale in comparison with atrocities committed by other nationals in the modern era. I propose that there is only one explanation for this exceptional self-control: Jewish internal solidarity and the presence of nonviolent taboos in Jewish society and culture. Israel may have created for its citizens unprecedented conditions of freedom, including the freedom to exercise force, but so far it has also remained Jewish to its core. The permanent Arab threat to the existence of the state has contributed significantly to the preservation of this Jewish instinct in the Israeli psyche.

The deeper we delve into the phenomenon of Jewish exceptionalism experienced by most Israelis, the more we rediscover the stiff Halakhic prohibitions against domestic violence, and even more so, the powerful psychosocial system of self-control and fear of civil war developed and experienced in the Diaspora. It appears to me that the origins of Jewish sensitivity to domestic violence go back to the tragedy of the Great Revolt against the Romans and to the intense civil war that divided the nation just before the Temple's destruction in A.D. 70. Though the Jewish civil war, as well as the rebellion against the Romans, was launched by ultra-Orthodox Jews—completely observant, loyal to God, and prepared to die in sanctification of His name—Jewish Orthodoxy looks upon them as sinners of the first order. In their hubris and baseless conviction that God would not allow His people to be destroyed, they tried to force the coming of the Messiah by desperate and insane acts.

The Second Temple Zealots staged domestic terrorism against Jerusalem's Jewish moderates, who opted for a compromise with the Romans, including the high priests and other prominent members of the community. And their hubris further led them to burn the food supplies of Jerusalem, in order to blackmail God into immediately dispatching the Messiah, lest the Temple be destroyed.[17] Even the late Rabbi Meir Kahane, when questioned about the zealots and his potential identification with them, vehemently rejected any such association. Kahane stated at that interview that Second Temple Zealots had sinned against God and the people and that he had no sympathy for them. Maintaining that he was a follower of the "central school" of historical Judaism, going all the way back to Abraham and King David, Kahane rejected any future involvement of his followers in a Jewish civil war.[18]

The great destruction in A.D. 70 and the subsequent disaster in A.D. 135 following the Bar-Kokhva revolt—the events largely responsible for the end to the nation's collective presence in Eretz Israel—were only the beginning of a painful history of crises, expulsions, humiliations, anti-Semitism, persecutions, and massacres. The Jews learned from these experiences that their communal survival required "Israel to be responsible for each other" and to refrain, as much as possible, from domestic conflicts. The experience of destruction and exile probably stands behind the three Talmudic oaths that forbid the nation from returning to Eretz Israel before the arrival of the Messiah. It is thus told in the Babylonian Talmud that with the destruction of the Second Temple, the Lord enforced a unique bargain with the Jewish people. In return for their survival, wherever they were to go, they swore (a) not to return en masse to their Holy Land; (b) to be loyal to the countries and governments of their dispersion, and (c) not to attempt to hasten the coming of the Messiah.[19]

The memories of the bloody civil war as well as the sanctification of the three oaths do probably stand behind the *haredi* approach to the question of violence. These experiences and commitments explain the strange phenomenon that Jews who have no problem stigmatizing the secular leaders of the state of Israel with titles such as "Nazis," "Amalek," or "Agents of the Catholic Inquisition" do nevertheless refrain from extreme violence and consider the use of firearms against Jews as a desecration of the name of God. As long as the Jewish people live in the Diaspora, a theological and existential concept that includes Jewish life in Israel—according to the *haredi* understanding of history—the use of intense violence equals a rebellion against God.

While secular and Orthodox Zionists have never shared the *haredi* approach to violence, a large number of them have not been able to disengage from its psychosocial manifestations. The most outstanding example in the modern era of a secular Jewish refusal to take part in a bloody civil war is the decision of Menachem Begin, the Irgun's commander between 1943 and 1948, not to fight rival Jews regardless of the other side's aggression. Begin made the same decision twice: during the Season's 1944 peak, when Irgun fighters were persecuted by the Haganah and even surrendered to the British, and in 1948, when the Irgun arms ship *Altalena* was destroyed under David Ben-Gurion's direct orders. Commemorating the two exceptional decisions in his memoirs, *The Revolt*, Begin wrote the unforgettable words:

> We said: civil war; never! A cruel fratricidal war was actually waged all over the country. But this was a one-sided fratricidal war and here was the key for the entire situation; the choice was between a disaster for us alone or a disaster for the entire nation. You know when a two-sided fratricidal war starts, but you never know when will it end. . . . the command [not to fight back] came from "somewhere," from the depths of Hebrew history. It was obeyed. At the beginning of the Revolt [Begin's] there was no domestic bloody war. We were all saved from the disaster of disasters. . . .
>
> To avoid domestic bloody war at all cost—this principle, distilled in the Season's sufferings, was followed by us years later, in *Altalena*'s test of blood and fire.[20]

Menachem Begin, a conscientious and merciful Jew, may have been particularly worried about the risk of large-scale domestic violence, but without the instinctive Israeli rejection of civil war one cannot understand the lack of extreme violence by the undergrounds of the 1950s, the minimal aggression of Gush Emunim's settlers against the government in the 1970s, the nonviolent reaction to Yamit's 1982 evacuation, and the shock over the murder of Peace Now activist Emil Greentzweig in 1983. A retrospective examination of the Hebron massacre and the Rabin assassination (in both of which the Diaspora-born Kahanist philosophy of violence played a key role) suggests that the two acts were committed under exceptional circumstances. Goldstein, as I argued earlier, was an admitted and devoted member of the extreme Kach movement, but the massacre was not part of the party's modus operandi. It was, instead, a product of a most exceptional combination of personal and theological crises. Rabin was murdered after two dramatic years of ultranationalist radicalization during which time the intervening factors of a devastating Palestinian terrorist campaign and a highly charged rhetorical conflict between the prime minister and settlers took place. Surely these unique conditions do not provide a methodological legitimation of the massacre and the assassination, but they place the two cases of extreme violence in proper behavioral perspective. There are a number of indications that the Rabin assassination shocked the Israeli extreme right almost as much as it stunned the left. The implied fear of civil war had a significant restraining effect on the nation as a whole, not just on its liberal constituents.[21]

While the powerful presence in Israeli culture of nonviolent taboos provides an explanation for most of the nation's exceptional containment of physical confrontation, another factor should also be credited for contributing to this effect—the determined action of past Israeli prime ministers against violent groups. It is true that a number of studies have expressed dissatisfaction with the government's illegalism and sluggish response to lawbreaking.[22] But in their reaction to domestic violence, Israeli prime ministers had almost always been aggressive and determined, occasionally perhaps too determined. David Ben-Gurion was unequivocal in his decision to crush the *Altalena* uprising, to establish the monopoly of the Israeli army, and maintain law and order in the newly created state. But if the "Old Man" had not been as suspicious as he was of the Irgun's subversive motivations (which, incidentally, never existed), the lives of innocent Jews might have, in my opinion, been spared. Golda Meir's initial response to the Black Panthers was also very aggressive, betraying arrogance, impatience, and overeagerness to put the socio-ethnic genie back into the bottle. But the decisive response by these two leaders made it unequivocally clear that domestic violence and extreme lawlessness would not be tolerated and that people who break the law would pay dearly.[23]

Menachem Begin and Yitzhak Shamir also reacted decisively to domestic violence. Following the Jewish Underground operations of 1980 and 1983, and despite indications that the terrorists were settlers from the right wing, the Israeli secret service was ordered to aggressively pursue the perpetrators. This attitude also prevailed in the 1983 murder of Peace Now activist Emil Greentzweig, murdered during an anti-Begin demonstration. Israel's police force was ordered to spare no effort or resources in bringing the killer to justice. Tragically, the only exception to this tradition of law enforcement seems to have been the Rabin government's sluggish response to the most extreme among the anti-Oslo activists. I believe that had the government acted more decisively against Kach, Kahane Chai, Eyal, and Mate Ma'amatz—separating them from the legitimate right-wing demonstrators, outlawing their parties, and prosecuting their leaders for incitement—the Hebron massacre and the Rabin assassination might have been avoided.

Taking into consideration the nation's powerful taboos against violence, the history of Israeli violence as presented in this volume, and identifiable future challenges to Israeli society, I believe it is possible to speculate informatively about the future of Israeli political violence. Since the parameters of Israeli collective behavior are likely to change in the long run, the assessment presented here is of a five- to ten-year duration. The examination is made along the four areas of violence identified in this book.

Socio-ethnic Violence

The socio-ethnic conflict between Sephardim and Ashkenazim made a significant contribution to Israeli political violence, highlighted by the 1959 Wadi Salib riots and the eruption in 1971–72 of riots by the Black Panthers. To these exceptional cases one should add the food riots of the mid-1950s, the atmosphere of violence surrounding the 1981 elections and the Lebanon War, and the rise of local, aggressive Sephardi groups in Tel Aviv and Jerusalem in the late 1970s. A close examination of these events suggests that the violence was primarily an expression of powerlessness. None of these anti-establishment protests, including that of the Black Panthers, were motivated by a desire for political power in Israel or an aggressive demand for power sharing. The intense rioting expressed, in my opinion, two simple outcries: the demand for a sympathetic hearing from the government and the Ashkenazi public, and assistance in closing the socio-ethnic gap.

While a number of indicators suggest that Israel's ethnic gap, expressed by the uneven distribution of wealth and power, still exists, the potential for the violent expression of frustration has declined significantly. The most important change in the Sephardi-Ashkenazi equation since the 1970s is the dramatic political mobilization of Sephardi Jews. Likud and Labor recruitment of numerous Sephardi activists for prestigious Knesset and government positions as well as the election of a large number of Sephardi mayors has greatly reduced their sense of alienation and lack of representation. The present Netanyahu government comprises, for example, five (of eighteen) Sephardi ministers, including the nation's defense and police ministries. The rate of Sephardi-Ashkenazi intermarriage has risen to well over 20 percent. The meteoric success of Shas, a party that brings together Sephardi and ultra-Orthodox elements, elected ten representatives to the fourteenth Knesset, and has become a prominent member of the governing coalition, is another reason for the relaxation of socio-ethnic tensions.

It appears that if the present commitment to closing the socio-ethnic gap and eliminating the cultural discrimination against Sephardi Jews had existed in the 1950s, the Wadi Salib and Black Panther riots would not have occurred. The Black Panthers succeeded in scaring Israeli society to such an extent that an integration process never before attempted was initiated. It is true that the 1981 election campaign produced a new socio-ethnic rivalry, but the tension indicated a temporary upsurge in anti-Labor sentiment and not a return to the 1970s. The elections of 1988, 1992, and 1996 were notably free of ethnic violence. Although Likud had maintained its dominance among Sephardi voters, the campaigns were nonviolent, relaxed, even cordial. Unlike 1981, Labor leaders had little trouble campaigning in Sephardi neighborhoods. Given the ongoing commitment of all Israeli parties to the elimination of the socio-ethnic gap, as well as the appeal of the Shas party and the Sephardi voter to Labor and Likud, the likelihood of ethnic violence appears low.

The only source of potential socio-ethnic friction is Shas's protest against the Israeli legal system and the state's prosecution of several Shas Knesset and cabinet members who have been involved in corruption scandals. In reacting to their prosecution, the party's spokespersons have repeatedly resorted to the ethnic discrimination argument with accusations that their leaders have been "framed" because of their Sephardi origins. Shas's denouncements peaked in the spring of 1997, following the attorney general's recommendation, which was not acted upon, to charge Arye Deri with an illegal effort to fix the nomination of the state's attorney general. Deri, Shas's uncontested leader, had already been involved in a five-year trial of corruption and embezzlement. Having been singled out for prosecution among four other suspects in the attorney general affair, including Prime Minister Netanyahu, Deri became a Shas martyr. With their ten Knesset seats, heavy government representation, and the charismatic leadership of former chief Sephardi

Rabbi Ovadia Yosef, Shas activists gained confidence. Threats of aggressive demonstrations and violence have increasingly become their stock-in-trade.

It is, however, my assessment that Shas is unlikely to be involved in any meaningful antigovernment violence. The party is presently an establishment organization, constantly sought after by the prime minister and opposition leaders. Its educational network, El Hama'ayan, is generously financed by the public purse, and many of its leaders hold well-paying government positions, including two cabinet ministries. Shas's carefully staged demonstrations reveal neither genuine popular anger nor violent energy. While the case of Arye Deri is likely to create more commotion before it is over, particularly if Deri is convicted, it does not possess a great potential for violence.

Ultra-Orthodox Violence

Our discussion of the ultra-Orthodox has yielded two major observations about past *haredi* violence that seem highly relevant for its future.

1. *Haredi* protest and violence—with the exception of intracommunal violence—stem from their ideo-theological rejection of the Zionist state and are unrelated to major historical events of Israeli society. *Haredi* violence consequently has an independent, internal rhythm that cannot be detected by observation of non-*haredi* events. A key feature of *haredi* violence is its reaction to local developments. The paving of a new road in Jerusalem bordering a *haredi* neighborhood, the beginning of archaeological excavations in areas identified as ancient gravesites, or the posting of offensive commercial ads in an ultra-Orthodox neighborhood may easily create the conditions for *haredi* rioting.

2. Because of their strict Halakhic prohibitions against the use of force as well as their tradition of communal restraint, the violence of *haredim* is expected neither to involve the use of firearms nor to escalate into massive destruction and sabotage. This "soft" violence is therefore unlikely to have a major impact on any segment of Israeli society.

The conclusion from these observations is that *haredi* violence in the future will most likely resemble that of the past. Israeli society will surely witness more ultra-Orthodox violence, but its timing and magnitude are difficult to predict. As in the past, the intensity and volume of *haredi* aggression will likely be determined by the nature of the perceived threat to the Orthodox community, the decisions of individual rabbis or rabbinical councils, the community's willingness to support the protest, and the response of secular authorities. There are significant indications that the recent rise in their Knesset representation and the greater *haredi* involvement with the Israeli government may reduce ultra-Orthodox extremism and violence. Paradoxically, students of extraparliamentary politics and violence know that greater self-confidence and a rising sense of power may remove the restraining inhibitions on small and vulnerable radical groups, thereby driving them to greater extremism and violence. It is presently impossible to foresee which trend will prevail.

Violence Between Israeli Arabs and Jews

The political violence of Israeli Arabs erupted in the second half of the 1970s. And yet, with the exception of Land Day, which escalated into unexpected killing, it never reached significant levels. The aftermath of Land Day seems to have been responsible for the furtive plans of the Islamic Arab Movement's founders, in the late 1970s and early 1980s, to engage in acts of anti-Jewish violence. But this underground activity, discovered and preempted by the state's security services, ended abruptly in a series of arrests,[24] and their failure subsequently redirected young Arab fundamentalists in Israel into nonviolent communal activism, an area in which they have had phenomenal success. During the first two years of the Intifada, the Palestinian uprising in the occupied territories, Israeli Arabs sided with the rebels. But the riots expressing this solidarity and the few cases of terrorist collaboration were easily contained.[25]

Two reasons seem to explain the low level of Israeli Arab violence:

1. The forceful and effective control exercised by the security forces over Israeli Arabs since the War of Independence and the unpleasant memories of the 1948–63 military government.
2. An increasing awareness among Israeli Arabs of the sociopolitical

> and economic benefits that can be gained from participation in the Israeli political system.[26]

Although these factors bode well for the future and promise limitations on violence, the explosive potential of Arab-Jewish relations should not be ignored. At stake is the partial legitimation accorded to the Zionist state by its Arab minority, the danger of future Israeli-PLO confrontations and its spillover effect on Israeli Arabs, the Arabs' complete identification with Palestinian demands in Jerusalem and the West Bank, and the explosive elements involved in being an ethnic minority among a suspicious and insecure Jewish majority. There are minority groups on each side of the ethnonationalist divide that consider the other party illegitimate and openly express the desire for the other community's destruction or expulsion. In recent years, the notion of cultural autonomy has become increasingly popular in certain Arab circles. While the idea has not yet been translated into specific demands, a number of Israeli experts are certain that it is only a matter of time. Israeli ultranationalist spokespersons are already warning against what they consider the inevitable next stage, a quest for irredentist secession.

The fears and suspicions raised over these controversial issues warrant a cautious expectation concerning violence. Considering the escalation leading to Land Day, a radicalization triggered by a small number of extreme activists, one should not rule out a similar future explosion. The great intensity of ethnic conflicts around the world and in the Middle East in particular, and their contagion effect, should also be considered a factor likely to produce violence.

Regardless of the likelihood of future Arab-Jewish confrontation, it is important to stress the power of mutual respect, stabilizing policies, and compromise. A magnanimous government policy toward Arab citizens, expressed in an understanding of their point of view and a genuine effort to treat them as equals, may dramatically reduce the likelihood of violence or eliminate it altogether.

Violence over the Question of Eretz Israel

There is little doubt that the deep ideological cleavage between the Israeli right and left over the question of Eretz Israel produced the largest amount of domestic violence in Israeli history. The Jewish-Palestinian confrontation in the occupied territories has contributed to a dramatic intensification of this violence both directly or indirectly. Given the past dynamics of Israeli political violence, the state of the peace process at the time of this writing, the intense settler-Palestinian hostility in Judea and Samaria, and the expected Palestinian terrorism, the central question is not about the likelihood of Israeli domestic violence but about its intensity and magnitude.

Long-range forecasting about this zone of political violence is particularly difficult because of the large number of unknown factors involving Israel's future relations with the Palestinians. One should be cautious about short-range projections too, but the presence of certain conditions and political facts may safely be assumed. For this reason, I suggest examining the prospects for political violence only during the tenure of the present Likud government and engaging in this venture through a careful portrayal of alternative scenarios. Since the likelihood of Jewish civil war in the full sense of the term—a war in which a significant number of Israelis will fight against the rest of the nation—does not really exist, I focus on four realistic alternative projections. The most significant factors in the development of these scenarios are the strategic decisions and policymaking of Prime Minister Benjamin Netanyahu.

Scenario 1. Jewish Bloodshed

This projection presupposes Netanyahu's full compliance with the Oslo Accords and a quick move on his part for their implementation. The scenario predicts that when confronted by a dead end to hardline negotiations with the Palestinians and facing mounting international hostility, Netanyahu, the former hawk, will alter course and adopt something similar to the Rabin-Peres peace policies. Securing Labor support, either through a national unity coalition or by outside endorsement, Netanyahu will implement an Israeli-Palestinian peace agreement based on a comprehensive territorial compromise and settlement evacuation. This projection may alternatively be called the Algerian Scenario, because it follows Charles de Gaulle's 1960 momentous decision to recognize the FLN and end the French occupation of Algeria.[27]

While this scenario would unquestionably please the Palestinians, the rest of the Arab world, the community of nations, and most Israelis, it would simultaneously drive the Israeli extreme right into desperation and intense struggle. In addition to his "betrayal" of Eretz Israel, Netanyahu would most likely become the subject of crises of rising expectations among tens of thousands of radical-right activists who had personally worked for his 1996 election. It is thus certain that the agreement with the Palestinian Autonomy would be deemed illegitimate by these activists. Rabbinical rulings against the government and personally against Netanyahu, which would put him at great personal risk, would be expected. While I do not foresee renewed rabbinical deliberations over *din moser* and *din rodef*—because of the painful memories of the Rabin assassination—I expect a bitter personal campaign and Netanyahu's portrayal as a "traitor" and "liar." I further expect that in response to the ruling of their rabbis, religious soldiers would disobey orders and a few career officers would be forced into retirement. As in the past, the antigovernment campaign and rhetorical violence would be spearheaded by the most extremist elements among the settlers, followers of the late Rabbi Kahane, Zo Artzenu, Mate Ma'amatz, Women in Green, and the Center to Stop the Autonomy Plan. An extensive mobilization among the settlers and their supporters from within the Green Line would be conducted.

Scenario 1 is expected to produce dual conflict: provocative violence against Palestinians and confrontation violence among Jews. It is likely that the desperate efforts of the extreme right to stop the peace process would involve provocative terrorism, i.e., terrorism launched to draw the other side into retributive action. The ultimate purpose of provocative terrorism is the transformation of a peaceful atmosphere of negotiation into a warlike situation in the hope that all peace overtures will be suspended indefinitely. In the past, Israeli extremists have been careful not to engage in systematic terrorist provocations. But following a Netanyahu "treason" and facing the imminent dismantling of their life accomplishments in Judea and Samaria, I expect the most extreme elements among the settlers to resort to this tactic. If not contained promptly, provocative settler terrorism would indeed trigger a Palestinian response and raise the number of casualties on both sides.

There would also be bloody confrontations between settlers and soldiers in Judea and Samaria and between right-wing supporters and policemen within the Green Line. The use of the army and police against rioters would only exacerbate an explosive situation, and an antigovernment ruling by the rabbis would fuel the fire. The threat of self-inflicted violence, in the form of Jewish suicides in response to the evacuation of settlements, should also be taken seriously. Following the ruling *yehareg velo ya'avor* (be killed but not sin), messianic individuals may undertake such desperate action as a last resort. While it has not previously occurred, acts of suicide have twice been seriously considered: in the 1982 evacuation of northern Sinai and during the 1994 planning of Tel Rumeida's evacuation. Acts of suicide, needless to say, are likely to trigger additional desperate acts, creating a snowball effect. Riots and demonstrationsin Jerusalem and Tel Aviv would be accompanied by many threats to the life of the prime minister.

It is important to stress, however, that the majority of the settlers and their rabbis would probably refuse to participate in the violent struggle, particularly if the government is strongly supported by public opinion polls and a significant Knesset majority. Responding to the "erroneous will of the people," most rabbis would not endorse extralegal struggle and would instead abide by "God's inexplicable decision." Only the most extremist organizations and a few radical rabbis would push for confrontation. Given the endorsement of the opposition and 75–80 percent support for the government in the polls, the settler struggle to stop the Israeli-Palestinian peace is expected to fail, but not before the loss of Jewish and Muslim lives.

Scenario 2. Israeli-Palestinian Bloodshed

While the first scenario foresees plenty of intra-Jewish violence, the second projects a heavy degree of Israeli-Palestinian violence. Conflict would take place after confrontations over building in Jerusalem and settlement expansions when Prime Minister Netanyahu slows implementation of the Oslo Accords and fails to honor all commitments of the Rabin-Peres government. As the government expands West Bank settlements and employs military force against the inevitable Palestinian rioting, and as these events are duly reported in the international media, degrading Israel's image abroad, incentives would be created for a comprehensive Palestinian uprising under the leadership of Yasser Arafat—who may then retreat to Egypt and declare a Palestinian state in exile. The intensification of violence would force the Israeli army to reoccupy the West Bank and Gaza, thereby creating an international crisis of the first order. Israel would shortly become a pariah state.

A brutal repression of the Palestinians would have significant repercussions in Israel proper. Represented in the streets by Peace Now and several smaller, extraparliamentary movements, the Israeli left is unlikely to remain an idle spectator to the crisis. Similar to their response to the 1982 invasion of Lebanon, left-wing activists could be counted on to organize a campaign of direct action, conducting vigils, demonstrations, and even rioting. While the left's confrontation with the police would probably not generate intense violence, an unruly right-wing backlash, fomented by overeager Likud activists and Kahanist hooligans, is anticipated. Scenes reminiscent of the winter of 1983, in which government supporters physically attacked Peace Now demonstrators, are likely. Physically threatened, and mindful of the murder of Peace Now activist Emil Greentzweig, young peace activists would feel compelled to enhance their defensive preparations for confrontation by arming themselves. Thus, scenario 2 features widespread street clashes between extremists on the right and the left, and the evolution of a deep sociopolitical rupture.

Scenario 3. Nonviolent Politics

The third scenario portrays Netanyahu's prudent and innovative policies appealing to and satisfying the Palestinians and the Israeli left without completely alienating the radical right. This scenario starts with a significant slowdown in Israeli building in Jerusalem, and presupposes a Likud-Labor understanding on the final settlement of the Israeli-Palestinian conflict and the state's future borders. The basis of the agreement is the understanding reached prior to the Rabin assassination by Yossi Beilin and Arafat's confidant, Abu Mazen. Beilin's most significant accomplishment was a Palestinian agreement for territorial compromise that would leave 70 percent of West Bank settlers in Israel and give the remaining 30 percent extraterritorial status in an independent Palestine. Beilin also discovered Palestinian readiness to turn Abu Dis, a village adjacent to Jerusalem, into the site of the future Palestinian government. The great attraction of the

Beilin–Abu Mazen understanding for right-wing ideologues is that it neither involves settler evacuation nor compromises on the Israeli claim to a "unified" Jerusalem. Given the mounting regional and international pressures, this understanding is likely to be Netanyahu's fallback position.

Scenario 3 assumes that the government is capable of gradually but methodically implementing the Oslo Accords, of reaching a de facto understanding about this course with Yasser Arafat, of implementing Israeli-Palestinian economic cooperation, and of negotiating final agreements in good faith. It also assumes a modest expansion of settlements that would reduce settler opposition without irritating the Palestinians—who have already been assured of the future establishment of a Palestinian state.

There is good reason to believe that although none of the parties would be completely happy with the course charted in this scenario, all sides would recognize an interest in avoiding confrontation and violence. The strategy would require Netanyahu to demonstrate great political skill, and would also require full Labor endorsement, consistent cooperation from Arafat, and possibly the permanent presence of an American mediator. Even under these optimal conditions, Jewish and Muslim extremists can be expected to make every effort to sabotage the emerging understanding. But decisive action by Israeli and Palestinian military forces could succeed in minimizing this opposition.

Scenario 4. Intermittent Violence

While the first three scenarios regard the violence (or nonviolence) generated in the course of future conflicts among Israelis and Palestinians as a by-product of Netanyahu's strategic execution, scenario 4 presupposes an inconsistent Israeli policy accompanied by repeated blunders and tactical readjustments. Based on Netanyahu's two-year track record as prime minister, he can be regarded as a conservative ideologue with pragmatic instincts, a bad sense of timing, and vulnerability to pressure from the extreme right. This final scenario features a prime minister who endeavors to isolate Arafat and hopes expand the Israeli presence in the occupied territories, and generally rejects the Palestinians as legitimate, trustworthy peace partners. He increasingly discovers, however, that this is difficult to accomplish, as violent exchanges with the Palestinians, the Arab world's hostility, and growing anger among Europeans and Americans severely damage Israeli interests and threaten to bring about his downfall. What does he do? He responds to pressures, plays for time, and makes a large number of tactical concessions. But Netanyahu's readjustments are often too little and too late.

The fourth scenario does not foresee lengthy confrontations with the Palestinians or the settlers. It also does not predict the collapse of the peace process. But it expects occasional crises with the Palestinians and the settlers, leading to small and medium-sized violent incidents. Scenario 4 assumes that as in the past, the prime minister would not have the good fortune or prudence to pacify all Palestinian and Israeli extremists all the time. Tactical mistakes, personal arrogance, extreme-right pressures, and unexpected terrorist incidents are bound to result in occasional bloody incidents. The overall projection here is that the next two years are likely to witness a slow and sluggish peace process, full of diversions and derailments. Some of these may involve individual fanatics in the stripe of Baruch Goldstein, Yigal Amir, or Hamas terrorists trying to destabilize the situation by massacres, assassinations, or suicide bombings.

At the time of this writing, March 1998, it is difficult to assess the likelihood of each scenario and select the one that will most likely dominate the Israeli scene. Cautiously evaluating the present stalemate following Netanyahu's determination to change the parameters of the Oslo Accords and minimize Israel's redeployment in the West Bank, it is my feeling that the last scenario is the most realistic of all alternatives. Whatever projection is finally realized, I am certain that by the year 2000, Israeli society, including the extreme right, will be increasing prepared for implementation of the Oslo Accords and accept the necessity of compromise in order to make a real peace with the Palestinians. I pray that the cost of waiting will not be too high.

APPENDIX

Violence, Political Violence, Political Violence in Israel

A Short Introduction to the Study of Political Violence

In 1907, George Sorel, a French engineer turned social thinker, published a book titled *Reflexions sur la violence.* His book had an enormous influence on an entire generation of socialist and fascist revolutionaries. Sorel, an ardent revolutionary socialist, looked for a way to rescue the Marxist model of violent revolution from historical irrelevance. The problem he encountered was that the original Marxist hope for inevitable revolution, born out of the alleged unavoidable class conflict between workers and capitalists, was quickly waning. The rise of strong unions capable of improving workers' conditions, which Karl Marx and Friedrich Engels did not foresee, took the revolutionary spirit out of the classical proletariat. It produced popular "reformist" thinkers such as Edward Bernstein, who doubted the necessity of physically destroying bourgeois society. Sorel's solution was to glorify the notion of violence in the mind of the workers and turn the idea of violent revolution into an end in itself. He reached the conclusion that the natural aggression of the workers, as well as their spontaneous violence at the workplace, most notably expressed in the French general strike, was a virtue of the first degree. He recommended that instead of feeling guilty about their unruly conduct, worker leaders should glorify workers' brutality and even encourage it. A myth of a positive, redemptive, virile violence was necessary, an alternative to the "soft" struggle methods recommended by reform Marxism. To reach this goal, Sorel made an argument almost unprecedented before his time—he presented violence as a *moral* force in history, an attitude and social behavior that are not only needed temporarily to destroy the exploiting classes but are also inherently good. Although Sorel believed that he was a genuine and devoted student of Marx and Engels, his argument made him an early proponent of fascism. His intellectual construct, to be precise, created the theoretical bridge between Marxist socialism and fascism.[1]

Sorel's importance in the intellectual history of violence is twofold. First, he developed and presented the concept of violence as a distinct social category, separate from concepts traditionally discussed by political philosophers such as power, force, war, revolution, rebellion, tyrannicide, and terrorism. Hannah Arendt identified this contribution in her seminal essay *On Violence*, maintaining that although violence had always been at the center of collective social behavior, it had not been conceptualized separately until Sorel.[2] Second, Sorel was instrumental in postponing for nearly sixty years the systematic study of violence by sociologists and political scientists. Because of his increasing identification as a fascist, the democratic thinking about violence remained dominated until the mid-1960s by the belief that political violence is exclusively the business of the fascist right or the communist left. The only group of social scientists who seriously studied political violence were a few sociologists interested in the dynamics of extremist movements. Rather than focus on violence as a universal form of social behavior, they were motivated by the need to explain the great appeal of modern fascism and revolutionary communism. The sociologists involved had indeed laid the foundations for the modern study of political violence, but they limited their research to that of the behavior of irrational crowds.[3] They regarded anti-establishment elites moved by irrational ideologies, as well as emotional masses mesmerized by charismatic demagogues, as solely responsible for political violence.[4]

The inclination of social and political scientists to study everything but violence was particularly evident after World War II. It reflected the optimistic belief that the world that had emerged out of the horrendous war was rational, ergo a world without violence. The same attitude that led many scholars to believe in the end of ideology[5] and the decline of religion[6] also created the conviction that violence as well was a matter of the past. No serious student of society and politics denied the presence of violence in the "old world" and in the Third World, but it was viewed as a childhood disease. Approaching political violence as a symptom of backwardness, not as a universal form of collective behavior deserving of systematic observation and study, very few recognized sociologists or political scientists believed that democratic, postindustrial society could ever again experience intense violence. This was probably the reason that the *International Encyclopedia of the Social Sciences*, the largest compendium of social and political knowledge, published in 1968, did not have an entry on violence or on political violence. Nor did it have one on terrorism.

The great awakening from the illusion of rational democracy and peaceful postindustrial society began in the last quarter of the 1960s and culminated at the beginning of the 1970s. The unexpected outbreak of student rebellions in the most prosperous learning centers of postindustrial society, the riots in black ghettos in the United States, the rise of violent protest against the Vietnam War, the evolution of small terrorist organizations in the West, and finally the reawakening of separatist violence in western and central Europe had shocked the political world.[7] The turmoil in the academic world was equally pervasive. Sociologists, political scientists, and historians who for years had taught and wrote about the end of ideology and the decline of violence were stunned by their most brilliant students who adopted old preachers of violence such as Lenin, Rosa Luxembourg, and Trotsky as well as new ones such as Franz Fanon and Che Guevara. What was especially disturbing was that these figures were not looked upon as mythical heroes of the past but as relevant contemporary theoreticians and instructors.

In 1968, U.S. President Lyndon Johnson formed a special committee to look into the roots of violence in the world's senior democracy. The committee asked sociologists, historians, and political scientists to explain the unexpected rise of violence in America and its causes. Less than a year later, Johnson's successor, Richard Nixon, had on his desk *Violence in America*, a devastating document edited by the sociologist Ted Robert

Gurr and the historian Hugh Davis Graham.[8] To their great dismay, the American academics discovered what they should have known a long time ago, that the history of the United States was *always* full of political violence and that despite its glorious Constitution and contributions to Western civilization as described by Alexis de Tocqueville, American democracy had never been devoid of violence, especially against minorities. American political scientists, so impressed in the 1950s with their democracy, discovered that for nearly one hundred years prior to the outbreak of the black ghetto riots, blacks had been victims of brutal repression by the white South under Jim Crow. Americans were painfully reminded of thousands of lynchings that had taken place without the intervention of the federal government or any other "democratic" authority for that matter. From rediscovering the repression of blacks, American collective memory moved to the rediscovery of the systematic genocide against Native Americans and of the vigilante attacks conducted for years against weak minorities such as Chinese, Japanese, and Mexicans. Gurr and Graham's report also had an interesting chapter on labor violence in America, ruthless violence conducted by capitalists against workers trying to unionize and counterviolence by workers, which relied on organized crime.

The academics who coauthored *Violence in America* did not discover in 1968 anything that was not already in their history books. It so happened that this 1968 sociopolitical exploration of the roots of American violence repeated previous similar cases in the history of science, especially in the history of the social sciences. A whole series of facts and information previously deemed irrelevant for the prevailing academic paradigm became, suddenly, enormously relevant.[9] In a short while, the study of political extremism and violence emerged as a theme of great interest in the social sciences. The simplistic belief that political violence is the exclusive property of fascism, Stalinism, or political backwardness disappeared immediately. Since the end of the 1960s, hundreds of books and thousands of scholarly articles on the subject of social and political violence have appeared. Political violence was not only put on the agenda of Western society but also became a subject of that society's self-examination. These interests and research have led to related studies of violence in the family, battered women, violence against children, and the relationship between criminal and political violence. The presence of violence in developed societies is today an uncontested fact.[10]

What then, are the findings? What do we presently know about political violence that we did not know before? What are the fruits of the accumulated scholarly knowledge on political violence? It appears to me that out of the large body of available academic writings, several critical findings are of special relevance to the present study of political violence in Israel.

1. The political world is not divided between black and white, between individuals and groups who are violent and nonviolent and between whom one can draw a distinct moral and behavioral line. Under certain circumstances even decent, nonviolent people, neither psychopaths nor sociopaths, may be dragged into using force for political purposes. Political violence is thus not a product of inherently violent people but of social and political circumstances of struggles for power.[11]

2. In spite of the observation above, it is possible to distinguish political cultures that are more violent than others. A nation has a violent political culture when it perceives violence as an integral part of the "legitimate" political repertoire and accepts it as an inseparable aspect of the general socialization of youth. A nonviolent political culture is a culture whose inhabitants look upon violent behavior as normatively illegitimate and have effective sanctions against its practice. It is furthermore marked by the presence of moral and psychological mechanisms that effectively prohibit or limit the use of physical force for social and political purposes.[12] The distinction between violent and nonviolent cultures is, of course, conceptual. In reality, it is possible to identify only *degrees* of violence and nonviolence.

3. Political violence is usually a developmental phenomenon. The passage from nonviolent to violent behavior is gradual. Extreme groups or movements do not become violent overnight but rather *radicalize* into violence. The two most significant components of this radicalization are (1) a process of delegitimization in which the social or political rival (usually a regime or another political group) is increasingly seen by the extreme

group as an unjust part of society and a threat to its existence;[13] (2) an experimentation over time with lesser forms of militancy and a slow moral disengagement with the commitment to nonviolence.[14]

4. With the exception of unstable individuals who may act on their own, political violence is a product of collective or "group" behavior. What are often involved are formal groups or social movements that struggle for power or informal social groups motivated by a certain world view and leaders who become their role models.[15]

5. Political violence does not just originate from *below*, from individuals who do not respect the law. Governments and government agencies are responsible for the generation of a large amount of violence. Violence from below is often triggered by previous violence from *above* (and if not violence, at least repression and arbitrariness). In our world, including our democratic world, plenty of violence is carried out in the name of law and order. What is at stake is the rather common governmental resort to "law enforcement" that far exceeds the law and the requirements of the public interest.[16]

6. Political violence is not always an expression of power, strength, self-confidence, or a desire for conquest. More often then usually recognized, it is an expression of weakness and inability to cope with social pressures.[17] It may thus be useful to distinguish between *violence of power* and *violence of powerlessness*. Violence generated by powerless people should not be looked upon as just a legal impediment but also as a desperate cry for help.

7. Political violence, especially in the form of assassinations, should often be looked upon as a *rhetorical device* developed in time of intense conflict to define the boundaries of the symbolic universe of the perpetrating movement.[18]

8. The historical role of violence is neither necessarily negative nor destructive. In the past, political violence served as a major vehicle for constructive reforms.[19] William O'Brien, a nineteenth-century Irish revolutionary and propagandist, said, "Violence is often the only way to make sure the government listens to the voice of moderation."[20]

9. Political violence is neither inherent nor inevitable. It is, instead, a form of collective behavior that depends on social and political factors. Just as it is possible to artificially raise the level of violence, so it is possible to contain it by intentional action. "Conflict management" may not be easy, given situations of deep social cleavage, but it is not impossible either.[21]

These findings, which represent only a small fraction of our knowledge on political violence, call for two operational conclusions that are of considerable relevance for the present study:

1. Since political violence is a behavioral pattern that in nonviolent societies develops over a long period of time, it is possible and desirable to identify (through research) previolent stages and warning signals for a future potential outbreak of violence.[22]

2. If violence is neither inherent nor hereditary but is rather a social product of previolent experiences that slowly evolve over time, then its potential prevention requires constant vigilance. Historical examples of evolution to violence in nonviolent societies make complacency about early indications of violence a risky attitude.[23]

What Is Political Violence?—Definitions and Conceptual Framework

What is violence? What is political violence? How can this phenomenon be defined, studied, and assessed? A short examination of the relevant literature suggests that there are many approaches to the study of violence and that the number of definitions is almost as large as the number of the definers. Yet out of this large body of writings it may be helpful to focus on two approaches to violence, a narrow approach that stresses the specific meaning of the term and a broader view that takes into consideration the causal processes that lead to the committing of violent acts.

Violence, according to the narrow definition, is the use of physical force against another person regardless of all conventions, social norms, and positive laws that define the legitimate use of force.[24] Political violence, according to this approach, is violence resorted to in a political context, i.e., for the purpose of taking over government, obtaining influence with the government, protesting government action, defending oneself against the government, and containing other individuals or groups who make claims on the government. The broad definition of violence is related to the concept of *violation* in its most general sense, i.e., the use of superior power to obtain something that is inherently not yours, is owned by other people, and is taken against their free will. Violence, according to the broad definition, also implies the use of force, but this force is not necessarily physical. Political violence, according to the broad definition, is the practice of violence for all the political purposes mentioned above. Regardless of its obvious advantages, however, this broad definition of violence is much too general to allow useful research. Violence, according to this definition, calls for intense value judgment and is unlikely to create the academic consensus necessary for the advancement of scientific knowledge.

Even a cursory examination of the findings of modern research reviewed earlier suggests that the narrow definition of violence, chosen for our research purposes, does not exhaust the social dynamics of violence in reality. This observation reveals further that political violence is not distinctively different from other forms of nonviolent political behavior. Political violence is, as we saw above, an advanced product of previolent political situations. It exists on a continuum that starts with mild forms of political militancy and extends to killing and terrorism. This is why a full understanding of political violence throughout a society requires reference to a whole range of neighboring concepts and phenomena that add up to a meaningful conceptual framework. This is also the reason I find it useful to acquaint the reader with the relevant concepts to be frequently used in the present study. My short dictionary addresses only violence from below.

Extraparliamentary Politics—A political behavior that usually involves direct action of social movements and extremist groups, protests, riots, aggressive demonstrations, and direct street appeal to the public and the media.[25] Extraparliamentary politics is not centered on the parliament or the executive, is not focused on election day, and is not run according to the rules of the game of the large political parties, major interest groups, and key social and political institutions. Extraparliamentary politics often leads to various degrees of illicit and extralegal activities and the use of physical force, and it may occasionally deteriorate to sabotage and terrorism.

Intentional and Unintentional Violence. Intentional violence is the premeditated use of violence for political purposes. The instigator of violence does not arrive at the use of force because of external incentives, accidents, or situations he does not control. He thinks about the use of force and plans his violent operations well in advance. Unintentional violence is an unplanned resort to the use of force. It results when a protest, extraparliamentary demonstration, or another form of collective behavior meets with stiff opposition, goes out of control, and becomes violent against the intent of its organizers.

Hooliganism is a pattern of violent street behavior designed to intimidate and act as propaganda. Hooligans rarely use firearms or resort to violence that kills. Their action is usually marked by fist fights, the use of nonlethal arms, vandalism, and property damage. Hooligans wish to take over the street from other hooligans, to intimidate weak rivals, or simply to protest. Although hooliganism presupposes a low degree of violence, it produces favorable conditions for higher and more intense forms of violence.

Revolutionary Violence. This is a form of violence operated with the intent of destroying the prevailing system of government and establishing an alternative regime. Revolutionary violence is the product of a deep crisis of legitimacy with the regime, which implies, among other things, a readiness to use firearms against representatives of the state. Revolutionary violence should not be confused with antigovernment violence conducted by an armed underground. Every secretly planned antiregime violence is an act of an "underground" violence, but not every underground violent act is revolutionary.

Vigilante violence. This is the practice of violent self-defense by citizens who feel the government does not protect them from those who threaten them. Vigilante violence is rarely associated with revolutionary violence or with a legitimacy conflict with the regime. Vigilantes who take the law (and guns) into their hands believe that they are administrating justice according to the law of the land and are doing what the government should have done if it had been functioning properly.[26]

Terrorism. Terrorism is a systematic political action involving three components: use of extreme violence (such as killing, maiming, or seriously wounding) or a credible threat to use it; an extranormal direction of this violence toward civilians of all categories in contradiction to all social conventions and national and international laws; the use of this extreme violence in a symbolic way, i.e., as a vehicle to instill fear in the minds a large public that is unlikely ever to be hurt by the terrorists.[27]

Assassination. A single act of political killing that the assassin does not consider to be part of a larger series of similar acts or a message to instill fear beyond the assassination itself.

Verbal Violence. This is the use of extreme language against an individual or a group that either implies a direct threat that physical force will be used against them or is seen as an indirect call for others to use it. Verbal violence is often a substitute for real violence, for it helps excited leaders to vent their frustration in less than a violent manner.[28] The problem of verbal violence is that it may incite followers who are incapable of distinguishing between real and verbal violence to engage in actual violence.[29]

An Ideology of Violence. This is the presence of a systematic body of political thinking that sees violence as a desired part of the group's behavior, admits its necessity, and glorifies it. Most violent groups do not have an ideology of violence. When the need for violence arises. it is justified by self-defense, the necessity of sheer survival, and the provocative violent behavior of the other side. An ideology of violence facilitates the path to actual violence by removing the sociopsychological barriers against the use of violence present in most societies.

The concepts presented above show that political violence is related to a variety of extremist behaviors and that it covers a vast territory, ranging from verbal violence to terrorism. Within this field one may comfortably place such forms of militancy as illicit riots and physical confrontation with the police, property damage, physical assaults, random killing, and political assassination. The first questions that students of extremist politics ask when observing violent political situations are as follows: Which category of violence is taking place? Which forms of previolent collective behavior preceded the existing situation? What are the scope and intensity of the violence under consideration?

The Facilitating Conditions of Political Violence

In addition to improving our understanding of the nature of political violence, present-day knowledge makes it possible to recognize the conditions and likelihood of its occurrence. While we are not yet at a stage of prediction or accurate forecasting, it seems possible to identify the facilitating factors that govern the likely evolution of violent situations. The question about the likelihood of political violence focuses on nonviolent political cultures, for violent political cultures already imply its massive presence. Using the working assumption that radical challenge groups usually generate violence *from below*, I suggest that the following six variables seem to be the most responsible for its evolution (or decline):

1. The strength of the antiviolence "immune-system" of the society under consideration. Every society that wishes to survive cannot allow its members to freely exercise violence and must have built-in mechanisms of violence control. The question that must be asked about each political society is: how strong is its antiviolence "immune-system"? Immune system is an appropriate collective name for all antiviolence religious norms existing in the society involved, antiviolence traditions, taboos, and voluntary social sanctions.[30] This antiviolence "immune system" excludes formal legislation (which is easy to make!) and focuses on informal but deeply ingrained social and cultural mechanisms.

2. The level of delegitimation experienced by the potentially violent group against its rivals. The deeper the sense of delegitimation experienced by an extreme group vis-à-vis the government or another political rival, the higher is its readiness to use physical force against the perceived foe. Intense delegitimation has in fact a double effect on the likelihood of violence. Not only does it increase the chances of violence against the object of delegitimation, but that object, sensing the imminent threat, is likely to consider counterviolence.

3. A rational conviction of extremist leaders that violence may best serve their interests. Modern research on political violence suggests that

many leaders and activists do not resort to violence emotionally but reach a decision about its use after a careful consideration of the risks and opportunities involved. The likelihood of violence depends, from this perspective, on the confidence of the group in its physical and material strength and on its assessment of its rival's response capabilities.[31] This equation has a special meaning in relation to the powers that be. The more effective a government is in maintaining law and order and in punishing its challengers, the less the chance that their leaders will opt for extranormal violence.[32] The weaker a regime is, the readier to turn a blind eye to violence, the more likely it will turn to violence itself.

4. Previous experience with violence. The more experienced a radical group is in the use of physical force, the more likely it will be to engage in extreme violence. An extraparliamentary movement whose members have already been through intense physical confrontations with the police and the military are much more likely to move to intense antiregime violence than protesters who have just discovered an issue to demonstrate about.[33] For a street hooligan with plenty of experience with nonlethal weapons, it is a lot easier to move into killing than for a freshman protester who has just been introduced into extraparliamentary politics. The same behavioral logic explains the observation that individuals long experienced with ethnic violence against an external group have lesser inhibitions than inexperienced members of the community in switching targets and using violence against their own kinsmen.[34]

5. The presence or absence of earlier violent stimulation. The likelihood that an extremist group will resort to violence increases dramatically if it has already been subjected to violence by its enemies. For its victims, the use of physical force produces pain, humiliation, stimulation for revenge, and especially legitimation to "an eye for an eye."

6. The presence or absence of inherently violent leaders. Although present-day research on political violence is still unable to explain the making of the violent personality, it recognizes its presence as an important facilitator in the creation of violent situations. What we do know is that violent leaders have been able single-handedly to turn nonviolent situations

into violent ones. Violent leaders are noted for the formulation of ideologies of violence for their followers or for putting their group's struggles within a symbolic framework of aggressive self-defense.[35]

In addition to the insights into the dynamics of political violence provided by the identification of the facilitating variables of violence, this identification may help officials to contain violence and reduce its destructive effects. A government determined to fight political violence should be able to reduce the likelihood of its eruption through prudent manipulation of the factors mentioned above. Disregard for the facilitating conditions or a denial of their presence may, however, increase the chances of violence dramatically. Manipulating the violence variables is not a simple task, because not all these factors are automatically working in the same direction. A nervous government that substitutes law enforcement with repression—hoping to eliminate political violence in a short time—may push the radical group involved to an acute crisis of legitimacy. Having no alternative but a humiliating surrender, the group may opt to engage in terrorism and political assassination. The containment of violence requires a *prudent* manipulation of the relevant variables. A government determined to reduce the level of domestic violence or its likelihood ought to study carefully the situation and dynamics of extremism and violence. Preventive action ought always to be preceded by cautious planning. The relevant questions about antiviolence policy, just as those about any other area of sensitive decision making, involve the timing, scope, and magnitude of government response.

Political Violence in Israel—The Analytical Framework

The discovery of political violence as a significant dimension of society has not skipped Israel. Although Israeli scholars have not yet exhausted the subject, they have systematically studied it in the last two decades. Taking the existing scholarly literature on Israeli political violence as a point of departure, as well as the relevant comparative literature, we find it useful to examine Israeli political violence through two analytical manipulations: (1) an identification of the main issues that led Israelis to use force for political purposes and their presentation as "areas of violence"; (2) an itemization of

Israeli history according to the presence, intensity of, or absence of political violence.

Areas of Violence. An observation of the issues that led Israelis to use force for political purposes in the nation's nearly fifty years of sovereign existence reveals four relevant areas:

1. *Violence generated by the political and ideological debate over the borders of Israel and the fate of the Palestinians.* What is involved is extremism and violence generated by the conflict between the Israeli political right and left over issues such as the territorial borders of the state, the question of peace with the Arabs, and its implications for Israeli democracy. This area covers the most significant public debate in the nation's history since the 1930s and aspects of this debate that could not be resolved by peaceful means.

2. *Violence born from a sense of socio-ethnic discrimination.* What is involved is the extremism and violence generated in Israel since the 1950s by Sephardi Jews, immigrants from Middle Eastern and North African countries, who responded violently to what they considered the "social-ethnic gap," the broad sense of social discrimination and the conviction that Israeli society is divided between the Ashkenazi haves and the Sephardi have-nots.

3. *Violence born out of the domestic tension between Israeli Jews and Arabs.* What is involved is militant collective action resorted to by Israel's Arab citizens in protest against government repression and the sense of unjust discrimination (with no direct bearing on the external Arab-Israeli conflict).

4. *Violence born out of the conflict between ultra-Orthodox and secular Israeli Jews.* What is involved are the occasional violent eruptions of ultra-Orthodox Jews against the Zionist government or against individuals and groups seen as desecrating the name of God.

I chose not to include in this book information on local political violence generated by marginal municipal and rural power struggles. The same logic led me also to exclude information on labor-related local cases of violence.

The identification of distinct "areas of violence" is somewhat artificial and is made for analytical purposes. In reality these areas are not mutually exclusive and in at least three of the four it is possible to identify interdependence and spillovers. Ethnic protest in the 1950s was, for example, isolated from all other conflicts (e.g., the Wadi Salib riots), but in the 1980s it was intensely interconnected with the political-ideological area and with the debate between Likud and Labor over the territorial borders of Israel and the Palestinian entity. Although no study of the contagion effect of political violence has been conducted yet in Israel—i.e., the imitation of violence exercised in one area by extremist groups active in another area—the comparative literature on violence suggests a significant interdependence and imitation.[36]

Episodes of political violence. A careful examination of Israeli political violence since 1948 suggests an eight-stage historical model for its organization and understanding.

1. *1948—On the Brink of Civil War.* Year one of the newly created state of Israel was the bloodiest in the history of the nation, with Jews openly killing Jews. Domestic violence between government forces, representing the ruling Labor movement and members of the right-wing Irgun and Lehi undergounds, reached crisis proportion in the fight over the arms ship *Altalena* and in the assassination of Count Folke Bernadotte, the U.N. mediator in the Middle-East.

2. *1949–1957—The Decline of Past Hatreds.* A period marked by the existence of a few small, antiregime groups and the discovery of three violent right-wing undergrounds. The formation of the undergrounds does not mark, however, the evolution of new challenges to the government but the decline of the old, bitter rightist rivals of the dominant Labor movement, which desperately tried to stop their political decline by unrealistic, almost helpless, violence.

3. *1957–1967—The Golden Age of Israel's Parliamentary Politics.* A period marked by total dominance of Israeli parliamentary politics and by an absence of extremist and violent groups. The only exception to the dominance of parliamentary politics of the time was a three-week eruption of

antigovernment rioting by Israeli Sephardim, easily suppressed by the establishment.

4. *1967–1973—The First Rebellion of the Extraparliamentary Periphery.* This period, begun after the 1967 Six-Day War, is marked by a vocal but small protest of Israeli peace groups, which failed to leave a significant impact on government policies in the occupied territories. The period is also marked by the maturation of the socio-ethnic protests of Israel's Sephardim, which, unlike the peace groups, had a significant impact on government policies. But even the Israeli Black Panthers, the carriers of the great protest, failed to establish an influential extraparliamentary movement that would permanently challenge Israel's parliamentary politicians from the periphery.

5. *1973–1978—The Second Rebellion of the Extraparliamentary Periphery.* This period, which began with the shock of the 1973 Yom Kippur War, is marked by an unprecedented intensity of Israeli extraparliamentary politics. The magnitude of political violence was low but the peripheral challenges to the political center were substantial. Permanent extraparliamentary movements such as Gush Emunim and Peace Now became established in Israel's periphery with the ability to significantly challenge parliamentary politics. There was also a dramatic rise in Arab extremism and violence and the evolution of Jewish verbal violence in the Kach movement.

6. *1978–1984—The Maturation of Political Violence.* A period marked by great intensification of the Israeli left-right ideological conflict, by violent expressions of this conflict in the streets, and by the rise within Israel's extreme right movements of factions and individuals ready to use terrorism and extreme violence against their rivals.

7. *1984–1992—The Containment of Political Violence and the Institutionalization of Extraparliamentary Politics.* A period marked by the presence of a National Unity government coalition between Likud and Labor and by an effective containment of the violence of the earlier period. The government and the extraparliamentary movements involved, with the active support of the public, are acting to control the violent factions. Nonvio-

lent extraparliamentary politics was not rejected, however, but became an institutionalized part of national politics.

8. *1992–1996—The Return of Political Violence and the Countdown for the Rabin Assassination.* A period marked by the "shocking" overtures of the Rabin government toward the PLO and by the determined effort of Israel's extreme right to stop the peace process through the use of intense, extraparliamentary tactics. The peaks of the struggle were the massacre of twenty-nine Palestinians in Hebron's Cave of the Patriarchs and the assassination of Prime Minister Yitzhak Rabin.

I wish to emphasize in conclusion that there is an arbitrary element in the itemization offered above. The eight-stage historical model presented has been decided upon not because of independent measures of political violence but owing to the occurrence of key events in the history of Israel that in my judgment changed the national agenda and the violence-producing controversies.[37]

NOTES

Chapter 1. On the Brink of Civil War

1. Shlomo Nakdimon, *Altalena* (Jerusalem: Edanim, 1978—in Hebrew), pp. 297-99.
2. Eliyahu Tavin, *The Second Front: The Irgun Tzevai Leumi in Europe 1946-1948* (Tel Aviv: Ron, 1973—in Hebrew), pp.157-66.
3. Nakdimon, *Altalena*, pp.103-4.
4. On the Irgun in general see J. Bowyer Bell, *Terror Out of Zion* (New York: St. Martin's Press, 1977).
5. Menachem Begin, *The Revolt* (Tel Aviv: Ahiasaf, 1978—in Hebrew), pp. 411-13.
6. Shmuel Katz, *Day of Fire* (Tel Aviv: Karni, 1966—in Hebrew), pp. 393-96.
7. Uri Brener, *Altalena* (Tel Aviv: Hakibbutz Hameuchad, 1978—in Hebrew), pp. 44-51.
8. Nakdimon, *Altalena*, pp.102-3.
9. Eliyahu Lenkin, *The Story of Altalena's Commander* (Tel Aviv: Herut, 1954—in Hebrew), pp. 278-79.
10. Begin, *The Revolt*, p. 213.
11. Ibid., pp. 214-16.
12. Nakdimon, *Altalena*, pp. 158-60.
13. Begin, *The Revolt*, pp. 216-18.
14. Michael Bar Zohar, *Ben Gurion*, vol. 2, in Hebrew (Tel Aviv: Am Oved, 1977), p. 778.
15. Ibid., p. 779.
16. Ibid.
17. Begin, *The Revolt*, p. 245.
18. Lenkin, *The Story of Altalena's Commander*, pp. 281-84.
19. Nakdimon, *Altalena*, p.199.
20. Ibid., pp. 179-84.
21. Uri Brener, *Altalena*, pp. 135-39.
22. Nakdimon, *Altalena*, p. 287.
23. Ibid., pp. 226-29.
24. Brener, *Altalena*, pp. 172-79.
25. Nakdimon, *Altalena*, pp. 254-55.

26. Ibid., p. 254.
27. Ibid., pp. 257-58.
28. Ibid., pp.277-78.
29. Brener, *Altalena*, pp. 221-23.
30. Nakdimon, *Altalena*, pp. 282-89.
31. Ibid., pp. 310-11.
32. Ibid., pp. 318-19.
33. Brener, *Altalena*, p. 248.
34. Ibid., p. 255.
35. Nakdimon, *Altalena*, pp. 374-94.
36. Ibid., pp. 336-39.
37. Ibid., p. 340.
38. Ibid., pp. 353-54.
39. Ehud Sprinzak, "*Altalena*: Thirty Years Later," *State, Society and International Relations* (in Hebrew), No. 14, 1980.
40. Ibid.
41. Ya'acov Shavit, *Jabotinsky and the Revisionist Movement 1925-1948* (London: Frank Cass, 1988), pp. 131-51.
42. Shabtai Teveth, *David's Zeal*, vol. 3 (Tel Aviv: Schoken, 1987—in Hebrew), pp. 46-55.
43. Conor Cruise O'Brien, *The Siege* (New York: Simon and Schuster, 1987), pp. 233-35.
44. Arye Naor, *David Raziel* (Tel Aviv: Ministry of Defense, 1990—in Hebrew), chap. 8.
45. Teveth, *David's Zeal*, pp. 161-64.
46. J. Bowyer Bell, *Terror Out of Zion*, pp. 39-6.
47. *David Raziel*, Ch.19.
48. Ibid., pp. 270-75.
49. Nathan Yelin-Mor, *The Fighters for the Freedom of Israel* (Tel Aviv: Shikmona, 1975—in Hebrew), pp. 71-84.
50. Begin, *The Revolt*, chap.3.
51. O'Brien, , pp. 25-58.
52. Yehuda Lapidot, *The Season: Hunting Brothers* (Tel Aviv: Jabotinsky Institute, 1994—in Hebrew), pp. 176-79.
53. Yitzhak Shamir, *Summing-Up* (Tel Aviv: Edanim, 1994—in Hebrew), pp.68-73.
54. Nakdimon, *Altalena*, p. 28.
55. Ya'acov Shavit, *Open Season* (Tel Aviv: Hadar, 1976—in Hebrew), pp. 103-4.
56. Lapidot, *The Season*, pp. 120-24.
57. Begin, *The Revolt*, chap. 6.
58. Lapidot, *The Season*, pp. 138-40.
59. Ibid., pp. 151-60.
60. Shavit, *Open Season*, pp. 130-36. The Haganah was aware of the plan to blow up the King David Hotel, but refused to admit it.
61. Ibid., pp. 136-42.
62. Benny Morris, *The Birth of the Palestinian Refugee Problem, 1947-1949* (Cambridge: Cambridge University Press, 1987), pp. 113-115.
63. O'Brien, *The Siege*, p. 282.
64. Bar Zohar, *Ben Gurion*, pp. 778-79.
65. Ibid., pp. 778-79.

66. Joseph Heller, *Lehi: Ideology and Politics* (Jerusalem: Keter, 1989—in Hebrew), pp. 435-37.
67. Kati Marton, *A Death in Jerusalem* (New York: Pantheon, 1994), pp. 11-12.
68. Ibid., pp. 13-14.
69. Ibid., p. 18.
70. Bar Zohar, *Ben Gurion*, p. 831.
71. Isser Harel, *Security and Democracy* (Tel Aviv: Edanim, 1989—in Hebrew), pp. 108-10.
72. Heller, *Lehi*, pp. 454-59.
73. Quoted in Marton, *A Death in Jerusalem*, p. 176.
74. Ibid., pp. 164-65.
75. Heller, *Lehi*, p. 459.
76. Ibid., pp. 519-25.
77. Harel, *Security and Democracy*, pp. 14-46.
78. Bar Zohar, *Ben Gurion*, pp. 831-34.
79. Harel, *Security and Democracy*, pp. 111-12.
80. Isser Harel, *The Truth About the Kastner Murder* (Jerusalem: Edanim, 1985), pp. 18-21.
81. Marton, *Death in Jerusalem*, pp. 233-34.
82. Ibid., pp. 246-47.
83. Ibid., p. 238.
84. Ibid., p. 255.
85. Shamir, *Summing Up*, pp. 97-98.
86. Personal interview with Eldad, February 28, 1985.
87. Harel, *The Truth about the Kastner Murder*, p. 41.
88. Ehud Sprinzak, *The Ascendance of Israel's Radical Right* (New York: Oxford University Press, 1991), pp. 33-34.
89. Harel, *Security and Democracy*, pp. 109-110.
90. Nakdimon, *Altalena*, pp. 415-16.

Chapter 2. Violence in the 1950s

1. Ora Shem Or, "No German Should Set a Foot in Tel-Aviv," *Yediot Aharonot*, September 4, 1949.
2. Gershom Schocken, "We and the Germans," *Ha'aretz*, September 2, 1949.
3. Tom Segev, *The Seventh Million: The Israelis and the Holocaust* (Jerusalem: Keter, 1991—in Hebrew), p.174.
4. Ibid., p.188.
5. Azriel Karlibach, "Amalek," *Ma'ariv*, October 5, 1951.
6. Yochanan Bader, *The Knesset and I* (Jerusalem: Edanim, 1979—in Hebrew), pp. 56-57.
7. Amos Perlmutter, *The Life and Times of Menachem Begin* (New York: Doubleday, 1987), pp. 99-117.
8. Begin's speech quoted in *Herut*, January 1, 1952.
9. *Ha'aretz*, January 8, 1952.
10. Menachem Begin in *The Knesset Proceedings*, vol.10 (Jerusalem: Knesset Publications, 1952), p. 906.
11. Michael Bar-Zohar, *Ben-Gurion*, vol. 2 (Tel-Aviv: Am Oved, 1977—in Hebrew), p. 923.

12. Ibid., p. 924.
13. Ibid., p. 925.
14. Isser Harel, *Security and Democracy* (Tel Aviv: Edanim, 1989—in Hebrew), p. 192.
15. Ibid.
16. Dov Shilansky, *In the Hebrew Prison* (Tel Aviv: Armony, 1977—in Hebrew), pp.10-33.
17. Nachman Ben-Yehuda, *Political Assassinations by Jews* (Albany, N.Y.: SUNY Press, 1993), p. 275.
18. "The Underground Movements in the State of Israel: Two Who Came Out of Dr. Scheib's Lecture," *Ma'ariv*, July 5, 1957 (author not identified).
19. Ibid.
20. "Underground Movements in the State of Israel: A War of Independence Hero Who Sought to Conduct a Revolution," *Ma'ariv*, July 12, 1957 (author not identified)
21. Michael Bar-Zohar, *The Man in Charge: Isser Harel and Israel's Security Services* (Jerusalem: Widenfeld and Nicholson, 1970—in Hebrew), p. 97.
22. Ibid., p.98.
23. "The Underground Movements . . . : Two Who Came Out . . .), *Ma'ariv*, July 5, 1957.
24. "The Underground Movements . . . , " *Ma'ariv*, July 12, 1957.
25. "The Underground Movements in the State of Israel: How Was the Effort to Attack the Knesset Aborted," *Ma'ariv*, July 19, 1957 (author not identified).
26. Harel, *Security and Democracy*, p. 186.
27. Avraham Daskal, "Extra-parliamentary Oppositional Behavior in the State's Early Days: B'rith Hakana'im and Malchut Israel" (M.A. thesis, Ramat Gan, Bar-Ilan University), p.56.
28. "The Underground Movements . . . ," *Ma'ariv*, July 19, 1957.
29. "Underground Movements in the State of Israel: B'rith Hakana'im Discovers a 'Secret Service Within a Secret Service,'" *Ma'ariv*, July 27, 1957 (author not identified).
30. Ibid.
31. Harel, *Security and Democracy*, p. 187.
32. Isser Harel, *The Truth About the Kastner Murder* (Jerusalem: Edanim, 1985—in Hebrew), pp.55-57.
33. Bar-Zohar, *The Man in Charge*, p.101. The damage to Heifetz's hand was small and he recovered soon thereafter.
34. Harel, *The Truth About the Kastner Murder*, pp. 255-56.
35. Ibid., pp. 58-73.
36. Daskal, "Extra-parliamentary Oppositional Behavior in the State's Early Days," p. 33.
37. On Greenwald, see Harel, *The Truth About the Kastner Murder*, pp. 113-19.
38. Quoted in Howard M. Sachar, *A History of Israel* (New York: Knopf, 1989), p. 374.
39. Segev, *The Seventh Million*, pp. 249-59.
40. Ibid., p. 248.
41. Harel, *The Truth About the Kastner Murder*, pp. 149-52.
42. Segev, *The Seventh Million*, pp. 249-59.
43. Ibid., pp. 254-55.
44. Ibid., pp. 265-68.
45. Ibid., p. 256.
46. Sachar, *A History of Israel*, p. 376.
47. Harel, *The Truth About the Kastner Murder*, p. 137.

48. Ibid., pp. 105-12.
49. Ibid., pp. 155-78.
50. Ibid., pp. 282-83.
51. Segev, *The Seventh Million*, pp. 288-90.
52. Harel, *The Truth About the Kastner Murder*, pp. 262-63.
53. Harel, *Security and Democracy*, chap. 11.
54. Eyal Kafkafi, "The Rift in Ein Harod . . . The Controversy Over Ein Harod's Relationship with Hakibbutz Hameuchad," in Pinchas Ginosar (ed.), *Studies in Israel's Reconstruction* (Sde Boker: Ben Gurion University, 1993—in Hebrew), pp. 427-54.
55. Bar-Zohar, *Ben-Gurion*, pp. 952-53.
56. The best documentation of the Seamen Rebellion can be found in a documentary film, *This Is How the Sea Became Stormy*," produced in 1952 by a group that called itself "the seamen loyalists convention."
57. David Ben-Gurion in *The Knesset Proceedings* (Jerusalem: Knesset Publications, October 28, 1951).
58. *Al Hamishmar*, November 23, 1951.
59. "This Is How the Sea Became Stormy."
60. Ibid.
61. *Al Hamishmar*, December 12, 1951.
62. "This Is How the Sea Became Stormy."
63. Ibid.
64. Ben-Yehuda, *Political Assassinations by Jews*, chap.7.
65. Interview with Dr. Shlomo Lev-Ami (Levi), June 25, 1994.
66. William A. Gamson, *The Strategy of Social Protest* (Homewood, Ill.: Dorsey, 1975), pp. 81-88.

Chapter 3. Thou Shalt Protest, Not Kill

1. On the *heredim* in general, see Menachem Friedman, *The Haredi Society* (Jerusalem: Jerusalem Institute for the Study of Israel, 1991—in Hebrew); Amnon Levy, *The Haredim* (Jerusalem: Keter, 1988—in Hebrew); Samuel C. Heilman and Menachem Friedman, "Religious Fundamentalism and Religious Jews," in Martin E. Marty and R. Scott Appleby, *Fundamentalisms Observed* (Chicago: University of Chicago Press, 1991).
2. Aviezer Ravitzky, *Messianism, Zionism and Jewish Religious Radicalism* (Tel Aviv: Am Oved, 1993—in Hebrew), pp. 36-39.
3. Ibid., pp. 40-44.
4. Charles S. Liebman and Eliezer Don-Yehiya, *Religion and Politics in Israel* (Bloomington, Ind.: Indiana University Press, 1984), chap.8.
5. Menachem Friedman, *The Haredi Society*, p. 64.
6. Ibid., p.65.
7. A. Yehuda Cohen, "Under Examination," in *Om Ani Homa* (Jerusalem: Neturei Karta, 1950—in Hebrew), part 2, p.70.
8. Amram Blau and Yoseph Sheinberger, "Our Duties and Obligations," "At a Crossroad," in *Om Ani Homa*, part 1. Shaul Schiff, "Rabbi Amram Blau explains: 'Why I flew Black Flags on Independence Day" *Hatzofe*, May 11, 1973.

9. Blau, "Our Duties and Obligations," p.31.
10. Levy, *The Haredim*, p.195. On the personality of Rabbi Amram Blau, see Menachem Michaelson, "Rabbi Amram Blau: The Eternal Rebel," *Yediot Aharonot*, July 7, 1974.
11. William Gamson, *The Strategy of Social Protest* (Homewood, Ill.: Dorsey, 1975), pp.81-88
12. Yoseph Shilhav and Menachem Friedman, *Expansion Within Seclusion: The Haredi Community in Jerusalem* (Jerusalem: Jerusalem Institute for the Study of Israel, 1985—in Hebrew), pp.56-58.
13. Abraham Farver, "Patterns of Haredi Attacks on non-Haredi Inhabitants in North-West Jerusalem as Part of the Struggle for the Area"(M.A. thesis, Institute of Criminology, Hebrew University of Jerusalem, 1987, in Hebrew).
14. Levy, *The Haredim*, pp. 214-16.
15. Gad Lior, "A Zone of Fire," *Yediot Aharonot—7 Days*, June 20, 1986.
16. Ibid.
17. Shahar Ilan, "The Meshi Road," *Kol Ha'ir*, February 10, 1989.
18. Eliezer Schulman, "Who, If not Meshi-Zahav?" *Hadashot*, February 2, 1989.
19. Ibid.
20. Yitzhak Rav-Yehiya, "The Pangs of Messiah, It Is Coming," *Yerushalaim*, June 30, 1989.
21. Amnon Levy, "Shtreimel, a Club and Kefiya," *Hadashot*, April 1, 1988.
22. Shahar Ilan, "The War of Hirsch against Meshi-Zahav," *Kol Ha'ir*, February 24, 1989.
23. Buki Na'eh, "Keshet Will Clean Up B'nai Brak's Abomination, and We Are Not Talking about Dry Cleaning," *Hadashot*, January 6, 1989.
24. *Ha'aretz*, February 20, 1989.
25. Ehud Sprinzak, *The Emergence of Politics of Delegitimation in Israel, 1967-1973* (Jerusalem: Eshkol Institute Publications, 1974—in Hebrew), p.11.
26. Uzi Benziman, "The Cossacks of God, *Ha'aretz*, January 6, 1989.
27. Numbers, chap.25.
28. Friedman, *The Haredi Society*, p.89.
29. Ibid., p. 91.
30. Ravitzky, *Messianism, Zionism and Jewish Religious Radicalism*, pp.89-93.
31. Friedman, *The Haredi Society*, p.69.
32. Avi Pozen, "The History of the Belz the-V," *Kol Ha'ir*, February 2, 1990; Levy, *The Haredim*, pp.209-11.
33. *Kol Ha'ir*, April 13, 1990.
34. Levy, *The Haredim*, pp.9-10.
35. Shahar Ilan, "The Chastity Belt Is Getting Tightened," *Kol Ha'ir*, March, 24, 1989.
36. Ibid.
37. Friedman, *The Haredi Society*, p.10.

Chapter 4. Challenge From the Left

1. Rael Jean Isaac, *Israel Divided* (Baltimore: Johns Hopkins University Press, 1976), chaps. 3-4; Ehud Sprinzak, *The Ascendance of Israel's Radical Right* (New York: Oxford University Press, 1991), chap. 2.

2. Nira Yovel-Davis, *Matzpen: The Israeli Socialist Organization* (Jerusalem: Hebrew University, Department of Sociology, 1977—in Hebrew), pp. 28-47.
3. Ibid., p. 84.
4. Ibid., pp. 82-85.
5. Ibid, p.23.
6. Ehud Sprinzak, *The Emergence of Politics of Delegitimation in Israel 1967-1972* (Jerusalem: Hebrew University, Eshkol Institute, 1973—in Hebrew), p.46.
7. Arye Bober (ed.), *The Other Israel: The Radical Case Against Zionism*, (New York: Anchor Books, 1972), introduction.
8. Sprinzak, *The Emergence of Politics of Delegitimation*, p.25.
9. Ibid., pp.50-51.
10. Ibid., pp.48-49.
11. "Siah' s Resolutions" (mimeograph, Tel Aviv, July 15, 1972).
12. Sprinzak, *The Emergence of Politics of Delegitimation*,. p. 34.
13. "Siah's Resolutions," July 15, 1972.
14. Sprinzak, *The Emergence of Politics of Delegitimation*, pp. 30-31.
15. Ibid., p.32.
16. Reuven Kaminer, "An Outline for Consideration," *Siah* (November 5, 1970), p. 17.
17. Siah Manifesto, April 19, 1970.
18. Sprinzak, *The Emergence of Politics of Delegitimation*, pp. 37-38.
19. Sam N. Leheman-Wilzig, *Stiff-Necked People, Bottle-Necked System* (Bloomington: Indiana University Press, 1990), pp. 29-30.
20. Yigal Mossinzon, *Cazablan* (Tel Aviv: Israeli Drama Center, 1960).
21. *Report of the State Investigation Commission for the Events at Wadi Salib in July 9, 1959* (Jerusalem: Government Printer, December 17, 1959), pp.3-6.
22. *Yediot Aharonot*, July 8, 1959.
23. *Report of the State Investigation Commission*, p.7.
24. *Yediot Aharonot*, July 10, 1959.
25. Ibid.
26. *Yediot Aharonot*, July 27, 1959.
27. Henriette Dahan-Kalev, "Self-Organizing Systems: Wadi Salib and the 'Black Panthers'—Implications for Israeli Society" (Ph.D. thesis, Hebrew University of Jerusalem, July 1991), pp.100-1.
28. *Report of the State Investigation Commission.*
29. Dahan-Kalev, *Self Organizing Systems*, pp.108-12.
30. *Report of the State Investigation Commission.*
31. Sprinzak, *The Emergence of Politics of Delegitimation*, pp.13-14.
32. Ibid., p.14.
33. Interviews with Shabtai Amadi, City of Jerusalem social worker, December 28, 1971; January 5, 1972.
34. Dahan-Kalev, *Self Organizing Systems*, pp.178-79.
35. Sprinzak, *The Emergence of Politics of Delegitimation*, p.14.
36. Ibid.
37. Dahan-Kalev, *Self Organizing Systems*, p.179.

38. Uzi Benziman, "This is how they make decisions; the government after the Panthers," *Ha'aretz Magazine*, August 3, 1973.
39. Interview with Panther leader Charlie Biton, December 12, 1971.
40. Interview with Nahum Barnea and Yehiel Limor, *Davar* and *Ma'ariv* correspondents, respectively, in Jerusalem, May 17, 1973.
41. Sprinzak, *The Emergence of Politics of Delegitimation*, p.17.
42. Dahan-Kalev, *Self Organizing System*, pp. 179-81.
43. Sprinzak, *The Emergence of Politics of Delegitimation*, p.22.
44. *Yediot Aharonot*, August 25, 1971.
45. Interview with Charlie Biton, December 12, 1971.
46. Dahan-Kalev, *Self Organizing Systems*, pp. 198-203.
47. Sprinzak, *The Emergence of Politics of Delegitimation*, p.18.
48. Ibid, pp.21-22.
49. Dahan-Kalev, *Self Organizing Systems*, pp.203-4.

Chapter 5. From Pioneering to Terrorism

1. Ehud Sprinzak, *The Ascendance of Israel's Radical Right* (New York: Oxford University Press, 1991), p. 319.
2. On Gush Emunim, see Sprinzak, *The Ascendance of Israel's Radical Right*, chaps. 3, 4, and 5; Gideon Aran, "Jewish Zionist Fundamentalism: The Bloc of the Faithful in Israel (Gush Emunim)," in Martin E. Marty and R. Scott Appleby, *Fundamentalisms Observed* (Chicago: University of Chicago Press, 1993); Gershon Shafat, *Gush Emunim* (Bet El: Bet El Library, 1996—in Hebrew).
3. Rabbi Zvi Yehuda ha-Cohen Kook, "This Is the State the Prophets Had Envisioned," quoted in *Nekuda* No. 86, April 26, 1985, pp.6-7.
4. Danny Rubinstein, *On the Lord's Side: Gush Emunim* (Tel Aviv: Hakibbutz Hameuchad, 1982—in Hebrew), pp.38-45.
5. Hava Pinchas-Cohen, "Gush Emunim—Early Days," *Nekuda* No. 69 (February 3, 1984), pp.4-11.
6. Peter Robert Demant, "Ploughshares into Swords: Israeli Settlement Policy in the Occupied Territories 1967-1977" (Unpublished Ph.D diss. submitted to the University of Amsterdam, 1988), pp.293-95.
7. Quoted in Nahum Barnea, "The Dervish," *Koteret Rashit* (Hebrew), May 16, 1984, p.15.
8. Sprinzak, *The Ascendance of Israel's Radical Right*, pp. 140-141.
9. Ibid.
10. Hans Kohn, "Messianism," *Encyclopedia of the Social Sciences* (New York: Macmillan, 1935); R. J. Zvi Verblovsky, "Messiah and Messianic Movements, "*The New Encyclopedia Britannica* (New York: Encyclopedia Britannica, 1981), vol.11.
11. Marty and Appleby, "Conclusion: An Interim Report on a Hypothetical Family," in *Fundamentalisms Observed.*
12. Menachem Friedman, *Society and Religion: The Non-Zionist Orthodoxy in Eretz Israel 1918-1936* (Jerusalem: Yad Ben-Zvi, 1978—Hebrew), pp.103-9.
13. Gideon Aran, "From Religious Zionism to Zionist Religion: The Origins and Culture of Gush Emunim, A Messianic Movement in Modern Israel" (Unpublished Ph.D diss., Hebrew University of Jerusalem, 1987—in Hebrew), chap.3.

14. Uriel Tal, "Foundations for a Political Messianic Trend in Israel," *Jerusalem Quarterly* No. 35 (Spring 1985), p.40.
15. Rabbi Zvi Yehuda ha-Cohen Kook, "Honest We Shall Be," in Yehuda Shaviv (ed.), *A Land of Settlement* (Jerusalem: 1977), pp.106-10.
16. Rabbi Shlomo Aviner, "And We Shall Not Betray Your Covenant," *Artzi* (Hebrew) No.1 (1982), pp.38-39.
17. Rabbi Zvi Yehuda ha-Cohen Kook, "This Is the State the Prophets Envisioned."
18. Sprinzak, *The Ascendance of Israel's Radical Right*, pp. 121-24.
19. Ibid, pp.117-21.
20. Rubinstein, *On the Lord's Side*, pp.147-56.
21. Menachem Livni, *Interrogation* (Court Documents, the Jewish Underground Trial, mimeograph), May 18, 1984.
22. Prison interview with Etzion, September 9, 1985.
23. Ibid.
24. Yitzhak Ganiram, *Interrogation* (Court Documents, the Jewish Underground Trial, mimeograph), May 5, 1984.
25. Uri Meir, *Interrogation* (Court Documents, the Jewish Underground Trial, mimeograph), April 30, 1984.
26. Livni, *Interrogation*, May 18, 1984.
27. Tzvi Ra'anan, *Gush Emunim* (Tel Aviv: Sifriyat Poalim, 1980), chap. 3.
28. David C. Rapoport, "Messianic Sanctions for Terror," *Comparative Politics* Vol.20, No.2 (January 1988), p.200.
29. Ibid., pp.200-201.
30. Livni, *Interrogation*, May 18, 1984.
31. Chaim Ben David, *Interrogation* (Court documents, the Jewish Underground Trial, mimeograph), April 30, 1984.
32. Prison Interview with Etzion, September 9, 1985.
33. Livni, *Interrogation*, May 18, 1984.
34. Interview with Rabbi Yoel Ban Nun, March 10, 1985.
35. Sprinzak, *The Ascendance of Israel's Radical Right*, pp.23-25.
36. Shabtai Ben Dov, *The Redemption of Israel in the Crisis of the State* (Safad: Hamatmid, 1960—in Hebrew); *Prophesy and Tradition in Redemption* (Tel Aviv: Yair, 1979).
37. Yehuda Etzion, "From the Flag of Jerusalem to the Redemption Movement," *Nekuda* No.94, December 20, 1985, p. 28.
38. Ibid.
39. Yehuda Etzion, *The Temple Mount* (Jerusalem: E. Caspi [private publisher], 1985—in Hebrew), p. 2.
40. Ibid., p. 4.
41. Yehuda Etzion, "To Fly, at Last, the Flag of Jerusalem, " *Nekuda* No. 93 (November 1985), p. 23.
42. Yehuda Etzion, "From the Laws of Existence to the Laws of Destination," *Nekuda* No. 75 (July 6, 1984), p. 26.
43. Livni, *Interrogation*, May 18, 1984.
44. Prison Interview with Etzion, September 9, 1985.
45. Livni, *Interrogation*, May 18, 1984.
46. Ibid.

47. *Licht's Report on Explosives* (Court Documents, the Jewish Underground Trial, mimeograph), May 22, 1984.
48. Sprinzak, *The Ascendance of Israel's Radical Right*, pp.155-58.
49. Yehuda Etzion, "I Felt an Obligation to Purify the Temple Mount," *Nekuda* No. 88 (June 24, 1985), pp. 24-25.
50. Richard Maxwell Brown, "American Vigilante Tradition," in Hugh Graham and Ted R. Gurr (eds.), *Violence in America* (New York:, Signet Books, 1969), pp.144-46; John H. Rosenbaum and C. Sederberg, "Vigilantism: An Analysis of Establishment Violence," *Comparative Politics* No.6 (1974).
51. Richard Maxwell Brown, " Legal and Behavioral Perspectives on American Vigilantism," *Perspectives in American History* No. 5 (1971), pp.95-96.
52. Giora Goldberg and Ephraim Ben Zadok, "Regionalism and Territorial Cleavage in Formation: Jewish Settlements in the Administered Territories," in *Medina, Mimshal Veyehasim Beinleumiim* (in Hebrew) No. 21 (Spring 1983).
53. Judith Carp, "Investigation of Suspicions Against Israelis in Judea and Samaria," *A Report of the Follow Up Committee* (mimeograph, in Hebrew), May 23, 1982.
54. David Weisburd and Vered Vinitzky, "Vigilantism as Rational Social Control: The Case of Gush Emunim Settlers," in Myron Aronoff (ed.), *Religion and Politics, Political Anthropology* vol. 3 (New Brunswick, N.J.: Transaction Books, 1993).
55. Ibid., p. 82.
56. Ibid., pp. 80-82.
57. Livni, *Interrogation*, May 18, 1984.
58. Ibid.
59. Shaul Nir, *Interrogation* (Court documents, the Jewish Underground Trial, mimeograph), May 9, 1984.
60. Gideon Aran, *Eretz Israel Between Religion and Politics: The Movement to Halt the Retreat in Sinai and its Lessons* (Jerusalem: Jerusalem Institute for the Study of Israel, 1985—in Hebrew), p. 22.
61. Haggai Segal, *Dear Brothers* (Jerusalem: Keter, 1987—in Hebrew), p.124.
62. Sprinzak, *The Ascendance of Israel's Radical Right*, pp. 102-3.
63. Aliza Weisman, *The Evacuation: The Story of the Uprooting of the Settlements in the Yamit Region* (Beth El: Beth El Library, 1990—in Hebrew), chap. 6.
64. Gideon Aran, *Eretz Israel Between Religion and Politics*, pp. 62-67; Haggai Segal, *Dear Brothers*, p. 131.
65. Gadi Wolsfeld, "Collective Political Action and Media Research Report," *Jerusalem Quarterly* No. 31 (Spring 1984), pp.140-41.
66. Segal, *Dear Brothers*, p.135.
67. Moshe Livne, "Israel Shelanu [Our Israel], the Rise and Fall of a Protest Movement" (Unpublished M.A. thesis, Tel Aviv University, 1977).
68. Ibid.
69. Mordechai Bar-On, *Peace Now* (Tel Aviv: Hakibutz Hameuchad, 1985—in Hebrew), pp. 120-121.
70. Ehud Sprinzak, "Extra-Parliamentary Politics in Israel," in Shmuel Stempler (ed.) *Nation and State: Israeli Society* (Tel Aviv: Ministry of Defense Publishers, 1989—in Hebrew) , p. 234.
71. The case of Greentzweig is discussed in chapter 6, pp. 205–206.

Chapter 6. The Kahanist Culture of Violence

1. Rabbi Meir Kahane, *Hillul Hashem* (A Kach mimeograph, n.d., in Hebrew).
2. On the strong anti-Gentile motive in Kahane's thinking, see Aviezer Ravitzky, "The Root of Kahanism: Consciousness and Political Reality, *Jerusalem Quarterly* No. 39 (1986).
3. Rabbi Meir Kahane, *Listen World, Listen Jew* (Tucson, Ariz.: Institute of Jewish Idea, 1975), pp. 121-22.
4. George Sorel, *Reflections on Violence* (New York: Collier Books, 1961); Franz Fanon, *The Wretched of the Earth* (New York: Grove Press, 1968).
5. Gerald Cromer, "The Debate About Kahanism in Israeli Society," *Occasional Papers* (New York: Harry Guggenheim Foundation, 1988), p.35.
6. In his *The Story of the Jewish Defense League* (Radnor, Pa.: Chilton, 1975), Kahane has a special chapter titled "Violence: Is This a Way for a Nice Jewish Boy to Behave?" in which he provides the rationale for the violence of the JDL. The reader is told that among its purposes, "Jewish Violence is meant to . . . destroy the Jewish neuroses and fears that contribute so much encouragement to the anti-Semite as well as Jewish belief in its own worthlessness. We want to instill self-respect and self-pride in a Jew who is ashamed of himself for running away, p. 142.
7. Howard M. Sachar, *A History of Israel* (Jerusalem: Steimatzky, 1976), pp.14-15, 38-41.
8. Meir Kahane, *Never Again: A Program for Jewish Survival* (New York: Pyramid Books, 1972), pp.74-101.
9. Ibid., pp. 72-104.
10. Ibid., pp. 151-74.
11. Rabbi Meir Kahane, *Israel's Eternity and Victory* (Jerusalem: Institute of Jewish Idea, 1973—in Hebrew); *Numbers 23:9* (Jerusalem: Institute of Jewish Idea, 1974—in Hebrew).
12. Rabbi Meir Kahane, *Forty Years* (Miami: Institute of Jewish Idea, 1983), pp. 6-7.
13. According to Kahane's logic, the only condition for complete salvation is a full repentance of the entire nation. His expected takeover of political power would have been a big step in the right direction, but since he did not plan to force repentance on the entire nation, "it would probably not satisfy God." He would try to tell the people about the disaster that awaited them, but if they chose not to listen, then even he would not be able to save them. Author's interview with Rabbi Kahane, June 12, 1988.
14. Janet Dolgin, *Jewish Identity and the JDL* (Princeton, N.J.: Princeton University Press, 1977), p.16.
15. Meir Kahane, *Never Again: A Program for Jewish Survival* (New York: Pyramid Books, 1972).
16. Robert I. Friedman, *The False Prophet: Rabbi Meir Kahane* (New York: Lawrence Hill Books, 1990), pp. 105-8.
17. Ibid., p. 115.
18. Quoted in Ehud Sprinzak, "Kach and Meir Kahane: The Rise of Jewish Quasi-Fascism," *Patterns of Prejudice* Vol. 19, Nos. 4-5 (1985), p. 2.
19. Robert I. Friedman, *The False Prophet*, pp. 114-15.
20. Rabbi Meir Kahane, *The Story of the Jewish Defense League* (Radnor, Pa.: Chilton, 1975), pp. 75-76.

21. Yair Kotler, *Heil Kahane* (Tel Aviv: Modan Books, 1985—in Hebrew), pp.99-102; Robert I. Friedman, *The False Prophet*, pp. 127-28.
22. Ehud Sprinzak, *The Emergence of the Politics of Delegitimation in Israel, 1967-1972*, (Jerusalem: Eshkol Institute, Hebrew University, 1973—in Hebrew), p. 26.
23. Ibid.
24. Kotler, *Heil Kahane*, pp. 153-60.
25. Robert I. Friedman, The False Prophet, pp. 149-53.
26. Kotler, *Heil Kahane*, pp. 26-17; also, Kahane, *The Story of the Jewish Defense League*, p.91.
27. Interview with Rabbi Kahane, April 18, 1973.
28. Meir Kahane, "The Activist Column: Reflections on the Elections," *Jewish Press*, June 3, 1977, p.20.
29. Meir Kahane, "The Activist Column: The Second Revolution," *Jewish Press*, October 20, 1978, p.28.
30. Rabbi Meir Kahane, *The Challenge: The Chosen Land* (Jerusalem: Center for Jewish Consciousness, 1973—in Hebrew), chap. 2.
31. Rabbi Meir Kahane, *Thorns in Your Eyes* (New York: Drunker, 1981—in Hebrew), p. 51.
32. For an excellent exposition of Kahane's political ideas, see his long interview in Raphael Mergui and Philippe Simonnot, *Israel's Ayatollahs: Meir Kahane and the Far Right in Israel* (London: Saqi Books, 1987), pp.29-90.
33. *Ha'aretz*, March 31, 1976.
34. Eli Reches, *The Arab Minority in Israel: Between Communism and Nationalism* (Tel Aviv: Hakibbutz Hameuchad, 1993—in Hebrew), pp. 80-81.
35. Majid al-Haj, "Strategies of Mobilization Among the Arabs in Israel," in Keith Kyle and Joel Peters, (eds.), *Whither Israel: The Domestic Challenges* (London: I.B. Tauris, 1993).
36. Quoted in Reches, *The Arab Minority in Israel*, p.81.
37. Ibid., pp.83-84.
38. Jacob M. Landau, *Israel's Arabs* (Tel Aviv: Ministry of Defense, 1971—in Hebrew), pp.111-24.
39. Reches, *The Arab Minority in Israel*, pp.112-14.
40. *Ma'ariv*, December 12, 1979.
41. Kahane, *The Challenge*, pp. 39-47.
42. Gershon Shafir and Yoav Peled, "'Thorns in Your Eyes': The Socio-Economic Basis of the Kahane Vote," in Asher Arian and Michal Shamir (eds.), *Elections in Israel 1984* (Tel Aviv: Ramot, 1986), pp.203-4.
43. Ilan Greilshammer, "The Likud," in Howard R. Penniman and Daniel J. Elazar (eds.), *Israel at the Polls* (Bloomington: Indiana University Press, 1986), pp. 89-91.
44. Ned Temko, *To Win or Die* (New York: William Morrow, 1987), pp. 257-58.
45. Ibid., p. 258.
46. Meron Benvenisti, *The West Bank Data Project* (Washington, D.C.: American Enterprise Institution, 1984), pp. 57-60.
47. Mordechai Bar-on, *Peace Now* (Tel Aviv: Hakibbutz Hameuchad, 1985—in Hebrew), p. 50.
48. Ibid., p. 54.

49. Ibid., pp. 58-59.
50. Quoted in Bar-On, *Peace Now*, pp.62-63.
51. Kahane, *The story of the Jewish Defense League*, pp.278-79; Janet Dolgin, *Jewish Identity and the JDL*, chap. 3.
52. Kahane, *The Story of the Jewish Defense League*, pp. 99-100.
53. For Kahane's own account of this strange association, see ibid., pp.185-91.
54. Kotler, *Heil Kahane*, pp. 103-8.
55. Kahane, *The Story of the Jewish Defense League*, pp. 141-42.
56. Kahane, *Hillul Hashem*, p. 3; *Listen Jew, Listen World*, pp. 88-89; *From the Knesset Stand: The Speeches of Rabbi Kahane in the Knesset* (Jerusalem: Kach Movement, n.d—in Hebrew), p.11.
57. Rabbi Meir Kahane, *The Jewish Idea* (Jerusalem: Institute of Jewish Idea, 1974), p. 14.
58. Kahane, *Hillul Hashem*, p.3.
59. Rabbi Meir Kahane, *Uncomfortable Questions to Comfortable Jews* (Secaucus, N.J.: Lyle Stuart, 1987), p. 269.
60. Quoted in Kotler, *Heil Kahane*, p. 257.
61. Nadav Shragai, "Going for the Action," *Ha'aretz*, November 27, 1984.
62. Quoted in Chaim Shibi, "Wherever There Is Blood Spilled You Find Kahane," *Yediot Aharonot*, August 2, 1985.
63. Quoted in Yair Avituv, "All Is Well in the Casbah," *Kol Hair*, August 12, 1991.
64. *Ha'aretz*, February 12, 1983.
65. Sprinzak, *The Ascendance of Israel's Radical Right*, pp. 155-158.
66. Cromer, "The Debate About Kahanism in Israeli Society."
67. Sprinzak, *The Ascendance of Israel's Radical Right*, pp. 245-46.
68. Ibid., pp. 159-64.
69. Ibid., pp. 164-65.
70. Ibid., pp. 247-48.

Chapter 7. After Oslo

1. Giora Goldberg, *The Israeli Voter 1992* (Jerusalem: Magnes Press, 1994—in Hebrew), pp. 212-14.
2. Eliezer Don Yehiya, "The Book and the Sword: The Nationalist Yeshivot and Political Radicalism in Israel," in Martin E. Marty and R. Scott Appleby (eds.), *Accounting for Fundamentalisms* (Chicago: University of Chicago Press, 1994).
3. "Emunim: To return to and proceed in the path of Zionist fulfillment," mimeographed leaflet, n.d..
4. Nadav Ha'etzni, "Golan Settlers Play with Fire," *Ma'ariv*, February 26, 1993.
5. Israel Harel, "Editor's Comment," *Nekuda*, no. 162, September 1992, p.11.
6. Yesha Rabbi's Communiqué, No.1, August 1992.
7. Elyakim Ha'etzni, "It Is Time to Wake Up from the Dreams," *Nekuda*, no. 162, September 1992, p.26.
8. Yehuda Etzion, "To Fly at Last the Flag of Jerusalem," *Nekuda,* no. 93, November 22, 1985.
9. Interview with Etzion, February 19, 1989.
10. "Identity Card," Chai Ve-Kayam, n.d..

11. On Ha'etzni, see Ehud Sprinzak, *The Ascendance of Israel's Radical Right* (New York: Oxford University Press, 1991), pp. 199-203.
12. Ha'etzni, "It Is Time," pp. 91-92.
13. Uriel Ben Ami, "Helpless in Ofra," *Dvar Hashavua*, November 8, 1985.
14. Elyakim Ha'etzni, "To Make It Impossible for the Zionist State to Betray Zion," *Nekuda*, no. 163, October 1992.
15. Elyakim Ha'etzni, "Crossing the Red Lines," *Nekuda,* no. 168, May 1993, p.35
16. Rabbi Shlomo Aviner, "Morality and the War Against Terrorism," *Yesha Rabbis' Communique* No. 9 (May 1993).
17. Elyakim Ha'etzni, "Civil Disobedience Now," *Nekuda*, no. 180, September 1994), pp. 25-27.
18. Ilan Lagaziel, "Political Violence in Israel's Extreme Right: Kach from Kahane's Assassination to the Oslo Agreements," (M.A. thesis, Hebrew University of Jerusalem, 1994), p. 91.
19. Ibid., p.87.
20. Leon Festinger, "When Prophecy Fails," in Stanley Schachetr and Michael Gazzaniga (eds.), *Extending Psychological Frontiers: Selected Works of Leon Festinger* (New York: Russel Sage Foundation, 1989).
21. David Rapoport, "Messianic Sanctions for Terror," *Comparative Politics* Vol. 20, No.2 (1988).
22. See testimonies and letters of praise in Michael Ben-Horin (ed.), *Baruch: The Man: Memorial Book for Dr. Baruch Goldstein, the Saint* (Jerusalem: special edition, 1995—in Hebrew), pp.369-433.
23. Nadav Ha'etzni, *Ma'ariv*, March 4, 1994.
24. *Report of the State Investigation Commission Studying the Massacre in Hebron's Cave of the Patriarchs* (Jerusalem: Government's Printer, 1994—in Hebrew), p.79.
25. Rabbi Meir Kahane, *Forty Years* (Miami: Institute of the Jewish Idea, 1983).
26. Nadav Ha'etzni, *Ma'ariv*, March 4, 1994.
27. *Report of the State Investigation Commission*, p.80.
28. Roni Shaked & Aviva Shabi, *Hamas* (Jerusalem: Keter, 1994—in Hebrew); Roni Shaked, "This Is How the Engineer Operated," *Yediot Aharonot Magazine*, October 21, 1994.

Chapter 8. To Kill a Prime Minister

1. *Report: The State Investigation Commission in the Matter of the Murder of the Late Prime Minister Yitzhak Rabin* (Jerusalem: The Government Printer, 1996—in Hebrew), pp.24-32.
2. Interview with settler leader Aharon Domb (Dompa), November 9, 1994.
3. This account is based on author's daily contact with Eitan Haber, Rabin's bureau chief, during the Tel Rumeida crisis.
4. Ehud Sprinzak, *The Ascendance of Israel's Radical Right* (New York: Oxford University Press, 1991), pp. 89-99.
5. Nadav Shragai, *Ha'aretz*, December 1, 1993.
6. Shragai, *Ha'aretz*, March 7, 1994.

7. Shlomo Dror, *Ha'aretz*, March 30, 1994.
8. Gideon Alon and Avirama Golan, in *Ha'aretz*, March 31, 1994; Orna Landau, *Hair*, April 8, 1994.
9. Gideon Alon, *Ha'aretz*, April 1, 1994.
10. The author was personally involved in writing one of these memoranda.
11. Avirama Golan, *Ha'aretz*, April 5, 1994.
12. Nadav Shragai, *Ha'aretz*, May 5, 1994.
13. Sprinzak, *The Ascendance*, p. 45.
14. Rabbi Dov Lior, Rabbi Daniel Shilo, and Rabbi Eliezer Melamed, "What Is the Rule About This Bad Government?" in Dana Arieli-Horowitz (ed.), *Religion and State in Israel, 1994-1995* (Jerusalem: Center for Jewish Pluralism, 1996—in Hebrew), pp.120-23.
15. Rabbi Ya'kov Ariel, "Defining Rodef," in Dana Arieli-Horowitz, *Religion and State 1994-1995*, pp. 136-37.
16. Nadav Shragai, *Ha'aretz*, November 23, 1995.
17. This is based on interviews with several Yeshiva students who asked that their names not be disclosed.
18. Shimon Shifer, *Yediot Aharonot*, September 11, 1995.
19. Shlomo Shamir and Reli Sa'ar, *Ha'aretz*, November 9, 1995.
20. Nadav Shragai & Shachar Ilan, *Ha'aretz*, Tzi Zinger, *Yediot Aharonot*, November 13, 1995.
21. Rabbi Shlomo Aviner, *The Prime Minister: Essays in Honor of the Kingdom of Israel and Eretz Israel* (Bet El: Bet El Publishing Services, 1996).
22. Shachar Ilan, "Hashavua: Rabin and Peres: Israel's Evil People: Yudenrat Men and Capos," *Ha'aretz*, November 12, 1995.
23. The author was present at the Goldstein commemoration.
24. Sprinzak, *The Ascendance of Israel's Radical Right*, p. 165.
25. Rabbi Yitzhak Ginzburg, "Baruch Hagever," in Michael Ben Horin (ed.), *Baruch Hagever* (Jerusalem: Special Publication, 1995—Hebrew), p.20.
26. Ibid., p.28.
27. Ibid., p. 44.
28. Ibid., pp. 28-29.
29. Ibid., p. 31.
30. Ibid., p.33.
31. Rabbi David Cohen, "To Take Revenge Aagainst the Gentiles," in Michael Ben Horin (ed.), *Baruch Hagever*, p.56.
32. Ibid., p. 67.
33. Ibid., p.88.
34. Ibid., p. 92.
35. *Ha'aretz*, September 22, 1994.
36. Ido Elba, "Examination of the Rulings about the Killing of Gentiles," in Michael Ben Horin (ed.), *Baruch Hagever*, p. 127.
37. Rabbi Mordechai Eliyahu, "letter," in *Tzfiya* I, 1985.
38. Sprinzak, *The Ascendance of the Radical Right*, p. 352, n.25.
39. Yigal Amir was known by his friends as a great Goldstein admirer. *Baruch Hagever* was one of three books found in his room after the Rabin assassination.

40. Benjamin Ze'ev Kahane, "A Cultural War," in Michael Ben Horin (ed.), *Baruch Hagever*, p. 256.
41. *Ha'aretz*, April 13, 1995; November 19, 1995.
42. *Ha'aretz*, November 20, 1995. Months after the Rabin assassination it was discovered that Eyal's head, Avishai Raviv, was an informant of the Shin Beth. The Israeli secret service had apparently bankrolled Eyal to obtain access to the secret meetings of the extreme right. Many critics of the service have since argued that this was a totally irresponsible operation because Raviv became a major antigovernment provocateur and was directly involved in the creation of the atmosphere that led to the Rabin assassination. Especially adamant were spokespersons of the extreme right who charge the service with direct responsibility for both the assassination and the anti-right smear campaign that followed it. While admitting the blunder involved in Raviv's employment, Shin Beth officials let it be known that Raviv was a useful agent, but one who could not be fully controlled. They erroneously believed that the damage of his employment was less than Raviv's contribution.
43. *Yediot Aharonot*, July 13, 1995.
44. Ibid.
45. Ibid.
46. Daliah Karpel, "Must Scream Gevald," *Ha'aretz Magazine*, January 17, 1995.
47. Nadav Shragai, *Ha'aretz*, December 2, 1993.
48. Zvi Gilat, "Operation 'Awanta'," *Yediot Aharonot*, February 4, 1994.
49. Nadav Shragai, *Ha'aretz*, July 31, 1995.
50. Dani Sade et al., "Zo Artzenu Fails Again," *Yediot Aharonot*, September 19, 1995.
51. Lili Galili, "No Need to Give the Barbecue Up," *Ha'aretz*, February 6, 1994.
52. Ravit Naor, "Moshe Feigelin, Zo Artzenu Chairman. . . ." *Ma'ariv Magazine*, August 18, 1995.
53. Amos Harel, "He Is not Impressed by the Law," *Kol Hair*, June 16, 1995.
54 Moshe Feigelin, "The ideological Failure and the Tactical Blunder," *Nekuda* No. 180 (September 1994), p.46.
55. Dov Elboim, "The Murder Curse," *Yediot Aharonot*, November 13, 1995.
56. Dimitry Prokofyev, "They Asked Me to Help Yigal Amir . . . ," *Yediot Aharonot*, December 18, 1995.
57. Arieli-Horowitz (ed.), *Religion and State in Israel*, p. 287.
58. This judgment is based on several interviews I conducted with Kahane supporters after the assassination.
59. *Report: The State Investigation Commission in the Matter of the Murder of the Late Prime Minister Yitzhak Rabin*, p.89.
60. Ibid.
61. David Lavi, *Ma'ariv*, November 6, 1995.
62. Yael Gvirtz, "Death's Perverted Servant," *Yediot Aharonot Magazine*, March 29, 1996.
63. *Report: The State Investigation Commission*, p.88.
64. Ariela Ringle-Hofman, "A Murderer's Breeding Place," *Yediot Aharonot Magazine*, November 10, 1995.
65. Yaron Kaner, "Eyal Seminar in Hebron, the Organizer: Yigal Amir," *Yediot Aharonot's Seven Days* (November 10, 1995).
66. *Ha'aretz*, November 19, 1995.
67. Buki Naeh, *Yediot Aharonot*, November 7, 1995.

68. *Ha'aretz*, November 10, 1995.
69 *Ha'aretz*, December 12, 1995.
70. Zvi Harel, *Ha'aretz*, December 12, 1995.
71. Yoram Yarkoni, *Yediot Aharonot*, December 11, 1995.
72. Yael Gvirtz, *Yediot Achronot*, March 29, 1996.
73. This conclusion is based on the official report of the state investigation commission of the Rabin assassination, on the entire press coverage of Amir's investigation, and on portions of the confidential part of the investigation shown to the author under the condition that no specific references be made.
74. Numbers 25.
75. Shaul Yisraeli, *Amud Hayemini Book* (Jerusalem: Eretz Hemdat, 1992—in Hebrew), chap. 15.
76. Yael Gvirtz, *Yediot Aharonot*, March 29, 1996.
77. See note 73 above.
78. Gvirtz, *Yediot Aharonot*, March 29, 1996.
79. Ibid.
80. *Yediot Aharonot*, November 24, 1995.
81. Gvirtz, *Yediot Aharonot*, March 29, 1995.
82. Ibid.
83. Ibid.
84. Zvi Harel, *Ha'aretz*, February 2, 1996.
85. Avihai Beker and David Lavi, "A Profile of a Jewish Killer," *Ma'ariv Magazine*, November 10, 1995.
86. Gvirtz, *Yediot Aharonot*, March 29, 1995.
87. See note 73 above.
88. *Report: The State Investigation Commission*, pp.85-87.
89. Reuven Shapira and Daliah Shchori, *Ha'aretz*, November 13, 1995.

Chapter 9. Jews Who Kill?

1. David Biale, *Power and Powerlessness in Jewish History* (New York: Schocken Books, 1986); Paul Breines, *Tough Jews: Political Fantasies and the Moral Dilemma of American Jewry* (New York: Basic Books, 1990).
2. Biale, pp. 72-73.
3. Ibid., 74-76.
4. Yosef Braslavski, *War and Defense of Eretz Israel Jews* (Tel Aviv: Hakibbutz Hameuchad, 1943—in Hebrew), p. 183.
5. Rami Rosen, "A History of Denial," *Ha'aretz Magazine*, November15, 1996.
6. Braslavski, p. 187.
7. Rosen, "A History of Denial."
8. Breines, *Tough Jews*, pp. 96-101.
9. Ze'ev Ivianski, "The Moral Issue," in David C. Rapoport and Yonah Alexander (eds.), *The Morality of Terrorism* (New York: Pergamon, 1982).
10. Albert Parry, *Terrorism: from Robespierre to Arafat* (New York: Vanguard, 1977), chap. 14.
11. Breines, *Tough Jews*, pp. 102-4. Reference is to Harriet and Fred Rochlin, *Pioneer Jews: A New Life in the Far West* (Boston: Houghton Mifflin, 1984).

12. Ibid., pp. 105-15. Reference is to Jenna Weissman Joselit, *Our Gang: Jewish Crime and the New York Jewish Community: 1900-1940* (Bloomington: University of Indiana Press, 1983).
13. Rosen, "A History of Denial."
14. Ibid.
15. Ibid.
16. Jean-Paul Sartre, *Anti-Semite and Jew,* trans. George J. Becker (New York: Schocken Books, 1965), pp. 117-18.
17. David C. Rapoport, " Terror and the Messiah: An Ancient Experience and Some Modern Parallels," in David C. Rapoport and Yonah Alexander (eds.), *The Morality of Terrorism* (New York: Pergamon Press, 1982).
18. Personal interview, June 7, 1988.
19. Aviezer Ravitzky, *Messianism, Zionism and Jewish Religious Radicalism* (Tel Aviv: Am Oved, 1993).
20. Menachem Begin, *The Revolt* (Tel Aviv: Achiasaf, 1978—in Hebrew), pp. 210-11.
21. This is based on personal interviews I conducted with several rabbis and major activists of the extreme right after the Rabin assassination.
22. Ehud Sprinzak, *Every Man Whatsoever Is Right in His Own Mind: Illegalism in Israeli Society* (Tel Aviv: Sifriyat Poalim, 1986—in Hebrew); Gadi Wolfsfeld, *The Politics of Provocation* (Albany: Suny Press, 1988).
23. On Ben-Gurion's leadership style (later followed by Meir), see Peter Y. Medding, *The Founding of Israeli Democracy* (New York: Oxford University Press, 1990), pp.214-20.
24. Thomas Meyer, *The Awakening of the Muslims in Israel* (Givat Haviva:, Center for Arab Studies, 1988—in Hebrew), chap. 3.
25. Ehud Ya'ari and Ze'ev Schiff, *Intifada* (Tel Aviv: Schocken Books, 1990—in Hebrew), chap. 7.
26. Sammy Smooha, "Class, Ethnic and National Cleavages and Democracy in Israel," in Ehud Sprinzak and Larry Diamond (eds.), *Israeli Democracy under Stress* (Boulder, Colo.: Lynne Reinner, 1993), pp.332-33.
27. Cf. Alistaire Horne, *A Savage War for Peace: Algeria 1954-1962* (London: Macmillan, 1977).

Appendix

1. Ze'ev Sternhell et al., *The Birth of Fascist Ideology: From Cultural Rebellion to Political Revolution* (Princeton, N.J.: Princeton University Press, 1994), chap. 1.
2. Hannah Arendt, *On Violence* (New York: Harcourt, Brace & World, 1969), pp. 9-12.
3. James Rule, *Theories of Civil Violence* (Berkeley: University of California Press, 1988), chap. 3.
4. Robert Park, "Human Nature and Collective Behavior," *American Journal of Sociology* Vol. 32 (1927); Herbert Blumer, "Collective Behavior," in J.B. Gittler (ed.), *Review of Sociology: Analysis of a Decade* (New York: Wiley, 1957); William Kornhauser, *The Politics of Mass Society* (Glencoe, Ill.: Free Press, 1959); Neil Smelser, *Theory of Collective Behavior* (New York: Free Press, 1962).
5. Daniel Bell (ed.), *The End of Ideology* (New York: Free Press, 1960).

6. Peter Berger, *Sacred Canopy: Elements of the Sociology of Religion* (Garden City, N.Y.: Doubleday/Anchor Books, 1968).
7. Ehud Sprinzak, "Delegitimization Processes in Democracy," *State, Government and International Relations* (in Hebrew) No.6 (Autumn 1974).
8. Ted R. Gurr and Hugh D. Graham (eds.), *Violence in America* (New York: Signet Books, 1969). Another pathbreaking study belonging to this era is David Rapoport's *Assassination and Terrorism* (Toronto: CBC Merchandizing, 1971).
9. On scientific paradigms and scientific revolutions, see Thomas S. Kuhn, *The Structure of Scientific Revolutions* (Chicago: University of Chicago Press, 1962).
10. Harry Eckstein, "Theoretical Approaches to Explaining Collective Political Violence," and Ekkart Zimmermann, "Macro-Comparative Research on Political Protest," in Ted R. Gurr (ed.), *Handbook of Political Conflict: Theory and Research* (New York: Free Press, 1980).
11. Joe R. Feagin and Harlan Hahn, *Ghetto Revolt* (New York: Macmillan, 1973); Charles Tilly, *From Mobilization to Revolution* (Reading, Mass.: Addison-Wesley, 1978), chap. 8; E.N. Muller, *Aggressive Political Behavior* (Princeton, N.J.: Princeton University Press, 1979); E.N. Muller and K. Opp, "Rational Choice and Rebellious Collective Action," *American Political Science Review* Vol. 80 (1986); Sidney Tarrow, *Democracy and Disorder* (New York: Oxford University Press, 1989).
12. Ted R. Gurr, *Why Men Rebel* (Princeton, N.J.: Princeton University Press, 1970), pp. 168-77.
13. Sprinzak, "Delegitimization Processes in Democracy"; Donatella Della Porta, *Social Movements, Political Violence, and the State* (New York: Cambridge University Press, 1995).
14. Albert Bandura, "Social Learning Theory of Aggression," in J.F. Knutson (ed.), *The Control of Aggression: Implications from Basic Research* (New York: Hawthorn, 1973); Albert Bandura, "Mechanisms of Moral Disengagement," in Walter Reich (ed.), *Origins of Terrorism* (New York: Cambridge University Press, 1990).
15. Smelser, *Theory of Collective Behavior*, chap. 1; William A. Gamson, *The Strategy of Social Protest* (Homewood, Ill.: Dorsey, 1975); pp. 14-15; Tilly, *From Mobilization to Revolution.*
16. William Gamson and J. McEnvoy, "Police Violence and Its Public Support," in James F. Short and Marvin E. Wolfgang (eds.), *Collective Violence* (Chicago: Aldin Atherton, 1972); Fred R. von der Mehden, *Comparative Political Violence* (Englewood Cliffs, N.J.: Prentice-Hall, 1973), pp. 37-54; Michael Stohl and George Lopez (eds.), *The State as Terrorist* (London: Alswych Press, 1984); Della Porta, *Social Movements, Political Violence, and the State*, chap. 3.
17. Emanuel Marx, *The Social Context of Violent Behavior* (London: Routledge and Kegan Paul, 1976), p. 74.
18. Nachmen Ben-Yehuda, *Political Assassinations by Jews* (Albany, N.Y.: SUNY Press, 1993), chap. 12.
19. Lewis A. Coser, *The Function of Social Conflict* (Glencoe, Ill.: Free Press, 1956).
20. Quoted in Arendt, *On Violence*, p. 79.
21. Dennis C. Pirages, "Political Stability and Conflict Management," in Gurr, *Handbook of Political Conflict.*
22. Ehud Sprinzak, "The Process of Delegitimization: Towards a Linkage Theory of Political Terrorism," *Terrorism and Political Violence* Vol.3, No.3 (1991), pp. 67–68.

23. Tom Bowden, *The Breakdown of Public Security* (Beverly-Hills, Calif.: Sage, 1977); Juan Linz, *The Breakdown of Democratic Regimes: Crisis, Breakdown and Reequilibrium* (Baltimore: Johns Hopkins University Press, 1978, pp. 14-23.
24. Joseph Fink, "Violence" in *The Hebrew Encyclopedia*, vol.3 (Tel Aviv: Massada, 1951).
25. Ehud Sprinzak, "Extra-parliamentary politics in Israel," in Shmuel Stempler (ed.), *Nation and State: Israeli Society* (Tel Aviv: Defense Ministry, 1989—in Hebrew).
26. J.N. Rosenbaum and P.C. Sederberg, "Vigilantism: An Analysis of Establishment Violence," *Comparative Politics* Vol. 6 (1974).
27. Thomas P. Thornton, "Terror as a Weapon of Political Agitation," in Harry Eckstein (ed.), *Internal War* (New York: Collier and Macmillan, 1964); Paul Wilkinson, *Political Terrorism* (London: Macmillan, 1975), chap. 1.
28. Von der Mehden, *Comparative Political Violence*, p. 113.
29. Feliks Gross, *Violence in Politics* (The Hague: Mouton, 1972), pp. 90-91.
30. Bandura, "Mechanisms of Moral Disengagement," pp. 161-63.
31. Gamson, *The Strategy of Social Protest*, pp. 81-88;. Muller and Opp, "Rational Choice and Rebellious Collective Action"; Tarrow, *Democracy and Disorder*.
32. Gadi Wolfsfeld, *The Politics of Provocation: Participation and Protest in Israel* (Albany: SUNY Press, 1988), pp. 171-73.
33. Bandura, "Social Learning Theory of Aggression."
34. Sprinzak, "The Process of Delegitimization," p. 61.
35. Ehud Sprinzak, "Violence and Catastrophe in the Theology of Rabbi Meir Kahane: The Ideologization of the Mimetic Desire," *Terrorism and Political Violence* Vol. 3, No.3 (Autumn 1991).
36. Manus I. Midlarsky, Martha Crenshaw, and Yoshida Fumihiko, "Why Violence Spreads," *International Studies Quarterly* Vol. 24, No.2 (1980).
37. Bar-Ilan's Sam Leheman-Wilzig took an alternative approach in his comprehensive study of protest patterns in Israel that is also highly relevant for the present study. Leheman-Wilzig offers periodization that he bases on objective measurement of riots and protests as reported in the press. A period in the history of Israeli protest begins, or ends, when a dramatic change in the frequency of protest events occurs. My decision not to follow Leheman-Wilzig's approach stems from the recognition that his impressive work relates only indirectly to the issue this study addresses, political violence in Israel. Leheman-Wilzig does not write, for example, about terror operations and underground activities that, when executed and discovered, have had an enormous political impact. He is also not interested in the rhetoric of violence and developments in Israel's ideologies of violence. While Leheman-Wilzig's research approach is fully legitimate, I find it less than helpful for understanding Israeli violence in the past, present, and future. Sam N. Leheman-Wilzig, *Stiff-Necked People, Bottle-Necked System*, (Bloomington: Indiana University Press, 1990), chap. 3.

BIBLIOGRAPHY

In Hebrew

Aran, Gideon. *Eretz Israel Between Religion and Politics: The Movement to Halt the Retreat in Sinai and its Lessons* (Jerusalem: Jerusalem Institute for the Study of Israel, 1985).

———. "From Religious Zionism to Zionist Religion: The Origins and Culture of Gush Emunim, A Messianic Movement in Modern Israel" (Unpublished Ph.D. diss., Hebrew University of Jerusalem, 1987).

Ariel, Rabbi Ya'kov. "Defining Rodef," in Dana Arieli-Horowitz (ed.), *Religion and State in Israel, 1994–1995* (Jerusalem: Center for Jewish Pluralism, 1996).

Aviner, Rabbi Shlomo. "And We Shall Not Betray Your Covenant," *Artzi*, no. 1, Jerusalem, 1982.

———. "Morality and the War Against Terrorism," Yesha Rabbis' Communiqué, no. 9, May 1993.

———. *The Prime Minister: Essays in Honor of the Kingdom of Israel and Eretz Israel* (Bet El: Bet El Publishing Services, 1996).

Avituv, Yair. "All Is Well in the Casbah," *Kol Ha'ir*, August 12, 1991.

Bader, Yochanan. *The Knesset and I* (Jerusalem: Edanim, 1979).

Barnea, Nahum. "The Dervish," *Koteret Rashit*, May 16, 1984.

Bar-On, Mordecahi. *Peace Now* (Tel Aviv: Hakibbutz Hameuchad, 1985).

Bar-Zohar, Michael. *Ben-Gurion*, vol. 2 (Tel Aviv: Am Oved, 1977).

———. *The Man in Charge: Isser Harel and Israel's Security Services* (Jerusalem: Wiedenfeld and Nicholson, 1970).

Begin, Menachem. *The Revolt* (Tel Aviv: Ahiasaf, 1978).

Beker, Avihai and David Lavi. "A Profile of a Jewish Killer," *Ma'ariv Magazine*, November 10, 1995.

Ben Ami, Uriel. "Helpless in Ofra," *Dvar Hashavua*, November 8, 1985.

Ben Dov, Shabtai. *Prophesy and Tradition in Redemption* (Tel Aviv: Yair, 1979).

———. *The Redemption of Israel in the Crisis of the State* (Safad: Hamatmid, 1960).

Ben Horin, Michael (ed.). *Baruch Hagever: Memorial Book for Dr. Baruch Goldstein, the Saint* (Jerusalem, special publication, 1995).

Benziman, Uzi. "The Cossacks of God," *Ha'aretz*, January 6, 1989.

———. "This Is How They Make Decisions: The Government After the Panthers," *Ha'aretz Magazine*, August 3, 1973.

Blau, Amram. "Our Duties and Obligations," in *Om Ani Homa* (Jerusalem: Neturei Karta, 1950).

Braslavski, Yosef. *War and Defense of Eretz Israel Jews* (Tel Aviv: Hakibbutz Hameuchad, 1943)

Brener, Uri. *Altalena* (Tel Aviv: Hakibbutz Hameuchad, 1978).

Carp, Judith. "Investigation of Suspicions Against Israelis in Judea and Samaria," *A Report of the Follow Up Committee* (mimeograph), May 23, 1982.

Cohen, A. Yehuda. "Under Examination," in *Om Ani Homa* (Jerusalem: Neturei Karta, 1950).

Cohen, Rabbi David. "To Take Revenge Against the Gentiles," in Michael Ben Horin (ed.), *Baruch Hagever* (Jerusalem,:Special Publication, 1995).

Dahan-Kalev, Henriette. "Self-Organizing Systems: Wadi Salib and the "Black Panthers"—Implications for Israeli Society" (Ph.D. diss., Hebrew University of Jerusalem, July 1991).

Daskal, Avraham. "Extra-parliamentary Oppositional Behavior in the State's Early Days: B'rith Hakana'im and Malchut Israel" (M.A. diss., Bar-Ilan University).

Elba, Ido. "Examination of the Rulings about the Killing of the Gentiles," in Ben Horin, Michael (ed.). *Baruch Hagever* (Jerusalem, special publication, 1995).

Elboim, Dov. "The Murder Curse," *Yediot Aharonot*, November 13, 1995.

Eliyahu, Rabbi Mordechai. "Letter," *Tzfiya I*, 1985.

Etzion, Yehuda. "From the Flag of Jerusalem to the Redemption Movement," *Nekuda*, no. 94, December 20, 1985.

———. "From the Laws of Existence to the Laws of Destination," *Nekuda*, no. 75, July 6, 1984.

———. "I Felt an Obligation to Purify the Temple Mount," *Nekuda*, no. 88, June 24, 1985.

———. "To Fly, at Last, the Flag of Jerusalem," *Nekuda*, no. 93, November 1985.

———. *The Temple Mount* (Jerusalem: E. Caspi, 1985).

Farver, Avraham. "Patterns of Haredi Attacks on non-Haredi Inhabitants in North-West Jerusalem as Part of the Struggle for the Area" (M.A. diss., Institute of Criminology, Hebrew University of Jerusalem, 1987).

Feigelin, Moshe. "The Ideological Failure and the Tactical Blunder," *Nekuda*, no. 180, September 1994.

Friedman, Menachem. *The Haredi Society* (Jerusalem: Jerusalem Institute for the Study of Israel, 1991).

———. *Society and Religion: The Non-Zionist Orthodoxy in Eretz Israel 1918–1936* (Jerusalem: Yad Ben-Zvi, 1978).

Galili, Lili. "No Need to Give the Barbecue Up," *Ha'aretz* February 6, 1994.

Gilat, Zvi. "Operation 'Awanta'," *Yediot Aharonot* February 4, 1994.

Ginzburg, Rabbi Yitzhak. "Baruch Hagever," in Michael Ben Horin (ed.), *Baruch Hagever* (Jerusalem: Special Publication, 1995).

Goldberg, Giora. *The Israeli Voter 1992* (Jerusalem, Magnes, 1994).

Goldberg, Giora, and Ephraim Ben Zadok, "Regionalism and Territorial Cleavage in For-

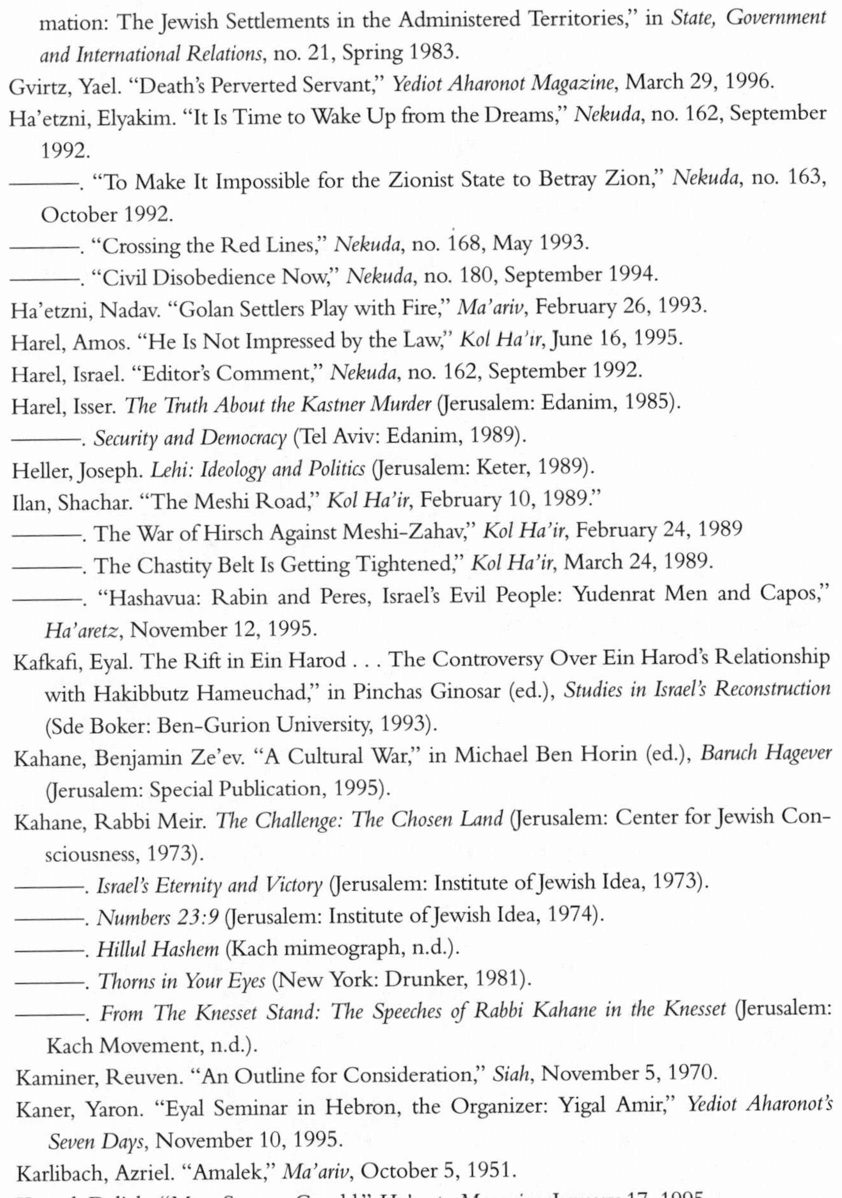

mation: The Jewish Settlements in the Administered Territories," in *State, Government and International Relations*, no. 21, Spring 1983.

Gvirtz, Yael. "Death's Perverted Servant," *Yediot Aharonot Magazine*, March 29, 1996.

Ha'etzni, Elyakim. "It Is Time to Wake Up from the Dreams," *Nekuda*, no. 162, September 1992.

———. "To Make It Impossible for the Zionist State to Betray Zion," *Nekuda*, no. 163, October 1992.

———. "Crossing the Red Lines," *Nekuda*, no. 168, May 1993.

———. "Civil Disobedience Now," *Nekuda*, no. 180, September 1994.

Ha'etzni, Nadav. "Golan Settlers Play with Fire," *Ma'ariv*, February 26, 1993.

Harel, Amos. "He Is Not Impressed by the Law," *Kol Ha'ir*, June 16, 1995.

Harel, Israel. "Editor's Comment," *Nekuda*, no. 162, September 1992.

Harel, Isser. *The Truth About the Kastner Murder* (Jerusalem: Edanim, 1985).

———. *Security and Democracy* (Tel Aviv: Edanim, 1989).

Heller, Joseph. *Lehi: Ideology and Politics* (Jerusalem: Keter, 1989).

Ilan, Shachar. "The Meshi Road," *Kol Ha'ir*, February 10, 1989."

———. The War of Hirsch Against Meshi-Zahav," *Kol Ha'ir*, February 24, 1989

———. The Chastity Belt Is Getting Tightened," *Kol Ha'ir*, March 24, 1989.

———. "Hashavua: Rabin and Peres, Israel's Evil People: Yudenrat Men and Capos," *Ha'aretz*, November 12, 1995.

Kafkafi, Eyal. The Rift in Ein Harod . . . The Controversy Over Ein Harod's Relationship with Hakibbutz Hameuchad," in Pinchas Ginosar (ed.), *Studies in Israel's Reconstruction* (Sde Boker: Ben-Gurion University, 1993).

Kahane, Benjamin Ze'ev. "A Cultural War," in Michael Ben Horin (ed.), *Baruch Hagever* (Jerusalem: Special Publication, 1995).

Kahane, Rabbi Meir. *The Challenge: The Chosen Land* (Jerusalem: Center for Jewish Consciousness, 1973).

———. *Israel's Eternity and Victory* (Jerusalem: Institute of Jewish Idea, 1973).

———. *Numbers 23:9* (Jerusalem: Institute of Jewish Idea, 1974).

———. *Hillul Hashem* (Kach mimeograph, n.d.).

———. *Thorns in Your Eyes* (New York: Drunker, 1981).

———. *From The Knesset Stand: The Speeches of Rabbi Kahane in the Knesset* (Jerusalem: Kach Movement, n.d.).

Kaminer, Reuven. "An Outline for Consideration," *Siah*, November 5, 1970.

Kaner, Yaron. "Eyal Seminar in Hebron, the Organizer: Yigal Amir," *Yediot Aharonot's Seven Days*, November 10, 1995.

Karlibach, Azriel. "Amalek," *Ma'ariv*, October 5, 1951.

Karpel, Daliah. "Must Scream Gevald," *Ha'aretz Magazine*, January 17, 1995.

Katz, Shmuel. *Day of Fire* (Tel Aviv: Ahiasaf, 1978).

Kook, ha-cohen, Rabbi Zvi Yehuda. "Honest We Shall Be," in Yehuda Shaviv (ed.), *A Land of Settlement* (Jerusalem: Young Mizrahi Generation, 1977).

———. "This Is the State the Prophets Had Envisioned," *Nekuda*, no. 86, April 26, 1985.

Kotler, Yair. *Heil Kahane* (Tel Aviv: Modan Books, 1985).

Lagaziel, Ilan. "Political Violence in Israel's Extreme Right: Kach from Kahane's Assassination to the Oslo Accords," (M.A. diss, Hebrew University of Jerusalem, 1994).

Landau, Jacob M. *Israel's Arabs* (Tel Aviv: Ministry of Defense, 1971).

Lapidot, Yehuda. *The Season: Hunting Brothers* (Tel Aviv: Jabotinsky Institute, 1994).

Lenkin, Eliyahu. *The Story of Altalena's Commander* (Tel Aviv: Herut, 1954).

Levy, Amnon. *The Haredim* (Jerusalem: Keter, 1988).

———. "Shtreimel, a Club and Kefiya," *Hadashot*, April 1, 1988.

Lior, Rabbi Dov, Rabbi Daniel Shilo, and Rabbi Eliezer Melamed. "What Is the Rule About This Bad Government?" in Dana Arieli-Horowitz (ed.), *Religion and State in Israel, 1994–1995* (Jerusalem: Center for Jewish Pluralism, 1996).

Lior, Gad. "A Zone of Fire," *Yediot Aharonot—7 Days*, June 20, 1986.

Livne, Moshe. "Israel Shelanu [Our Israel], the Rise and Fall of a Protest Movement" (Unpublished M.A. diss., Tel Aviv University, 1977).

Meyer, Thomas. *The Awakening of the Muslims in Israel* (Givat Haviva: Center for Arab Studies, 1988)

Michaelson, Menachem. "Rabbi Amram Blau: The Eternal Rebel," *Yediot Aharonot*, July 7, 1974.

Mossinzon, Yigal. *Cazablan*, (Tel Aviv: Israeli Drama Center, 1960).

Na'eh, Buki. "Keshet Will Clean Up B'nai Brak's Abomination and We Are Not Talking About Dry Cleaning," *Hadashot*, January 6, 1989.

Nakdimon, Shlomo. *Altalena* (Jerusalem: Edanim, 1978).

Naor, Arye. *David Raziel* (Tel Aviv: Ministry of Defense, 1990).

Naor, Ravit. "Moshe Feigelin, Zo Artzenu's Chairman . . . " *Ma'ariv Magazine*, August 18, 1995.

Pinchas-Cohen, Hava. "Gush Emunim—Early Days," *Nekuda*, no. 69, February 3, 1984.

Pozen, Avi. "The History of the Belz the-V," *Kol Ha'ir*, February 2, 1990.

Prokofyev, Dimitry. "They Asked Me to Help Yigal Amir . . . ," *Yediot Aharonot*, December 18, 1995.

Ra'anan, Tzvi. *Gush Emunim* (Tel Aviv: Sifriyat Poalim, 1980).

Ravitzky, Aviezer. *Messianism, Zionism and Jewish Religious Radicalism* (Tel Aviv: Am Oved, 1993).

Rav-Yehiya, Yitzhak. "The Pangs of Messiah, It Is Coming," *Yerushalaim*, June 30, 1989.

Reches, Eli. *The Arab Minority in Israel: Between Communism and Nationalism* (Tel Aviv: Hakibbutz Hameuchad, 1993).

Report: The State Investigation Commission for the Events at Wadi Salib on July 9, 1959, (Jerusalem: The Government Printer, December 17, 1959).

Report: The State Investigation Commission Studying the Massacre in Hebron's Cave of the Patriarchs (Jerusalem: The Government Printer, 1994).

Report: The State Investigation Commission in the Matter of the Murder of the Late Prime Minister Yitzhak Rabin (Jerusalem: The Government Printer, 1996).

Ringle-Hofman, Ariela. "A Murderer's Breeding Place," *Yediot Aharonot Magazine*, November 10, 1995.

Rosen, Rami. " A History of Denial," *Ha'aretz Magazine*, 15 November 1996.

Rubinstein, Danny. *On the Lord's Side: Gush Emunim* (Tel Aviv: Hakibbutz Hameuchad, 1982).

Sade, Dani et al. "Zo Artzenu Fails Again," *Yediot Aharonot* September 4, 1994.

Schiff, Shaul. "Rabbi Amram Blau Explains: 'Why I Flew Black Flags on Independence Day," *Hatzofe*, May 11, 1973.

Schoken, Gershom. "We and the Germans," *Ha'aretz*, September 2, 1949.

Schulman, Eliezer. "Who, If Not Meshi-Zahav?" *Hadashot*, February 2, 1989.

Segal, Haggai. *Dear Brothers* (Jerusalem: Keter, 1987).

Segev, Tom. *The Seventh Million: The Israelis and the Holocaust* (Jerusalem: Keter, 1991).

Shafat, Gershom. *Gush Emunim* (Bet El: Bet El Library, 1996).

Shamir, Yitzhak. *Summing-Up* (Tel Aviv: Edanim, 1994).

Shavit, Ya'acov. *Open Season* (Tel Aviv: Hadar, 1976).

Sheinberg, Yoseph. "In a Crossroad," in *Om Ani Homa* (Jerusalem: Neturei Karta, 1950).

Shem Or. Ora. "No German Should Set Foot in Tel Aviv," *Yediot Aharonot*, September 4, 1949.

Shibi, Chaim. "Wherever There Is Blood Spilled You Find Kahane," *Yediot Aharonot*, August 2, 1985.

Shilansky, Dov. *In the Hebrew Prison* (Tel Aviv: Armony, 1977.)

Shilhav, Yoseph and Menachem Friedman. *Expansion Within Seclusion: The Haredi Community in Jerusalem* (Jerusalem: Jerusalem Institute for the Study of Israel, 1985).

Shragai, Nadav. "Going for the Action," *Ha'aretz*, November 27, 1984.

Sprinzak, Ehud. *The Emergence of Politics of Delegitimation in Israel, 1967–1973* (Jerusalem: Eshkol Institute, 1974).

———. "Delegitimation Processes in Democracy," *State, Government and International Relations,"* No.6, Autumn, 1974.

———. Altalena: Thirty Years Later," *State, Society and International Relations*, No. 14, 1980.

———. *Every Man Whatsoever Is Right in His Own Eyes: Illegalism in Israeli Society* (Tel Aviv: Sifriyat Poalim, 1986).

———. "Extra-Parliamentary Politics in Israel," in Shmuel Stempler (ed.), *Nation and State: Israeli Society* (Tel Aviv: Ministry of Defense, 1989).

Tavin, Eliyahu. *The Second Front: The Irgun Tzvai Leumi in Europe 1946–1948* (Tel Aviv: Ron, 1973).

Teveth, Shabtai. *David's Zeal*, vol. 3 (Tel Aviv: Schocken, 1987).

Weisman, Aliza. *The Evacuation: The Story of the Uprooting of the Settlements in the Yamit Region* (Beth El: Beth El Library, 1990).

Ya'ari, Ehud and Ze'ev Schiff. *Intifada*, (Tel Aviv: Schocken, 1990).

Yelin-Mor, Nathan. *The Fighters for the Freedom of Israel* (Tel Aviv: Shikmona, 1975).

Yisraeli, Rabbi Shaul. *Amud Haymini Book* (Jerusalem: Eretz Hemdat, 1992).

Yovel-Davis, Nira. *Matzpen: The Israeli Socialist Organization* (Jerusalem: Hebrew University, 1977).

In English

al-Haj, Majid. "Strategies of Mobilization Among the Arabs in Israel," in Keith Kyle and Joel Peters (eds.), *Whither Israel: The Domestic Challenges* (London: I.B. Tauris, 1993).

Aran, Gideon. "Jewish Zionist Fundamentalism: The Bloc of the Faithful in Israel (Gush Emunim)," in Martin E. Marty and R. Scott Appleby, *Fundamentalisms Observed*, (Chicago: University of Chicago Press, 1993).

Arendt, Hannah. *On Violence* (New York: Harcourt, Brace and World, 1969).

Bandura, Albert. "Social Learning Theory of Aggression," in J.F. Knutson (ed.), *The Control of Aggression: Implications from Basic Research* (New York: Hawthorn, 1973).

———. "Mechanisms of Moral Disengagement," in Walter Reich (ed.), *Origins of Terrorism* (New York: Cambridge University Press, 1990).

Bell, Daniel (ed.). *The End of Ideology* (New York: Free Press, 1960).

Bell, J. Bowyer. *Terror Out of Zion*, (New York: St. Martin, 1977).

Benvenisti, Meron. *The West Bank Data Project* (Washington, D.C.: American Enterprise Institute, 1984).

Ben-Yehuda, Nachman. *Political Assassinations by Jews* (Albany: SUNY Press, 1993).

Berger, Peter. *Sacred Canopy: Elements of the Sociology of Religion* (Garden City, N.Y.: Doubleday/Anchor, 1968).

Biale, David. *Power and Powerlessness in Jewish History* (New York: Schocken, 1986).

Blumer, Herbert. "Collective Behavior," in J.B. Gittler (ed.), *Review of Sociology: Analysis of a Decade* (New York: Wiley, 1957).

Bober, Arye (ed.). *The Other Israel: The Radical Case Against Zionism* (New York: Anchor Books, 1972), Introduction.

Bowden, Tom. *The Breakdown of Public Security* (Beverly Hills, Calif.: Sage, 1977).

Breines, Paul. *Tough Jews: Political Fantasies and the Moral Dilemma of American Jewry* (New York: Basic Books, 1990).

Brown, Richard Maxwell. "Legal and Behavioral Perspectives on American Vigilantism," *Perspectives in American History*, no. 5, Spring 1983.

———. "American Vigilante Tradition," in Hugh Graham and Ted R. Gurr (eds.), *Violence in America* (New York: Signet, 1969).

Coser, Lewis A. *The Function of Social Conflict* (Glencoe, Ill: Free Press, 1956).

Cromer, Gerald. "The Debate About Kahanism in Israeli Society," *Occasional Papers* (New York: Harry Guggenheim Foundation, 1988).

Della Porta, Donatella. *Social Movements, Political Violence, and the State* (New York: Cambridge University Press, 1995).

Demant, Peter Robert. *Ploughshares into Swords: Israeli Settlement Policy in the Occupied Territories 1967–1977* (Unpublished Ph.D. diss., University of Amsterdam, 1988).

Dolgin, Janet. *Jewish Identity and the JDL* (Princeton, N.J.: Princeton University Press, 1977).

Don-Yehiya, Eliezer. "The Book and the Sword: The Nationalist Yeshivot and Political Radicalism in Israel," in Martin E. Marty and R. Scott Appleby (eds.). *Accounting for Fundamentalism* (Chicago: University of Chicago Press, 1994).

Eckstein, Harry. "Theoretical Approaches to Explaining Collective Political Violence," in Ted R. Gurr (ed.), *Handbook of Political Conflict: Theory and Research* (New York: Free Press, 1980).

Fanon, Franz. *The Wretched of the Earth* (New York: Grove Press, 1968).

Festinger, Leon. "When Prophecy Fails," in Stanley Schachter and Michael Gazzaniga (eds.), *Extending Psychological Frontiers: Selected Works of Leon Festinger* (New York: Russell Sage Foundation, 1989).

Friedman, Robert I. *The False Prophet: Rabbi Meir Kahane* (New York: Lawrence Hill, 1990).

Gamson, William A. *The Strategy of Social Protest* (Homewood, Ill: Dorsey, 1975).

Gamson, William and J. McEnvoy, "Police Violence and Its Public Support," in James F. Short and

Gresilshammer, Ilan. "The Likud," in Howard R. Penniman and Daniel J. Elazar, *Israel at the Polls* (Bloomington: Indiana University Press, 1986).

Gross, Feliks. *Violence in Politics* (The Hague: Mouton, 1972).

Gurr, Ted R. *Why Men Rebel* (Princeton, N.J.: Princeton University Press, 1970).

Heilman, Samuel C. and Menachem Friedman. "Religious Fundamentalism and Religious Jews," in Martin E. Marty and R. Scott Appleby (eds.), *Fundamentalisms Observed* (Chicago: University of Chicago Press, 1991).

Horn, Alistaire. *A Savage War for Peace: Algeria 1954–1962* (London: Macmillan, 1977).

Isaac, Rael Jean. *Israel Divided* (Baltimore: Johns Hopkins University Press, 1976).

Ivianski, Ze'ev. "The Moral Issue," in David C. Rapoport and Yonah Alexander (eds.), *The Morality of Terrorism* (New York: Pergamon, 1982)

Kahane, Rabbi Meir. *Never Again: A Program for Jewish Survival* (New York: Pyramid, 1972).

———. *The Jewish Idea* (Jerusalem: Institute of Jewish Idea, 1974).

———. *Listen World, Listen Jew* (Tucson, Ariz.: Institute of Jewish Idea, 1975).

———. *The Story of the Jewish Defense League* (Radnor, Pa.: Chilton, 1975).

———. "The Activist Column: Reflections on the Elections," *Jewish Press*, June 3, 1977.

———. "The Activist Column: The Second Revolution," *Jewish Press*, October 20, 1978.

———. *Forty Years* (Miami: Institute of Jewish Idea, 1983).

———. *Uncomfortable Questions to Comfortable Jews* (Secaucus, N.J.: Lyle Stuart, 1987).

Kohn, Hans. "Messianism," *Encyclopedia of the Social Sciences* (New York: Macmillan, 1935).

Kornhauser, William. *The Politics of Mass Society* (Glencoe, Ill.: Free Press, 1959).

Kuhn, Thomas S. *The Structure of Scientific Revolutions* (Chicago: University of Chicago Press, 1962).

Leheman-Wilzig, Sam N. *Stiff-Necked People, Bottle-Necked System* (Bloomington: Indiana University Press, 1990).

Liebman, Charles S. and Eliezer Don-Yehiya. *Religion and Politics in Israel* (Bloomington: Indiana University Press, 1984).

Linz, Juan. *The Breakdown of Democratic Regimes: Crisis, Breakdown and Reequilibrium* (Baltimore: Johns Hopkins University Press, 1978).

Marton, Kati. *A Death in Jerusalem* (New York: Pantheon, 1994).

Marty, Martin M. and Scott R. Appleby. "Conclusion: An Interim Report on a Hypothetical Family," in Marty, Martin M. and Scott R. Appleby (eds.). *Fundamentalisms Observed* (Chicago: University of Chicago Press, 1993).

Marx, Emanuel. *The Social Context of Violent Behavior* (London: Routledge and Kegan Paul, 1976).

Medding, Peter Y. *The Founding of Israeli Democracy, 1948–1967* (New York: Oxford University Press, 1990)

Mergui, Raphael and Philippe Simonnot. *Israel's Ayatollahs: Meir Kahane and the Far Right in Israel* (London: Saqi, 1987).

Midlarsky, Manus I., Martha Crenshaw, and Yoshida Fumihiko. "Why Violence Spreads," *International Studies Quarterly*, vol. 24, no. 2, 1980.

Morris, Benny. *The Birth of the Palestinian Refugee Problem 1947–1949* (Cambridge: Cambridge University Press, 1987).

Muller, E.N. *Aggressive Political Participation* (Princeton, N.J.: Princeton University Press, 1979).

Muller, E.N. and K. Opp. Rational Choice and Rebellious Collective Action," *American Political Science Review*, vol. 80, 1986.

O'Brien, Conor Cruise. *The Siege* (New York: Simon and Schuster, 1986).

Park, Robert. "Human Nature and Collective Behavior," *American Journal of Sociology*, vol. 32, 1927.

Parry, Albert. *Terrorism: From Robespierre to Arafat* (New York: Vanguard, 1977).

Perlmutter, Amos. *The Life and Times of Menachem Begin* (New York: Doubleday, 1987).

Pirages, Dennis C. "Political Stability and Conflict Management," in Ted R. Gurr (ed.), *Handbook of Political Conflict: Theory and Research* (New York, Free Press, 1980).

Rapoport, David C. *Assassination and Terrorism* (Toronto: CBC Merchandize, 1971).

———. "Terror and the Messiah," in David C. Rapoport and Yonah Alexander (eds.) *The Morality of Terrorism* (New York, Pergamon Press, 1982).

———. "Messianic Sanctions for Terror," *Comparative Politics*, vol. 20, no. 2, January 1988.

Ravitzky, Aviezer. "The Root of Kahanism, Consciousness and Political Reality," *The Jerusalem Quarterly*, no. 39, 1986.

Rosenbaum, John H. and C. Sederberg. "Vigilantism: An Analysis of Establishment Violence," *Comparative Politics*, no. 6, 1974.

Rule, James. *Theories of Civil Violence* (Berkeley, University of California Press, 1988).

Sachar, Howard M. *A History of Israel* (Jerusalem, Steimatzky, 1976).

Sartre, Jean-Paul. *Anti-Semite and Jew*, (New York, Schocken Books, 1965).

Shafir, Gershon and Yoav Peled. "'Thorns in Your Eyes':The Soco-Economic Basis of the Kahane Vote," in Asher Arian and Michal Shamir (eds.), *Election in Israel 1984* (Tel Aviv, Ramot Publishing Co., 1986).

Shavit, Ya'acov. *Jabotinsky and the Revisionist Movement 1925-1948* (London, Frank Cass, 1988).

Smelser, Neil. *Theory of Collective Behavior* (New York, Free Press, 1962).

Smooha, Sammy. "Class, Ethnic and National Cleavages and Democracy in Israel," in Ehud Sprinzak and Larry Diamond (eds.), *Israeli Democracy Under Stress* (Boulder, Colo., Lynne Reinner, 1993)

Sorel, George. *Reflections on Violence* (New York, Collier Books, 1961).

Sprinzak, Ehud. "Kach and Meir Kahane: The Rise of Jewish Quasi-Fascism," *Patterns of Prejudice*, vol. 19, nos. 4-5, 1985.

———. *The Ascendance of Israel's Radical Right* (New York: Oxford University Press, 1991).

———. "The Process of Delegitimization: Towards a Linkage Theory of Political Terrorism," *Terrorism and Political Violence*, vol. 3, no. 1, Spring, 1991.

———. "Violence and Catastrophe in the Theology of Rabbi Meir Kahane: The Ideologization of the Mimetic Desire," *Terrorism and Political Violence*, vol. 3, no. 3, Autumn 1991.

Sternhell, Ze'ev et al. *The Birth of Fascist Ideology: From Cultural Rebellion to Political Revolution* (Princeton: Princeton University Press, 1994).

Stohl, Michael and George Lopez (eds.). *The State as Terrorist* (London, Alswych Press, 1984).

Tal, Uriel. "Foundations for a Political Messianic Trend in Israel," *The Jerusalem Quarterly*, No.35, Spring 1985.

Tarrow, Sidney. *Democracy and Disorder* (New York: Oxford University Press, 1989).

Temko, Ned. *To Win or Die* (New York: Morrow, 1987).

Thornton, Thomas P. "Terror as a Weapon of Political Agitation," in Harry Eckstein (ed.), *Internal War* (New York: Collier and Macmillan, 1964).

Tilly, Charles. *From Mobilization to Revolution* (Reading, Mass.: Addison-Wesley, 1978).

Verblovsky, R.J. Zvi. "Messiah and Messianic Movements," *The New Encyclopedia Britannica* (New York: Encyclopedia Britannica, 1981).

Von der Mehden, Fred R. *Comparative Political Violence* (Englewood Cliffs, N.J.: Prentice-Hall, 1973).

Weisburd, David and Vered Vinitzky. "Vigilantism as Rational Social Control: The Case of Gush Emunim Settlers," in Myron Aronoff (ed.), *Religion and Politics: Political Anthropology*, vol. 3, (New Brunswick, Transaction Books, 1993).

Wilkinson, Paul. *Political Terrorism* (London: Macmillan, 1975).

Wolfgang, Marvin E. (ed.). *Collective Violence* (Chicago: Aldin Atherton, 1972).

Wolfsfeld, Gadi. "Collective Political Action and Media Research Report," *Jerusalem Quarterly*, No.31, Spring 1984.

———. *The Politics of Provocation: Participation and Protest in Israel* (Albany: SUNY Press, 1988).

Zimmermann, Ekkart. "Macro-Comparative Research on Political Protest," in Ted R. Gurr (ed.), *Handbook of Political Conflict: Theory and Research* (New York: Free Press, 1980).

Newspapers

Al Hamishmar
Davar
Dvar Hashavua
Ha'aretz
Hadashot
Hatzofe
Kol Ha'ir
Ma'ariv
Yediot Aharonot
Yerushalaim

INDEX